RUSSIA'S IMPERIAL END
ITS GEOPOLITICAL CONSEQUENCES

RUSSIA'S
IMPERIAL ENDEAVOR AND ITS GEOPOLITICAL CONSEQUENCES

The Russia-Ukraine War ▸ Volume Two

Edited by Bálint Madlovics
and Bálint Magyar

CEU PRESS

Central European University Press
Budapest – Vienna – New York

© The editors, 2023

Published in 2023 by
Central European University Press

Nádor utca 9, H-1051 Budapest, Hungary
Tel: +36-1-327-3138 or 327-3000
E-mail: ceupress@press.ceu.edu
Website: www.ceupress.com

An electronic version of this book is freely available thanks to the libraries supporting CEU Press's Opening the Future initiative. More information and links to the Open Access version can be found at *ceup.openingthefuture.net*.

This work is licensed under
a Creative Commons Attribution-NonCommercial-NoDerivatives 4.0
International License.

Cover design and typesetting by Éva Szalay

ISBN 978-963-386-651-1 (paperback)
ISBN 978-963-386-652-8 (ebook)

A CIP record for this title is available from the Library of Congress.

Table of Contents

Chronology of Modern Russia (1985–2022)   vii

Kirill Rogov: Preface   xv

I. Russia's Patronal Autocracy: Elites, Society, and Ideology in War Mode   1

Nikolay Petrov: The Evolution of Russia's Patronal System: Elites During the War and After Putin   3

András Rácz: Socially Inclusive and Exclusive Warfighting: Comparing Ukraine and Russia's Ways of War   27

Zoltán Sz. Bíró: The Falsification of History: War and Russian Memory Politics   51

Kostiantyn Fedorenko: Enter the "Bloody Clown": Ukraine's Volodymyr Zelensky in the Lens of Russia's Media Machine   77

Péter Krekó, Boglárka Rédl: Authoritarian Deflation: How Russia Lost the Information War against the West   105

II. Geopolitical Structures and the War: The Changing Position of Russia and Ukraine   125

Kálmán Mizsei: In the Gravitational Tensions of East and West: The Systemic and Geopolitical Integration Patterns of Ukraine and Moldova   127

Dóra Győrffy: Neo-Backwardness and Prospects for Long-Term Growth: The Effects of Western Sanctions on Russia and the Changing Embeddedness of Ukraine in the World Economy   165

Tamás Lattmann: From Partner to Pariah: The Changing Position of Russia in Terms of International Law   183

Oksana Mikheieva, Viktoriya Sereda, Lidia Kuzemska: Forced Displacement of Ukrainians during the War: Patterns of Internal and External Migration (2014–2022)   199

III. The International Community: Patronal and Non-Patronal Responses to the War — 229

Zsombor Zeöld: Crescent Rising? The Baltic, Romanian, and "V3" Reaction to the 2022 Russia-Ukraine war — 231

Bálint Madlovics, Bálint Magyar: Hungary's Dubious Loyalty: Orbán's Regime Strategy in the Russia-Ukraine War — 255

Anatoly Reshetnikov: Defensive Submission, Lucrative Neutrality, and Silent Detachment: Post-Soviet Patronal Autocracies in the Shadow of the Russian Invasion — 287

Gyula Krajczár: The Russia-Ukraine War and China: Neutrality with Imperial Characteristics — 311

Contributors — 327

Index — 333

Chronology of Modern Russia (1985–2022)

- *March 11, 1985*: Mikhail Gorbachev is elected General Secretary of the Communist Party of the USSR. Continuing the policy of Yuri Andropov (1982–1984), he makes significant changes in personnel within a short period of time. In one year, he replaces 70% of the ministers in the federal government, and half of the senior officials in the member republics.
- *February 25 – March 6, 1986*: The 27th Congress of the Communist Party of the Soviet Union meets. In his speech, Gorbachev describes the Brezhnev years as the "era of stagnation." At the same time, he promises a comprehensive reform of the economic management system, and the democratization of the country.
- *April 26, 1986*: An explosion occurs at the Chernobyl nuclear power plant, just 130 kilometers from Kyiv. The Soviet authorities are slow to inform the public, but the country's political leadership later realizes that it has no right to conceal important public affairs. The disaster leads to a major change in the authorities' information policy. Openness in the public sphere, *glasnost*, takes on a new political meaning.
- *December 16, 1986*: Gorbachev personally calls Andrei Sakharov, who has been living in exile in Gorky, and informs him that he can return to Moscow.
- *February 9, 1987*: The Soviet authorities announce the imminent release of nearly 100 political prisoners.
- *December 8, 1987*: The Soviet-US agreement on the destruction of medium- and short-range land-launched missiles is signed in Washington.
- *February 4, 1988*: The Supreme Court of the Soviet Union rehabilitates the prisoners of the third Moscow Trial (1938), including Nikolai Bukharin. This marks the beginning of the legal rehabilitation of the victims of the "great trials."
- *March 14–18, 1988*: Gorbachev visits Yugoslavia. The Communist Party of the Soviet Union and the League of Communists of Yugoslavia issue a joint declaration ("Dubrovnik Declaration") in which the Soviet side publicly recognizes for the first time that all communist and workers' parties have the right to determine the direction of their country's social and political development. This is essentially a denunciation of the "Brezhnev Doctrine."
- *May 15, 1988*: The withdrawal of Soviet troops from Afghanistan begins. The operation is completed by February 15 the following year.
- *June 28 – July 1, 1988*: The 19th Congress of the USSR is held. This conference is the zenith of Gorbachev's "perestroika" policy; afterward, the Gorbachev center gradually begins to lose the initiative.

- *December 1, 1988*: The Supreme Soviet of the USSR amends the Constitution and passes a law establishing a Congress of People's Deputies of 2,250 members.
- *March 26, 1989*: Elections to the Congress of People's Deputies are held. The elections, which are held under compulsory plurality voting, are won in many places by independent or opposition candidates against the Communist Party candidate. The first session of the Congress begins two months later.
- *November 9, 1989*: The Berlin Wall comes down, putting German unity at the center of European politics.
- *December 12–24, 1989*: The second session of the Congress of People's Deputies meets. The Deputies pass a resolution declaring the 1939 Molotov-Ribbentrop Pact legally invalid from the moment of its inception.
- *March 1990*: Elections for the Congress of People's Deputies of Russia and the Supreme Soviets of the 14 other member republics are held in the member republics.
- *March 12–15, 1990*: An extraordinary session of the Congress of People's Deputies of the USSR meets. The Constitution is amended, removing the clause on the leading role of the Communist Party of the USSR. This legally opens the way for the establishment of a multi-party system.
- *October 15, 1990*: Gorbachev is awarded the Nobel Peace Prize.
- *March 17, 1991*: A referendum is held on the future of the Soviet Union. Six of the 15 member republics—Georgia, Armenia, Estonia, Latvia, Lithuania, and Moldova—boycott participation. Where the referendum is held, turnout reaches 80%, with 76% voting in favor of preserving the Soviet state.
- *April 1991*: The drafting of a new federal treaty begins in Novo-Ogaryovo. After months of negotiations, the treaty is signed on August 20.
- *June 12, 1991*: Boris Yeltsin is elected president of the Russian republic. Unlike Gorbachev, who was elected President of the Soviet Union by the members of the Congress of People's Deputies (i.e., a body), Yeltsin is elected by citizens with the right to vote.
- *August 19-21, 1991*: A coup is attempted by conservative forces against Gorbachev. The State Committee on the State of Emergency (SCSE) tries to prevent the signing of a new treaty of alliance by isolating the Soviet president. The attempt fails, and the leaders of the coup attempt are arrested.
- *December 8, 1991*: In Belovezhskaya Pushcha, the leaders of three Soviet republics—Russia, Ukraine, and Belarus—sign a document declaring the dissolution of the Soviet Union, the fifth point of which states that the contracting parties will respect the borders, territorial integrity, and sovereignty of their countries. The parliaments of all three Soviet republics ratify the agreement within two weeks.

- ***January 2, 1992***: The Russian economic reform, devised by Yegor Gaidar and his colleagues, is launched. The "shock therapy," following the Polish model, is designed to liberalize prices and trade, to prepare and launch privatization, and to restore macroeconomic balance. One of the results of the reforms is an annual inflation rate over 2,600%.
- ***December 12, 1993***: A referendum is held on Russia's new constitution. At the same time, the State Duma and the Federal Council—the lower and upper chambers of the new bicameral parliament, the Federal Assembly—are elected. This is the first parliamentary election in Russian history that is not only multi-party, but also universal, equal, direct, and secret.
- ***December 5, 1994***: The Presidents of Ukraine, Russia, the United States, and the Prime Minister of Great Britain sign the *Budapest Memorandum*. In return for Kyiv's renunciation of its nuclear weapons, the powers guarantee the inviolability of Ukraine's borders, its territorial integrity, and sovereignty. This is the second international agreement in which Moscow guarantees respect for Ukraine's borders.
- ***December 11, 1994***: The first Chechen war begins. The conflict is brought to an end with the signing of the Khasavyurt Agreement on August 31, 1996.
- ***December 17, 1995***: Duma elections are held. The Communists have the largest faction, but they control only just over a third of the seats, so they pose no real threat to the political will of the President.
- ***June 16, 1996***: Presidential elections are held with no winner emerging in the first round. In the second round, held on July 3, Boris Yeltsin wins by a significant margin (53.82%) over the Communist candidate, Gennady Zyuganov (40.31%).
- ***May 31, 1997***: The Treaty of Friendship, Cooperation, and Partnership between Russia and Ukraine is signed. Clause 2 of the Treaty reiterates that the Parties shall respect each other's borders, territorial integrity, and sovereignty. This is Russia's third such guarantee.
- ***August 17, 1998***: Prime Minister Sergei Kiriyenko announces that the state is unable to pay the equivalent value of maturing short-term government bonds. Payments are suspended for three months. A week after the announcement, Yeltsin dismisses Kiriyenko, but his nominee is rejected by a majority in parliament. The political crisis, triggered by the state's bankruptcy, ends with the election of Yevgeny Primakov as Prime Minister.
- ***August 9, 1999***: Vladimir Putin is appointed Prime Minister of Russia. The decision is approved by the State Duma on August 16.
- ***September 4–16, 1999***: A series of bombings attributed to Chechens shake Russia. They occur first in Buynaksk (September 4), then twice in Moscow (September 9 and 13), and finally in Volgodonsk (September 16). The authorities

declare the events Chechen terrorist attacks from the start, but there are still serious doubts about this.
- *October 1, 1999*: The second Chechen war begins.
- *December 19, 1999*: Duma elections are held. The Communists win again, but with 44 fewer seats than four years earlier. However, a few months later the parties with the second and third largest factions (United Russia and Fatherland-Holy Russia, respectively) merge to form United Russia, creating the largest parliamentary faction.
- *December 31, 1999*: Boris Yeltsin resigns as President. He is replaced as acting president by Prime Minister Vladimir Putin.
- *March 26, 2000*: Putin wins the first round of presidential elections, with 52.94% of the vote.
- *September 11, 2001*: Terrorist attack against the United States. Putin is among the first to call the US President and assure him of Russia's support.
- *January 28, 2003*: Ukraine and Russia conclude a delimitation treaty on their common borders. This is the fourth Russian guarantee of respect for Ukraine's borders.
- *July 2, 2003*: Platon Lebedev, a close associate of Mikhail Khodorkovsky and head of the MENATEP group, which holds the majority of the shares in the Yukos oil company, is arrested.
- *October 25, 2003*: A commando raid arrests Russia's richest man, Mikhail Khodorkovsky, majority owner of the Yukos oil company. This is the beginning of the "Yukos affair."
- *December 7, 2003*: Duma elections are held. The election is won by the United Russia party, which wins 223 seats out of 450. However, by "buying" the non-party deputies, it gains a constitutional majority. This is the first election in which no liberal or social-liberal party seeking broad cooperation with the West has been elected to the lower house.
- *March 14, 2004*: Presidential elections are held. Putin wins the election by a large margin (71.31%) in the first round.
- *November 21, 2004*: The fraudulent victory of the Moscow-backed Viktor Yanukovych as President of Ukraine triggers the Orange Revolution in Ukraine.
- *February 10, 2007*: Putin attends the Munich Security Conference, where he delivers a memorable speech sharply criticizing what he sees as a unipolar world order.
- *March 2, 2008*: Presidential elections are held. Putin is barred from standing for a third consecutive term by a constitutional restriction. He is replaced by his political front man, Dmitry Medvedev, who wins the first round with 70.28% of the vote.

Chronology of Modern Russia (1985–2022) • xi

- *August 2008*: The global financial crisis hits Russia.
- *August 7–12, 2008*: The five-day Russian-Georgian war takes place. Under pressure from the European Union, Moscow withdraws its troops from the Georgian mainland. However, on August 26, it recognizes Abkhazia and South Ossetia, which are part of Georgia under international law, as sovereign states.
- *April 8, 2010*: In Prague, Russian President Dmitry Medvedev and US President Barack Obama sign the START III treaty on the further limitation of military offensive weapons.
- *December 4, 2011*: Duma elections are held. The election is won by the United Russia party, but the vote counting is rigged to give the party at least an absolute majority (after the constitutional majority it won in the previous two elections). According to some calculations, some 14 million votes were "redirected" to the ruling party to achieve this. The apparent fraud triggers a wave of protests in several major cities in Russia, which lasts for months.
- *March 4, 2012*: Presidential elections are held. Putin is re-elected president of Russia after a four-year hiatus. The official results show Putin winning with 63.60% of the vote, but model calculations suggest that 10–11% of this are fictitious, i.e., non-existent votes. The opposition admits that Putin won in the first round, but not by as much as the official results suggest.
- *Summer 2012:* Shortly after Putin's inauguration in May, the State Duma passes a series of repressive laws and amendments. The most notable of these is the addition of a "foreign agent" clause to the law on the operation of NGOs.
- *2012–2013:* Opinion polls show a steady decline in Putin's popularity.
- *February 26, 2014*: For the first time, unmarked Russian army troops appear in Crimea. They occupy the peninsula, and prepare for the referendum on Crimea's independence, which takes place two weeks later (March 16, 2014).
- *March 18, 2014*: Russia annexes Crimea and Sevastopol as the 84th and 85th subjects of the Russian Federation.
- *Second week of April, 2014*: In three provinces of eastern Ukraine—Kharkiv, Luhansk, and Donetsk—as in Crimea, the Russian army's unmarked soldiers appear and, with the help of some of the local population, instigate a rebellion in the region. They are not successful in Kharkiv oblast, but they manage to control 30% of the other two oblasts by the beginning of 2015.
- *May 2, 2014*: A serious incident in Odessa between forces supporting and opposing the new Kyiv leadership (emerging in the wake of the Euromaidan Revolution) takes place, resulting in the death of dozens of people. Pro-government protesters fear that pro-Russian demonstrators are trying to force a turnaround in Odessa, as they did in eastern Ukraine a few weeks earlier. An impartial investigation into the incident has not been carried out to this day.

- ***September 19, 2014***: The first Minsk Agreement is signed.
- ***August 2014 – February 2015***: Protracted heavy fighting in eastern and southeastern Ukraine. Russian regular forces are occasionally involved in the fighting, but Moscow denies this.
- ***February 12, 2015***: The second Minsk Agreement is signed between representatives of the Ukrainian central authorities and the separatists in eastern Ukraine. The German Chancellor and the French President accept that Russia is not part of the conflict but as much a guarantor of the agreement as Germany and France. The agreement is aimed at halting months of fighting and providing a framework for resolving the status of the breakaway territories in eastern Ukraine.
- ***September 18, 2016***: In accordance with the amendment to the Constitution made during Medvedev's presidency, a new State Duma is elected after five years instead of four. This time, the lower house of parliament is won by the United Russia party with a constitutional majority. However, this result requires a higher percentage of fraud in the vote aggregation than ever before.
- ***March 18, 2018***: Presidential elections are held. The official results show that Putin wins with an unprecedented 76.69% of the vote.
- ***June 25 – July 1, 2020***: A week-long "All-Russian vote" on constitutional change takes place. The "All-Russian vote" is an *ad hoc* legal measure with the function of preventing legal agitation against the amendments. The constitutional amendment has essentially one purpose: to allow Putin to remain president after 2024. Nevertheless, the constitution is amended in 206 places. The official results show that 76.69% of the voters support the amendments.
- ***August 20, 2020***: Traveling on a plane from Tomsk to Moscow, Russian opposition politician Alexei Navalny is poisoned with a binary nerve agent, Novichok, by the Russian secret service (FSB). The plane makes an emergency landing in Omsk, where Navalny's life is saved by paramedics who arrive at the scene. After many months, he makes a recovery, thanks to his treatment in Germany.
- ***January 17, 2021***: Alexei Navalny returns to Moscow, where he is immediately arrested. Three major nationwide protests against the authorities' actions take place in late January and early February. The protests are violently crushed by the authorities.
- ***September 17–19, 2021***: The Duma elections, which are postponed for three days, are again won by the United Russia party, this time with a constitutional majority. Model calculations show, however, that more than 50% of the officially counted votes cast for the party are fictitious votes.
- ***Autumn 2021***: In autumn 2020, Russia again starts to mass a significant military force, estimated at 150–170 thousand troops, on the northern and eastern borders of Ukraine.

- ***December 15, 2021***: The Russian Foreign Ministry hands over a draft treaty to US and NATO representatives. In it, Russia expects a halt to further NATO expansion, the withdrawal of NATO infrastructure to its pre-July 1997 state, and a moratorium on the deployment of strike weapons capable of reaching Russian territory. Both the military organization and the United States reject Moscow's first two demands as groundless, while on the third they indicate their willingness to negotiate.
- ***February 21, 2022***: Russia recognizes the Donetsk and Luhansk People's Republics as sovereign states.
- ***February 24, 2022:*** Russia attacks Ukraine.

Compiled by Zoltán Sz. Bíró.

Preface
Kirill Rogov

The Russia-Ukrainian war, which looks to be a tragedy for Ukraine and an institutional catastrophe for Russia, represents a remarkable event in political history for many reasons. One of them is that the causes for this war stem from a divergence of the two countries' political regimes, which have arisen on the basis of very similar social orders shaped by similar "stubborn structures" and historical experiences. The divergence of these regimes, which may have seemed insignificant, even accidental and easy to remedy (as perceived from Moscow) at the start, has through several iterations transformed into devastating fight.

As Magyar and Madlovics astutely observe in Volume One of this book, the Russo-Ukrainian conflict can only prospectively be designated as a conflict between democracy and autocracy. At the time of Russia's full-scale invasion, Ukraine was still neither a consolidated nor a liberal democracy. In more precise terms, this clash can be defined as a conflict between a patronal democracy and a patronal autocracy. The concept of patronalism, introduced by Henry Hale and further developed in the book by Magyar and Madlovics,[1] highlights this connection between the political regimes of the two countries and the established social orders in which these regimes are rooted and which have so much in common.

But we can go even further in this comparison. In the countries that emerged from the former Soviet republics, we can observe three main paths of post-Soviet political developments. The Baltic States quickly and consistently integrated into Europe after the collapse of the USSR, successfully reproducing European institutional models. In the second group of countries, Soviet party-based authoritarianism transformed into personalistic patronal autocracy without any transition period (Kazakhstan, Turkmenistan, Uzbekistan) or such transformation occurred after a brief period of instability (Azerbaijan, Belarus, Tajikistan). In this group of countries, unified patronal pyramids of undivided economic and political power formed quickly or existed from the beginning, having matured under the shell of the Soviet institutional system.

Finally, the third type of political regime can be defined as competitive oligarchy (a term coined by Robert Dahl in his seminal work).[2] In terms of Henry Hale's framework, within such polities multiple patronal pyramids emerge, competing with each other and ensuring political pluralism in the society through this competition. The further dynamics of these regimes resemble a series of cycles, as one oligarchic group endeavors to "capture" the state and integrate other pyramids under its supreme patronage, encounters broad political mobilization (the so-called "color revolutions"), and suffers defeat. This is what Magyar and Madlovics refer to as the "regime cycles" of patronal democracies–cycles which prevent autocratic breakthroughs but lead back only to oligarchic competition, and not to liberal democracy.[3]

This trajectory is seen in such post-Soviet countries as Ukraine, Moldova, Georgia, and Armenia. However, it is important to highlight the oft-overlooked fact that in the 1990s Russia also gravitated towards this type of political regime. One could observe at that time a sufficiently pluralistic political and party environment, competitive elections with unpredictable outcomes, and oligarchic groups that established their own media machines while forming political and administrative clienteles. There was also significant autonomy and variation in the actual political regimes of the Russian regions—the other dimension of political diversity. Only a decade later, with the arrival of Putin in the early 2000s, the process of dismantling this pluralistic system commenced. The Putin administration's conflict with the most powerful and ambitious oligarchic group, Mikhail Khodorkovsky's Yukos, was the culmination of these efforts. As a result, by the second half of the 2000s, the process of constructing a unified pyramid of political power and overall economic patronage was complete.

Interestingly, a form of grassroots political mobilization also occurred in Russia in 2011–2012. As in other semi-democratic post-Soviet countries, mass protests in Moscow were driven by discontent over the perceived unfairness of elections and citizens' attempts to restore meaning to electoral procedures. However, due to the absence of competing elite groups capable of supporting grassroots mobilization through media and administrative resources, this attempt failed.

It is remarkable that from the very beginning, Putin's struggle to consolidate economic and political power in Russia has been intertwined with attempts to interfere in a similar battle for patronal autocracy within Ukraine. As early as the 2004 Ukrainian presidential elections, Putin actively supported an attempt to organize an authoritarian power transition in Ukraine but found himself on the losing side. All through Yushchenko's presidency, Putin invested in the opposition and bribed the Ukrainian power and security elites, hoping to bring Ukraine back to the path of autocratic consolidation that he had pursued in Russia. A subsequent attempt to consolidate patronal autocracy during Yanukovych's presidency encountered powerful resistance from citizens and elites alike. And a further attempt to divide Ukraine along the lines of patronal democracy and patronal autocracy based on geographical principles—East versus West—also failed in 2014.

Equally astonishing is the fact that Putin's attempts to support Ukrainian "patronal autocracy"—or, more precisely, the autocratic *attempts* within a patronal democracy—from outside, which triggered reciprocal counter-mobilization in Ukraine, led to the divergence of the Ukrainian political order and its "detachment" from the Russian model, in a sense establishing the framework for Ukrainian political identity while consolidating Ukrainian diversity.

Thus, the current war is in fact a sort of externalization of the internal conflict that defines the pendulum dynamics and regime cycles of patronal regimes. The roots of this war lie more in domestic than in international politics. This is a war between the united forces of patronal autocracy and a coalition of forces advocating patronal pluralism and the anti-patronal demands of civil society. In other words, this is a war between two institutional and political potentials that exist in post-Soviet societies within the Orthodox sphere where we find predominantly competitive oligarchical regimes with their pendulum dynamics.

In fact, the same theme is taken up in this volume by Kálmán Mizsei, who suggests in his chapter that "Russia's opposition to EU membership is actually greater than its opposition to NATO." Indeed, as the experience of the Baltic and CE countries demonstrates, the prospects for EU membership can elicit a sustainable coalition based on the interests of influential elite groups and demands from below. And such a coalition has the potential to overcome the trap of patronalism. Indeed, it was precisely the Association Agreement with the EU, which was supposed to be signed by Ukraine, which became the cause of Putin's attempts to change the course of Ukrainian politics, leading to the Euromaidan protests.

In the second half of 2010s, institutional divergence from Russia became the main vector of reforms in Ukraine. Although the direction of these reforms was largely shaped by the "gravitational field" of the European Union, they also relied on the clear demands of Ukrainian society. These demands became evident during President Zelensky's triumphant election campaign. As András Rácz convincingly illustrates in his chapter, the war unleashed by Putin in Ukraine has become the setting not only of military conflict but also of institutional competition. While Russia, in its military organization, seeks to showcase the advantages of patronal autocracy and its potential for top-down mobilization and normalized violence, Ukraine strives to compensate for Russia's initial economic and military advantage through resources of horizontal mobilization and networks of trust, inclusiveness, and crowdfunding.

Ukraine, however, has not been the sole theatre of Putin's incursions into the internal affairs of neighboring states. It is worth noting Putin's past and present attempts to interfere in the internal struggle between the two vectors of political evolution in Georgia, and to a lesser extent in Moldova and Armenia. Moreover, the chapters in this volume discussing the responses to the war in Ukraine on the part of the countries of Central and Eastern Europe can also shed light on how Putin's invasion resonates with political divisions in those countries. The gravitational field of "Putinism" emerges as a significant phenomenon influencing the domestic political dynamics of countries such as Bulgaria, Slovakia, Czech Republic, and, of course, Hungary. What is more, the question of supporting Ukraine and the associated costs thereof reveals vulnerabilities in democracy and the political order in Central and Eastern European countries.

Another significant challenge to the research agenda posed by this war and its consequences for the political regime in Russia concerns the definition of the regime's present nature. Within the pages of this volume, contemporary Hungary, Kazakhstan, and Russia are equally classified as patronal autocracies. However, the actual practices of their political regimes differ considerably. Indeed, over the past 15 months, political persecutions in Russia, accompanied by lengthy prison sentences, have become a commonplace occurrence, with political repression itself becoming a mass phenomenon. But does this signify a move toward totalitarianism as it is sometimes defined? Could personalized, non-party-based totalitarianism, not grounded in a comprehensive ideological doctrine, ever exist? The volume's first chapter by Nikolay Petrov provides insights into this question by tracing the internal changes in Putin's patronal pyramid.

Two phenomena that predominantly characterize the dynamics of the Russian political regime since the onset of the war have been a sharp rise in repression and a significant expansion in the ideological control over society. Both are intertwined with the central, one might say existential, challenge facing the regime now—justifying the initiated war, the reasons and objectives of which remain unclear even to loyal groups within Putin's camp. Three contributions in this volume address this critical issue. Zoltán Sz. Bíró discusses Putin's models of falsifying history, essentially constructing a "crash course" in Putin's historical mythology which places confrontation with the hostile West at the center of the historical existence of the Russian state. Meanwhile, Kostiantyn Fedorenko on the one hand and Péter Krekó and Boglárka Rédl on the other delve into the patterns and narratives of Kremlin propaganda, which operates not so much on the basis of arguments but rather creates a parallel, fake reality.

These narratives, however, would have exerted only a limited influence on Russian society (as they did prior to the war) had they not been bolstered by the repressive apparatus of the Putin regime, ensuring the coerced loyalty of the majority of the Russian population. While primarily intended to justify Putin's invasion of Ukraine within the Russian context, these narratives have found broad dissemination and resonate with the rhetoric of numerous political leaders in both

East and West, such as Orbán and Erdoğan. This context allows us to define the current political regime in Russia as an "illiberal dictatorship" having emerged on the basis of a patronal autocracy. Usually, patronal autocracies either entirely do without the ideological mobilization of citizens as a means of legitimacy, or the rhetoric of "defending sovereignty" plays merely an additional and instrumental role (as has largely been the case for much of Putin's rule). However, in an illiberal dictatorship, the balance of legitimacy sources changes, while its external aggression justifies the growing role of political mobilization and repression in ensuring its stability. Increasing repression and the development towards dictatorial rule in Russia can be visualized in the triangular framework developed by Magyar and Madlovics as well (Figure 1).[4]

Figure 1. The regime trajectory of modern Russia.

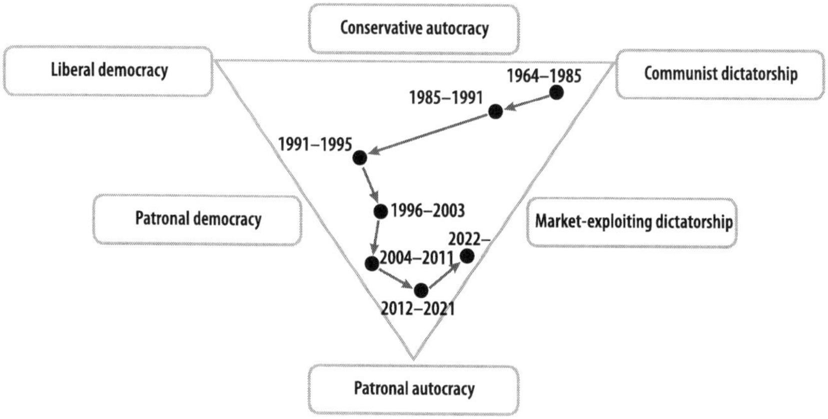

Source: Magyar and Madlovics (2022, 222).

This second volume based on the two editors' conceptual framework offers a unique view on the war by analyzing its structural consequences for Russia, its political and economic system, and the geopolitical order that is being shaken by Putin's imperial endeavor.

Notes

[1] See Henry E. Hale, *Patronal Politics: Eurasian Regime Dynamics in Comparative Perspective* (Cambridge: Cambridge University Press, 2015); Bálint Magyar and Bálint Madlovics, *The Anatomy of Post-Communist Regimes: A Conceptual Framework* (Budapest–New York: CEU Press, 2020).

[2] Robert A. Dahl, *Polyarchy: Participation and Opposition* (New Haven: Yale University Press, 1971).

[3] See Madlovics and Magyar's introductory chapter "Ukrainian Regime Cycles and the Russian Invasion," in *Ukraine's Patronal Democracy and the Russian Invasion: The Russia-Ukraine War, Volume One*, edited by Bálint Madlovics and Bálint Magyar (Budapest–Vienna–New York: CEU Press, 2023), 3–53.

[4] Bálint Magyar and Bálint Madlovics, *A Concise Field Guide to Post-Communist Regimes: Actors, Institutions, and Dynamics* (Budapest–Vienna–New York: CEU Press, 2022), 222–26.

I.
Russia's Patronal Democracy: Elites, Society, and Ideology in War Mode

The Evolution of Russia's Patronal System: Elites During the War and After Putin

Nikolay Petrov

1. The structure of Putin's single-pyramid network

The future of the Russian political regime after the departure of Vladimir Putin is now of concern to many. In a situation where there is no clarity regarding the mechanisms for the transfer of power, just as there are no well-functioning institutions of bureaucracy and political competition,[1] attention is naturally drawn toward the elites in Russia.

In the patronal autocracy built by Putin, actors with formal and informal positions are organized into a single-pyramid patronal network.[2] However, if we look at the structure of the elite we can observe that the state apparatus plays a dominant role. The bureaucracy consists of three main groups: the security forces, technocrats, and political managers. Regional actors can be singled out as a special category. The growth of personal rule by the chief patron, which has especially accelerated since 2014, has had depersonalization as its obverse side, a situation where the influence of any figure in the system is determined not so much by their person as by their position. Naturally, we are not talking about the name of the position, but about its functionality, which is rather variable according to the chief patron's whim.

If we look at the ratings of the 100 leading politicians in Russia, which have been compiled monthly by experts and published by *Nezavisimaya Gazeta* for many years,[3] it turns out that there have been no noticeable changes since the start of the war in Ukraine. Indeed, we see the same picture as before the war.[4] Meanwhile, it is intuitively clear that this cannot be so, and that serious changes are taking place in the higher echelons of Russia's patronal system. In most cases, it is difficult to talk about shifts in influence; rather, shifts in media coverage are noticeable. The personal, targeted sanctions imposed by Western countries and the selection of persons who have fallen under them have added practical interest to the problem.

War is a crash test, and so far everything suggests that the Russian patronal system is passing it very successfully. At the very least, not only key, but simply notable figures in power and business have remained in their places, and everyone is either actively or passively demonstrating their loyalty to Putin. This contrasts surprisingly with the role of the oligarchs, whose informal position and influence has greatly deteriorated during this period, and with the sharp split in opinions among the cultural, scientific, and media elite, which has not yet become part of the state apparatus.

This can be explained simply: the modern Russian political and administrative elite is highly depersonalized and represents parts of a common mechanism that are well adjusted to each other. Figuratively speaking, these people are cogs, not individuals, and they are not capable of acting in an individual capacity, unlike some cultural figures with more autonomy.

The elements of Putin's state-based single-pyramid network, however, have a functional specialization within the framework of large blocs, according to which it is convenient to consider the situation with the Russian elites now and in the future. As a first approximation, five such blocs can be distinguished: (1) oligarchs; (2) security bureaucrats; (3) technocratic bureaucrats; (4) bureaucrats-political managers; and (5) regional actors.

2. Oligarchs: in the double grip of Putin and Western sanctions

2.1. *Enumeration: an overview of Russian oligarchs and major entrepreneurs and their position on the war*

Oligarchs can be conditionally divided into "Yeltsin," "Yeltsin-Putin," and "Putin" categories according to the origin of their fortunes/initial accumulation of capital (Table 1). Among the first and second are those who were allowed to leave Russia, leaving part of their assets, but taking away their cash: these include Roman Abramovich and the "tankers" (viz. TNK-BP oil company), i.e., Mikhail Fridman, German Khan, Petr Aven, Alexey Kuzmichev, Dmitry Rybolovlev, and others.

At the end of the 2000s, with the creation of state corporations, a class of *state oligarchs* emerged alongside private oligarchs. This group consists of officials close to Putin, who control colossal resources on behalf of the state. State oligarchs are a hybrid of business bureaucrats and "private" oligarchs, who control *de jure* private companies. Importantly, state oligarchs are not on the *Forbes* list, but the financial flows they dispose over and their lifestyles are fully commensurate with their private counterparts and their influence far greater. Their position, on the one hand, is more secure against the vicissitudes of the market, while on the other, they can lose almost everything they have with one stroke of the pen, if the president dismisses them. It is they who control the most important sectors of the Russian economy and who comprise the greater part of the silovarchs. Daniel Treisman proposed the term "silovarch" in 2006, combining the words oligarch and siloviki, for those of them who have a security or intelligence background.[5] They represent the majority in Putin's single-pyramid network.

Table 1. Grouping the Russian oligarchs according to the source of their wealth.

Group of oligarchs (according to period of initial wealth accumulation)		Key members of the group (with corresponding major company or—if applicable—ranking in the Forbes 2022 list of Russian billionaires)[6]
"Yeltsin" (1991–98)		Vladimir Lisin (#1), Vladimir Potanin (#2), Mikhail Fridman (#6), Vagit Alekperov (#10), German Khan (#14), Dmitry Rybolovlev (#19), Alexey Kuzmichev (#20), Petr Aven (#29)
"Yeltsin-Putin" (1999–2003)		Vladimir Lisin (#1),[7] Alexey Mordashov (#5), Alisher Usmanov (#7), Andrey Melnichenko (#9), Roman Abramovich (#17), Viktor Vekselberg (#22), Oleg Deripaska (#50), Andrey Kostin (VTB)
"Putin" (2003–)	state oligarchs	Sergey Chemezov (Rostec); Igor Sechin (Rosneft); Nikolai Tokarev (Transneft); Alexey Miller (Gazprom); German Gref (Sberbank); Igor Shuvalov (VEB.RF)
	private oligarchs	Leonid Mikhelson (#4), Gennady Timchenko (#8), Arkady Rotenberg (#53), Yuri Kovalchuk (#71)

State oligarchs control a significant part of the oil and gas sector (Alexey Miller of Gazprom, Igor Sechin of Rosneft, Aleksandr Dyukov of Gazprom Neft), the military-industrial complex (Sergey Chemezov of Rostec), the nuclear complex (Alexey Likhachev of Rosatom), the three largest banks (German Gref of Sberbank, Alexey Kostin of VTB, and Igor Shuvalov of VEB.RF), as well as the most important infrastructure companies (Nikolai Tokarev of Transneft, and Oleg Belozerov of Russian Railways).

Turning to the private oligarchs, by being included in the sanctions lists after the start of the invasion they have lost a significant part of their resources and are now busy trying to save the rest. This is not only about their money and influence in the West but also about their usefulness in the Russian system—a usefulness which has decreased in proportion to the decrease in their independent resources. Of particular note has been Roman Abramovich, who initiated several appeals from eminent people to lift sanctions from him and who took on a mission of mediation between Moscow and Kyiv. Other oligarchs in a similar position include Petr Aven and Mikhail Fridman.[8] Those who have been living in London for a long time and have fallen under sanctions are now trying to sell their shares in Alfa-Bank, the last assets they have in Russia. It should be noted that a number of oligarchs—including Abramovich, Fridman, Viktor Vekselberg, and German Khan—originally came from Ukraine, which, however, has not had a significant effect on their public position regarding the war.

The line between private oligarchs (or *chastniki* "private traders") and state oligarchs has blurred even more, and today it is not so much the state that depends on the oligarchs as the oligarchs who depend on the state. As will be shown below, the role of the oligarchs as the determining actors in political competition ("state capture") has been reversed, and they have become clients under the chief patron Putin ("oligarch capture"), only to lose even their limited bargaining positions as a result of the war.

There is also a special group of wealthy businessmen of Russian origin who have made their fortunes over the last 10–20 years but who have not had close relations with the authorities. In other words, these people can be seen as major entrepreneurs rather than oligarchs.[9] Since these major entrepreneurs, with their autonomous economic positions built mainly in the IT sector, do not conform to a patronal autocracy, where they would either be adopted into the single-pyramid network or be exposed to the predatory actions of the state,[10] many of them left Russia long before the war and continue to live abroad even now. Without being exhaustive, we may list some of the most important members of this group as follows:

- Pavel Durov (#3 in the *Forbes* 2022 list), the founder of the VKontakte social network and Telegram messenger (left in 2014 for Dubai);
- brothers Dmitry Bukhman (#12) and Igor Bukhman (#13), founders and owners of Playrix, one of the world's largest manufacturers of computer games (left in 2016 for Israel and UK);
- Yuri Milner (#15), owner of DST Global, former co-owner and chairman of the board of directors of Mail.Ru Group (left in 2014 for Israel and USA);
- Nikolay Storonsky (#16), founder of the fintech company Revolut (left in 2006 for London);
- Valentin Kipyatkov (#34) and Sergey Dmitriev (#30), co-founders and co-owners of the international software company JetBrains (left in 2000 for Prague);
- Timur Turlov, founder and main shareholder of Freedom Holding Corp. (left in 2014 for Kazakhstan);
- Arkady Volozh, co-founder of Yandex, "father of Runet" (left in 2014 for Israel).

Connections to the Russian aggression against Ukraine should be noted: many of the major entrepreneurs left the country in 2014, and Milner, Storonsky, and Turlov renounced their Russian citizenship in 2022. Those who still had assets in Russia have disposed of them, like Volozh. Unsurprisingly, most of the major entrepreneurs have condemned the war, although loud anti-Putin statements are not made out of fear for relatives and employees still in Russia. Among the oligarchs, members of the Yeltsin group have reacted most publicly to the Western sanctions (especially those oligarchs outside Russia, who did not understand why they were sanctioned in the first place). Many of them cautiously spoke out against the war, avoiding, however, clear identification of those responsible for its unleashing. Only Oleg Tinkov, a banker in the West, came out with a loud condemnation of the war, and was immediately forced to sell his business in Russia at a deep discount.[11]

2.2. The changing role of the oligarchs: from state capture to oligarch capture and the war

The changing role of oligarchic business within the Russian elite is well illustrated by a table compiled in 2021 by Andrey Yakovlev (Table 2).[12] The only clarification that I would like to offer in connection with recent events is the complete absence of an independent role for oligarchic business now. The role of the oligarchs, as determined by their financial resources, has noticeably decreased during Putin's last two presidential terms (2012–2018, 2018–), although these resources themselves have grown. This can be explained by the shift in power between the oligarchs and Putin's security forces (the so-called *siloviki*), which—just as ants harvest aphids— began to "harvest" the oligarchs during this period. In other words, with the outbreak of the war in Ukraine, the role of Russian oligarchs in Putin's network has become purely instrumental.

Table 2. The role of different elite groups in the ruling coalition in Russia.

Main groups	1996-1998	1999-2003	2004-2011	2012-present
Oligarchic business	Major partner	Main partner	Junior partner	Limited influence
Top federal bureaucracy	Junior partner	Main partner	Main partner	Junior partner
Siloviki	Limited influence	Junior partner	Main partner	Major partner

Source: Yakovlev (2021).

Immediately before the start of the war in Ukraine and a few hours after it began, the Kremlin demonstrated two hypostases of the Russian elite: first, a meeting of the Security Council with the participation of the top political, administrative and security elites, and then a meeting between Putin and representatives of various business circles. On the one hand, it was demonstrated who bears or shares responsibility with Putin for war crimes in Ukraine. On the other hand, with regard to the oligarchs (with whose representatives Putin had last met a year earlier in March 2021), the meeting was both a review of the ranks and an oath of allegiance to the leader. It is difficult to say who was not invited to the meeting, and who, having been invited, did not come for some reason. It is only known that Abramovich flew from the Cote d'Azur, and, being late for a general meeting, received a private audience instead. However, it is also revealing to look at the absent figures from among those who were usually present at such meetings: Lisin, Deripaska, Rotenberg, Timchenko, Kantor, Prokhorov, Usmanov, and Vekselberg. The participants of the meeting, which took place on the day the full-scale invasion began on February 24, 2022, were later subject to Western sanctions without exception.

Three months later, in June, at the height of the war, only six of the Russian oligarchs attended the traditional St. Petersburg economic forum: Vekselberg, Deripaska, Yevtushenkov, Mikhelson, Mordashov, and Pumpyansky. Several more of them showed up for Putin's speech during the Russian Union of Industrialists and Entrepreneurs (RSPP) congress on March 16, 2023: the same lineup plus Andrey Melnichenko, Vladimir Potanin, and Herman Khan, who had returned from London.

The absence of the others, however, in nowise implies a challenge to the system, but rather a reluctance to appear in a public setting once again. The Russian oligarchy went into deep shadow, and many of those who fell under the sanctions left their official positions in companies and transferred them to close relatives or other (strictly loyal) people. The RSPP, which used to be the "trade union of the oligarchs," has turned into a purely business association, with bureaucrats or top managers operating as the oligarchs' front men, rather than the actual owners of companies.[13]

According to the latest *Forbes* rating, Moscow ranked sixth in the world in terms of the number of billionaires living there (61 people) and third in terms of their combined wealth (USD 307 billion), second only to New York and Paris.[14] On the other hand, oligarchic business in an authoritarian state, largely controlled by people from the special services (see below), is associated with high risks, which are multiplied many times over in times of crisis. An example is the series of mysterious deaths of top managers in the oil and gas industry in 2022. In mid-April, the deaths of former top managers of Gazprombank and Novatek and their families occurred almost simultaneously in Moscow and Spain and were framed as murder-suicides on the part of the former executives.[15]

At LUKOIL, antiwar statements made by Vagit Alekperov, the president of the company, led to sharp changes in top management, followed by the death of Alekperov's right-hand man, Ravil Maganov, who allegedly fell out of a window at the Kremlin hospital on September 1—Alekperov's birthday.[16] The symbolism and demonstrative cruelty of these deaths suggests that these are not just business showdowns with the elimination of interfering figures, but signals sent to those remaining and, more broadly, to the entire oligarchic business community, to dissuade them from excessive independence.

At the same time, the war has placed the Russian oligarchs in a vise, with Putin exerting pressure from one side and the West from the other. The personal sanctions imposed on large and small oligarchs alike, having played a certain role in Western countries (apparently related to political considerations of the popularity of "punishing the guilty"), have made the oligarchs much more dependent on the Kremlin than they were before the war. The Kremlin, in turn, has become much less susceptible to the aspirations of the oligarchs, on whom both the current state and the prospects for the development of the Russian economy depend less than before.

Widespread personal sanctions against private oligarchs launched a process of semi-real redistribution of property in Russia, fraught with serious negative consequences. They have also led to significant personnel changes at major companies, as Vagit Alekperov (LUKOIL), Andrey Guryev (Phosagro), Vladimir Yevtushenkov (System), Dmitry Konov (SIBUR), Dmitry Mazepin (Uralkali), Andrey Melnichenko (SUEK and EuroChem), Vadim Moshkovich (Rusagro), Vladimir Rashevsky (SUEK) and others left their positions due to sanctions.

At the RSPP congress in March 2023, the composition of the board of the RSPP changed significantly, with 15 people—including such figures as Alisher Usmanov (USM), Leonid Fedun (LUKOIL), Dmitry Konov (SIBUR), and Araz Agalarov (Crocus Group)—leaving their positions.[17] Of those who have come in to replace them, only the name of Sergei Kogogin, the general director of truck and bus manufacturer Kamaz, has been mentioned so far. It is also characteristic that, at the moment of submitting this manuscript, two weeks after all the changes took place, there was still no information about the new composition of the leadership of the RSPP either on the organization's website or in the media.

The fate of the above-mentioned Alekperov is also revealing. In May 2022, he ceded the post of president of LUKOIL to Vadim Vorobyov, a former associate of the deputy chief of staff of the Russian presidential administration, Sergey Kiriyenko. According to the Brief telegram channel, Alekperov received permission to remotely control the strategic direction of LUKOIL and obtained a "24 month moratorium on Rosneft's attempts to take over the company." In exchange, Alekperov agreed to support the special operation in Ukraine and transferred his core energy assets to the management of one of the state corporations.[18] The resignation of LUKOIL's vice president and co-owner Leonid Fedun, announced soon after, means, in fact, a change not only in the top management, but also in the company's ownership.

2.3. "Chaebolization" in Russia: large conglomerates in the service of the chief patron

Until now, we have considered the Russian ruling class according to the logic of corporations, and by means of dichotomies such as state versus private ownership and power versus economic position. Meanwhile, the boundaries between corporations in recent years have become less and less rigid in Russia, and have less and less influence in determining the structure of the elite space. On the one hand, the radically replaced leadership of corporations plays a more instrumental, rather than a relatively independent, political role. On the other hand, corporations have begun to perform a variety of functions that go far beyond their main original field of activity, structurally resembling the chaebols, or affiliated conglomerates, of developmental states which merge various spheres of social action.[19] In this sense, in the more than two decades of Putin's rule, one can see (1) an initial phase of centralization, when there was deregionalization through corporatization, and (2) an ongoing, second phase of centralization, which also involves decorporatization through "chaebolization." The main difference between Russian "chaebols" and the original chaebols of South Korea is, of course, the lack of a bargaining position among the Russian conglomerates vis-à-vis Putin, who exercises direct control over them and over the centralization process in general.[20] At this point, we must finally mention that among Russian corporations there is one mega-corporation, the Russian secret service (FSB), which itself is a complex conglomerate of loosely centralized structures, and which under Putin has spread into all other large corporations in order to facilitate control.

The trend towards the formation of "chaebols" arose in 2008, with the transition to the so-called tandem (when Putin was temporarily replaced as president by his political front man Dmitry Medvedev), and has intensified in recent years. These comprise a combination of power and property in the same hands, which allows the chief patron to control the most important areas of activity and the country as a whole, regardless of political upheavals. In addition to Rostec, the companies that have undergone this procedure include Gazprom, Rosneft, Rossiya Bank, VTB, Rosatom, and the Kurchatov Institute. The chaebols are led by Putin's closest associates: Alexey Miller (Gazprom), Sergey Chemezov (Rostec), Igor Sechin (Rosneft), Andrey Kostin (VTB), Sergey Kiriyenko and Alexey Likhachev (Rosatom), and Yuri and Mikhail Kovalchuk (Kurchatov Institute and Rossiya Bank). On both a one-time and/or permanent basis, Russian chaebols have performed various non-core economic and political functions, for example: Gazprom has been used in geopolitical and geostrategic projects, for exerting control over the media, and in creating a network of theme parks called "Russia – My History"; Rosatom has been used in the operation of the Northern Sea Route, the elimination of pollution, the management of Sakhalin, and the management of the Vladivostok seaport; and Rosneft has been used in foreign policy projects in Venezuela, the launch of the Zvezda shipbuilding complex in the Far East and genetic research, etc.

With regard to Putin's cadres, the chaebols are not even assigned on a conglomerate basis but through symbioses: mergers of financial, political, power, and other resources according to the functional specialization of the respective elites, acting or able to act as a single team. Sometimes, as, for example, in the case of Igor

Sechin, who in 2012 exchanged his deputy prime minister's post for the position of state oligarch and chairman of Russia's third largest company, Rosneft, the close relationship between public administration, business, and security becomes especially visible.

Similar metamorphoses occurred with German Gref, who in 2007 moved from the position of minister of economics to the head of Sberbank; and more recently, with Igor Shuvalov, first deputy prime minister under Putin and then Medvedev (2008-2018), who became the head of another large bank and development institution, VEB.RF.

The role of chaebols in Russia, and especially Rostec, is greatly increasing in the context of the current protracted war and difficult confrontation with the West, as they are relied on to ensure the smooth functioning of the now-sanctioned military-industrial complex, of which Rostec is the core. As a result, experienced individuals, such as Manturov, who was appointed deputy prime minister in July 2022 and made responsible both for production and for the building of supply and distribution chains during the recent pandemic, are in great demand.

In the ordinary world, large property ensures continuity and serves as a guarantor of stability in the event of a change in political power. In Putin's Russia, where property rights are conditional and colossal state property is reserved for colleagues and clients of the president, things are not so. Putin's departure could provoke a colossal redistribution of property—both state-owned, cut into huge chunks, and private, as the above-mentioned example of LUKOIL shows. This means that those who today control these huge pieces of property are not interested in Putin's departure: they are interested in maintaining the status quo for as long as possible. At the same time, however, in a situation of weak institutions and aging "oligarchs" (for the most part, Putin's peers) the longer the status quo persists, the lower the managerial efficiency and the higher will be the risks of destabilization as a result of retirement for natural reasons and a one-time mass change of state oligarchs and "private traders."

3. Bureaucrats: *siloviki*, technocrats, and political managers

3.1. The siloviki *bureaucrats and Putin's "Praetorian Guard"*

As power in Russia shifts from informal to semi-formal positions, the war is the time of the *siloviki* bureaucrats who operate the instruments of state power such as the Russian Armed Forces, the Prosecutor General's Office, and the intelligence service. However, they also act on command: they are instrumental, and do not cope very well with this instrumental role. For the most part, they are not public, and although information about the removal from office or even the arrest of high-ranking military and FSB officials appears every now and then, it is still difficult to verify such news. What is known for sure is that with the changes in the heads of the Prosecutor General's Office and the Rosgvardiya/Internal Troops large-scale purges were carried out in the internal forces. At the end of 2021, Putin replaced the official responsible for the personnel of the security forces.

Unlike the oligarchs, the security forces are all Putin's, and many of them are already second generation. Therefore, two sub-groups of *siloviki* bureaucrats may be distinguished: the "old" ones appointed during the transition to and exit from the Putin-Medvedev tandem, and the "new" ones appointed during Putin's last two presidential terms (Table 3). However, the difference between the "old" and "new" *siloviki* is not only in the length of service and, accordingly, in the degree of control over the corporations[21] they lead. The categorization also marks, as a rule, the difference in age. Many of the veteran *siloviki*, including Bastrykin, Patrushev, and Bortnikov, have crossed the 70-year mark, and although Putin annually extends their service life, which makes their leash very short, they are more than likely to be replaced under Putin. In 2014-2016, the leadership of half of the power corporations was radically updated, and the departure of the remaining old-timers during the transition from a serious confrontation with the West to a relatively stable regime could take place at any moment.

Table 3. Grouping of siloviki bureaucrats according to the period of their emergence.

Group of siloviki bureaucrats (period of appointment)	Members of the group (with institutions and dates of appointment)
"Old" (2007–2012)	Alexander Bastrykin (Investigative Committee, 2007), Nikolai Patrushev (Security Council, 2008), Alexander Bortnikov (FSB, 2008), Vladimir Kolokoltsev (Ministry of Internal Affairs, 2012), Sergei Shoigu (Ministry of Defense, 2012), Valery Gerasimov (Ministry of Defense, 2012)
"New" (2012-2022)[22]	Viktor Zolotov (Rosgvardiya, 2016), Dmitry Kochnev (Federal Guard Service, 2016), Alexey Rubezhnoy (Presidential Security Service, 2016), Igor Krasnov (Prosecutor General, 2020), Sergey Korolev (FSB, 2021), Dmitry Mironov (presidential staff, 2021), Alexander Kurenkov (Ministry of Emergency Situations, 2022).

With the outbreak of the war, the *siloviki*, for the most part, went into the shadows. Of the security officials who have promoted themselves in the war, it is worth mentioning Ramzan Kadyrov, the head of Chechnya and at the same time the head of a semi-independent power structure (a "sub-sovereign mafia state"),[23] and Yevgeny Prigozhin, who conducted operations with his "private army" called PMC "Wagner."

The main public conflict within the power community is now taking place along the lines of the state security forces and the "private" entities, represented by Kadyrov and, for a year and a half, Prigozhin.[24]

Special mention should be made of the phenomenon of the Praetorian Guard, Putin's most trusted personal guards and aides-de-camp, which actively began to grow a few years ago. It began with Viktor Zolotov, the longtime head of the Presidential Security Service (SBP), who was appointed deputy commander of the Internal Troops in 2013, then commander of the Internal Troops in 2014, and finally commander-in-chief of the National Guard of Russia (Rosgvardiya) in 2016. In 2016, Evgeny Zinichev, Alexey Dyumin, Dmitry Mironov, Sergey Morozov and Igor Babushkin were appointed to the posts of governors. At the same time, a scheme was usually employed for the interim formal appointment of Putin's clients for a month or two to some high public post (e.g., deputy minister with an assigned rank of general) and only then to the post of governor, perceived by appointees as a bridge to a federal career. This is what happened in the case of Zinichev (who first became deputy director of the FSB, and then minister of emergency situations) and in the case of Mironov (who moved in 2021 to the post of assistant to the president in charge of personnel issues of the military and security forces).

After the full-scale invasion began, we learned about Putin's new guards in high positions: Alexander Kurenkov, appointed minister of emergency situations, and Roman Gavrilov, who resigned as deputy head of the Rosgvardiya, where he carried out a large-scale purge of the organization's leadership. In short, Putin's praetorians are now responsible for the personnel of the security forces (Mironov), and they head two key armed forces: Rosgvardiya (Zolotov) and the Ministry of Emergency Situations (Kurenkov), as well as two regions: Tula (Dyumin) and Astrakhan (Babushkin).

The leadership of the highest courts complements the *siloviki* bureaucrats. The chairman of the Supreme Court, 79-year-old Vyacheslav Lebedev, belongs to the main old-timers—indeed, he was appointed to this post under Gorbachev. The chairman of the Constitutional Court, 80-year-old Valery Zorkin, also took up his post in 1991, then returned to it after a ten-year hiatus in 2003. Both play a largely symbolic role, on the one hand ensuring stability and continuity, and, on the other hand, allowing the Kremlin to keep full control over the judiciary, either through them or directly through the Commission for the Preliminary Review of Candidates for the Position of Federal Judges under the President, whose work is controlled by Maxim Travnikov, the head of the Office of the President for Public Service and Personnel.

The question of whether the security forces (or at least one or two power corporations) could act in a concerted manner against the Kremlin would have to be answered in the negative. This is extremely unlikely due to their disunity (the security forces are not directly connected to each other, but through Putin), as well as the presence of multiple control mechanisms. These include external controls by the FSB and through interdepartmental competition, and internal controls through quasi-checks and balances in the leadership of the power corporations themselves. In addition, the Kremlin ensures that power corporations are not headed by individuals exhibiting too much authority or independence, thereby preventing any cracks in the unity of the single-pyramid patronal network.

3.2. Technocrat bureaucrats: from being grey to being invisible

The government of Prime Minister Mikhail Mishustin is perhaps the most technocratic and apolitical of all Russian cabinets since 1991. Assuming office in 2020 represented a sharp advancement and a radical change in duties for both Mishustin and many members of his cabinet. The new government leadership took on the role of crisis managers, who were tasked with creating a mobilization management system in a short period of time.

Having received *carte blanche* at the beginning to appoint "his" deputy prime ministers, Mishustin strengthened the position of his team step-by-step, replacing a number of ministers he inherited (November 2020), carrying out large-scale replacements in the government apparatus (January 2021), and gradually updating the composition of deputy ministers and heads of services and agencies. The result was greater unity of command and the weakening of some traditionally strong clients (like Sobyanin, Sechin, Kovalchuk, and Rotenberg).

Even before the start of the war in Ukraine, both the head of the government, Mishustin, and the head of the Presidential Executive Office, Anton Vaino, somewhat faded into the background, allowing their deputies to assume center stage, both formally and in practice. In the government, this involved the First Deputy Prime Minister Andrei Belousov, Deputy Prime Minister for Construction and Regional Development Marat Khusnullin, Deputy Prime Minister for Social Policy Tatyana Golikova, and Deputy Prime Minister for Energy Alexander Novak; in the AP, we find in similar role assumed by the First Deputy Chief of Staff of the Presidential Administration Sergey Kiriyenko. With the start of the war, Mishustin and Vaino withdrew even further into the shadows.

None of the high-ranking "technocratic" bureaucrats have publicly criticized the war or resigned in protest, which can be considered Putin's most important achievement. Anatoly Chubais, the former presidential special representative for relations with international organizations, and Alexei Kudrin, the head of the Accounts Chamber, "begged" Putin for permission to leave; the former resigned in March 2022, while the latter left in November to work for the Yandex IT company. The chairman of the Central Bank, Elvira Nabiullina, who, according to rumors, also asked to resign, was nominated by Putin to a new five-year term instead, a month after the start of the war.[25]

Although several deputy ministers left the government, no one was loud or critical. The only exception was Natalya Poklonskaya, an exotic figure in Russian politics. She was once the face of the "Crimean spring," as well as the deputy head of the foreign ministry agency Rossotrudnichestvo after February 2, 2022. She was dismissed by June the same year and transferred to the post of adviser to the Prosecutor General, which excludes public statements.

In mid-March, FIDE president and former deputy prime minister in the Medvedev government, Arkady Dvorkovich, gave a resonant interview to the American edition of *Mother Jones*, in which he spoke out against the military operation in Ukraine.[26] For this, he was accused of treason and forced to resign as chairman of the Skolkovo Foundation.

In the single-pyramid network there is no room for independent action, any disagreement with orders is regarded as a betrayal and disloyalty. To add to this, the Russian system has now been placed on a martial law footing. It can be assumed that many internally do not agree with what is happening but, firstly, the members of the Federal Assembly cannot make independent assessments and actions, and, secondly, all dissidents remain essentially hostages. Dvorkovich and Chubais are retirees. All this means that there is no independent elite in Russia, and after the collapse of the regime, there will be no one to count on.

3.3. "Political manager" bureaucrats: domesticated parties and the propaganda machinery

The political manager bureaucrats can be seen as an extensive superstructure, which includes (1) a significant part of Sergey Kiriyenko's Presidential Administration bloc, (2) the State Council, which is under the responsibility of Presidential Aide Igor Levitin and the head of the Office of the Presidential Administration for ensuring the affairs of the State Council, Alexander Kharichev, and (3) remote structures of the lower and upper houses of the Federal Assembly with their speakers Vyacheslav Volodin and Valentina Matvienko. This also includes the leaders of political parties in the State Duma, whose already limited role, with the start of the war, has become completely unobtrusive.[27]

This is a very competitive area with confrontation taking place within the frame-work of two macro-groups of the elite: one led by Putin's major shadow businessman, Yuri Kovalchuk, and the other led by the oligarch Igor Sechin, chairman of Rosneft using power resources given by law enforcement. Among the relatively independent figures in relation to Kiriyenko (in charge of domestic politics) are Vyacheslav Volodin, who has his own clientele (which has noticeably decreased since 2016, when he moved from the post of first deputy head of the Presidential Administration to the State Duma), Andrei Turchak, the main party functionary of United Russia, and Valentina Matvienko, the first deputy speaker of the Federation Council since September 2020.

Political parties, including United Russia, have been pushed to the sidelines of a system which comprises a dominant party with a largely domesticated, marginalized and fragmented opposition.[28] Apart from trying to promote the "New People" party as a new political force on the conditionally liberal flank, and weakening the positions of a younger and more radical faction in the leadership of the Communist Party, the Kremlin has not implemented any projects in the field of party building. Everything has worked out with the Communist Party (KPRF) so far, but the problem of replacing its leader, 78-year-old Zyuganov, has not yet been solved. At the same time, the replacement of the deceased Zhirinovsky as the leader of the right-wing populist Liberal Democratic Party of Russia (LDPR) by the scandalous politician-businessman Leonid Slutsky shows that the Kremlin is not going to take any drastic steps against its "opposition" parties. As for the "New People" party, a project connected with businessman Yuri Kovalchuk, it is hardly possible to expect its development under conditions of war.

Gennady Zyuganov has been the leader of the Communist Party of the Russian Federation since 1995. Grigory Yavlinsky has headed the Yabloko party since its founding in 1993 (as chairman of the party until 2008, and then as its informal undisputed leader). Sergey Mironov has been heading "A Just Russia" (SRZP) in its various reincarnations since 2003. Only two politicians can be considered newcomers to the posts of party leaders: Sergey Nechaev, who created the "New People" political party in 2020, and Leonid Slutsky, who replaced the LDPR leader Vladimir Zhironovsky, who led the party from 1992 until his death in 2022.

Without exception, all Duma parties at the federal level have publicly expressed complete unanimity regarding the war. If in the previous composition of the State Duma there were several people capable of going against the current, the current Duma has seen all decisions regarding the annexation of the occupied Ukrainian regions adopted unanimously.

At the regional level, there were attempts to adopt a more critical attitude within the KPRF, but these were quickly suppressed. Yabloko stands somewhat apart, publicly—albeit cautiously—condemning the war, but both its political positions and its electoral support are very weak; indeed, the party has not been represented in the State Duma since 2007.

An important part of political management is the information and propaganda sector. Regarding the heads of the three main TV channels, two of them, like the leaders of the parties, have been in their posts since the end of the Yeltsin era. These are Konstantin Ernst, general director of Channel One since 1999, and Oleg Dobrodeev, permanent head of the All-Russian State Television and Radio Company since 2000. Both are full holders of the Order of Merit for the Fatherland, having been awarded all four classes. The third person is Alexei Zemsky, the general director of NTV, who replaced his predecessor in 2015, who left for health reasons. We should also mention Margarita Simonyan, who has headed the Russia Today international news agency since its inception in 2013. The media is also supervised by the indefatigable Aleksey Gromov, one of Putin's former press secretaries and the first deputy chief of staff of the Presidential Administration since 2012.

The two largest players in the media market are Gazprom-Media Holding, whose general-director since 2020 is Alexander Zharov, who previously headed Russia's main internet and media censor Roskomnadzor, while its chairman since 2007 is Alexey Miller; and the National Media Group, controlled by Yuri Kovalchuk, whose chairman since 2014 is Alina Kabaeva, the alleged mother of Putin's children.

It is rather difficult to judge the changes since the beginning of 2022 within the political management bloc, an area that is already lacking in public transparency. A proper assessment is hindered by two factors. First, just before the start of the war and in its first two or three months, the main and only concern of the Kremlin was the war, and all decisions in the domestic political sphere, including personnel, were put on hold. At one time, there was even an active discussion of the possibility of abandoning elections and other peacetime routines under conditions of the country's *de facto* transition to martial law.[29] The internal political paralysis ended by May 2022, when the idea of a blitzkrieg campaign had to be completely abandoned and a transition was made to the option of a protracted war.

Secondly, with the full-scale invasion of Ukraine and a sharp confrontation with the West, the importance of demonstrating the consolidation of the elites has increased, and Putin is trying in every possible way to avoid high-profile reshuffles and public manifestations of dissatisfaction with this or that figure. Instead, his practice is to change the authority and functionality of individual figures in political management without changing their official positions. This is more typical for the military and the security forces in general, but it also takes place in relation to the bureaucrats of the political bloc. Certain figures can fall out of the public space, sometimes for a long time, giving rise to rumors of disgrace, resignation, even arrest, and then suddenly reappear.

A typical example is Dmitry Kozak, deputy head of the Presidential Administration, one of Putin's most trusted associates back in St. Petersburg, and an effective crisis manager. One of the most prominent figures in the maneuvering before the war (since the Donbass and Ukraine in general were part of his area of responsibility), he disappeared from sight shortly after the start of the war, just as negotiations stalled and the transition to a protracted war took place. There were rumors of his disagreement with Putin over the conditions for ending the war and even talk of his house arrest. Officially, authority for overseeing the Donbass and the newly occupied territories was transferred from Kozak to Kiriyenko. However, a year later, at the time of this writing, it is known that Kozak continues to work from his office in the Kremlin. According to rumors, he is being considered as a candidate for the position of chairman of the Accounts Chamber, vacated with the departure of Alexei Kudrin in November 2022.[30] While the political managers at the very top are virtually irremovable, the replacement of leaders at the next level sharply intensified following the outbreak of the war. This concerns the removal of rectors of large, and especially liberal, universities, and directors of leading art museums: Iosif Reichelgauz ("School of Modern Drama," June 2022), Alexei Agranovich ("Gogol Center," June 2022), Viktor Ryzhakov ("Contemporary," June 2022), Vladimir Mau (RANEPA, January 2023), Zelfira Tregulova (Tretyakov Gallery, February 2023), Vladimir Gusev (State Russian Museum, February 2023), Sergey Zuev (Moscow Higher School of Social and Economic Sciences (Shaninka), March 2023), and Marina Loshak (Pushkin State Museum of Fine Arts, March 2023). In place of strong professionals and bright and independent personalities, little-known officials began to make an appearance: the "children" of Putin's elite, that is, people from pro-Kremlin youth movements.

The political management bloc, along with that of media and culture, has undergone perhaps the greatest changes in Putin's bureaucracy since the beginning of the war. However, these changes have taken place at the middle and grassroots levels, where the Kremlin has diligently cleaned out everyone who has not made public expressions of support for the war unleashed in Ukraine. Many representatives of the intellectual elite left the country altogether; others replaced by competitors who took advantage of the moment. At the same time, at the very top in this bloc, there is not only remarkable stability, demonstrating the evolutionary nature of the changes that have taken place, but also complete business control by the most trusted people from Putin's inner circle.

4. Regional governors: from self-governance to a lower level of state administration

The governors of the Russian regions were the first large group of the elite on which the model of constant rotation and decoration was tested, with the replacement of governors from among the local elite with so-called "Varangians" who had nothing to do with the region. According to Alexander Kynev's calculations, in the most massive series of these "Kiriyenko" governor replacements, which took place in 2016-2018, some 57% of the 47 newly appointed regional heads were "Varangians."[31]

It is these appointees who are now approaching the time for re-election. In May 2022, five regional heads were replaced, and in all five cases the status quo was maintained: in three regions, Varangians were replaced by Varangians, while in the other two, local heads were replaced by other locals.

Most of the newly appointed officials, as well as their predecessors, underwent special training at the "school of governors"—the management reserve program of the Russian Presidential Academy of National Economy and Public Administration (RANEPA). At the same time, however, most of them also had work experience at both the federal and regional level.

Previously, the Kremlin proceeded from the fact that a department head of a federal ministry and, even more so, a deputy minister, who made a career in Moscow, could easily cope with regional leadership. Now, apparently, the managerial skills that have been developed at the regional level are required of regional heads. The question is what caused the Kremlin to change its position: disappointment in the ministerial technocrats or situational complications?

The principle of maintaining the status quo when replacing regional heads is true not only in relation to the connection between the new governor and the local elite, but also in relation to large patronal networks—however, not in relation to the individual regions, but in relation to the overall national balance. Most of the new regional heads are Kiriyenko's people, which does not negate their dual loyalty (to him and to Putin). One of the new heads is associated with Sobyanin's circle, another is associated with Igor Sechin, while the Saratov governor, Roman Busargin is, as always, Volodin's protégé. Prior to his appointment, Busargin was the head of the regional government; he is of "one flesh" with the local elites and did not study at the above-mentioned "school of governors." At the same time, however, there is a point of view according to which Busargin's appointment is situational and testifies not so much to the strength of Volodin's position as the speaker of the State Duma, but to the fact that Igor Sechin and Yuri Kovalchuk each promoted their own candidate and, unable to divide Saratov between them, the region remained with Volodin's man.

According to one telegram channel, it is against the backdrop of the regional struggle between Igor Sechin and Yuri Kovalchuk, each of whom has his own "sub-network," his own alternative approaches to development and management, including that of the regions, that the main intrigues in the series of appointment made on May 10 should be seen.[32] It was from the party of Kovalchuk that the regions—the Kirov and Ryazan regions—received the Kiriyenko technocrats-political strategists.

In the last two weeks of March 2023, Putin replaced three more regional heads, and the replacement model this time turned out to be new. Firstly, two of the three departing regional heads were so-called party governors, one representing the

Liberal Democrats (LDPR) and the other A Just Russia (SRZP). According to the informal party quota system, which has been in operation since 2012, although the overwhelming majority of governors are represented by United Russia, the other major parties also have representation within the corps of governors, including the Communist Party of the Russian Federation (KPRF), which now has three, the Liberal Democrats, which now have only one (although they had three at their peak), and the SRZP, which has now lost one of the two it had previously.

However, instead of extending the party quota to the "New People" party, which entered the Duma in 2021, the Kremlin decided to dismantle or at least reduce party representation altogether. And this was not due to a lack of loyalty on the part of the so-called "systemic" (or domesticated) opposition parties, which are absolutely obedient to the Kremlin. On the contrary, it is because under the conditions of complete unity around Putin, it becomes difficult and meaningless to emphasize any party differences.

The second way in which this most recent replacement of regional heads was new is that this generation of governors comprises not only officials who have completed courses at the Civil Service Academy but also includes people who have gained experience working at the regional level. Two of them worked for several months as government officials in the so-called People's Republics of Lugansk and Donetsk (DNR and LNR). The third individual was in charge of integrating the new regions into the government apparatus. Thus, all three constitute members of the "Donbas generation."

Lastly, a course has been set for a sharp rejuvenation. The new appointees are not even forty—these are people whose entire careers have been spent under the Putin regime. They are executives and are used to being cogs in the management machine. At the same time, they do not and cannot have their own teams, nor do they have obligations to the regional elite. They are obedient to those who sent them to the regions: the Kremlin and the power corporations.

When a new governor forms his team, two approaches are employed: (1) a number of key officials of the administration are factually appointed by the federal center (this applies to such areas as finance, state regulation of tariffs, education, and health care);[33] and (2) other positions are filled in part by the governor himself and in part by the corporation or federal elite group standing behind him.

Recently, local self-government, which comprised an independent branch of government under the 1993 constitution, has been turned into a lower level of the state administration. Only six directly elected mayors of regional centers remain in the country, all in Siberia and the Far East. Moreover, in the largest of the centers that remained with elected mayors, Novosibirsk, direct elections were abolished quite recently, in February 2023.[34] In most regions, mayors are appointed by a competition commission *de facto* controlled by the governor.

What has been said about the regional elites means one very important thing: in the event of a sharp weakening of the Center, as happened in the late 1980s and early 1990s, the regional level will be unable to play the role of a "safety net," picking up the power that has fallen from above. As a result of political engineering carried out during Putin's twenty-odd years in power, which aimed at strengthening the control of the Center, the regional elites are extremely weakened and lack consolidation. It will take time to restore their viable form and independence— a year or two, maybe more.

5. Conclusion: from informal to bureaucratic patronalism and the future of Putin's single-pyramid network

The first thing to say is that there is no elite existing as an amateur stratum with some kind of independence in Putin's patronal system. The single-pyramid network does not comprise an elite of strong personalities; rather, with the weakening of informal and the strengthening of formal elements, it resembles more and more a party state-like nomenklatura. The governing class is fragmented, not to say atomized, and at the same time built into a rigid mechanistic structure, which sharply limits its ability to act independently. The structure of the system works for this, just like the selection of personnel and their coaching (and not just strict control and repression).

The representatives of the so-called "liberal wing" in the structures of power deserve special mention. Indeed, this wing has been gone for a long time, since 2012, and certainly since 2014. Those figures who were once part of it and remain in power to this day, such as Alexei Kudrin, German Gref, and Elvira Nabiullina, differ little from other technocrat managers, showing their liberalism in strictly defined places and amounts allowed by the system. There were no public resignations of status liberals in connection with the outbreak of the war, and only Anatoly Chubais left an insignificant post in the Presidential Administration (AP), and the country as well, without commenting on his resignation in any way. Yeltsin's son-in-law Valentin Yumashev, who was a pro bono adviser to the president during Putin's entire tenure, also left the AP.

In the first year of the war, changes in the upper echelon of the elite were minimal, although changes in power competences were noticeable as the transition to a state of war took place (Table 4). Among oligarchs, whose dependence on the Kremlin has sharply increased since the start of the war in Ukraine and the adoption of tough sanctions by the West, these changes have been greater; among bureaucrats, including technocrats, political managers, and security forces *(siloviki)*, the changes have been less noticeable.

Under the conditions of the war in Ukraine and the paramilitary situation inside Russia itself, the role of the security forces within the bureaucracy has increased to a relative degree—not so much in an individual capacity, but at a corporate level. Their role, as in the case of other bureaucrats, is rather instrumental.

Table 4. Changing power competences of various groups in Putin's patronal network during the war.

Elite group	Change of influence	Specific features of the change
Oligarchs	decrease	widespread change of managers and owners, increasing danger of raiding
Technocrat bureaucrats	increase	operators of domestic institutions in war mode (progressive nationalization of the economy and growing role of budgetary resources)
Security bureaucrats (*siloviki*)	increase/stagnation (on a high level)	corporate-institutional strengthening rather than personal (limited autonomy)
Political manager bureaucrats	stagnation (on a low level)	"business as usual"

A split in the elites or even a visible intensification of the competitive struggle between their various groups is not observed as of April 2023. At the same time, in a situation witnessing a reduction in the "pie" of rents distributed among them, tougher competition seems inevitable as early as 2023.

This past year with Russia in a state of war has not only highlighted aspects of the personnel policy that existed before, but has also given rise to new practices. At the same time, most of the relocations and new appointments over the year were connected with the war and its support in one way or another. Despite the relatively small number of public replacements and the general stability of the personal composition of Putin's single-pyramid network, the latter is undergoing tectonic shifts associated with the forced redistribution of power and property. The once very active group of Yeltsin-era oligarchs is leaving the stage quite quickly, while the influence of the Putin-era ones is increasing. The replacement of personnel, which is piecemeal as a rule, is reactive, leading to isolated areas of rejuvenation, but does not solve the general problems of the system.

As for the future, the current configuration of the elite will have a great influence on the possible variety of scenarios. Instead of positing various kinds of speculative constructions, I will offer one of the conclusions made by my colleagues and I based on the results of a network analysis of Putin's political elite.[35] We asked ourselves whether there were such actors or connections in the network under consideration, the removal of which would destroy it as a whole or render the system disconnected. It turned out that formally speaking there were three players—Putin, his chief of staff Alexey Gromov, and Moscow mayor Sergey Sobyanin—whose exclusion would cause the network to lose its connectivity. However, what parts of the network would be dismantled in this case? It turns out that the elite network would lose only those players who have no other connections than those that connect them with the aforementioned actors, namely, the director of the FSB—Alexander Bortnikov, the general director of the All-Russian State Television and Radio Broadcasting Company—Oleg Dobrodeev, and the deputy prime minister of Russia for construction and regional development—Marat Khusnullin.

This means that the network has every chance of remaining stable even in the event of Putin's hypothetical withdrawal from it. The reason for this is the breadth of horizontal ties that have formed in the upper echelon of the Russian elite. Of course, in this situation, factionalism may increase, and ties between communities, which are now largely closed on the leader of the network, will become rarer. Nevertheless, the level of development of informal intra-elite ties may be sufficient to prevent or minimize intra-elite splits that are characteristic of autocracies

Notes

1. Vladimir Dubrovskiy, "Why Is the Russian Bureaucracy Failing in the Face of War?" *Review of Democracy*, February 24, 2023, https://revdem.ceu.edu/2023/02/24/why-is-the-russian-bureaucracy-failing-in-the-face-of-war/.
2. See Bálint Madlovics and Bálint Magyar's introductory chapter "Ukrainian Regime Cycles and the Russian Invasion," in *Ukraine's Patronal Democracy and the Russian Invasion: The Russia-Ukraine War, Volume One*, edited by Bálint Madlovics and Bálint Magyar (Budapest–Vienna–New York: CEU Press, 2023), 3–53.
3. See for example the final rating of the 100 leading Russian politicians in 2022: Dmitry Orlov, "100 Ведущих Политиков России в 2022 Году" [100 leading politicians in Russia in 2022], *Nezavisimaya gazeta*, January 9, 2023, http://www.ng.ru/ideas/2023-01-09/7_8629_100.html.
4. On the picture before the war, see Nikolay Petrov, "Putin's Neo-Nomenklatura System and Its Evolution," in *Stubborn Structures: Reconceptualizing Post-Communist Regimes*, ed. Bálint Magyar (Budapest–New York: CEU Press, 2019), 179–215.
5. Triesman's article first appeared as a working paper in 2006, and was published a year later in *Orbis*. See Daniel Treisman, "Putin's Silovarchs," *Orbis* 51, no. 1 (2007): 141–53.
6. Forbes' list of billionaires included 88 people in 2022, almost thirty percent less than a year before (123 people). "88 российских миллиардеров. Рейтинг Forbes" [88 Russian billionaires. The Forbes rating], *Forbes.ru*, 2022, https://www.forbes.ru/milliardery/463151-88-rossijskih-milliarderov-rejting-forbes-2022.
7. Lisin is listed in both the "Yeltsin" and the "Yeltsin-Putin" group as his wealth accumulation spanned through both of these periods.
8. "Abramovich Is Suing the EU. He's Not the Only One," *POLITICO*, June 3, 2022, https://www.politico.eu/article/roman-abramovich-sue-eu-sanctions-assets-visas-vladimir-putin-russia-war-ukraine-mikhail-fridman-petr-aven-alisher-usmanov/.
9. On the conceptual difference, see Magyar and Madlovics, *The Anatomy of Post-Communist Regimes*, 164–68.
10. Magyar and Madlovics, *The Anatomy of Post-Communist Regimes*, 168–78.
11. Anton Troianovski and Ivan Nechepurenko, "Russian Tycoon Criticized Putin's War. Retribution Was Swift.," *The New York Times*, May 1, 2022, sec. World, https://www.nytimes.com/2022/05/01/world/europe/oligarch-putin-oleg-tinkov.html.
12. Andrei Yakovlev, "Composition of the Ruling Elite, Incentives for Productive Usage of Rents, and Prospects for Russia's Limited Access Order," *Post-Soviet Affairs* 37, no. 5 (2021): 417–34.
13. On the concept of front men, see Magyar and Madlovics, *The Anatomy of Post-Communist Regimes*, 180–83.
14. "Москва вошла в тройку городов с самыми богатыми миллиардерами" [Moscow joined the top three cities with the richest billionaires], *RBK*, April 9, 2023, https://www.rbc.ru/business/09/04/2023/6432b5b79a7947de26b86fe7.
15. Chloe Taylor, "Deaths of 2 Russian Oligarchs within 48 Hours Add to Wave of Executives Found Dead in 'Suspicious' Circumstances," *Fortune*, April 25, 2022, https://fortune.com/2022/04/25/deaths-russian-oligarchs-wave-executives-found-dead-gazprom-novatek/.
16. "Ravil Maganov: Russian Lukoil Chief Dies in 'Fall from Hospital Window,'" *BBC News*, September 1, 2022, sec. Europe, https://www.bbc.com/news/world-europe-62750584.
17. "Агаларов и Федун выйдут из правления РСПП" [Agalarov and Fedun leave the board of the RSPP], *RBK*, March 14, 2023, https://www.rbc.ru/business/14/03/2023/64103fea9a79477849294a69.
18. "«Он тихо офигевает от всего происходящего»: когорту санкционных отставников пополнил Вагит Алекперов" ['He is quietly going nuts over everything that is happening': Vagit Alekperov has joined the cohort of sanctions-retireees], *Biznes Online*, April 21, 2022, https://www.business-gazeta.ru/article/547711.

19   See David Murillo and Yun-dal Sung, "Understanding Korean Capitalism: Chaebols and Their Corporate Governance," Position Paper (ESADEgeo Center for Global Economy and Geopolitics, September 2013).

20   On the bargaining position of chaebols in South Korea, see David C. Kang, "Bad Loans to Good Friends: Money Politics and the Developmental State in South Korea," *International Organization* 56, no. 1 (2002): 177–207.

21   By "corporation" I mean both power institutions (coercive state power) and economic corporations led by *siloviki*, in line with (1) the idea of "privatizing" power resources of the state, and (2) the idea of power and ownership and the lack of separation of spheres, as explained in Magyar and Madlovics, *The Anatomy of Post-Communist Regimes*.

22   It should be mentioned that the composition of the *siloviki* is influenced by the large-scale *siloviki* re-shuffling carried out in 2016, in advance of the 2018 presidential election.

23   See Magyar and Madlovics, *The Anatomy of Post-Communist Regimes*, 121–23.

24   On August 23, 2023, Prigozhin was presumed dead in a plane crash in Tver Oblast, north of Moscow, along with nine other people.

25   "Russia Central Banker Wanted Out over Ukraine, But Putin Said No," *Bloomberg*, March 23, 2022, https://www.bloomberg.com/news/articles/2022-03-23/russia-central-banker-wanted-out-over-ukraine-but-putin-said-no.

26   Arkady Dvorkovich, Former top Kremlin official who chairs global chess federation decries Russia's war on Ukraine, interview by Daniel King, *Mother Jones*, March 14, 2022, https://www.motherjones.com/politics/2022/03/chess-grandmasters-putin-russia-ukraine-war/.

27   On the role of Russian parties before the war, see Zoltán Sz. Bíró, "The Russian Party System," in *Stubborn Structures: Reconceptualizing Post-Communist Regimes*, ed. Bálint Magyar (Budapest–New York: CEU Press, 2019), 319–52.

28   Magyar and Madlovics, *A Concise Field Guide*, 69–72.

29   Andrey Pertsev, "В России из-за войны могут отменить выборы губернаторов, говорят источники «Медузы»" [Gubernatorial elections in Russia may be cancelled because of the war, sources tell Meduza], *Meduza*, March 4, 2022, https://meduza.io/feature/2022/03/04/v-rossii-iz-za-voyny-mogut-otmenit-vybory-gubernatorov-govoryat-istochniki-meduzy.

30   "Дмитрий Козак стал основным кандидатом на пост главы Счетной палаты" [Dmitry Kozak has become the main candidate for the post of head of the Accounts Chamber], *RBK*, January 20, 2023, https://www.rbc.ru/politics/20/01/2023/63ca64b59a7947f808dbf1e8.

31   A. V. Kynev, "Феномен губернаторов-«варягов» как индикатор рецентрализации (опыт 1991—2018 гг.)" [The phenomenon of governor-"varangians" as an indicator of recentralization. Experience of 1991-2018], *Полития: Анализ. Хроника. Прогноз (Журнал Политической Философии и Социологии Политики)* 93, no. 2 (2019): 125–50.

32   "Сечин и Ковальчук не поделили Саратов, поэтому он остался у Володина. По слухам, в губернаторы прочили Ольгу Баталину и Дениса Филиппова" [Sechin and Kovalchuk were unable to divide Saratov, so it remained with Volodin. According to rumors, Olga Batalina and Denis Filippov were expected to be governors], *Biznes-vektor*, May 17, 2022, https://www.business-vector.info/sechin-i-kovalchuk-ne-142037/.

33   "Подписан закон о единой системе публичной власти в субъектах России" [The law on a unified system of public authority in the constituent entities of Russia was signed], President of Russia, official website, December 30, 2021, http://kremlin.ru/acts/news/67399.

34   "Lawmakers Abolish Direct Mayoral Elections in Novosibirsk," *Meduza*, February 20, 2023, https://meduza.io/en/news/2023/02/20/lawmakers-abolish-direct-mayoral-elections-in-novosibirsk.

35   Е.А. Иванов, К.В. Мельников, and Н.В. Петров, "Неформальная Структура Элитного Пространства России (Опыт Сетевого Анализа)," *Полития: Анализ. Хроника. Прогноз (Журнал Политической Философии и Социологии Политики)* 104, no. 1 (2022): 72–91.

Socially Inclusive and Exclusive Warfighting: Comparing Ukraine and Russia's Ways of War
András Rácz

1. Introduction

A full-scale escalation of the Russia-Ukraine war has been going on since February 24, 2022.[1] Since then, Ukraine has been fighting for its survival and is mobilizing every possible resource both at home and abroad. Meanwhile, Russia is officially still not at war, but is conducting a "special military operation," which intends to limit the effect of the war on Russian society to the bare possible minimum. This discrepancy between how Ukraine and Russia have been fighting this war constitutes the focus of the present chapter.

Hence, I intend to provide a comparative overview of the wider political, social, and sociological aspects of how Ukraine and Russia are fighting this war. It is not about military sociology, however; the generally scarce availability of data about both the Russian and the Ukrainian forces, combined with operational security considerations and increased secrecy since February 2022, make any military sociological research currently impossible. Hence, while the chapter discusses how the armed forces are used on the strategic level, and how the two societies relate to their own armies, it can barely touch upon the relations within the militaries themselves.

In terms of methodology, the overall availability of data constitutes a serious limitation in conducting in-depth research on countries and societies that are actively engaged in a high-intensity, all-out war. The war also affects the legal context of the accessibility of data. With Ukraine having declared martial law on February 25, 2022, a great deal of information has become classified, and it is hard to verify any official data released by the government or its related institutions. On the Russian side, although the country is officially not at war, since February 2022 control over the media and limitations on freedom of speech have progressed even further, to be discussed in detail below. Under such circumstances, accessing and verifying official data from either of the fighting sides has become extremely complicated, and one needs to have realistic ambitions about the extent to which official data can be used to describe the actual situation.

Moreover, particularly when discussing military-related developments, one needs to take into account the "fog of war" effect, as well as the operational security considerations of both fighting sides. Deliberate disinformation and propaganda conducted by the fighting parties add additional layers of complications to this already complex methodological situation.[2]

This chapter relies to a large extent on information provided by third parties, or by actors that are independent of the fighting sides. Regarding primary sources, this includes declarations and speeches from third country officials, journalists, experts, and NGO-activists, as well audio-visual material produced by independent reporters accessing the frontlines. Still, the "fog of war" prevails and hampers any in-depth analysis of the actual military situation. Consequently, this methodological caveat stemming from the limited accessibility of reliable information constantly needs to be observed and factored in.

Instead of focusing on the changing position of the elites in the war,[3] this chapter intends to answer how the Russian and Ukrainian states are presenting the war to their own societies, and how they have been striving to get their societies involved or disengaged, starting from the first day of the full-scale Russian invasion. Hence, both the overall framing of the war as well as its military objectives have been studied in detail. Another, highly indicative aspect of involving society is the phenomenon of volunteering, i.e., how the two states rely on volunteers to expand their combat capabilities beyond the regular armed forces.

The chapter is composed of five main parts. Following a short introduction, the text first studies how the two fighting states and administrations are framing the war for their own domestic audiences. The second part compares how the Russian and Ukrainian leaderships present their military objectives to their respective publics and how these objectives have changed over time. Thereafter the phenomenon of volunteering is discussed in detail, focusing particularly on combat-related volunteering. The fourth part focuses on how the Russian and Ukrainian governments are trying to internationalize the war by forging alliances and how they present this to their domestic publics. The study ends with a short, concluding part.[4]

2. Framing the war: "special military operation" vs. patriotic war

When Russian President Vladimir Putin *de facto* declared war on Ukraine,[5] following the massive invasion on February 24, 2022, he did not *de jure* declare war. Instead, he announced the launch of a so-called "special military operation." By not calling it a war, Putin apparently intended to limit the fighting to the exclusive task of the Russian armed forces, leaving the public as unaffected as possible. Based on the information obtained about Russia's initial plans, Moscow calculated on a short, Blitzkrieg-type military operation, which was supposed to end approximately one week after its commencement. In other words, the Kremlin framed the attack as an action much smaller and much more limited than a war, because it was actually planned to be so.

Consequently, martial law was not declared in Russia, nor was even a partial mobilization announced. The country's economy was not set on a war footing either. The Russian regime was so confident that it did not even bother to relocate the country's approximately USD 300 billion foreign exchange reserves deposited in the West, which were swiftly frozen by EU sanctions.[6]

However, once it turned out that Ukraine's state, army, and society did not collapse and instead of a rapid victory the war had turned into a long, grinding struggle, the Kremlin confronted a major political dilemma about framing the war. On the one hand, abandoning the "special military operation" narrative and declaring war on Ukraine would enable Russia to concentrate much more human and economic resources for the fight. Doing so has long been demanded by radical nationalist circles among the Russian elites and society. On the other hand, openly declaring war would also mean admitting that the Kremlin had seriously miscalculated the attack and its consequences. As of February 2023, Moscow is still maintaining the "special military operation" narrative, although the partial mobilization ordered in September 2022, as well as several measures taken in order to strengthen state control over the economy,[7] indicate that the Kremlin is gradually setting the country on a *de facto* war footing, despite not calling it a war.

Meanwhile, the Russian President's narrative about the role of the West in the conflict has remained consistent: since the beginning of the escalation, Putin has framed this war as a conflict between Russia and the collective West, particularly NATO. Already in his speech of February 24, 2022,[8] Putin accused the West of misleading and tricking Russia by ignoring Moscow's security interests and by not keeping alleged promises about not expanding NATO. These claims were reiterated a year later,[9] supplemented by the accusation of Western biological laboratories deployed in Ukraine, Western instructors training Ukrainian neo-Nazis, and a number of other accusations. Hence, after a year of fighting, the official framing of the international context of the war has become only more radical.

Contrary to Russia's exclusive approach, Ukraine has from the very beginning framed the war and the need to defend the country in a fully inclusive way. In his speech on the eve of the invasion, President Volodymyr Zelensky called on the whole Ukrainian people to stand up and defend the homeland; he even summoned those Ukrainians working abroad to return home. Moreover, the president addressed the Russian people specifically as well, refuting accusations that Ukrainians were Nazis or that Ukraine posed any threat to Russia.[10] He also called for the solidarity of the whole international community, with him and his officials giving several interviews to the international media even in the very early days of the war, even when their personal safety was at risk.

Another difference reflecting the way in which the Ukrainian government has framed the events is that Kyiv introduced martial law already on February 25, 2022, so the country has been in a state of war for more than a year. This has allowed the government to mobilize reservist soldiers, ban the travel of military-aged men abroad, nationalize economic assets, and limit freedom of the media and freedom of speech, including the possibility of banning pro-Kremlin political parties.[11] Hence, by declaring martial law, the Ukrainian government has, by definition, included the whole society in the war, because martial law affects very many aspects of everyday life.

3. Setting and pursuing the war objectives: offensive vs. defensive strategy

In his already mentioned speech at the start of the invasion, Putin enumerated several ambitious military objectives for the "special military operation" to present and justify the war primarily to the Russian public. The first was to protect the people of the so-called Donetsk and Luhansk National Republics (DNR and LNR), unilaterally recognized by Russia as independent states on February 21, from an alleged genocide continuously committed by Ukraine. This genocide claim has been present in Russia's narrative about the war ever since 2014, even though it has not been substantiated by any independent international organizations.[12] Nevertheless, this narrative resonated well within Russian society because of the eight years of propaganda that preceded the attack in 2022.

He also pledged to de-nazify and de-militarize Ukraine. Without publicly elaborating the details of "de-nazification," accusing Ukraine of being ruled by a Nazi regime has again been a persistent element of Russia's narratives of the war ever since the change of power in Kyiv in February 2014. The fact that President Petro Poroshenko was elected democratically on May 25, 2014 and that Russia recognized him as the legitimate president did not interfere with the continuous repetition of the Nazi accusations. Calling Ukraine and its people Nazis has been an integral part of how Russia has framed the conflict ever since 2014;[13] hence, by defining "de-nazification" as one of the key military objectives the Kremlin could well count on this well-established Nazi-narrative.

Based on the events of the early days of the full-scale escalation, "de-nazification" in fact meant the objective of killing or capturing Zelensky and probably other members of his government too. In the first days after February 24, 2022, several Russian special operation and diversionary groups operated in Kyiv and attempted to neutralize the Ukrainian president.[14] There were reportedly two assaults against

Zelensky's compound in Kyiv, but both failed.[15] Meanwhile, the third main objective, the demilitarization of Ukraine, meant militarily defeating Ukraine's armed forces.

In order to realize these objectives, Russia launched a full-scale attack against several of Ukraine's regions, entering the country along four main axes (from the north, the north-east, the east, and also the south), with altogether seven thrusts. Hence, Russia's initial objectives covered the whole territory of Ukraine: they intended to conquer Kyiv, Kharkiv, Odesa, possibly also Dnipro and Zaporizhzhia, and planned to cut Ukraine off completely from both the Azov Sea and the Black Sea.

However, after the siege of Kyiv failed, Russia officially downscaled its territorial objectives. On March 29, Moscow declared that it had given up the fight for Kyiv, Chernihiv, and the whole north and north-east, and was concentrating on the Donbas instead.[16] This shift was presented to the Russian public as if it was a deliberate choice and not a necessity dictated by the military defeat at Kyiv. This decreased ambition level enabled Russia to better concentrate her forces, resulting in the capture of Mariupol, Severodonetsk, and Lysychansk in late spring and summer of 2022.

However, Russia could not realize even these downscaled objectives: in August, Ukraine launched a counterattack in the Kherson region, and liberated most of the Kharkiv region in September. As a reaction to these Ukrainian successes, Russia hastily organized four quasi-referenda in the occupied parts of Donetsk, Luhansk, Zaporizhzhia, and Kherson regions on September 23–27 on their joining the Russian Federation. By referring to the results of these "referenda," Moscow swiftly declared the annexation of these four regions of Ukraine. Still, regardless of the claimed annexation, Russia was forced to withdraw its forces from the right bank of the River Dnipro, including the city of Kherson, in mid-November. Since then, Russia's military objectives have been essentially limited to the capture of the entire Donbas as well as to defend the parts of Zaporizhzhia and Kherson regions that it still occupies.

In short, since the beginning of the full-scale invasion, Russia's military objectives have been factually reduced to a considerable degree, even though in the official narrative the "denazification" and "demilitarization" slogans are still frequently repeated. In other words, the original Russian ambitions to directly control the whole of Ukraine, including capturing large parts of its territories and changing its government, have been reduced to annexing four regions of Ukraine, while the core narratives surrounding the "special military operation" have remained the same.

Meanwhile, Ukraine's war objectives have developed along a fundamentally different trajectory. As Ukraine has been fighting a defensive, rather than an offensive, war, the evident goal to achieve after February 2022 has been first to stop the Russian aggression, and thereafter to start regaining the occupied territories. Taking into account the size and scale of the Russian attack, this evidently required the involvement of the whole Ukrainian society from the very first day of the aggression. Hence, both Zelensky and members of his administration have been very active in communicating with Ukrainian society about the war since February 24, 2022. Since then, Zelensky has addressed the population in video messages every night, discussing various aspects of the war and encouraging the Ukrainian people to keep fighting.[17]

An interesting phenomenon is that, before February 2022, Ukraine did not make notably active efforts to regain either the occupied Donbas or the Crimea. The loss of *de facto* control over these territories in 2014 was never recognized by Kyiv, but no offensive actions for regaining them were taken either. Shortly after the invasion, Zelensky even voiced the possibility of reaching a compromise on the status of the Crimea in exchange for stopping the Russian invasion.[18]

However, since late summer 2022,[19] the official rhetoric started to change. More and more Ukrainian officials, including the president and the military leadership, started to talk about the need to regain all the occupied territories, including the ones that Russia seized in 2014, thus also the Crimea. Most recently, Zelensky reiterated this intention at the World Economic Forum in Davos.[20]

Hence, Ukraine's war objectives have become considerably broader since the beginning of the full-scale Russian invasion. This is in sharp contrast with how Moscow has been setting her objectives, which have factually shrunk from controlling the whole of Ukraine to holding the four occupied eastern regions and the Crimea.

Parallel to Moscow's changing military objectives, a new element of Russian strategy emerged from October 2022 on: systematic, large-scale attacks on Ukraine's civilian infrastructure. By using the Ukrainian attack on the Kerch Bridge on October 8, 2022 as a pretext, Russia launched—from 10 October on—a massive air and missile campaign against Ukraine's critical civilian infrastructure, namely the energy infrastructure and the components related to it.[21] As far as can be determined from open sources, the objective of this campaign has been to deprive the Ukrainian population of electricity, heating, and running water during the winter, and thus break their morale.[22] A likely secondary objective has been to induce another massive wave of Ukrainian refugees to flee the country, and thereby put further pressure on the West, hoping to weaken the political resolve behind Ukraine's international support.

Russia used thousands of ballistic and air-launched missiles, as well as cruise missiles and also drones supplied by Iran (to be discussed later in detail); even a few of Moscow's brand new hypersonic Kinzhal missiles were launched. Although Ukraine's energy infrastructure suffered widespread and severe damage, and the winter was marred by long electricity blackouts and other supply interruptions, the Russian campaign did not manage to break either the Ukrainian population or Western support for Kyiv.

Meanwhile, it is worth noting that so far Ukraine has refrained from similar attacks against Russia's civilian infrastructure, even though Ukraine would also be entirely capable of hitting such targets in Russia's border regions. Ukraine hit a few oil industry facilities in the border regions,[23] but these attacks[24] were more related to hampering Russia's war effort than targeting the Russian civilian population. Hence, the attitude towards hitting civilian infrastructural targets constitutes another difference between how Russia and Ukraine have been fighting this war.

4. Getting the whole society involved: inclusive vs. exclusive warfighting

4.1. From patriotic volunteering to criminal recruitment

Another aspect in which Ukraine's and Russia's way of fighting differs is how the two states operate their military recruitment systems and particularly on how they channel in or rely on the phenomenon of volunteering. Volunteering has been an integral and crucially important part of Ukraine's war effort ever since 2014. Back then, following the Russian occupation of the Crimea, several volunteer battalions were established, often partially composed of Maidan activists. These volunteer formations, albeit badly trained and equipped, played a key role in halting the spread of the Russian-instigated separatism in Eastern Ukraine.[25] During the mid-2010s, these volunteer units were integrated either into the army or into the National Guard, but the phenomenon of volunteering for defending the country continued unabated.

Even before the full-scale Russian invasion, on January 1, 2022, Ukraine set up a separate command for creating Territorial Defense Forces[26] (commonly called *teroborona*, which is the abbreviation of the official Ukrainian expression *territorialna oborona*). This newly established branch of the armed forces was supposed to be composed of both reservists and volunteers, who signed up to defend their own neighborhoods against a possible attack and also to assist the regular army in its duties, including enforcing public order, manning checkpoints, and other duties. Each of Ukraine's 26 regions was supposed to set up a separate territorial defense brigade, with a size of 3,500 soldiers, composed of battalions with 600 soldiers each.[27] Most volunteers received only rudimentary infantry training before the full-scale escalation broke out. Nevertheless, the *teroborona* units of Kyiv and the Kyiv region played an important role in stopping the Russian invasion, and also in neutralizing the Russian sabotage groups that infiltrated the capital, though they suffered severe losses. Since spring 2022, territorial defense units can also be deployed in regions other than their home, meaning in practice that *teroborona* forces—which were originally meant to be mere auxiliaries to the regular army—can also be sent to the frontline. Despite the severe losses suffered by many territorial defense units, the phenomenon of volunteering has persisted.

Besides the territorial defense units, tens of thousands of Ukrainians also volunteered for the regular military units, particularly such people who had previous military experience, so their skills could be refreshed relatively easily. The willingness to volunteer to fight is so widespread that Ukraine decided to set up a new type of unit in February 2023, the so-called storm brigades *(gvardiya nastupu)*, intended specifically to participate in the liberation of the Russian-occupied territories. The main difference compared to the *teroborona* units is that the storm brigades are subordinated to the Ministry of Interior and are not intended for auxiliary duties, but for combat operations.[28] While the exact number of these volunteers is classified, in mid-February a Ukrainian official said that 15,000 people had already applied.[29] In early March, a Ukrainian member of parliament, Andrey Zhupanin, spoke of about 20,000 people who had already joined the storm brigades.[30]

In addition to this, Ukraine also has foreign volunteers fighting on her side. One of the most numerous groups is the Georgians, some of whom have been in combat since 2014 in the framework of the so-called Georgian legion. There are also anti-Russian Chechen volunteers, who joined Ukraine's fight against Russia also in 2014.

The most interesting phenomenon, however, is the so-called International Legion, which is a separate unit of the Territorial Defense Forces created by President Zelensky already on February 27, 2022, that is, on the fourth day of the invasion.[31] Setting up such a unit served as a framework for channeling foreign military expertise and manpower into the war effort. According to official information from March 2022, altogether some 20,000 volunteers from more than 52 countries had already joined the International Legion,[32] not only to fight but also to provide cyber security help or medical assistance.

Meanwhile, on the Russian side, volunteering has turned out to be a fundamentally different phenomenon, which has shown considerable differences depending on the various phases of the war. During the initial phase of the Russian aggression against Ukraine, in 2014, tens of thousands of genuine volunteers arrived from Russia to Ukraine to fight against Kyiv. Their motives varied greatly: the predominant majority of them wanted to fight the allegedly fascist Ukrainian government; others were hardline nationalists; and there were also religious fanatics among them.[33] However, once the frontlines stabilized and maneuver warfare transformed into a grinding, trench war, most of the surviving Russian volunteers either returned home or joined the separatist armed forces. This was also in line with Russia's intention to centralize control over the initially rather chaotic separatist formations and warlords.

When the escalation started in 2022, Russia, unlike Ukraine, initially did not continue the volunteering tradition originating from 2014. Instead, as was already stated above, Moscow tried to keep the "special military operation" as an exclusive task of the regular armed forces. Once human losses started to mount and the Russian army started to desperately need more manpower, the Russian Ministry of Defense opted for a volunteer-based recruitment: they tried to convince reservists, particularly those with relatively fresh military experience, to sign up again for a fixed term of service and go fight in Ukraine. While some call this phenomenon a covert mobilization,[34] initially there was no element of coercion involved; hence, the term "recruitment" describes reality better. The Russian recruitment system tried to motivate reservists with generous financial and other benefits. However, this recruitment effort did not deliver the expected results due to the insufficient number of volunteers.

Another attempt also failed to bring in the required number of volunteers: the use of the so-called BARS system. In 2021, Russia created a new system of reservists, the so-called Combat Army Reserve of the Country or BARS *(Boyevoy Armeyskiy Rezerv Strany)*[35]—the word *bars* in Russian also stands for "snow leopard." The intention was to recruit men to take up a three-year long reservist contract, which also included the possibility of being deployed in combat operations, in exchange for regular salary as well as significant combat pay and bonuses. BARS reservists were also provided with the necessary training; moreover, as many of them were former officers and soldiers, their former skills only had to be refreshed. Still, the system could not fulfill the plan to recruit 100,000 reservists;[36] as only some 40,000 men signed up, and not all of them could be trained before the invasion. Moreover, once Russia started to deploy BARS units, it quickly turned out that these soldiers often did not receive the promised payments,[37] were mistreated by the regular army, and in many cases were not provided the necessary equipment, weaponry, and support. All these recruitment failures, combined with battlefield losses in Ukraine, led to the partial mobilization in September 2022.

However, the phenomenon of volunteering did not disappear on the Russian side but was simply channeled into the paramilitary Wagner Group instead of the regular armed forces. From summer 2022 on, the Wagner Group, led and owned by the late oligarch Yevgeny Prigozhin, started to recruit convicts from Russian penitentiary facilities. As of January 2023, approximately 40,000 prison inmates had been recruited with the promise of an amnesty and decent payment in exchange for six months of armed service in Ukraine. However, these new volunteers were often sent into battle with minimum or no training and insufficient equipment. Both captured Wagner fighters and the Ukrainian soldiers combatting them often described the convicts as having been used simply as cannon fodder, with a complete disregard for the number of casualties among them.[38] As of February 2023, the Wagner Group had lost at least 30,000 fighters, of whom approximately 9000 were killed.[39] As news about the fate of the volunteer inmates reached the Russian prisons, the Wagner Group started to face serious problems with recruiting new convicts from December 2022 on; later, in early February 2023, the group stopped recruiting prisoners completely.[40] In August, leading prisoner's rights activist Olga Romanova claimed that the total number of convicts recruited for the war could be up to 80,000, and at least 20,000 ex-convicts from Wagner already returned to civil life.[41]

The palpable disregard for human life in Russian military strategy indicates a fundamental difference between Russian and Ukrainian forces. While the Ukrainian advance is also hampered by the fact that the main bottleneck for them is manpower (the main resource that Western countries cannot send), the Russian army is able and willing to risk larger masses of soldiers on the front line. And although this attitude, as I mentioned above, discourages volunteerism, several semi-official private groups have been mobilized on the Russian side in addition to the Wagner Group. Russia officially bans the creation of private armies and private military companies, but there are more than 40 "volunteer" groups active on the battlefield, according to Russian Deputy Defense Minister Nikolai Pankov.[42] Among them are troops of private military companies belonging to different commands. The PMC Redut has been on the ground since February 2022 is connected to Russia's military intelligence, while the company Potok is owned by the state gas export giant Gazprom.[43] This illustrates well the Russian patronal system's tendency to rely on informal collusion rather than separation of the spheres of social action (political, economic, and communal).[44] Recent legal changes to allow Russian governors to establish military organizations during wartime[45] also seem to be a desperate step to increase mobilization, but one that empowers Russian sub-patrons vis-à-vis the chief patron and makes it even more difficult for Putin to control his single-pyramid patronal network.

At the same time, it is also apparent that irregular forces, which proliferate out of necessity, are often difficult to incorporate into the Russian military hierarchy. The most prominent example was Prigozhin's attempted coup d'etat in June 2023, the purpose of which was to get the leadership of the regular armed forces removed, including Minister of Defense Sergei Shoigu and Chief of the General Staff Valery Gerasimov, and secure that the Wagner Group can avoid subordination to the ministry. Albeit Prigozhin survived the failed coup attempt and in August he even ambitioned new deployments to Africa,[46] he was killed in an air crash on August 23, 2023 in Russia, together with six other Wagner commanders.[47] This is highly likely to put the moderate autonomy of the Wagner Group to an end.

4.2. Crowdfunding for weapons and equipment in Ukraine and Russia

A particularly interesting aspect of combat-related volunteering is how bottom-up campaigns are organized both in Ukraine and abroad to support the Ukrainian armed forces. Within Ukraine, the state has actively supported and encouraged various bottom-up volunteer campaigns to help the war effort. Ukraine's National Bank immediately opened a dedicated bank account for receiving donations from abroad,[48] and so did several other state organizations and NGOs endorsed by the state. Non-governmental organizations managed to collect not only money, but also procure weapons and equipment for the army. Some of these NGOs already existed since 2014, such as the Come Back Alive Foundation,[49] which collects private donations for military purposes, but even this one has considerably upgraded its activities since February 2022. As of February 2023, the Come Back Alive Foundation is one of the largest non-state buyers of arms for the Ukrainian armed forces. Another one is the Serhiy Prytula Charity Foundation, also operating since 2014, which has purchased more than 4,500 drones, 1,000 military vehicles, 70 large UAV complexes, and several other types of equipment for the armed forces, based predominantly on crowdfunding.[50] Of course, no NGO would be able import and transfer weapons and military equipment on such a scale without direct state support; hence, these foundations, and several other smaller ones can also be factored into the phenomenon of state-managed volunteering.

Crowdfunding-based support for Ukraine's military has also occurred outside the country. In May 2022, the Lithuanian public collected money for a Turkish TB-2 Bayraktar attack drone. The campaign was preliminarily approved by both the Turkish and Lithuanian defense ministries. The first such Bayraktar was named Vanagas,[51] after the codename of a legendary Lithuanian anti-Soviet resistance fighter, who symbolized the struggle against Moscow. The word means "falcon" in Lithuanian. Shortly thereafter, in summer 2022, Poland followed suit, and the local population collected money for another Bayraktar. This drone was named "Marik," after the colloquial name of the occupied Ukrainian city of Mariupol.[52] In Czechia, locals collected money first for a modernized T-72 tank named "Tomáš" to be sent to Ukraine.[53] Thereafter, once Russia started its air campaign against Ukraine's civilian infrastructure, Czechs started to collect money for a highly-mobile anti-aircraft system to be deployed against the Iranian drones used by Russia. The system, named "Viktor," is composed of twin 14.5 millimeter anti-aircraft heavy machine guns built upon a Toyota pickup, manufactured by a Czech defense company. As of January 2023, 15 such systems have been crowdfunded.[54]

Meanwhile, crowdfunding for the armed forces in Russia became widespread only after September 2022, thus after the partial mobilization. The sudden mobilization of approximately 300,000 Russian men quickly shed light on the grave shortages of protective gear, basic military equipment, and even clothing in the Russian army. Relatives of the mobilized soldiers quickly started to collect money for the missing clothes and equipment; hundreds of social media channels popped up, and various crowdfunding campaigns started.[55] As of early 2023, these campaigns are still going on, but the focus has gradually shifted from essential personal equipment to more advanced contributions, such as satellite dishes, batteries, and other electronic goods.[56]

Unlike the Ukrainian, Lithuanian, Czech, and Polish cases, in Russia crowdfunding campaigns cannot provide weapons for the armed forces because the state does not support such initiatives due to both legal and political reasons. Official support for such campaigns would mean the state admitting that there are shortages in equipment, let alone weaponry. Hence, Russian crowdfunding campaigns are limited to non-lethal goods and some dual-use equipment such as commercial drones.

Crowdfunding of military equipment (and particularly weapons) constitutes a very high level of active social involvement and direct contribution of the local (or international) public to the war effort. As of February 2023, Ukraine has clearly been a lot more successful in mobilizing civil society both at home and abroad for assisting its military than Russia. Of course, the difference in the legal framing of the war, namely, that Russia is officially conducting only a special military operation, while Ukraine is under martial law, constitutes a key variable in the social mobilization potential of the two governments.

For Ukraine, Western military assistance, including crowdfunded projects, is of crucial importance. Hence, the state needs to keep corruption down in order not to endanger the influx of supplies. The corruption scandal that erupted in January 2023 over the misuse of donated money and equipment by some Ukrainian officials indicated, on the one hand, that problems related to the misuse of Western assistance are widespread. On the other hand, the swift reaction of the government demonstrated that the state intends to actively step up against such schemes: several of the accused officials were immediately replaced, and a large-scale investigation was launched.[57] Later that year, Zelensky said that "cynicism and bribery during war is treason," and dismissed all the heads of Ukraine's regional army recruitment centers on corruption charges.[58]

5. Internationalizing the war: isolation vs. alliance-seeking in the West

Another key difference in how Russia and Ukraine have been fighting this war is manifested in the approaches taken to get the international community involved. Russia, initially planning for a short war, did not put much effort into forging any alliances. Apart from directly involving Belarus, which was anyways necessary for the attack on Kyiv and Chernihiv, Moscow did not try to set up any international coalition to support its "special military operation." A spectacular indicator of the absence of any such effort was the voting in the UN General Assembly on February 23, 2022, immediately after Moscow's unilateral recognition of the DNR and LNR, calling for the immediate withdrawal of Russian forces from Ukraine. In addition to Russia herself, only six countries voted against the resolution: Belarus, Eritrea, Mali, Nicaragua, North-Korea, and Syria.[59] Even Russia's closest military allies in the Collective Security Treaty Organization, such as Kazakhstan and Kyrgyzstan, did not vote in favor of Russia, but only abstained from the voting.

Once the invasion started, Russia's support decreased even further: on March 2, 2022, only four countries voted against condemning Russia's aggression against Ukraine: Belarus (which was a co-belligerent), Syria, North Korea, and Eritrea,[60] meaning the onslaught was beyond the red lines of even Nicaragua and Mali, which did not condemn the DNR/LNR recognition a week earlier. While 35 countries abstained, this did not mean that any of them would actively support Russia's actions. Russia did not manage to gain more support for the claimed annexation of the four Ukrainian regions either. The act was not recognized by any other UN member states, except Syria and North Korea.[61] Additionally, in the UN General Assembly vote held on October 12, 2022, only four countries voted against condemning Russia: Belarus and Nicaragua joined ranks with Damascus and Pyongyang.[62] Hence, Russian diplomacy failed to widen the country's international support base.

When it comes particularly to the West, Putin's February 24 invasion speech clearly accused the collective West of striving to weaken, and possibly even destroy, Russia. This narrative has been fully in line with the increasingly anti-Western directions of Russia's foreign policy which have been prevalent ever since Putin's 2007 speech at the Munich Security Conference. Hence, from this perspective it is hardly surprising that the Kremlin has also been framing the present war as part of Russia's long, historical struggle against the West, in which Moscow is in a deepening partnership with Beijing.[63]

Regarding military allies, Moscow started to look for capable partners only from the summer of 2022 on, when it became apparent that it could not address certain shortcomings in the Russian army on its own. The most important success Moscow achieved was that Iran agreed to provide Russia with military unmanned aerial vehicles (UAVs), including both attack and reconnaissance drones. Meanwhile, as of February 2023, strong international pressure[64] has prevented Moscow from obtaining ballistic missiles from Iran, even though in 2022 Moscow strove to procure such systems too. In addition to Iran, North Korea is also supporting Russia by transferring artillery ammunition.[65] Belarus has been a close ally of Russia also in terms of arms transfers: Russia is documented to have received old, reactivated T-72 tanks from Belarus,[66] as well as BMP-2 infantry fighting vehicles and military trucks.[67] China has reportedly supplied small amounts of assault rifles, body armor, and commercial drones to Russia, although Beijing has attempted to conceal these goods as dual-use products.[68]

Contrary to Russia's isolation and very limited military support received from abroad, Ukraine from the very beginning of the full-scale invasion has been actively striving to get the whole international community involved and to internationalize the conflict as much as possible. Since the very first day of the escalation, Zelensky as well as several other Ukrainian leaders have been addressing the international community practically on a daily basis, asking for support and assistance. The effort to get the international community, particularly the West, involved on the Ukrainian side is not a new phenomenon; doing so has been a consistent strategy of subsequent Ukrainian administrations ever since spring 2014, when Russia attacked the Crimea. However, the full-scale invasion brought this strategy to a new level.

Since February 2022, Ukraine has enjoyed an unprecedented degree of international support in its fight against Russian aggression. In terms of diplomatic support, using the UN General Assembly voting as an indicator once again, approximately two-thirds of all UN member states actively favor Ukraine.[69] In the public eye, while Zelensky is generally regarded as a hero in the West and became *Time Magazine*'s Person of the Year in 2022,[70] Putin is seen as a war criminal, against whom the International Criminal Court in The Hague issued an arrest warrant in March 2023.[71]

Regarding military support, in the framework of the Ukraine Defense Contact Group, informally called the "Ramstein Group," more than forty countries have been regularly participating in and contributing to strengthening Ukraine's defenses by various means.[72] One needs to add that, as of February 2023, Ukraine's war effort is very strongly dependent on the continuous flow of Western military support. Hence, aiming to keep the West involved on Ukraine's side is not a choice, but a factual must for Kyiv. Regardless, the overall attitude towards seeking international support and building coalitions for the war effort constitutes an important difference between the Russian and Ukrainian policies.

Due to the overall secrecy surrounding many details of arms shipments, it is not possible to conduct a detailed comparison of the supplies received by Ukraine and Russia. The shipments to Russia, in particular, are opaque, mainly because any country supplying Moscow with weapons risks widespread international sanctions. But not all shipments to Ukraine are transparent either: there are a number of countries that supply weapons to Kyiv without announcing it. These shipments become public only when the weapons are spotted on the battlefield. This was the case, for example, with the GAIA Amir armored vehicles supplied by Israel: the first systems were spotted in November 2022,[73] but the Israeli government has still not formally admitted to sending these vehicles. Officially, it was only in March 2023 that

Israel authorized the sale of defensive military equipment to Ukraine, specifically, electronic warfare devices for use against Iranian-made drones.[74] Hence, the Amirs were most probably sent via an intermediary country. However, even such an indirect transfer requires an export license, only this was not made public in the media. Another example of unpublicized arms deliveries to Ukraine are the Finnish-made Patria Pasi XA-185 armored vehicles, supplied to Ukraine probably since summer 2022,[75] but without any announcement from the Finnish government.

Due to the lack of transparency, it is not possible to compare either the numbers or the value of the military assistance received by Russia and Ukraine. Meanwhile, one may still compare the types of weapon systems received from abroad, based either on the official announcements of the transfers or on the given weapon system having been spotted in Ukraine (Table 1).

Table 1. Types of heavy weapons received by Ukraine and Russia from abroad since February 2022.

Types of heavy weapon systems and military equipment documented to be received from abroad	Ukraine	Russia
Tanks	X	X
Armored fighting vehicles	X	-
Infantry fighting vehicles	X	X
Armored personnel carriers	X	-
Military trucks	X	X
Tube artillery	X	-
Rocket artillery	X	-
Mortars	X	-
Artillery ammunition	X	X
Anti-tank missiles	X	-
Combat aircraft	X	-
Combat helicopters	X	-
Attack drones	X	X
Reconnaissance drones	X	X
Loitering ammunitions ("suicide drones")	X	X
Air-to-ground missiles	X	-
Air defense systems	X	-
Anti-aircraft guns	X	-
Electronic warfare equipment	X	-
MEDEVAC vehicles	X	-
Personal protective equipment	X	X
Military uniforms	X	X

Source: Trebesch et al. (2023), own compilation.

All in all, the table above demonstrates that Ukraine can rely on a much wider support base and receives a considerably wider range of weapons than Russia has managed to secure for herself. We should also note that beyond heavy weapons, Ukraine has received high-tech AI-based military software from the West as well, which has given an advantage to Ukraine on the battlefield.[76] Adding to this the Western sanctions on Russia, which severely restrict technology transfer, it seems only a slight exaggeration to accept a journalist's comment that the war in this field is a clash between "digital" and "analog" armies.[77] Meanwhile, it is worth noting that Russia is not completely left without external military assistance either, even though Ukraine receives a much wider variety of weaponry.

6. Conclusions

The policies of Russia and Ukraine differ fundamentally in terms of getting their own societies, as well as the international community, involved in support of their respective war efforts. This is summarized in Table 2. Russia has been employing a two-track approach that intends to ensure the continuous general support of the public but intends to keep society directly involved or affected to the smallest possible extent. This duality is manifested on the one hand in the narratives of "de-nazification," "protecting the people of the Donbas," and later in "the whole West is against us" discourses, which are all intended to create a rallying-around-the-flag effect, thus ensure lasting public support for the regime.

Table 2. Comparative summary of Russia and Ukraine's ways of war.

	Russia: **socially exclusive warfighting**	**Ukraine:** **socially inclusive warfighting**
Framing the war	"special military operation" (a matter of the armed forces)	a patriotic war (a matter of the whole nation)
War objectives	offensive strategy ("de-nazification," targeting civilian infrastructure)	defensive strategy (forcing Russia out of Ukraine's territory, no targeting of civilian infrastructure)
Combat-related volunteering	limited (partial mobilization and criminal recruitment)	mass movement (mobilization of society)
Crowdfunding	limited (domestic campaigns for non-lethal and dual-use equipment)	extended (international campaign for military equipment as well)
International alliances	isolation (limited support from other dictatorships)	alliance-seeking (widespread support from the West)

On the other hand, the still maintained "special military operation" framing and the absence of martial law and general mobilization all serve the purpose of keeping the direct effects of the war as far away from society as possible. The origins of this approach can be traced back to February 24, 2022, when Russia launched its full-scale invasion against Ukraine. Since back then Moscow planned to conduct a very short and relatively bloodless operation, the Kremlin apparently thought that it was simply not necessary to mobilize Russian society, neither in the political nor in the military sense. The same logic also explains why the Kremlin has not been successful in building up any significant international coalition behind the attack on Ukraine: it simply did not deem forging alliances necessary for a war that would last for only a few days.

Once it turned out that the war was going to be neither quick nor bloodless, amending the narrative framing and starting to call the "operation" a war would mean admitting that the Kremlin originally miscalculated with its offensive. The need to refrain from admitting any mistakes also explains why the Kremlin has presented the defeat outside Kyiv as an intentional re-focusing on the Donbas. Similarly, the Kremlin does not publicly address the discrepancy between the Ukrainian territories it claims since the unilateral annexations and the ones it actually holds. Hence, the military objectives have been tacitly downgraded to capturing the rest of the Donbas and defending the still Russian-held territories of the Kherson and Zaporizhzhia regions, while the official narrative about these regions fully belonging to Russia has remained unchanged.

Very similar considerations, i.e., the reluctance to get wider society involved, have been manifested also in the partial mobilization, which was ordered in September 2022 only after Russia had lost significant parts of the territories it occupied in Ukraine in August-September. Before that, instead of mobilizing its reservists, Russia tried to amend its combat losses by intensifying various volunteer-based recruitment schemes, albeit without much success. Since September, the contrast between the "special military operation" framing and the partial mobilization has created a strong contradiction which Russian society needs to face for interpreting the conflict. The intention to keep society involved to the least possible extent and to hide the weaknesses of the Russian army has resulted in the Kremlin's unwillingness to endorse any wider social movements and crowdfunding campaigns that would like to support the armed forces.

Ukraine has been conducting a fundamentally different policy about getting society involved in the war. From the very first day of the full-scale Russian invasion, the Ukrainian leadership aimed to mobilize both the domestic public as well as international partners to support Ukraine. There has been no effort to confine the effects of the war at all; instead, the objective is to the get society as much and as actively involved as possible. The introduction of martial law and general mobilization, as well as the very active and mobilizing messages of the president and the government, all serve the same purpose. Hence, the Ukrainian policy line is much more coherent than the one employed by Russia. This credibility helps Ukraine mobilize widespread international support for its war effort, and also to extensively rely on the phenomenon of volunteering, including crowdfunding, for the military.

Taking into account the political rigidity and inertia of the Russian system, combined with the upcoming presidential elections which limits the Kremlin's domestic maneuvering space, it is unlikely that Russia will change its two-track approach, regardless of the growing discrepancies. The Ukrainian policy is also unlikely to change, because from Kyiv's perspective this strategy, i.e., to mobilize both domestic and foreign societies, has proven successful so far. Hence, differences are highly likely to prevail.

Notes

1. András Rácz Ph.D. is Senior Fellow of the German Council on Foreign Relations (DGAP) and Senior Lecturer of the Corvinus University in Budapest. The views presented here are solely his own. Background research for the article was made possible by the support of the János Bolyai Research Fellowship provided by the Hungarian Academy of Science, in the framework of the research project titled "The role and place of proxy warfare in Russian military thinking and practice."
2. As an illustration, it is worth citing a Russian military blogger who claimed that his own country's military officials are encouraged to stage videos to exaggerate success, e.g. by "destroying" the same target multiple times and claiming that multiple targets were destroyed. See Jon Jackson, "Russian Military Told to Stage Videos to Exaggerate Success: Report," *Newsweek*, August 11, 2023, sec. World, https://www.newsweek.com/russian-military-told-stage-videos-exaggerate-success-ukraine-1819237.
3. To be analyzed by Nikolay Petrov in his chapter in this volume.
4. It is important to note that the chapter focuses on the military-related aspects of warfare and the direct military engagement of the two societies. Hence, the wider social consequences of the war, such as displacement, emigration, or unemployment are beyond of the focus of this study. Another limitation of the present chapter is that it focuses on developments since February 2022. Hence, events that occurred before that, including the 2014 occupation of the Crimea and parts of the Donbas, are not discussed in detail; they are mentioned only when they are necessary as a context for more recent developments. The Russian and Ukrainian names mentioned in the text are transliterated to English based on their respective equivalents; if a Ukrainian geographical name has both Russian and Ukrainian versions (such as Kiev or Kyiv), the latter is used here.
5. President of Russia, "Address by the President of the Russian Federation," *President of Russia*, February 24, 2022, http://en.kremlin.ru/events/president/news/67843.
6. "Half of Russia's Foreign Exchange Reserves Frozen Due to Sanctions — Finance Minister," *TASS*, March 13, 2022, https://tass.com/economy/1421403.
7. Polina Ivanova, "Russia Prepares to Mobilise Economy for Longer War in Ukraine," *Financial Times*, July 7, 2022, https://www.ft.com/content/fe233252-69fa-4259-8b35-a34d8738b968; Yevgeni Gontmakher, "The Russian Economy Mobilizes for War," *GIS Reports*, December 5. 2022, https://www.gisreportsonline.com/r/russia-economy-mobilization/.
8. President of Russia, "Address by the President of the Russian Federation."
9. President of Russia, "Presidential Address to Federal Assembly," *President of Russia*, February 21, 2023, http://en.kremlin.ru/events/president/news/70565.
10. Paul Sonne, "Ukraine's Zelensky to Russians: 'What Are You Fighting for and with Whom?'" *Washington Post*, February 24, 2022, https://www.washingtonpost.com/national-security/2022/02/23/ukraine-zelensky-russia-address/.
11. On this issue, see Bálint Madlovics and Bálint Magyar, "Ukrainian Regime Cycles and the Russian Invasion," in *Ukraine's Patronal Democracy and the Russian Invasion: The Russia-Ukraine War, Volume One*, edited by Bálint Madlovics and Bálint Magyar (Budapest–Vienna–New York: CEU Press, 2023), 3–53.
12. The International Court of Justice, at the request of Ukraine, investigated the Russian claims and found no evidence on the alleged genocide or on any preparations for it. See the relevant ICJ ruling from March 16, 2022: Lara Van Dousselaere, "The Court Indicates Provisional Measures."
13. EUvsDisinfo. "Key Narratives in Pro-Kremlin Disinformation: 'Nazis'" *EUvsDisinfo*, September 20, 2022, https://euvsdisinfo.eu/key-narratives-in-pro-kremlin-disinformation-nazis/.
14. Manveen Rana, "Volodymyr Zelensky: Russian Mercenaries Ordered to Kill Ukraine's President," March 24, 2023, https://www.thetimes.co.uk/article/volodymyr-zelensky-russian-mercenaries-ordered-to-kill-ukraine-president-cvcksh79d.
15. "Russians Twice Tried to Storm Zelensky's Compound in Early Hours of War, Aide Says," *The Times of Israel*, April 29, 2022, https://www.timesofisrael.com/russians-twice-tried-to-storm-zelensky-compound-in-early-hours-of-war-report/.

16. Nebi Qena and Yuras Karmanau, "Moscow Says It Will Curb Assault on Kyiv, Chernihiv; Russian Troops Seen Withdrawing," *The Times of Israel*, March 29, 2022, https://www.timesofisrael.com/moscow-says-it-will-curb-assault-on-kyiv-chernihiv-russian-troops-seen-withdrawing/.
17. President of Ukraine, "Video Collection — Official Web Site of the President of Ukraine," *Official Website of the President of Ukraine*, https://www.president.gov.ua/en/videos/videos-archive.
18. Anchal Vohra, "Ukraine Is Serious About Taking Back Crimea," *Foreign Policy*, February 22, 2023, https://foreignpolicy.com/2023/02/22/ukraine-crimea-russia-take-back/.
19. "Ukraine War Must End with Liberation of Crimea – Zelensky," *BBC News*, August 10, 2022, https://www.bbc.com/news/world-europe-62487303.
20. "REPLAY: Ukraine's Zelensky Speaks at Davos World Economic Forum," *France 24*, January 18, 2023, https://www.france24.com/en/video/20230118-replay-ukraine-zelensky-speaks-at-davos-world-economic-forum.
21. Benjamin Jensen, "Crippling Civilian Infrastructure Has Long Been Part of Russian Generals' Playbook – Putin Is Merely Expanding That Approach," *The Conversation*, October 14, 2022, http://theconversation.com/crippling-civilian-infrastructure-has-long-been-part-of-russian-generals-playbook-putin-is-merely-expanding-that-approach-192226.
22. Brian (Chun Hey) Kot and Steven Feldstein, "Two Deeply Troubling Trends from Ukraine's Year of War," *Carnegie Endowment for International Peace*, February 22, 2023, https://carnegieendowment.org/2023/02/22/two-deeply-troubling-trends-from-ukraine-s-year-of-war-pub-89086.
23. "Russia Says Ukrainian Helicopters Hit Oil Refinery," April 4, 2022, https://www.aa.com.tr/en/energy/oil/russia-says-ukrainian-helicopters-hit-oil-refinery/35021.
24. Reuters, "Russian Refinery Says It Was Struck by Drones from Direction of Ukraine," *Reuters*, June 22, 2022, https://www.reuters.com/world/europe/fire-broke-out-russias-novoshakhtinsk-oil-refinery-2022-06-22/.
25. Dominique Arel and Jesse Driscoll, *Ukraine's Unnamed War: Before the Russian Invasion of 2022* (Cambridge University Press, 2023).
26. "Ukraine's New Military Branch: Citizens Protecting Their Neighborhood," *Politico*, February 13, 2022, https://www.politico.eu/article/ukraine-russia-military-citizen-reservist-defense/.
27. Maksym Butchenko, "Ukraine's Territorial Defence on a War Footing," *ICDS*, April 13, 2022, https://icds.ee/en/ukraines-territorial-defence-on-a-war-footing/.
28. "Для освобождения оккупированных территорий: специальные штурмовые бригады создают в Украине — как попасть в их ряды" [For the liberation of the occupied territories: special assault brigades are created in Ukraine – how to join their ranks], *Freedom*, February 4, 2023, https://uatv.ua/dlya-osvobozhdeniya-okkupirovannyh-territorij-spetsialnye-shturmovye-brigady-sozdayut-v-ukraine-kak-popast-v-ih-ryady/.
29. Natalya Kava, "Много желающих: МВД будет формировать штурмовые бригады "Гвардии наступления" и после 1 апреля" [There are many who want to: the Ministry of Internal Affairs will form assault brigades of the "Offensive Guard" after April 1], *РБК-Украина*, February 12, 2023, https://www.rbc.ua/ukr/news/bagato-ohochih-mvs-bude-formuvati-shturmovi-1676218800.html.
30. Gábriel Dienes, "Az a béke, amiről a magyar kormány beszél, Ukrajna tragédiája lenne, mondta az ukrán parlamenti képviselő Budapesten" [The peace that the Hungarian government is talking about would be a tragedy for Ukraine, stated a Ukrainian parliamentarian in Budapest], *444*, March 4, 2023, https://444.hu/2023/03/04/az-a-beke-amirol-a-magyar-kormany-beszel-ukrajna-tragediaja-lenne-mondta-az-ukran-parlamenti-kepviselo-budapesten
31. Ministry of Foreign Affairs of Ukraine, "Join the International Legion of Defence of Ukraine!" 2022, https://fightforua.org.
32. "Volunteer Fighters from 52 Countries Join International Legion," *Ukrinform*, March 11, 2022, https://www.ukrinform.net/rubric-ato/3426983-volunteer-fighters-from-52-countries-join-international-legion.html.

33. Arkadiusz Legieć, "Profiling Foreign Fighters in Eastern Ukraine: A Theoretical Introduction," in *Not Only Syria? The Phenomenon of Foreign Fighters in a Comparative Perspective*, (Chisinau: IOS Press, 2017), 22–30; Andras Racz, "The Elephant in the Room: Russian Foreign Fighters in Ukraine," in *Not Only Syria? The Phenomenon of Foreign Fighters in a Comparative Perspective*, (Chisinau: IOS Press, 2017), 60–73.
34. Reuters, "Russia Is Conducting Covert Mobilisation Campaign, Ukraine Spy Chief Says," *Reuters*, June 25, 2022, https://www.reuters.com/world/europe/russia-is-conducting-covert-mobilisation-campaign-ukraine-spy-chief-2022-06-25/.
35. Sam Cranny-Evans, "Understanding Russia's Mobilisation," September 28, 2022, https://www.rusi.org/explore-our-research/publications/commentary/understanding-russias-mobilisation.
36. "Why Russia Is Urgently Forming a Combat Army Reserve BARS?" September 13, 2021, https://bulgarianmilitary.com/2021/09/13/why-russia-is-urgently-forming-a-combat-army-reserve-bars/.
37. "'We Were Nothing to Them': Russian Volunteer Reservists Return from War against Ukraine Feeling Deceived," *Radio Free Europe/Radio Liberty*, August 12, 2022, https://www.rferl.org/a/russia-volunteers-ukraine-treatment-minimal-training-war/31985377.html.
38. Yaroslav Trofimov, "Russia's Wagner Troops Exhaust Ukrainian Forces in Bakhmut," *WSJ*, March 5, 2023, https://www.wsj.com/articles/russias-wagner-troops-exhaust-ukrainian-forces-in-bakhmut-b58e726c.
39. "White House: Wagner Group Has Suffered over 30,000 Casualties in Ukraine," *Reuters*, February 17, 2023, https://www.reuters.com/world/europe/white-house-wagner-group-has-suffered-over-30000-casualties-ukraine-2023-02-17/.
40. Pjotr Sauer, "Wagner Mercenary Group Will 'Decrease' as Prisoner Recruitment Ends, Says Boss," *The Guardian*, February 15, 2023, https://www.theguardian.com/world/2023/feb/15/wagner-mercenary-group-will-decrease-as-prisoner-recruitment-ends-says-boss.
41. Anastasia Tenisheva, "Murders, Drugs and Brawls: Russia's Pardoned Ex-Convicts Return Home After Fighting in Ukraine," *The Moscow Times*, August 18, 2023, https://www.themoscowtimes.com/2023/08/18/murders-drugs-and-brawls-russias-pardoned-ex-convicts-return-home-after-fighting-in-ukraine-a82175.
42. Paul Sonne, "Wagner Founder Rebuffs Order Over Fighter Contracts With Russian Military," *The New York Times*, June 11, 2023, https://www.nytimes.com/2023/06/11/world/europe/wagner-russia-defense-ministry-contract.html.
43. Mark Krutov and Sergei Dobrynin, "Who's Who Among Russia's Mercenary Companies," *Radio Free Europe/Radio Liberty*, May 23, 2023, https://www.rferl.org/a/russia-other-mercenary-companies-ukraine/32424520.html; "It's Not Just Wagner. At Least Three Gazprom-Linked Private Military Companies Now Have Fighters in Ukraine," *Meduza*, May 16, 2023, https://meduza.io/en/feature/2023/05/16/it-s-not-just-wagner.
44. Bálint Magyar and Bálint Madlovics, *A Concise Field Guide to Post-Communist Regimes: Actors, Institutions, and Dynamics* (Budapest–Vienna–New York: CEU Press, 2022).
45. "Russian Lower House Votes to Allow Governors to Create Their Own Military Organisations during Wartime," *Novaya Gazeta Europe*, July 25, 2023, https://novayagazeta.eu/articles/2023/07/25/russian-lower-house-votes-to-allow-governors-to-create-their-own-military-organisations-during-wartime-en-news.
46. "Wagner Making 'Africa Even More Free', Says Prigozhin in First Post-Rebellion Video," *The Guardian*, August 22, 2023, https://www.theguardian.com/world/2023/aug/22/wagner-prigozhin-recruiting-post-russia-rebellion-video-africa-putin.
47. "Wagner chief Prigozhin was on plane that crashed in Russia, aviation agency says," *CNN*, August 23, 2023, https://edition.cnn.com/2023/08/23/europe/russia-wagner-prigozhin-plane-crash-intl/index.html.
48. "NBU Opens Special Account to Raise Funds for Ukraine's Armed Forces (Updated)," *National Bank of Ukraine*, March 1, 2022, https://bank.gov.ua/en/news/all/natsionalniy-bank-vidkriv-spets-rahunok-dlya-zboru-koshtiv-na-potrebi-armiyi.

49 Come Back Alive Foundation, "About the Foundation – Come Back Alive," https://savelife.in.ua/en/about-foundation-en/.
50 "Serhiy Prytula Charity Foundation," https://prytulafoundation.org/en.
51 "Lithuanian Bayraktar Arrived in Ukraine," *European Pravda*, July 8, 2022, https://www.eurointegration.com.ua/eng/news/2022/07/8/7142874/.
52 "Ten Bayraktar dla Ukrainy został kupiony dzięki Polakom. Dostał symboliczne imię" [This Bayraktar for Ukraine was bought thanks to Poles. It was given a symbolic name], *Onet Wiadomości*, October 17, 2022, https://wiadomosci.onet.pl/swiat/ten-bayraktar-dla-ukrainy-zostal-kupiony-dzieki-polakom-ma-juz-imie/p9sjnzn.
53 "Ukraine War: Czech Crowdfunding Buys 'Tomas the Tank' for Ukraine," *BBC News*, October 3, 2022, https://www.bbc.com/news/world-europe-63121649.
54 "Czech Crowdfunding Successfully Raised Funds to Purchase 15 Viktor for Ukrainian Army," *MilitaryLeak*, January 2, 2023, https://militaryleak.com/2023/01/02/czech-crowdfunding-successfully-raised-funds-to-purchase-15-viktor-for-ukrainian-army/.
55 "Russians Buy Boots and Body Armor for the Troops, as the Kremlin Tries to Fix the Campaign's Problems," *CNN*, December 22, 2022, https://edition.cnn.com/2022/12/22/europe/russians-crowdfund-soldiers-ukraine-cmd-intl/index.html.
56 For one such recent campaign, see, for example: https://vk.com/uralza?w=wall-212936965_1267.
57 "Ukraine Fires Officials amid Corruption Scandal, as Allies Watch Closely," *The New York Times*, January 24, 2023, https://www.nytimes.com/2023/01/24/world/europe/ukraine-corruption-firing-western-aid.html.
58 Dan Peleschuk, "Ukraine Sacks Army Recruitment Chiefs in Anti-Graft Shakeup," *Reuters*, August 11, 2023, sec. Europe, https://www.reuters.com/world/europe/ukraine-fire-all-regional-military-recruitment-chiefs-zelenskiy-2023-08-11/.
59 "Ukraine: UN Members Endorse Resolution to End War," *DW*, February 23, 2023, https://www.dw.com/en/ukraine-un-members-endorse-resolution-to-end-war/a-64799465.
60 General Assembly Vote on Ukraine | United Nations (2 March 2022), United Nations, YouTube video, 2:04, March 2, 2022, https://www.youtube.com/watch?v=THDHTlaSb50.
61 Hyonhee Shin, "N.Korea Backs Russia's Proclaimed Annexations, Criticises U.S. 'Double Standards,'" *Reuters*, October 3, 2022, https://www.reuters.com/world/asia-pacific/nkorea-backs-russias-proclaimed-annexations-criticises-us-double-standards-2022-10-03/.
62 Bill Chappell, "Only 4 Countries Side with Russia as U.N. Rejects Annexations in Ukraine," *NPR*, October 13, 2022, https://www.npr.org/2022/10/13/1128642820/un-rejects-russian-annexations-ukraine.
63 Stefan Lehne, "After Russia's War against Ukraine: What Kind of World Order?" *Carnegie Europe*, February 28, 2023, https://carnegieeurope.eu/2023/02/28/after-russia-s-war-against-ukraine-what-kind-of-world-order-pub-89130. See also Gyula Krajczár's chapter in this volume.
64 "Russia and Iran Hesitate over Co-Operation as West Warns of Costs," *Financial Times*, March 6, 2023, https://www.ft.com/content/b9361eae-5b05-4c17-8c59-7fb11e2579fe.
65 Victor Cha, "North Korea Sends Ammunitions to Russia," November 7, 2022, https://www.csis.org/analysis/north-korea-sends-ammunitions-russia.
66 "Belarus Sends 20 T-72 Tanks to Russian Belgorod Region," Army Recognition, October 13, 2023, https://www.armyrecognition.com/defense_news_october_2022_global_security_army_industry/belarus_sends_20_t-72_tanks_to_russian_belgorod_region.html.
67 "More War Equipment on Belarus-Russia Trains, This Time It's Vehicles," *RailFreight.com*, November 16, 2022, https://www.railfreight.com/specials/2022/11/16/more-war-equipment-on-belarus-russia-trains-this-time-its-vehicles/.
68 Eric Banco and Sarah Anne Aarup, "'Hunting Rifles' — Really? China Ships Assault Weapons and Body Armor to Russia," *Politico*, March 16, 2023, https://www.politico.com/news/2023/03/16/chinese-rifles-body-armor-russia-ukraine-00087398.

69 See the previously referred votes.
70 "2022 Person of the Year: Volodymyr Zelensky," *Time*, December 7, 2022, https://time.com/person-of-the-year-2022-volodymyr-zelensky/.
71 "Ukraine Conflict: What War Crimes Is Russia Accused Of?" *BBC News*, March 10, 2023, sec. World, https://www.bbc.com/news/world-60690688.
72 Christoph Trebesch et al., "The Ukraine Support Tracker: Which Countries Help Ukraine and How?" *Kiel Working Papers*, 2218 (2023), https://www.ifw-kiel.de/publications/kiel-working-papers/2022/the-ukraine-support-tracker-which-countries-help-ukraine-and-how-17204/.
73 Joe Saballa, "Ukrainian Army Spotted Using Israeli-Made Armored Vehicles," *The Defense Post*, November 14, 2022, https://www.thedefensepost.com/2022/11/14/ukrainian-army-israel-armored-vehicles/.
74 "In First, Israel Said to Authorize Sale of Defensive Military Equipment to Ukraine," *The Times of Israel*, March 16, 2023, https://www.timesofisrael.com/in-first-israel-said-to-authorize-sale-of-defensive-military-equipment-to-ukraine/.
75 Dylan Malyashov, "Finnish-Made Armored Vehicles Spotted in Ukraine," *Defence Blog*, September 28, 2022, https://defence-blog.com/finnish-made-armored-vehicles-spotted-in-ukraine/.
76 David Ignatius, "How the Algorithm Tipped the Balance in Ukraine," *The Washington Post*, December 19, 2022, sec. Global Opinions, https://www.washingtonpost.com/opinions/2022/12/19/palantir-algorithm-data-ukraine-war/.
77 Balázs Bozzay, "A mesterséges intelligencia már nemcsak a célpontot mutatja meg, hanem a hadműveletet is megtervezi [Artificial intelligence not only shows the target, but also plans the operaion]," *Telex*, May 15, 2023, https://telex.hu/tech/2023/05/15/mesterseges-intelligencia-haboru-orosz-ukran-palantir-most-kezdjuk-csak-latni-mire-is-kepes-a-mesterseges-intelligencia-egy-haboruban.

The Falsification of History: War and Russian Memory Politics

Zoltán Sz. Bíró

1. History in the service of self-legitimation

Putin started talking about historical issues years before the full-scale invasion of Ukraine. He gave a long lecture to CIS leaders on the antecedents of World War II;[1] he wrote a lengthy essay on the same subject,[2] followed by another on World War II;[3] then, he tried to prove on historical and cultural grounds that there was no Ukrainian people.[4] In June 2022, at the opening of an exhibition dedicated to Peter I, he also argued that the Tsar did not "take" the areas where St. Petersburg stands today from the Swedes but "took them back." He added that the Russians now shared the same fate as their predecessors: they had to defend the country's sovereignty, and regain their ancestral territories.[5] In the circumstances of the war, which was then in full swing, this obviously meant that what was happening in Ukraine was nothing less than the reassertion of the Russians' ancestral possessions and the strengthening of their sovereignty.

This idea was a rather open admission that the war was not about the "de-Nazification" and "demilitarization" of Ukraine, as Moscow had proclaimed in the early stages of the war, but about the reclamation of ancient Russian lands. But whatever the background to the war against Ukraine, there can be little doubt that in preparing for it, in persuading Russian society, the ruling elite attached enormous importance to the transformation of historical memory. The president himself played his part in this work. His many statements on historical issues were an attempt to set Russian society on the right course, which meant that, following his example, the self-critical view of history of the nineties, which had discarded the false tradition of self-celebration, was once again dominated by bias and insensitivity to the pain of others. This did not mean that views that differed from those that the authorities found salutary could not be expressed, but it did mean that the Kremlin tried to dominate public discourse on historical issues by all means. Unbiased and self-critical academic works could still be published (the Brezhnev era did not return in this respect), but they were unable to counterbalance the increasingly false narratives of the state propaganda machine. Historical memory became, in the hands of the authorities, a valuable tool of legitimation as well as ideological and emotional preparation for the war against Ukraine.

2. Falsifying Soviet history: rewriting the memory of World War II to resurrect the concept of "sphere of influence"

2.1. Whitewashing the Soviet Union: Putin's speech to CIS leaders (2019)

Putin's first spectacular display of interest in history was his lecture to the heads of state at the CIS summit in December 2019 on the background to and causes of World War II. The surprised colleagues probably did not understand why they had to listen to all this; they had not come to Moscow for such a lecture, but since they were there, they listened. The Russian president probably thought what he said was important because he had been outraged by the European Parliament's resolution on the importance of European remembrance, adopted shortly before, in mid-September. Among other things, the resolution states that "the Second World War—the most destructive war in European history—broke out as a direct consequence of the infamous German-Soviet Non-Aggression Treaty of 23 August 1939 (the Molotov-Ribbentrop Pact) and the secret protocols annexed to it."[6] From which Putin might have inferred that, in the eyes of the European Parliament, Hitler's Germany and Stalin's Soviet Union bore equal responsibility for the outbreak of the war. This is not the case, at least in the sense that the extent of their responsibility is the same. The responsibility is shared, but the extent of it differs. The pre-war policy of the Soviet Union can be rightly criticized in many respects, but the decision to go to war was taken by Hitler: not by the Soviet Union, but by Germany.

However, Putin's position is that the Soviet Union bears no responsibility for the outbreak of the war. Hence, he was outraged by the European Parliament's resolution, and decided not to let it pass unchallenged. In his speech to the leaders of the CIS countries, he tried to prove that the Soviet-German non-aggression treaty was not unusual or outrageous at the time, as other countries had concluded such treaties. Indeed, there are many similar examples from the pre-war period, but we are not aware of any non-aggression treaty that had a secret clause like the Soviet-German pact, especially one in which the parties divided up the territory of sovereign states. Putin, however, generously forgot this detail in his presentation, and instead began a lengthy analysis of the "cruel and cynical" 1938 Munich Convention. He argued the Convention was more responsible for the outbreak of the war than the later Soviet-German non-aggression treaty. In other words, Putin did nothing other than try to shift the blame for the outbreak of war onto the Western powers.

In his presentation, Putin told the story of the Munich deal as if the Soviet Union alone had been willing to defend Czechoslovakia, but the Western powers would not let it happen. No doubt both the French and the British were distrustful of Moscow, but the reverse was also true. In other words, it is a gross exaggeration to say that Stalin had no desire to do anything other than rush to the aid of Czechoslovakia, in concert with the French and British. Putin accuses the Western leaders of cynicism, but there is no hard evidence that the Soviet Union was really prepared to come to Prague's defense. In fact, it was only a pretext, not a reason, for Moscow's inaction that the Poles and the Romanians did not allow the Red Army to cross their territory. This circumstance can be invoked, as Putin did, but it does not follow that Stalin really wanted to help Prague. He was as cynical as his Western colleagues in this matter. The Soviet dictator, like British Prime Minister Neville Chamberlain and French President Édouard Daladier, was just buying time and would have been more than happy to see the Western powers and Germany at odds over Czechoslovakia. Of course, the reverse was also true. In other words, it is hardly closer to the truth to do as Putin did and put all the blame for the outbreak of war on the Western powers, claiming that they were no different from us, or, going even further, that they committed the "original sin." The situation was much more complex than that. What happened in Munich was ultimately the result of the deep and mutual distrust that characterized relations between the Soviet Union and the Western powers of the time, and which prevented them from joining forces at that time.

Another central topic of Putin's presentation was pre-war Polish politics. The Russian president went so far as to blame the Poles for the outbreak of World War II. But this is as unfounded as the unilateral blaming of the Western powers. The pre-war policies of the Poles can be criticized for a number of reasons but to accuse them of having caused the outbreak of the world war is without foundation. Nevertheless, Putin tried to support this claim on two grounds: first by the fact, mentioned earlier, that it was they (together with the Romanians) who refused to allow the Soviet army to march through their territory, thus preventing the defense of Czechoslovakia; and, second, by claiming that they themselves were the beneficiaries of the Munich decision, because they had gained territory from Czechoslovakia.[7] These, Putin said, were serious crimes that Warsaw itself had contributed significantly to the outbreak of the war. The only problem with the condemned land grab is that the territory annexed by the Poles (part of the Cieszyn region and a narrow strip of the Tatra Mountains) was a fraction of the size of the territory the Soviet Union acquired as a result of the Molotov-Ribbentrop Pact. The former was barely 1,000 km^2, while the latter was just over 400 times that. Putin is therefore either unable or unwilling to distinguish between Poland's opportunistic seizure of part of a long-disputed territory considered essential for the defense of the country and the Soviet Union's active collusion with Nazi Germany and the resulting acquisition of vast territories.

Even more questionable is the Russian president's defense of the Soviet army's invasion and annexation of eastern Poland. According to Putin, the Soviet forces' entry into eastern Poland on September 17, 1939 "saved a great many lives." This claim may have been true for a while, but it did not change the fate of the tens of thousands of people deported in three waves by the Soviets from the occupied

Polish territory in 1940. The total number, as far as we know today, was 276,000.[8] And the alleged "saving of lives" to which Putin referred did not change the plight of the almost 22,000 Polish military officers taken prisoner by the Soviets and executed by the Soviet secret police (NKVD) in the Katyn Forest and two other places in April 1940.

Putin's presentation did not include these facts. He discussed the period as if neither the deportations nor the executions had taken place. His omissions, however, weaken rather than strengthen his argument, as does his attempt to trivialize the significance of the territories acquired under the Molotov-Ribbentrop Pact. Putin presented to his fellow presidents what happened before the war as if there had been no secret clause in the agreement between the two totalitarian states, and the Soviet Union had not acquired vast territories, while violating the sovereignty of a series of countries.

2.2. Whitewashing Stalin and Molotov: Putin's essay "75 Years of Great Victory" (2020)

Putin already indicated in a speech to the CIS presidents that he intended to write a long and thorough essay on the background to the war. Accordingly, in June 2020, he published his paper "75 Years of the Great Victory: A Shared Responsibility for History and the Future."[9] In it, as might have been expected, he returned to the history of the Munich Agreement, as well as to his position that the war was inevitable because of the concessions made to Hitler at the time, and not because of the subsequent German-Soviet pact.

In his essay, Putin also detailed how both the British and the French had delayed reaching an agreement with the Soviet Union, and cited as evidence that the Western military delegation that negotiated in Moscow in August 1939 consisted exclusively of second-line generals without any substantive authority. Putin is right about that, but the full picture is that neither Paris nor London wanted to enter into a military alliance with Moscow at that time. Their aims were much more modest then. All they wanted was a guarantee that the Soviet Union would not assist Nazi Germany in any way. Stalin, however, refused to give such assurances and instead made his delegates play that such a promise could only be made if they entered into an alliance. But he did not want an alliance, nor did he want Moscow to be blamed for it. Stalin therefore instructed Kliment Voroshilov, the People's Commissar for National Defense, who led the Soviet delegation, to clarify at the outset of the negotiations whether the Western delegation, like the Soviets, had the authority to sign any agreement. If not, they should be asked, with surprise, why they have come. And if they reply that they have only been authorized for preparatory negotiations, they should be asked whether they have a detailed plan in place in case their ally, the Soviet Union, is attacked. If they do not have one, then they should be asked on what basis they want to deal with us. And if they still wish to negotiate further, Stalin's briefing continued, the negotiations must be confined to clarifying the question of principle as to whether the Red Army would be allowed to pass through Poland and Romania. "If it should turn out that the passage of our army through Poland and Romania is out of question, it must be declared that without the fulfillment of this condition an agreement is impossible."[10] In other words, it is clear from Stalin's briefing, which has been publicly available for more than 30 years, that not only were the Western powers reluctant to reach an agreement with the Soviet Union, but the reverse was also true. Yet Putin does not want to know about this important fact. The reason is that if he had presented the background to the negotiations in a credible way, it would have been difficult to prove unilateral responsibility on the part of the West.

Even more revealing of Putin's true intentions is the way he presented Molotov's visit to Berlin and his meeting with Hitler in November 1940. According to the Russian president, the Soviet People's Commissar for Foreign Affairs made new territorial and other demands that the Germans would certainly not accept, so that Moscow would not have to join the Tripartite Pact. In reality, however, the reverse was the case. What Molotov asked the Germans to do was meant very seriously by the Soviet leadership. Stalin, who had sent Molotov to Berlin, wanted to get a clearer picture of the German view on a number of issues, but also wanted to extend his influence, with Hitler's approval, into new areas. It was in this spirit that Stalin and some members of his political entourage (Molotov, Voroshilov, and Anastas Mikoyan) assigned the tasks of the People's Commissar for Foreign Affairs. It is clear from the document of the negotiating instructions that the Soviet leadership considered this path important and wanted to win Hitler's agreement on a number of issues. Among other things, Moscow tried to persuade the German leadership to withdraw its troops from Finland and to stop demonstrations there that threatened Soviet interests. The directive also required Molotov to clarify the views of the Axis powers on Greece and Yugoslavia, and to come to an agreement with his German counterparts that any future decisions on Romania and Hungary would be subject to Moscow's prior agreement. Molotov's mandate also extended to persuading the Germans to follow a similar procedure with regard to Turkey. But the main purpose of the visit of the People's Commissar for Foreign Affairs was to get Berlin to accept that Bulgaria belongs to the sphere of influence of the Soviet Union and that the Red Army could move in. In other words, the negotiating instructions make it clear that this was not a case of imitated demands, but of demands that were really important to Moscow.

However, the Germans did not accept the Soviet demands, so no new agreement was reached. The bottom line is that it was not at all a case of Moscow deliberately making unfulfillable demands just to avoid having to sign the tripartite agreement, as Putin claimed in his essay, but of Molotov's failure to follow through on the ideas set out in the negotiating directive. At the same time, Moscow had no real intention of joining the tripartite agreement, because it did not want to reduce its room for maneuver, but it was keen to gain new territory.[11] Putin was obviously trying to present Molotov's trip to Berlin as if it had not been another attempt to acquire territory, because he thought it would be easier to disguise the imperialist aims of the Molotov-Ribbentrop Pact and to make it look as if it had been imposed under duress and solely for the country's security needs. But we know that this was not the case. Molotov's negotiation in Berlin is the most convincing refutation of this. It is no coincidence that when the Nuremberg Tribunal was set up after the war, the Soviet Union named three areas that could not be mentioned in any way in the trial. One of these was the pre-war foreign policy of the Soviet Union, in particular the Molotov-Ribbentrop Pact, Molotov's visit to Berlin in 1940, and the incorporation of the Baltic States into the Soviet Union.[12] These issues seem to have been an embarrassment even immediately after the war, and Putin also found it better not to talk about them. Rather, he chose to give an interpretation of what happened that made the indefensible excusable.

2.3. Putin's epigones: Russian politicians in the service of the falsification of history

Putin was not the only one who did his part to make the memory of World War II as effective a political tool in the hands of the Russian ruling elite as it was before the war against Ukraine. Several leading Russian politicians joined the President. The task was clear: to transform the interpretation of the great Patriotic War so that it could be used as effectively as possible for current political purposes. To do this, Russian society had to be convinced that everything the Soviet Union had done before, during, and after the war was exemplary in every respect, and that there was no reason to criticize it. It also meant breaking with the view that had developed in the Gorbachev years and intensified under Yeltsin, which was capable of being critical of the Soviet past in more than one respect, including Moscow's role in World War II.

This abandonment of self-criticism began early in Putin's second presidency, but the process accelerated in the second half of the 2010s. One spectacular episode was Putin's speech at the inaugural meeting of the organizing committee for the 75th anniversary of the end of World War II in December 2019. The Russian president called for a credible account of the war, because he believed that some countries and international organizations had been trying to falsify history for some time, even giving the impression that Nazi Germany and the Soviet Union bore equal responsibility for starting the war.[13] Of course, as mentioned above, there is no question of equal responsibility, just as there is no question of equal responsibility for the war as a whole, but there are still cases where Moscow can be held responsible. Even the fact that Soviet society undoubtedly made the greatest sacrifice in the fight against fascism cannot change this. Moscow should not forget the policy pursued by the Soviet Union between 1939 and the summer of 1941, and the responsibility it bore as a consequence. In Putin's Russia, however, the need for critical introspection is becoming less and less acknowledged. The cult of the memory of World War II, the first version of which emerged in the late Brezhnev years and then faded away, began to be revived in 2005. Initially, it was entirely understandable and proportionate to the losses suffered, while its content was defined by a sense of shock and compassion for the victims' relatives. Over time, however, war remembrance increasingly became a political instrument of the regime, which went hand in hand with a loss of sensitivity to the pain of other political communities. This inevitably led to increasingly sharp clashes in the politics of memory. The dispute was most acute with Russia's immediate western neighbors.

On the approaching 80th anniversary of the Molotov-Ribbentrop Pact, the Kremlin launched a striking information campaign to rehabilitate the agreement. From Minister of Foreign Affairs Sergey Lavrov to Minister of Culture Vladimir Medinsky, key politicians in Putin's regime have spoken out. Sergei Ivanov, former Minister of Defense, former head of the President's office and a member of the Russian National Security Council in 2019, was a key speaker as well, just like Sergey Naryshkin, who was then, as now, both Director of the Foreign Intelligence Service and President of the Russian Historical Society. All of them felt it important to defend the treaty and its secret supplementary protocols, which had been condemned by the Congress of Soviet People's Deputies under Gorbachev and declared invalid from the moment of its drafting. The resolution, adopted on December 24, 1989, stated that Stalin and Molotov had negotiated the secret protocols without informing Soviet society, the Party Central Committee, the Supreme Soviet (the parliament of the time), or the Soviet government of the outcome of the negotiations, and that they had therefore not been ratified. The resolution stated that the protocols "in no way reflected the will of the Soviet people." The secret deal was used by Stalin and his immediate entourage, the resolution said, to "issue ultimatums to other states and to put pressure on them by force."[14]

Despite the decision taken under Gorbachev, Ivanov, at a conference on the prehistory of World War II, also held in 2019, directly recommended to Russian society to "be proud of the Molotov-Ribbentrop Pact."[15] In a long interview with *Izvestia*, Naryshkin blamed the Western powers and Poland for the outbreak of the war.[16] At the opening of an exhibition on the period, Lavrov saw fit to point out that the Soviet Union had signed the non-aggression pact in August 1939 out of necessity because Britain and France refused to enter into an alliance.[17] Even if we were to accept the foreign minister's position (which is certainly not true in the form in which it is stated) the question still remains unanswered: why was it necessary to conclude a secret agreement with Nazi Germany on the partition of Eastern Europe? The fact that London and Paris delayed making an alliance with Moscow does not explain in any way the signing of the secret protocols, even less so because the Kremlin was also delaying the agreement. If the Soviet side had been keen to make a deal with the Western powers (and they were not, because it was hardly possible to make a secret deal with them on the partition of Eastern Europe) they would not have made excuses—but they did. In any case, this did not disturb the Russian Foreign Minister in the least in his attempt to blame the Western powers alone for the failure to reach an agreement.

Of all the Russian politicians in the chief patron's court, Vladimir Medinsky went furthest in discussing the 1939 pact, writing a lengthy article in its defense. The very title of his essay, published by *RIA Novosti* in 2019, is revelatory: "The Diplomatic Triumph of the Soviet Union."[18] From the beginning of his article, the author, who considers himself a serious historian, felt it important to point out that the Soviet regime had made a serious mistake in concealing the supplementary protocols. But not because it was a mistake to keep such an important issue secret, but because there was no reason to do so, because there was nothing to be ashamed of in the protocols. According to the Minister, similar agreements with Hitler had been signed by other states. One such pact was the Munich Agreement of 1938, when Czechoslovakia was forced by the four major powers in Europe to hand over its most valuable military and economic territories to Germany. This was done, Medinsky says, in the hope that Hitler's aggression would then turn eastwards. However, the author is not the least bit bothered by the fact that the Western powers have long regarded the Munich agreement as a serious failure and have made no excuses for their decision. There is no authoritative Western historian or politician who defends the Munich agreement. The Russian Minister of Culture, on the other hand, does just the opposite when he states that, "in the specific foreign policy situation of the summer of 1939, the Soviet Union was right to agree to the non-aggression pact" and that it was "a forced step on the Soviet side, a legitimate agreement with an undisputed enemy."

After all this, the question rightly arises as to what was the point of excusing the pact in 2019, which was once firmly condemned. What was in it for the regime? Probably most of all, by reinterpreting the events of 80 years ago and essentially returning to the Stalinist tradition, the Russian ruling elite gained a reference point for a Russian foreign policy that was increasingly at odds with the West. For this foreign policy made the concept of the "sphere of interest" almost an official position. The concept refers to the idea that only a few great powers have full and unlimited sovereignty. These are the powers that decide the fate of the smaller states in their "spheres of interest" by common agreement. This view, which has become popular again in Moscow, challenges one of the most important principles of international law—the sovereign equality of states.

3. The falsification of Ukrainian history: legitimizing the war through politics of memory

Before the full-scale invasion, Putin was concerned not only with the history of World War II but also with the history of the Ukrainians. In his essay "On the Historical Unity of Russians and Ukrainians," published in the summer of 2021, Putin attempted to deduce the inevitability of close cooperation between Russia and Ukraine, and to justify the absurdity of the opposition between the two peoples.[19] He did this by placing the blame for the current situation solely on the Ukrainians, and more specifically on the Ukrainian political elite that came to power in 2014. Although there were some self-critical remarks in the essay, they are so general that they can be seen as no more than a simple rhetorical device.

3.1. Denial of the existence of an independent Ukrainian people

According to Putin, those who some people consider Ukrainians speak a little differently from Russians, but ultimately they are no different. It is only because of the intrigue of external forces that there are Ukrainians at all; and if it were not for the external forces working on this, Ukrainians would not exist.

Undoubtedly, there are many similarities between the two peoples, but it in no way follows that they do not exist in distinct ways. It can hardly be denied that they share similar languages, beliefs, and culture. It is even true that the Ukrainian language was not as different from the Russian language in the past as it is today, but there is still plenty of evidence that they are not the same language. This is immediately shown by the difference in the writing of the two languages, where the calligraphy of many letters differs, as well as the vocabulary and grammar of the two languages. These differences became increasingly apparent from the 16th to 17th centuries. It is typical that for almost half a century the reports written by the Hetmans to Moscow (they were obliged to report when the "left-bank Ukraine," i.e., the territories east of the Dnieper, came under Russian control) were systematically translated into Russian so that they could be understood in Moscow. This practice only ceased after the official correspondence between "Great Russian" (meaning Russian) and "Little Russian" (meaning Ukrainian) began to converge, but this convergence never meant the complete disappearance of differences.

There are many similarities in the beliefs and cultures of the two peoples, despite the fact that the different groups of Eastern Slavs were controlled by different powers from quite early on, essentially from the mid-13th century. Nevertheless, the great majority of them remained Eastern Orthodox Christians, whether they lived in the territory of the Lithuanian Principality or the Golden Horde and its successor kingdoms. After a while, however, differences between the Kyiv and Moscow versions of Orthodoxy became apparent, but these were not significant, if only because for a long time no one prevented the various politically controlled groups of Eastern Slavs from exchanging church books among themselves. There were some periods, such as the first half of the 17th century, when Moscow tried to prevent the admission of church books "printed in Lithuania," but after a while, they gave up on this practice. The distance between the two ecclesial communities was also created by the fact that the Metropolitan of Kyiv did not immediately come under the control of the Moscow Patriarchate after the Russian acquisition of the eastern Ukrainian territories in 1654. For many decades, until 1686, the Patriarch of Constantinople was in charge of this function.

However, the linguistic and religious proximity of Russians and Ukrainians in no way implies the identity of the two peoples, as Putin claims. The main reason is that, in the formation of a modern political nation, not only do ethnic and linguistic affinities and cultural proximity play a major role but social traditions, ideas about the past, legal norms, and forms of interaction within a given community as well. If we take these circumstances into account, we cannot fail to notice the significant differences between the social organization of Ukrainians and Russians, which were already evident by the 17th century. The everyday life of the Ukrainians and their social organization was influenced by the Rzeczpospolita, the set of traditions of the common Polish-Lithuanian state which took deep root at local level and which the Ukrainians came to regard as their own. The transformation of the local legal system in the 18th century speaks volumes about the strength of these traditions. Although the Russian imperial government took the initiative, the models that determined the reform of the judiciary in "Little Russia" were taken from the Polish legal and institutional system, and from certain rules in Lithuanian statutes. The system thus established continued to operate until 1864, when the empire's judicial system underwent a comprehensive overhaul. For a long time, the cities in these territories were governed by Magdeburg law. Overall, these particular circumstances gave rise to a very different social experience from that available to people in the rest of the empire.

Putin's essay is full of inaccuracies, half-truths, and omissions, in addition to problems of approach and methodology. It is striking that the Russian President never deigns to call the first state of the Eastern Slavs "Kyivan Rus" in the way historiography is accustomed to, but instead always uses the formula "Old Rus." This is no coincidence: it is an indication that Kyiv cannot have anything to do with the first Slavic state, which he claims was held together by a common language, extensive economic ties, and the rule of the princes of the Ryurik dynasty. However, this is certainly not true in this form, if Putin is thinking of the time of the formation of the Kyivan Rus in the ninth to tenth centuries. The Normans, who played an important role in the founding of the state, spoke their own old Scandinavian language, while the Finno-Ugric, Baltic, and Turkic tribes living here spoke their own. What Putin speaks about is a development of a few centuries later, when the Old Slavic language had a truly unifying role. Nor can we speak of the unifying role of economic relations in an age of natural farming, nor of the cohesive power of the Ryurik dynasty in a state without primogeniture. Putin also ignores the fact that in the 16th and 17th centuries at the latest, the groups of Eastern Slavs controlled by the various powers began to separate linguistically, creating Ukrainian and Belarusian languages alongside Russian.

According to Putin, the separation of Ukrainians was not the result of changes within the group, but was an externally inspired and controlled process, instigated at different times by the Poles or the Austrians and, now, by the "collective West." "The image of a Ukrainian people separated from the Russians was created and strengthened among the Polish elite and certain sections of the Belarusian intelligentsia," Putin says, adding that "there was no historical basis for this, nor could there have been." The Russian president is also outraged by the widespread condemnation in Ukraine today of the crimes of the Soviet regime, some of which cannot be attributed to the USSR or the Soviet Union, and especially not to Russia today. That may be so, and examples can be found, but the persuasive force of Putin's claim is considerably weakened by the fact that in his long essay he makes no reference whatsoever to Holodomor, the great famine of 1932–1933. There is now a general consensus among Russian, Ukrainian, and Western historians of the period that the Holodomor had 7–7.5 million victims in the Soviet Union as a whole, of whom some 3–3.5 million were probably Ukrainian. Instead, the debate today is simply whether what happened was the result of Moscow's deliberate policy of punishment against Ukrainians, or whether it was a joint martyrdom of the peoples of the Soviet Union—Russians, Ukrainians, and Kazakhs, for which the responsibility lies largely with the Stalinist leadership of the country.

3.2. Questioning Ukraine's borders

Apart from denying the recognition of Ukrainians as an independent people, Putin obviously needed the long historical prelude to convincingly explain his other main thesis, which can be summarized briefly as follows: when the Soviet Union broke up, it should have been ensured that each member state could take with it only as much territory as it had taken with it as a member of the federal state. According to the Russian president, after the former Soviet Member States annulled the treaty that created the Soviet Union at the end of 1922, they lost the legal basis on which they subsequently acquired new territories. He argues that the borders and the ownership of certain territories should in any case have been negotiated at the time of the break-up of the Soviet Union.

But this is an utterly irresponsible position. Fortunately, at the time of the break-up of the Soviet Union, the republics were led by leaders who were aware of the serious risks of this proposal. Indeed, the idea of redrawing the borders came up in the autumn of 1991, when the future of the federal state was already in doubt after the attempted coup against Gorbachev. It was then that the Burbulis Memorandum was published, which called for a revision of the internal borders of the Soviet Union, separating the member republics. The document, signed by a member of the Russian government, immediately provoked protests from Ukraine and Kazakhstan, and the memorandum, which was considered semi-official, was withdrawn by Moscow. Had it not, who knows what would have happened on the territory of the nuclear-armed Soviet Union. But fortunately that did not happen and they did not start arguing about borders. Instead, in the declaration signed in Belovezhskaya Pushcha on December 8, 1991, which dissolved the Soviet Union, Article 5 stated that the parties to the agreement respect each other's borders and the inviolability of their territories, i.e., they recognize the former Soviet internal borders as international borders without any changes. Putin's *ex post* reasoning is unacceptable not only because it would have seriously jeopardized the process of "dismantling" the Soviet Union if it had been implemented, but also because it was unworkable. If everything had to revert to the 1922 situation, there would have been enormous chaos within moments. For who, for example, would have gained the territories that the Soviet Union had acquired in the early stages of World War II as a result of the Molotov-Ribbentrop Pact and the subsequent invasion of eastern Poland? Would the 200–250 kilometer-wide strip of land in the western part of what is now Ukraine and Belarus, acquired in the autumn of 1939, have been returned to Poland? And if it had, how would the Germans have reacted to the new situation? Would they have reclaimed the territories they had ceded to Warsaw after the war, upsetting the European territorial order established after World War II?

Putin apparently never considered that the eastern borders of Ukraine today are not where they were when the Soviet Union was founded. If the 1922 situation was restored as Putin proposed, Crimea would have been part of Russia, but most of the Rostov region (including Taganrog, Shahti, and Gukovo), which is now under Moscow's control, would be Ukrainian. These territories were transferred from the Ukrainian republic to the Russian only in 1923–1924. Not to mention the fact that the internal territorial order, which survived with minimal changes until the break-up of the Soviet Union, was not established until 1936. It was only then that the three Transcaucasian republics of Armenia, Azerbaijan, and Georgia gained the status of member republics, just as the internal borders of the Soviet Union in Central Asia were not finalized until that time. If Putin's idea had been accepted in 1991, not only all of Kazakhstan, but also Russian Turkestan, including today's Kyrgyzstan, Uzbekistan, Tajikistan, and Turkmenistan, would belong to Russia today, because these territories were still part of the Russian republic when the Soviet Union was founded.

The unmanageable consequences of Putin's idea could go on and on, but perhaps we can see from what we have seen so far how unrealistic and false his proposal is. So is his claim that "the transfer of the Crimean territory belonging to the Russian Soviet Federative Socialist Republic to the Ukrainian Soviet Socialist Republic in 1954 was carried out in flagrant violation of the legal norms in force at the time." This is simply not true. As long as the Soviet Union existed, all decisions involving territorial changes, whether in republics or in counties, were always taken on the basis of decisions of the Presidium of the Central Executive Committee of the All-Union Central Executive Committee, and later of the Presidium of the Supreme Soviet of the USSR, or of the Presidium of the Supreme Soviet of the republics concerned. The transfer of Crimea was no exception.

Putin's long essay was probably intended to do nothing more than to provide a historical basis for what he had done to Ukraine up to 2021 (when the essay was published), including the annexation of Crimea; and to make it clear to everyone that as long as he is President of Russia, he will not let Ukraine go. The Russian chief patron does not consider Ukraine to be a fully sovereign country, despite the fact that the Russian state committed itself to this in the 1991 agreement that ended the Soviet Union.

Indeed, Putin's job as Russian head of state is not to write history papers and decide whether there are Ukrainians or not. That is not his business. Instead, it is his job as the leader of Russia to honor all the agreements that have been signed in his country's name in the past. And that is true even if he believes that there are no Ukrainians because whether or not he accepts their existence at the moment, the Ukrainian state exists. In fact, the sovereignty of Ukraine has been recognized and enshrined in international treaties by Russia on five separate occasions:

1. the agreement on the dissolution of the Soviet Union and the creation of the Commonwealth of Independent States, signed in Belovezhskaya Pushcha on December 8, 1991 (Article 5);
2. the Budapest Memorandum signed on December 5, 1994;
3. the Treaty of Friendship, Cooperation and Partnership between Russia and Ukraine signed on May 31, 1997 (Article 2);

4. the delimitation treaty on the borders of Russia and Ukraine, signed on January 28, 2003 (already during Putin's first presidency);
5. the extension of the delimitation treaty for another ten years in autumn 2008 without any textual modification.

Putin should have been concerned with this and not with writing historical treatises. Nevertheless, the Russian president felt a strong and recurring urge to justify historically everything he did against Ukraine. Even the speech he delivered three days before issuing the order to attack Ukraine was full of historical references. All of this gives the impression that Putin is convinced that he can rely on history, or a rather biased interpretation of it, to absolve himself of everything he and his army have done in this war.

4. The impact of manipulation: the politics of memory and the fallout of war propaganda in Russian society

4.1. The revival of the Stalin cult and Russian memory politics

Since the mid-1990s, the Levada Center, an independent public opinion polling institute in Moscow, has been tracking who Russian society considers to be the most important figures in Russian history. Stalin was already popular at the time of the first survey, but not as popular as he became in the early 2000s. In 1994, Russians still considered Lenin and Peter I to be far more important historical figures than Stalin. The two topped the list until 2003, but even then the dictator, whom the poet Osip Mandelstam referred to only as the "Caucasian Highlander," was close behind. By 2008, Pushkin had temporarily become the favorite of Russians, followed in a close second by Peter I, Stalin, and Lenin.[20] It was the first survey to measure Stalin as a more important figure than Lenin, and this has not changed since. On the contrary, the distance between them has grown. Since 2012, Russian public opinion has been unchanged: Stalin is considered the most outstanding Russian historical figure of all time.[21]

What could be the reason for all this? It is difficult to give a clear answer. If we were to rely only on this survey, which is repeated every few years, there would be no reason to link Stalin's enduring popularity with Putin's policies. Indeed, the polls conducted under his terms (2003, 2008, 2012, 2017, and 2021) show no significant difference. The polls in these years showed that 36-42% of respondents considered Stalin to be the most significant historical figure during this period. The "surge" in Stalin's acceptance took place before Putin, between 1994 and 1999. In these five Yeltsin years, Stalin's approval rating jumped from 20 to 35 percent. This would suggest that Putin's policies have nothing to do with the growing acceptance and respect for Stalin.

However, there are other types of surveys available. One of these, from the early 2000s, sought to find out how Russian society views Stalin as a person and how it judges his historical role. According to research also conducted by the Levada Center, in 2003, during the second half of Putin's first presidency, only just over half of those polled had an appreciative view of the role Stalin played in the country.[22] In 2019, however, this proportion reached 70%, while only 19% were critical.[23] In other words, in a decade and a half, Stalin's public image improved significantly, and Putin's policies must have had something to do with this change. This can be assumed based on another part of the survey as well, which measured how attitudes to Stalin correlated with the respondents' political views. This research revealed that among those who voted for Putin in the 2018 presidential election, there were proportionally more people who had a positive opinion of Stalin than among those who voted for the communist candidate.[24] In other words, for some time now there have been two distinct Stalinisms in Russia: the one represented by the Communist Party (in fake or domesticated opposition); and the one represented by the state. The latter still does not praise Stalin openly and directly, but many of its decisions, its struggle in the field of memory politics, and its methods have led to a social norm that is not to condemn Stalin but to respect him. Today, it is much more exceptional to condemn the "wise leader of the people" than to praise him.

This is closely linked to the memory politics of the Putin era, a patronal policy that has become increasingly important for the regime as time has gone by. From the moment patriotism was made the national ideal of the regime, the importance of the past has increased significantly. The regime began to demonstrate its continuity with centuries of Russian history, with an emphasis on reconciliation and national unity; at the same time, it began to fight vigorously (and for some time even with the tools of punitive legislation) against alternative and self-critical interpretations of the past. This duality was visible already in the years preceding the centenary of the 1917 revolutions. In his 2016 presidential message, Putin spoke of the need for Russia to "learn the lessons of history, above all, for reconciliation, for strengthening the social, political, and civic consensus that has been achieved today." He added that the misuse of historical tragedies, "speculation on them," was inadmissible.[25] Duma President Vyacheslav Volodin was even more explicit a few weeks later. Recalling the events of 1917, he warned that the memory of "dramatic events of the past must not become another source of division in Russian society."[26] These and other political statements made it clear that the ruling elite was strongly afraid of the upcoming centenary of the 1917 revolutions. In their statements, they warned against drawing parallels between the present and the events of a hundred years earlier. The Russian regime, fearful of "color revolutions," used the centenary not to rethink the causes and consequences of the revolutions, but to contrast what happened in 1917 with what they propagated as the most valuable feature of Putin's system, i.e., its stability.

While the regime is clearly afraid of certain periods of the past, it also sees history as a serious tool for autocratic consolidation. Accordingly, it has been increasingly assertive in defending what it considers to be the only correct historical memory. The 15-year cultural strategy adopted in spring 2016 identified as one of the most dangerous challenges facing Russia "the distortion of historical memory, the negative perception of significant periods in Russian history, and the spread of false claims about Russia's historical backwardness."[27] The doctrine of information security of the country, also adopted in 2016, similarly stressed the importance of protecting historical memory. The document said that neutralizing informational and psychological pressures on the country, including attempts to "dismantle the historical foundations and patriotic traditions associated with the defense of the homeland," was key.[28]

All this showed precisely that the Russian political leadership came to the realization relatively early on that comprehensive control of the "Russian cultural space" required various preventive measures, invoking the protection of national history. This intention was first expressed in the foreign policy concept adopted in 2008. It was here that the idea that the state has a duty to act against the "rewriters of history" was first put forward, because those who do so try to foment confrontation in international relations and spread the idea of revanchism.[29] In the spirit of this idea, the then President Dmitry Medvedev set up a commission to stop the "falsification of history."[30] Although the committee was set up, with several historians on board, it did not make much of a mark in the years that followed. This may have been one of the reasons why Vladimir Medinsky, who was dismissed as culture minister in 2020 and then appointed Putin's advisor on memory policy, initiated the creation of a new commission with similar tasks in 2021. The new committee, created in late July with staff from several ministries and agencies (including the Foreign Ministry, the National Security Council, the Federal Security Service, the Interior Ministry, and the Investigative Committee) was tasked with analyzing the "activities of foreign structures" that threaten Russia's interests and preparing effective "counter-propaganda events."[31] Although it was given the name "Committee for Historical Clarification," it did not include any historians, unlike its predecessor in 2009. It is in the hands of the clients and servants of the regime to decide what a threat to "correct" historical memory is, to initiate bills to protect the "rightly interpreted" past, and, in time, they will feel empowered to shape the historical narrative to be followed.

The conspicuous activity of the regime in interpreting the events of the past that it considers important serves only one purpose: to dominate historical memory. To do this, it needs historians less and less. As there is a growing acceptance of historical continuity in Russia, it is not surprising that Feliks Edmundovich

Dzerzhinsky, the founder of the Cheka (the first Soviet state security agency) was given a bust in Simferopol, the capital of annexed Crimea in 2021,[32] and that only a minority of people in Moscow considered him a "murderer" and "one who belongs to the dark side of history," as opposed to the majority which opined either that "the past should neither be erased nor sharply criticized" or that Dzerzhinsky indeed "did a lot for the country" and was "a significant revolutionary."[33] It is similarly unsurprising that the vast majority of Russian society has an appreciative opinion of Stalin, and a growing proportion of people believes that his repression of the most diverse sections of society was justified in part or in whole.[34] From the regime's perspective, in this environment it is much easier to make the majority of people believe that the war against neighboring Ukraine is for the greater good, because it is in fact a continuation of the Great Patriotic War.

4.2. Tuned for war: loyalty signaling of the Russian public during the Russian-Ukrainian war

The Levada Center began measuring the Russian public's attitude to the "special military operation" at the outbreak of the war. Since then, the results of its multi-perspective measurements have been published on a monthly basis. These show that the Russian society's attitude to the war hardly changed between March and December. In March, 53% of respondents strongly supported the "special military operation" and a further 28% supported rather than opposed it; that is, 81% of respondents agreed with the decision of the political leadership. Meanwhile, only 14 percent of those polled said the war was a failure in one way or another.[35] Four months later, in July, the situation barely changed: more than three quarters of respondents still supported Putin's war. Compared to March, the proportion of those who unconditionally approved of military action was down by 5 percentage points (48%), while 28%, if not enthusiastically, also supported the decision. The proportion of those who strongly opposed the war rose slightly, as did the proportion of those who were less strongly opposed, but even together they accounted for just under 18% of the population.[36] By December, this changed only minimally, with the proportion of those in favor falling from 76 to 71 percent, while those against rose to 21%.[37] This essentially means that the partial mobilization ordered at the end of September failed to bring about any significant change.

Meanwhile, more than two thirds of those polled in July said "yes" when asked if things were going well in the country. This is surprising because in November 2021, just four months before the war, only 44 per cent thought so.[38] By December 2022, the result was little changed from the summer. Even though the war had been going on for ten months, and more than 300,000 people had been conscripted, 63% of respondents still thought that things were going well for the country.[39]

In other words, these polls suggest that the majority of Russians believe that things are going well with the war and that everything is fine. It is hard to believe that this is the actual situation: that the majority of Russian society is much more satisfied with the way the country is run during the war than it was during peacetime.

But it is not only these numbers that seem surprising. Putin's public perception took a similar unexpected turn. This is most apparent when the researchers offered a shortlist of Russian politicians, including the president, to the respondents, who were then asked to say whose actions they approve of. When asked this question in July 2021, 61% said they supported Putin's actions; a year later, the corresponding number was 83%. Putin's support rose to a higher level only in 2014-2015, during the Crimea euphoria, when 88-89% of respondents were satisfied with his actions.[40] To add to the overall picture, since the outbreak of the war, not only has Putin's support increased significantly, but also that of the prime minister, the government, and even the generally distrusted State Duma.[41]

Similarly surprising changes have been recorded by another major Russian polling agency, the FOM (Фонд "Общественное мнение," Public Opinion Foundation), which operates under the supervision of the Kremlin. One of its recurrent research topics is to gauge how respondents perceive the mood of those around them, whether they consider it to be "calm" or "tense." One might think that with the outbreak of war, the survey would record a spectacular increase in the proportion of "tense" people, but the results show the opposite. By July, the proportion of those responding "calm" had risen to 62%, while the proportion of "tense" responses had fallen to 32%. This result is all the more striking because before the war, respondents still saw "tense" people as the majority (50–55%) and "calm" people as the minority (39-44%). This was the case until April 2022, when those responding "calm" became increasingly dominant, first temporarily and then permanently from May onwards.[42]

Therefore, a growing proportion of people in Russia were "calm," and the fact that the war is not yet over does not change that? Of course, it could be argued that respondents are misperceiving the mood of their environment. This is possible, but even if that were the case, it would need an explanation. It could also be argued that the FOM, an institute under the patronal control, has manipulated the data, but this is contradicted by the fact that the independent Levada Center has come to a similar conclusion when it asked people about their mood. Finally, it could be argued that, where there is no democratic public sphere, it is a mistake to assume that people will answer such sensitive questions about their loyalty to the authorities with what they really think. For let us not forget that the Putin regime was repressive even before the war. From the beginning of 2021, perhaps in preparation for war, it launched an extensive attack on the remaining institutions of civil society and the independent media that still operate. Under these circumstances, it is reasonable to think that many people are afraid to respond honestly, while at the same time they are less and less able to inform themselves from sources independent of the authorities.

In this light, what the polling results definitely show is that the war has resulted in a significant increase in the loyalty, or rather the *signaled* loyalty, of Russian society to Putin's regime. This is also evidenced by the fact that while in the three years before the war slightly less than half of those polled thought that the country was heading in the right direction, after ten months of war almost two thirds of them thought so. In other words, nearly a fifth of the population changed their opinion as a result of the war, which is the only way to explain this turnaround. In itself, this would not be particularly surprising, since a spectacular increase in loyalty to the authorities in wartime, or "rallying around the flag," is not unknown elsewhere. The main differences are two: the autocratic context in which these answers are given, which count as loyalty signaling towards the increasingly oppressive regime; and that in Russia this phenomenon has so far proved to be strikingly spectacular and enduring. Further evidence of this is that while before the war only 26% of the people would have been prepared to vote for the unpopular ruling party, United Russia, by the summer of 2022 this figure had risen to 39%.[43]

The suspicion that the answers are not necessarily honest is reinforced by the fact that questions formulated in different ways but essentially about the same thing do not produce identical answers. Let us take the three questions that probed people's loyalty to the regime:

1. "Do you approve of Putin's actions?" (This is a closed question, because Putin's name is on a list of politicians, and that is how you have to give your opinion.)
2. "Are things going in the right direction in the country?"
3. "Which politicians do you trust the most?" (This is an open-ended question. No one's name appears on the questionnaire. It is up to the respondent to choose which ones.)

If we look at the evolution of the responses to these three questions since 2014, we see that their dynamics have been similar for some time. This was the case until the summer of 2018, when the announcement of the increase in the retirement age was made. Since then, however, it seems that trust in Putin, when asked in an open-ended way, has fallen much more than in the first two questions, even though they are ultimately about perceptions of the regime and the president as well. There was also a drop in the other two questions, with fewer people approving of Putin's actions and fewer people thinking that things were going well in the country, but in neither case was the drop as large as for the third question.

Since the start of the full-scale invasion, repeated polls have shown that loyalty to the regime has begun to grow again. This is apparent on all three issues, but the magnitude of the increase is far from the same. Support for Putin's actions, when asked as a closed question, has increased much more than when asked as an open question. For the former, the Russian president was at the top in 2015. Then, almost 90% of those polled approved of his actions. But that support had plummeted to below 60% by the end of 2020, before rising again with the war against Ukraine, and by July it was 83%, almost back to its peak seven years earlier. The picture that emerged from the answers to the open-ended question was also the most positive for Putin in 2015. Then, 67% of respondents thought of Putin as a politician they trusted. This indicator fell to one third of that number by the summer of 2020 (23% at its lowest) and then started to slowly increase, but never exceeded 33% before the war. However, with the start of the war, it immediately shot up to 43% and then started to fluctuate between 35 and 42 percent.[44] In other words, when researchers ask open-ended questions about confidence in Putin, we find that his support is always much lower than when they ask closed-ended questions. At the same time, we can also see that the full-scale invasion has not come close to restoring Putin's former popularity in open-ended surveys to the extent that it has done in the closed question. This is important because the majority of pollsters believe that the real public perception of the Russian president is more accurately reflected by a questioning method where respondents are not influenced in any way, not even by a list put in front of them, but are left to decide for themselves.

4.3. Public opinion in an oppressive regime: conformists, believers, and the "silent majority"

Several contradictions in the perception of the war in Russian society can be detected. This is shown by the results of the research published in the summer of 2022 by Russian Field, a Moscow-based public opinion research institute now in its sixth year.[45] The data, collected at the end of July, shows that Russian society is really only consistent on one issue: following Putin's lead. Among other questions, the researchers asked whether the "special military operation" in Ukraine should be continued. Fifty-two percent of the respondents said "yes," while 38% would support the start of peace talks. But when asked if they would support Putin making peace tomorrow, 65% said "yes," with only 17% of respondents expressing strong opposition. However, when asked if they would support Putin issuing orders to attack Kyiv again, 60% of respondents said "yes."

From all this, it seems that a large part of the Russian population either has no independent opinion on the war, or, if it does, prefers not to reveal it, but instead to conform to the supposed expectations of the authorities. This is probably what the Russian Field researchers expected, because they included a question in the survey to get an idea of what the respondents really think. That question was: What would be the three most important decisions you would make if you woke up tomorrow morning and found yourself to be Putin? Survey respondents were not asked to choose from a list of alternatives, but to formulate their own answers. Most of them (208) would have ordered an end to military operations in Ukraine. They were followed by those who would have called for immediate peace negotiations (145). But there were almost as many who would have annexed eastern Ukraine to Russia without any prior negotiations (142), in stark contrast to the former, followed closely by those who would have raised salaries and pensions (134), and then those who would have either resigned immediately or shot themselves in the head (93). Finally, there were sixty-four respondents who would have immediately reinstated the lower retirement age. These responses seem to suggest that support for the war may not be as clear-cut as the surveys of the Levada Center and FOM suggest.

Of course, it is not clear from the Russian Field research whether those who support the war in their responses do so out of conviction or out of caution or fear. Nor is it clear whether those who might be assumed to support the war out of conviction are informed or misguided people: whether they can make arguments in defense of their position, or they simply go with the word of authority because they are negligent, cynical, or simply unable to form their own opinions on important public issues. None of this is clear from these surveys.

Although the figures on the high level of support for the war and the fact that it is barely declining in substance may seem absurd, we cannot be sure that they are mainly due to the fear of the respondents. Probably just as important is the fact that the propagandists in power have sensed something that makes this war very much supportable in the eyes of many Russians. This could be the Russians' undying nostalgia for empire, or some painful memory, some kind of believed humiliation, some kind of resentment. After all, we are talking about a community that has been persuaded for many years, and apparently not unsuccessfully, that the West humiliated Russia in the 1990s, brought it to its knees, but that now, with this war, "we are showing them that we are strong again." For years now, the authorities have also been saying that the "collective West" is trying to destroy Russia, envying its resources and natural endowments, so that nothing good can be expected from it (and it is in decline anyway). The persistent support for the war shows that the years of intense ideological "molding" of Russian society, the indoctrination that has turned the majority of Russians against the West and the Western-oriented Ukrainians, has had its effect.

If one has followed the evening political programs on Russian central TV channels for the past eight years, and the incessant vilification of Ukrainians, they will not be surprised at how many people are afraid to speak out or accept the views of the authorities uncritically. According to research published by the Levada Center in December 2022, among those who are mainly informed by television news and political programs, 86% supported, strongly or less strongly, Russian military operations in Ukraine. The proportion was much lower among those who are informed by various Telegram channels (61%). The proportion of those who support Russian aggression also differs significantly by age group. The youngest generation, those aged 18 to 24, show a 59% support rate, while they are the most likely to strongly condemn the war as well (23%). By contrast, the oldest generation, those aged 55 and above, are 79% in favor of what Russia is doing in Ukraine.[46]

All this suggests that the regime has so far succeeded in convincing the elderly and the TV-informed section of the population, to the greatest extent, that the war is for a good cause: that it is a continuation of the Great Patriotic War against fascism in Ukraine. The fact that they are the most convinced of this is probably due to the fact that the slogans used by the authorities during and before the war are in many ways the same as the ideological clichés they heard in their youth, in the late Soviet years, and which now sound all too familiar. However, this mechanism does not explain why younger generations are ready to accept the narrative offered by the regime. The generation between 40 and 54 is 71% in favor of war, compared to 65% of those between 25 and 39.[47] In other words, the Putin system is operating not only with ideological memories of the Soviet era, but also with something else that makes the war against Ukraine seem understandable and acceptable, even to those who were children at the time of the break-up of the Soviet Union and who spent their youth in the Yeltsin period.

It is difficult to determine at this stage what the possible motives for supporting the war, or the ratio between conformists and "believers," might be. Research by Russian Field has shown that two thirds of respondents would be willing to support the war financially, but when asked how much they would offer, two thirds of respondents also say "nothing." And when asked if they would personally participate in the war, less than a third say "yes," and only 12% say "definitely yes."[48] These responses also show that very few people consider the war to be their own business. The majority would prefer to end it as quickly, and to keep themselves as far away from it, as possible.

However, this might not be the full picture in Russia. It is worth recalling that Russian Field's survey, conducted in the summer of 2022, interviewed more than 27,000 people, but only produced 1,609 completed questionnaires. In fact, more than 24 thousand refused to participate, and more than a thousand changed their minds while filling in the questionnaire. It is likely that the "silent majority" rates are similar for the other polling agencies (the Levada Center, FOM, and VCIOM) except that they do not report the rates of non-respondents. By contrast, Russian Field has conducted 10 surveys since the start of the full-scale invasion, and on each occasion has reported the proportion of those who were consulted and those who actually participated. This number in no case has been more than ten percent. But there were also examples of only 5.3% of those asked completing the questionnaire, which effectively meant that only one in 20 of those contacted were willing to participate. Under these circumstances, with such a high rate of refusal to participate in the survey, it is extremely difficult to get a credible picture of what Russian society really thinks about the war.[49]

What is known is how those who support or simply acknowledge Russia's war against Ukraine justify it or on what grounds they soothe their consciences. We can find out about this from a study by two Russian sociologists, Svetlana Erpyleva and Veronika Ptitsyna, published back in mid-July.[50] The aim of their research was not to establish the proportions between different types of explanations, but to collect and organize the types of explanations themselves. In the course of their work, they came across six distinct explanations, the first four of which almost literally echo the ones that have long been propagated by the regime. One of them is that "Russia has been threatened by NATO, the West, and their ally Ukraine (for a long time), and the Russians are now doing nothing but defending themselves and showing that they are a force to be reckoned with." Another explanation, also often repeated, is that "Ukraine, incited by the West, was preparing to attack the Donbas, Crimea, and even Russia, and when Russian forces attacked Ukraine, they did nothing but preempt the Ukrainians." There are also a good number of people who believe that this war is being waged because "the Russian-speaking Donbas has been living under conditions of Ukrainian aggression for eight years and the Russians are only defending this region and its inhabitants." Many also claim that the "war is against the fascists/Nazis and the fascist/Nazi (Ukrainian) state." Others explain their support for the war in terms of their loyalty to Russia, saying that "whatever the causes and consequences of the war, we must be with our country in time of war." And quite a few also argued, as if to deflect responsibility, that "the war obviously had its causes, even if they are incomprehensible to ordinary people, but the president and the political elite are aware of them."

These recurring types of explanations prove more than anything else that the ideological work that has been going on for years, including the transformation of historical memory, has not been in vain. The majority of Russians, if the results of opinion polls are to be believed, give credit to everything that the regime wants them to believe.

Notes

1. "Путин назвал истинных виновников второй мировой войны" [Putin named the true culprits of the Second World War], *Rossiyskaya Gazeta*, December 20, 2019, https://rg.ru/2019/12/20/reg-szfo/putin-nazval-istinnyh-vinovnikov-vtoroj-mirovoj-vojny.html.
2. Vladimir Putin, "75 лет великой победы: общая ответственность перед историей и будущим" [75 years since the great victory: A shared responsibility before history and the future], President Rossii, June 29, 2020, http://kremlin.ru/events/president/news/63527. The study is also published in English: Vladimir Putin, "The Real Lessons of the 75th Anniversary of World War II," The National Interest (The Center for the National Interest, June 18, 2020), https://nationalinterest.org/feature/vladimir-putin-real-lessons-75th-anniversary-world-war-ii-162842.
3. Vladimir Putin, "Быть открытыми, несмотря на прошлое" [Let's be candid, despite the past], President Rossii, June 30, 2021, http://kremlin.ru/events/president/news/65899.
4. Vladimir Putin, "Об историческом единстве русских и украинцев" [On the historical unity of Russians and Ukrainians], President Rossii, July 19, 2021, http://kremlin.ru/events/president/news/66181.
5. "Путин заявил, что на долю России выпало «возвращать и укреплять земли»" [Putin declared that it is Russia's lot to return and strengthen the land], *RBK*, June 9, 2022, https://www.rbc.ru/politics/09/06/2022/62a1fef99a79478be49a944d.
6. "Европарламент выполнил политический заказ Польши" [The European parliament has carried out a political task for Poland], *Rossiyskaya Gazeta*, September 22, 2019, https://rg.ru/2019/09/22/evroparlament-vypolnil-politicheskij-zakaz-polshi.html.
7. "Путин Назвал Истинных Виновников Второй Мировой Войны."
8. See N. L. Pobol and P. M. Polyan, *Сталинские депортации: 1928-1953* [Stalin's deportations: 1928-1953] (Mezhdunarodnyy fond "Demokratiya," 2005), 791.
9. Putin, "75 Лет Великой Победы."
10. "Инструкция народному комиссару обороны СССР К. Е. Ворошилову, 7 августа 1939 г." [Instructions to the People's Commissar of Defense of the USSR K. Ye. Voroshilov, August 7, 1939], in *Документы внешней политики СССР* [Documents of USSR foreign policy], vol. 22, bk. 1 (Moscow: Mezhdunarodnye otnosheniya, 1992), 584.
11. On Molotov's 1940 visit to Berlin, see "Директивы И.В.Сталина В.М.Молотову перед поездкой в Берлинв ноябре 1940 г." [I.V. Stalin's directives to V.M. Molotov before his trip to Berlin in November 1940], *Novaya i noveyshaya istoriya*, no. 4 (1995).
12. Boris L. Khavkin, "К истории публикаций советско-германских секретных документов (1939-1941)" [On the history of the publication of the Soviet-German secret documents (1939-1941)], in *Великая Отечественная война: происхождение, основные события, исход* [The great fatherland war: origin, main events, outcome] (Moscow: MGIMO University, 2010), 236.
13. "Заседание Российского организационного комитета «Победа»" [Meeting of the Russian organizing committee Victory], President Rossii, December 12, 2019, http://kremlin.ru/events/president/news/62293.
14. "Постановление Съезда Народных Депутатов СССР «О Политической и Правовой Оценке Советско-Германского Договора о Ненападении От 23-Го Августа 1939 г.»" [Decree of the Congress of People's Deputies of the USSR "On the political and legal evaluation of the Soviet-German Non-Aggression Treaty of August 23, 1939"] in *Второй съезд народных депутатов СССР, 12-24 декабря, 1989 г.* [Second Congress of the Peoples' Deputies, December 12-24, 1989], vol. 4 (Moscow: Izdanie verkhovnogo soveta SSSR, 1990), 256-79, 378-81.
15. "Сергей Иванов предложил гордиться пактом Молотова-Риббентропа," [Sergey Ivanov suggested being proud of the Molotov-Ribbentrop pact], RBK, September 16, 2019, https://www.rbc.ru/rbcfreenews/5d7f90b49a79475cbfb95e55.

16 "«Система коллективной безопасности рушится не «под собственным весом»" [The collective security system is not collapsing under its own weight], *Izvestiya*, September 2, 2019, https://iz.ru/915277/izvestiia/sistema-kollektivnoi-bezopasnosti-rushitsia-ne-pod-sobstvennym-vesom.

17 "Немые свидетели: в Москве открылась выставка о начале войны" [Silent witnesses: an exhibition about the beginning of the war has opened in Moscow], *RIA Novosti*, 20190820T1912, https://ria.ru/20190820/1557709491.html.

18 Vladimir Medinskiy, "Дипломатический триумф СССР" [The diplomatic triumph of the USSR], *RIA Novosti*, August 23, 2019, https://ria.ru/20190823/1557826932.html.

19 Putin, "Об историческом единстве русских и украинцев."

20 "Самые выдающиеся личности в истории," [The most important figures in history], Levada Center, June 21, 2021, https://www.levada.ru/2021/06/21/samye-vydayushhiesya-lichnosti-v-istorii/.

21 "Самые выдающиеся личности в истории."

22 "В марте этого года исполняется 50 лет со дня смерти Сталина. Как Вы считаете, какую роль сыграл Сталин в жизни нашей страны?" [In March of this year it will be 50 years since the death of Stalin. What role do you think he played in the life of our country?], Levada Center, March 3, 2003, https://www.levada.ru/2003/03/03/v-marte-etogo-goda-ispolnyaetsya-50-let-so-dnya-smerti-stalina-kak-vy-schitaete-kakuyu-rol-sygral-stalin-v-zhizni-nashej-strany/.

23 "Уровень одобрения Сталина россиянами побил исторический рекорд" [Stalin's approval level among Russians has broken a historical record], Levada Center, April 16, 2019, https://www.levada.ru/2019/04/16/uroven-odobreniya-stalina-rossiyanami-pobil-istoricheskij-rekord/.

24 "Уровень одобрения Сталина россиянами побил исторический рекорд."

25 "Послание Президента Российской Федерации от 01.12.2016 г. б/н" [Message of the President of the Russian Federation from December 1, 2016], President Rossii, January 30, 2023, http://kremlin.ru/acts/bank/41550.

26 "Володин рассказал, какой должна быть память о событиях 1917 года" [Volodin reports what should be remembered regarding the events of 1917], *RIA Novosti*, January 11, 2017, https://ria.ru/20170111/1485467637.html.

27 "Стратегия Государственной Культурной Политики На Период До 2030 Года" [Strategy for the state cultural policy until 2030], 2016, http://static.government.ru/media/files/AsA9RAyY-VAJnoBuKgH0qEJA9IxP7f2xm.pdf.

28 "Доктрина Информационной Безопасности Российской Федерации" [Doctrine of information security of the Russian Federation], *Rossiyskaya Gazeta*, accessed February 7, 2023, https://rg.ru/documents/2016/12/06/doktrina-infobezobasnost-site-dok.html.

29 "Концепция Внешней Политики Российской Федерации," [Concept of foreign policy of the Russian Federation], *Rossiyskaya Gazeta*, accessed February 7, 2023, https://rg.ru/documents/2008/05/26/koncepciya-dok.

30 "Указ Президента Российской Федерации от 15 мая 2009 №549 О Комиссии при Президенте Российской Федерации по противодействию попыткам фальсификации истории в ущерб нитересам России" [Decree of the President of the Russian Federation No. 549 of May 15, 2009 on the commission reporting to the President of the Russian Federation to counter attempts to falsify history to the detriment of Russia's interests], http://special.kremlin.ru/acts/bank/29288.

31 "Указ Президента Российской Федерации от 30.07.2021 № 442 О Межведомственной комиссии по историческому просвещению" [Decree of the President of the Russian Federation No. 442 of July 30, 2021 on the interdepartmental commission on historical education], http://publication.pravo.gov.ru/Document/View/0001202107300042?index=0&rangeSize=1.

32 Anna Shukhina, "Отремонтированный памятник Дзержинскому открыли в Симферополе" [The renovated memorial to Dzerzhinsky has opened in Simferopol], *Izvestiya*, September 13, 2021, https://iz.ru/1221058/2021-09-13/otremontirovannyi-pamiatnik-dzerzhinskomu-otkryli-v-simferopole.

33 "Москвичи о памятнике Дзержинскому" [Muscovites regarding the Dzerzhinsky memorial], Levada Center, May 19, 2021, https://www.levada.ru/2021/05/19/moskvichi-o-pamyatnike-dzerzhinskomu/.
34 "Самые выдающиеся личности в истории."
35 "Конфликт с Украиной" [The conflict with Ukraine], Levada Center, March 31, 2022, https://www.levada.ru/2022/03/31/konflikt-s-ukrainoj/.
36 "Конфликт с Украиной: июль 2022 года," [The conflict with Ukraine: July 2022], Levada Center, August 1, 2022, https://www.levada.ru/2022/08/01/konflikt-s-ukrainoj-iyul-2022-goda/.
37 "Конфликт с Украиной: оценки декабря 2022 года" [The conflict with Ukraine: assessment in December 2022], Levada Center, December 23, 2022, https://www.levada.ru/2022/12/23/konflikt-s-ukrainoj-otsenki-dekabrya-2022-goda/.
38 "Одобрение институтов, положение дел в стране, доверие политикам" [Approval of institutions, the state of affairs in the country, and trust in politicians], Levada Center, December 2, 2021, https://www.levada.ru/2021/12/02/odobrenie-institutov-polozhenie-del-v-strane-doverie-politikam-i-elektoralnye-rejtingi-partij-2/.
39 "Одобрение институтов, положение дел в стране, доверие политикам."
40 "Доверие политикам, одобрение институтов и положение дел в стране" [Trust in politicians, approval of institutions and the state of affairs in the country], Levada Center, July 2, 2021, https://www.levada.ru/2021/07/02/doverie-politikam-odobrenie-institutov-i-polozhenie-del-v-strane-3/.
41 "Одобрение институтов и рейтинги политиков," Levada Center, December 22, 2022, https://www.levada.ru/2022/12/22/odobrenie-institutov-i-rejtingi-politikov-2/.
42 "Настроение окружающих" [The mood of those around us], https://media.fom.ru/fom-bd/d292022.pdf.
43 Kirill Rogov, "Широкий фронт неадекватности. Социальные настроения лета 2022 года" [A broad front of inadequacy. Social moods in summer 2022], Re: Russia, May 8, 2022, https://re-russia.net/analytics/015/.
44 "Одобрение институтов и рейтинги политиков."
45 ""Военная Операция" На Украине: Отношение Россиян. Восьмая Волна (28-31 Июля)" [The military operation in Ukraine. The attitude of Russians. Eigth wave (July 28-31), Russian Field, July 2022, https://russianfield.com/nuzhenmir.
46 "Конфликт с Украиной," December 23, 2022.
47 "Конфликт с Украиной."
48 ""Военная Операция" На Украине."
49 ""Специальная Военная Операция" в Украине: Отношение Россиян. 10 Волна (29 Ноября — 5 Декабря)" [The special military operation in Ukraine. The attitude of Russians. 10th wave (November 29 – December 5)], Russian Field, December 2022, https://russianfield.com/yubiley.
50 Svetalana Erpyleva and Veronika Ptitsyna, ""Возможно, Он Дед, Который Не Выпил Таблетки": Шесть Аргументов Оправдания Войны в Рассуждениях Россиян" [Maybe he's a granddad who's off his meds: Six arguments justifying the war according to Russian reasoning], July 15, 2022, https://re-russia.net/expertise/011/.

Enter the "Bloody Clown": Ukraine's Volodymyr Zelensky in the Lens of Russia's Media Machine

Kostiantyn Fedorenko

1. The war against reality

The role of Russia's propaganda machine in the development and consolidation of Putin's patronal autocracy has been thoroughly discussed in the literature. Peter Pomerantsev, one of the most vocal experts on the Russian media machine, has traced this role from the 2000s, when he worked on Russian television,[1] to what he calls "the war against reality" in his second book.[2] The ever-present mix of ideologemes used by journalists without actually believing in them, combined with a strong stylistic inspiration from Western media, has grown into a powerful machine justifying and whitewashing Russian foreign interventions and contributing to Russia's isolation from the Western world. Russian émigré activist Masha Gessen has written extensively about the consolidation of the media under Kremlin control and its weaponization against the critics of the regime.[3]

Those Western experts who are familiar with the Russian discourse often, and correctly, cite Viktor Pelevin's best-selling 1999 novel *Generation P* (released in English as *Babylon*), dedicated to the (re-)construction of reality by media and PR experts, when describing the processes in Russia. In Pelevin's book, both the government and the opposition are controlled by media "creators," while the real politicians do not even exist: they are simply three-dimensional models. The tumultuous and traumatic reality of the 1990s and early 2000s in Russia, manifested in Pelevin's early books, has contributed to the public disbelief in politics and ideologies. Ironically, this allowed Vladimir Putin to grow a titanic media machine by seizing and destroying pre-existent independent media[4]—and, eventually, to use the full power of this machine to justify his political practice, which, in turn, has become ever more influenced by ideology, particularly that of Russian nationalists such as Ivan Ilyin.[5] Thus, the hollow postmodern engine—described by Pomerantsev, but now much more consolidated than during his time in Russia—is now operating with the inclusion of modernist ideas. The present chapter will explore, in particular, its application both towards the current President of Ukraine, Volodymyr Zelensky,[6] and towards the country of Ukraine under his rule. It is split in two parts; the first part will examine Russian propaganda between Zelensky's election in 2019 and the start of the full-scale war against Ukraine on February 24, 2022, while the second will cover Russian wartime propaganda.

Ukraine has been one of the primary targets of the Russian media engine since the Orange Revolution of 2004, when, by a number of accounts, Putin became afraid of a similar "color revolution" in Russia.[7] This attention only grew due to the 2014 Euromaidan protests, initially caused by Ukraine's president Viktor Yanukovych not signing a prepared association agreement with the European Union in exchange for financial support from Russia—as quickly became known. Euromaidan, therefore, was from the beginning directed at preventing Ukraine's geopolitical movement towards Russia. As the protests intensified following the regime's use of force against the activists, the anti-regime and, by extension, anti-Russia (however, not necessarily *anti-Russian*) attitudes at the Euromaidan only increased.[8] This, of course, necessitated a reaction from Russia—and it came, first in the form of a harsh medial critique of the protesters, then via material assistance to Ukrainian riot police.[9] Finally, when the protesters won, Russia moved to direct—archaic, even—actions with the annexation of Crimea and the spread of clearly Russian-controlled separatist movements in Eastern Ukraine. These, too, were actively promoted and celebrated by the media.[10]

2. Pre-invasion developments: Russian illusions and the negative framing of Zelensky

2.1. Early support for Zelensky as a "convenient partner"

The post-Euromaidan regime in Ukraine, led by Petro Poroshenko, was a target of concentrated hate and fake news development[11] by the Russian media. However, during the 2014 snap presidential elections in Ukraine, Poroshenko was treated relatively mildly by the Russian media machine, as he was seen as a moderate by RBC,[12] and was immediately recognized as a legitimate president by the Kremlin. However, his policies in office reversed this attitude. In 2019, Poroshenko lost the presidential election run-off to Volodymyr Zelensky, a popular comedian and media manager. The campaign was quite heated, with both sides resorting to the production of fakes. For instance, Zelensky was accused of being a drug addict,[13] whereas he briefly referred to a pre-existing Russian fake about Poroshenko being an alcoholic.[14] More importantly, in the run-off, Poroshenko briefly used billboards that framed the choice as one between himself and Putin, clearly implying Zelensky to be a pro-Russian candidate. Although these billboards resulted in a scandal and were ordered removed,[15] Poroshenko's public supporters continued implying that Zelensky was either connected to or would "sell out" Ukraine to Russia.

When one looks at Russian media discourse around Ukraine's 2019 presidential elections, it also seems that Russia's preferences were on the side of Zelensky, as shown by claims that Poroshenko's loss would mean the failure of his "policy of hatred against Russia."[16] Furthermore, he was touted as a slightly preferable candidate even by some of the media of the so-called Lugansk and Donetsk "people's republics,"[17] created by Russia on the captured territories of Eastern Ukraine. The media of these unrecognized entities are generally extremely confrontational towards Ukraine and its politicians, except for openly pro-Russian figures; it is therefore remarkable that a strong contender in post-2014 Ukrainian elections received relatively milder treatment. Considering that LNR and DNR media operate under the observation and control of the Russian special services,[18] and seeing how Zelensky was treated by the Russian media, it is clear that he was indeed the candidate preferred by the Kremlin.

This could have been reinforced by another factor: popular recognition and cultural integration. Zelensky was not just any comedian; he earned his initial media fame in the so-called *Club of the Funny and Inventive* (*KVN, Klub veselykh i nakhodchivykh*)—a long-running, extremely popular TV show on Russia's *Channel One*, where teams would play out comedic sketches on stage. Zelensky was the captain of the Krivbas – Krivoi Rog (Kryvyi Rih) team. Subsequently, this team was renamed "95 Kvartal" (95th District), and then left the show to start their own production. KVN actors would often perform with Russian politicians present in the audience and even taking the stage; back then, Zelensky actually played on stage while Putin was in attendance. In other words, he was known to the Russian public, and, having played in a Russian television show, could have been perceived as Russia-friendly.

Many commentators—both in Russia and in Ukraine—did not, however, regard Zelensky as an independent candidate. He was considered to be a political "front man" for Igor Kolomoisky,[19] a powerful Ukrainian oligarch who controlled the 1+1 TV channel which aired Zelensky's shows for a long time. It was Kolomoisky, then, who was regarded as a candidate for Ukraine's chief patron position, and not Zelensky. Potentially, we could argue that Putin expected Kolomoisky as a businessman to be approachable for finding solutions to Ukraine's future that would have benefited Russia (thus allowing Putin to claim geopolitical success and further cement his position as an autocrat) and Kolomoisky personally. However, what followed went entirely opposite to Putin's plans.

2.2. Shattering Russian illusions

Zelensky's first New Year's address broadcast to the Ukrainian people was controversial. In a stark departure from his predecessor, Poroshenko—who underwent an ideological transformation in favor of Ukrainian nationalism during his term and, in particular, led the "decommunization" policy regarding Soviet memorials and toponyms—Zelensky offered the vision of a Ukraine "where the name of the street doesn't matter because it is lit and paved. Where it makes no difference, at which monument you're waiting for the girl you love."[20] Generally, his address emphasized the solidarity of Ukrainian citizens regardless of their religious, linguistic, political, and other differences.

In particular, he stressed that those who voted for him and those who did not are one people, as well as highlighting that the Ukrainian passport that every citizen carries does not identify whether someone is a "patriot" or a *maloros*." The latter means "little Russian"—initially the Russian Empire's way to refer to Ukrainians, today utilized by some in Ukraine as a slur for those Ukrainians who are either pro-Russian or even tolerant of Russian culture. Zelensky's speech led to criticism from more nationalist-minded Ukrainians who felt his liberal view threatened Ukraine's identity and future.[21]

The views expressed by Zelensky in this address seem to have been quite conciliatory towards Russia, too. Although he did make reference to Ukrainian soldiers including those in captivity, he never once referred to Russia itself. *RIA Novosti*, a major Russian news agency, reported on his address positively with an article entitled "Zelensky urged Ukrainians to unite in his New Year's address" and stressed in the story that Zelensky used both the Russian and Crimean Tartar languages.[22] Natalya Poklonskaya, who was, at that time, the deputy head of the Russian parliamentary committee for international affairs, stated with regards to Zelensky's address that he "tried to restore peace to the country" and that "she was glad about the changes in Ukraine."[23]

This conciliatory attitude persisted for a while; in summer 2020, for instance, Zelensky called the Russian and Russia-controlled separatist forces that shelled a Ukrainian unit "that side" ("Ukraine should always know the price of *that side's* 'promises'"). For this lack of explicitness, he was criticized by a number of Ukrainian politicians,[24] as well as journalists and activists.

However, at the same time, already during summer 2020, Viktor Medvedchuk, whose child's godfather is Vladimir Putin, and who has been employed by Russia to foster Russian influence in Ukraine[25]—something many Ukrainians had already commented on even earlier—claimed that Zelensky "cannot bring peace" to Ukraine.[26] Medvedchuk also stated that the Minsk agreements had been "fully destroyed," and that direct negotiations with Russia, as well as with representatives of the separatist republics, were required. This was to be understood as Russia's position—and indicated an ongoing shift in Russian attitudes towards Zelensky.

Furthermore, some signs point to this shift happening earlier than mid-2020. For instance, a report on the state of affairs in the unrecognized republics of Donbas in 2019 claimed that the local media was running a "disinformation campaign," according to which Zelensky "would implement reintegration by deporting pro-Russian minded civilians to other parts of Ukraine."[27]

This campaign, according to the report, even preceded those international developments that were bound to make Russia disappointed in Zelensky. In late 2019, Zelensky met Putin during the Normandy Four summit. The idea of the meeting proved extremely controversial in Ukraine, and Zelensky's phrase at the time ("I want to look into Putin's eyes")—together with an earlier desire to "meet Putin somewhere in the middle" and the claim that it is "enough just to stop shooting" to achieve peace—were frequently cited by Ukrainian patriots to express disappointment in their new president.[28] However, this rhetoric may have led Putin to believe that Zelensky was open to concessions.

In autumn 2019, Ukraine signed agreements regarding the Donbas conflict based on the so-called "Steinmeier Formula." According to this plan, elections would have been held by officials from the separatist administrations, and before the Russian military forces were to leave Donbas. This triggered a wave of mass protests in Ukraine under the slogan "No to capitulation!" The plan was eventually not implemented—most likely due to activist pressure in Ukraine, although the general public, according to one poll, did not know enough about the Steinmeier Formula to be able to render an assessment.[29] Nevertheless, Russia may have believed that the Minsk peace process had genuinely begun to move forward towards conflict resolution under Zelensky. At this point, their likely goal was to reintegrate Donbas into Ukraine and, through this densely populated region and the possible threat of restarting the conflict, influence Ukraine's foreign policy.

Arsen Avakov, Ukraine's Minister of the Interior at the time, claimed that during the Normandy Four meeting, Vladislav Surkov—then the Kremlin figure responsible for Donbas policy—threw papers on the table and screamed, "That's not what we agreed on!"[30] We do not have enough information to corroborate this claim; nevertheless, the 2019 Normandy Four summit was generally received with disappointment in Russia.[31] The 2020 Normandy Format talks in Berlin failed as well. During them, Russia pushed for the Steinmeier Formula once again, in addition to demanding that Ukraine's decentralization reform include special status for the then-occupied Donbas areas as well as incorporate certain specific Russian demands into this status. Moreover, Russia expected the legalization of the separatist forces in the guise of a "people's militia" and stressed the importance of conducting elections prior to Ukraine regaining full control over the area.[32] Regardless of Zelensky's personal views (which apparently had been conciliatory as late as 2020), these ideas would not and could not have found popular support in Ukraine.

2.3. The shift to criticism: Zelensky as the opposite of a "good" chief patron

Consequently, Russian media messaging about Zelensky towards the end of 2020 turned negative, in sharp difference to the pre- and early post-election coverage he had received. In December 2020, the Russian nationalist online resource *Vzglyad* (Outlook) summed up the early Russian messaging about Zelensky: "During the year after the presidential elections in Ukraine, Russian state media and government-affiliated politologs[33] avoided personal attacks on President Zelensky, while still criticizing the overall state of affairs in the country. [...] A new person had come on the scene, received solid popular support, spoke Russian and was far from Russophobia, did not care about Ukrainian national bugbears like Stepan Bandera and tomos,[34] and promised to achieve a sustainable peace in Donbas through compromise—what was bad about that?"[35] The same article then goes on to comment on the change: "Now, however, Vladimir Aleksandrovich Zelensky's portrayal in the Russian media has become much less sympathetic—not neutral but clearly negative." *Vzglyad* explains this by the fact that Ukraine's policy towards Russia and the Russian language had remained the same.

Of course, this exemplary article does not lack disinformation; in particular, it cites a pro-Russian MP in Ukraine who noted that because Ukraine decided against buying the Russian COVID-19 vaccine Sputnik V, "[Zelensky] will become an accomplice in the murder of his own citizens,"—something, the article concludes, "the citizens themselves will likely understand." However, no mass attitudes of this kind appeared in Ukraine. Moreover, the article claims that Ukraine was "close to a political collapse," as international financial institutions would soon withdraw their support for Ukraine and the country would lose its visa-free movement with the EU, while a default on Ukraine's debts loomed on the horizon. None of this came to fruition—yet these topics were actively discussed across Russian media.

In a slightly earlier article, *Vzglyad* expressed Russian disappointment in Zelensky as follows: "Observers have even had the feeling that Petro Poroshenko continues to rule in Ukraine—having only undergone liposuction and stopped his abuse of alcohol."[36] As for Zelensky's movement, "his party supporters saw it as a potential fortress for multinational and multicultural Ukraine, capable of overcoming numerous cleavages in society. However, Zelensky's political apathy and cowardice [...] led to [...] disgrace and failure." In the author's opinion, "average or pro-Russian voters" were leaving Zelensky's party for the (pro-Russian) Opposition Platform. He concludes rather dramatically: "Now the main intrigue is how Zelensky leaves his position—through elections or through another Maidan." This kind of phrasing is strange for both a liberal and a patronal democracy, since it is understandable and normal that presidents leave their positions; however, for Russia, as a patronal autocracy, it serves as a sign of weakness.

The negative framing of Zelensky meant that he was portrayed as the opposite of a chief patron. Since the ideal for the Russian media is a Putin-type leader, Zelensky was described using imagery opposite to that which Putin is associated with in the Russian media: (1) a weak leader, instead of a strong one; (2) a foreign puppet, instead of the leader who defends national sovereignty; and (3) a traitor who acts against the national interest and the people's will, instead of ruling by them.

A weak leader. Zelensky's weakness became a leitmotif in Russian media messaging. From a more radical corner of the Russian commentariat, he was called a "nonentity" who has zero influence in a country which is going downhill.[37] On the other hand, the more moderate *Gazeta.ru* claimed that Zelensky "actually did demonstrate a readiness for dialogue," yet commented that little had substantially changed in the Donbas conflict, while reflecting on Zelensky's failures in domestic politics.[38] In other words, the material expressed similar ideas, even if it was written in a much more professional style and targeted a smarter audience.

A number of Russian media outlets compared Zelensky's performance to that of Vasyl Holoborodko—the fictional history teacher turned President of Ukraine that Zelensky played in the *Servant of the People* (*Sluha narodu*) TV series. This is true of the aforementioned *Gazeta.ru* material as well as of *Ogonek*'s similar review of Zelensky's first year in power in May 2020, where the journalists compared Zelensky's real-life readiness to acquiesce to IMF demands to his fictional hero's emotional and explicit refusal to do so.[39] *Ogonek* even repeats the same tropes; according to them, Zelensky fostered an initial optimism for change, but then continued Poroshenko's nationalist policies. All of the cited materials have one more thing in common: they all combine Zelensky's undeniable failures in power (no reduction in oligarchic influence, slow pace of reforms, etc.) with his refusal to follow Russian demands regarding the Donbas conflict or to change Ukraine's domestic sociocultural policies to Russia's satisfaction, thereby framing the latter as an undeniable failure too.

A foreign puppet. Russian media outlets are keen to write about "external governance" in Ukraine—regularly mentioning, for instance, George Soros and his affiliates, just like their right-wing counterparts abroad do.[40] In March 2020, *Vzglyad* claimed that Zelensky was shifting Ukraine's foreign policy from relying on Western support to "relying on its own forces," thus displacing the "globalists" (another word characteristic of Western right-wingers) and "grant-eaters" in the process. The author also claimed that the Ukrainian oligarchy was "interested in restoring trade relations with Russia."[41] However, the abovementioned articles from later in 2020, where there are no more expectant signs of Zelensky's willingness to become "independent" of "the West," indicate that these hopes did not come to fruition. Later in 2020, *Regnum.ru* claimed that "vital interests of America demand the transformation of Ukraine into anti-Russia," that this was the reasoning behind the "coup" in 2014, and that the governments of Ukraine have been tasked with fulfilling these American interests ever since. They claimed that "it is naïve to believe that it is possible to cancel the results of a bloody coup by throwing ballots in a box."[42]

This article is useful for us in three ways: first, it continues the topic of Western "external governance" in Ukraine, but now without any hope for a change that would benefit Russia. Second, the article includes a caricature of Zelensky saying "anything for your money!" to a clearly identifiable American in a suit and a blue bowtie with stars. Zelensky's appearance in this caricature makes clear reference to his Jewish origins, as he is portrayed with a large nose and ears, a well-known motif from historical anti-Semitic caricatures. Finally, the idea of Ukraine being groomed as "anti-Russia" by the Western elites was already prevalent among the more nationalist Russian media even back then. However, in July 2021, Putin published an article "Towards the Historical Unity of Russians and Ukrainians," where he uses this trope.[43] It was also mentioned several times in his 2022 speeches.[44]

This article, some experts say, marked Putin's decision to "return" Ukraine under Russian influence. Its content is a mixture of facts, interpretations, and Russian historical myths presented as a set of truths; something very characteristic of the post-Soviet media space. Putin's article was based on a number of tropes that Russian media had already employed about Ukraine earlier; at the same time, it provided a clear template for what Russian media should say about Ukraine in the future.

A traitor. Putin's article does not refer to Zelensky specifically, but it does mention the May 2021 bill on indigenous people in Ukraine—penned by Ukraine's president—which excludes Russians from the list. Moreover, the article claims that the Western partners "reined in" the Ukrainian representatives during the talks on the Donbas conflict, thus precluding any movement towards peace. The Ukrainian representatives, according to Putin, "do not intend to seriously discuss either the special status of Donbas or safeguards for the people living there. They prefer to exploit the image of the 'victim of external aggression' and peddle Russophobia. They arrange bloody provocations in Donbas. In short, they attract the attention of external patrons and masters by all means." The "anti-Russia project" can only be maintained by the "constant cultivation of the image of an internal and external enemy. And I would add—under the protection and control of the Western powers. This is what is actually happening." Ukraine does not exhibit "complete dependence" but is under "direct external control," while the remnants of its economy are "exploited" by the West. The Western authors of the "anti-Russia" project set the Ukrainian political system in such a way that "presidents, members of parliament, and ministers" change but the goal of enmity towards Russia remains.

The article then goes on to claim that the Ukrainian government is acting against the will of the people, with millions of Ukrainians allegedly not accepting the "anti-Russia project" and being persecuted as a result. Towards the end of the article, Putin makes a not-so-vague threat: "We will never allow our historical territories and people close to us who live there to be used against Russia. And to those who will undertake such an attempt, I would like to say that this way they will destroy their own country."

The trope regarding millions of Ukrainians opposing an anti-Russian foreign policy has been continuously used by the Russian media since 2014. Considering how Russia expected to conquer Ukraine in a blitzkrieg in 2022—in the first days, even addressing Ukrainian soldiers to give up and not take orders from "nationalists"[45]—it is very likely that Putin genuinely believed this. And it is evident that in July 2021 at the latest, Putin was already clearly done with Ukraine's current government. In October of that year, when meeting then Israeli Prime Minister Bennett, he stated about Zelensky: "What kind of Jew is he? He's an enabler of Nazism,"[46] further reinforcing the idea that Putin himself started to believe the Russian propaganda machine.

Taken overall, the messaging of Russian pro-government media reporting on Zelensky in 2020 had shifted towards the negative. However, more neutral or even positive messages were not completely uncommon at the time. A good illustration of this is an article by *Moskovskii Komsomolets* in the summer of 2020, praising Zelensky's humanism in response to a hostage situation in Lutsk and his behavior when receiving the bodies of Ukrainians who had died in Iran. The article ends with the words: "He is a weak president and a good man."[47] Of course, in 2022, and even in 2021, such mixed messages about Zelensky would have been unthinkable.

3. The invasion: Russia's military application of fake news

3.1. Noisemaking and the communication preparations for war

We have seen that Russia had already decided Zelensky was incapable of rapprochement by mid-2021 at the latest, and that its media reflected this change. Russian troops had already amassed on Ukraine's borders, first in the spring of 2021, and then once again in the autumn of that year. The initial attack plans, which assumed Russian forces would transition to stabilization operations in the occupied central, eastern, and southern Ukraine by the tenth day of the invasion,[48] were based on the assumption that the West would not interfere to a significant extent. Meanwhile, Russia kept denying the invasion as late as in February 2022.[49]

Russian mass media were actively utilized in forming the necessary informational background to prepare its population for the invasion. Western intelligence services and politicians made repeated warnings in the winter of 2021 that Russia might conduct a false flag operation to justify its invasion;[50] presumably these reports made such an operation useless, yet Russia invaded anyway. In his early morning speech announcing the start of the attack on February 24,[51] Putin mentioned the threat of NATO expansion and alleged Western attempts at forming a unipolar world, together with the threat of a potential NATO attack, as some of the explanations necessitating the "special operation." He also mentioned the "genocide" of the people residing in Donbas and the prospect of a Ukrainian attempt to retake the occupied part of Donbas, as well as Crimea and "a number of other Russian territories," by force. Furthermore, he also claimed Ukraine was now aiming to obtain nuclear weapons. His general goals—repeated constantly by himself and other Russian politicians—stressed the intention to "demilitarize and de-nazify" Ukraine. The latter, considering the claim about "radical nationalists" in power, can and should be read as implying regime change.

All of these stories were, of course, presented in the Russian media in the run-up to the aggression. Furthermore, a more exotic story—about Ukraine being used by the US to host secret laboratories developing biological weapons—was repeated by the Russian media a number of times.[52] This particular conspiracy theory was, in fact, even amplified by China[53] and by the notorious QAnon movement.[54]

In other words, Russia alluded to five distinct motivations behind the aggression:

- NATO's willingness to go to war with Russia;
- Ukraine's own willingness to retake its territories and even possibly capture some more;
- genocide of the people of Donbas;
- Ukraine's alleged intentions to acquire a nuclear weapon;
- Ukraine's alleged development of a biological weapon.

These points have been used together as well as individually. It is not the first time Russia has produced a number of different versions behind a certain event; one notorious case is related to the downing of the Dutch MH-17 passenger airplane over Donbas.[55] This technique is called noisemaking, or "censorship through noise," and is employed to create "an atmosphere of general confusion and distrust";[56] "to leave the mind exhausted and confused."[57]

Moreover, for the receiver of such propaganda, the situation is made more complex by the state of war. According to interviews conducted by *PS Lab*, Russians tend to believe that since Russian decision-makers intervened in Ukraine, they must have had a good reason to do so. Kropivnitskii and Denisenko, reviewing this study, provide an analogy with previous studies regarding Americans who supported the decision to intervene in Iraq based on similar psychological mechanisms of "inferred justification"—i.e., argumentation for the intervention was not based on specific facts, but on the idea that these facts must exist and be available to the decision-makers, otherwise they would not have made such a decision.[58]

3.2. Silencing the opposition media behind the front

In late March 2022, Zelensky was interviewed by several Russian opposition media outlets, presenting the Ukrainian point of view on current events. This interview was quite fair and compassionate towards Ukraine. The notorious Roskomnadzor—the Russian state agency regulating the internet and media—immediately reacted, prohibiting Russian media from publishing this interview and threatening legal sanctions.[59]

The monopolization of media space in Russia was finalized earlier that March, following the attack on Ukraine; in early March, the broadcast of *Dozhd* (Rain) TV, the only clearly pro-opposition television channel, was stopped, and the same happened to the moderately liberal *Ekho Moskvy* (Echo of Moscow) radio station.[60] On March 4, *Meduza*, a popular online news website, was blocked by Roskomnadzor together with reputable Western media like *BBC* and *Deutsche Welle*.[61] In late March 2022, *Novaya Gazeta* (New Newspaper)—whose editor Dmitriy Muratov was awarded the Nobel Peace Prize in 2021—suspended its operations until the end of the Russian aggression. In April, emigrant journalists of the newspaper launched a new online project—*Novaya Gazeta. Evropa* (New Newspaper. Europe), but access to their website has also been banned by Roskomnadzor.[62] Several smaller online media have also been blocked in what constitutes a 180 degree turn in Russian state media policy.

During Putin's rule, moderately liberal media were always allowed to exist, even though some of the more inquisitive journalists ended up targeted by the regime. William Andrews Evans, for instance, describes *Ekho Moskvy* as a radio station that sought to include both official and oppositional narratives as a strategy of adaptation; and under these conditions, the station was allowed to exist for the bulk of the Putin era.[63] These rules were overwritten in 2022. Were *Dozhd* and *Meduza* not banned in early March, it is unclear whether they would have risked their legal status organizing an interview with Zelensky. Although they remained essentially Russian media, targeting, first and foremost, the Russian audience, legally they were in a limbo, and have subsequently become emigrant media—albeit clearly targeting Russians at home as well. For instance, every article on *Meduza* now starts with a header explaining how to share that article with people in Russia via PDF download or printing. Nevertheless, the coverage of these media—although not without their problems, as some Ukrainians highlight[64]—is not the focus of the present chapter. In the *Meduza*, *Novaya Gazeta* and *Dozhd* of 2022, Ukraine's point of view was represented—even if with caveats. This was not something possible in the Russian mainstream media of 2022.

In fact, the Russian domestic situation has now started to reflect the wartime logic of the media politics that the Russian authorities have imposed in the "LNR" and the "DNR." There—as well as in the newly annexed territories of Ukraine in

2022—media representing an alternative viewpoint has become unthinkable. In fact, these regions have even jammed Ukrainian FM radio stations, in contrast to other Russia-supported unrecognized states in the region, such as Transnistria, Abkhazia, and South Ossetia, where FM stations from Moldova and Georgia, respectively, are readily available.[65] As journalist Sergei Vysotskii describes the overall changes that occurred in 2022, "the LDNR has swallowed up Russia."[66]

3.3. Demoralization and covering up war crimes with fake news

As we know, Ukraine successfully fought off the first wave of the invasion, stabilized the situation on the frontlines, and retook a significant part of the occupied territories. Zelensky himself changed in the process. He is now a worldwide celebrity and a symbol of resistance, having been awarded several titles like *Time*'s Person of the Year 2022; he even looks and talks differently and there are few signs of his 2020 conciliatory attitudes left. Instead, Russian propaganda now paints Zelensky with pure black colors, describing him, alternatively or simultaneously, as a coward, a bloodthirsty barbarian, and a puppet of the West. The following section will review current attitudes towards Zelensky by the Russian media mouthpieces.

The earliest piece of fake news about Zelensky produced after the start of the full-scale Russian aggression against Ukraine was related to his having escaped Ukraine. Already on day 2 of the aggression, Russian media started claiming that Zelensky was abroad.[67] The next day, the speaker of the Russian parliament, Vyacheslav Volodin, claimed Zelensky was in Lviv.[68] In March, Ilia Kiva, a notorious ex-MP of the Ukrainian parliament, also claimed that Zelensky had escaped abroad.[69] Although there is no quantitative analysis of war-related fakes in 2022 in the Russian media available yet, the claim about Zelensky leaving his position seems to have been one of the most frequently repeated stories both in traditional media and on popular pro-Russian Telegram news channels. So much so that Zelensky himself had to react and confirm his location several times.[70]

The purpose of this fake was loud and clear: if Zelensky had left, the morale of Ukrainians would have taken a hit, and it would have been easier for the Russian army to fulfil its intended blitzkrieg goals. This is exactly why Zelensky's decision to confirm his location was necessary. Information inertia caused the Russian media to continue claiming that Zelensky's video addresses were filmed against a green screen, rather than on the streets of Kyiv, numerous times[71]—particularly when Zelensky visited the frontlines, like during his December visit to Bakhmut.[72]

Russia has continued to exploit the claim that Zelensky was a drug addict. This trope originated in the 2019 Ukrainian presidential campaign and was amplified by Zelensky's run-off opponent, Poroshenko.[73] The claim (which was never substantiated) was then picked by Russian propaganda; *Vice* claims that it "first surfaced from pro-Kremlin disinformation outlets" in late 2021, as Russia amassed its army on the borders of Ukraine.[74] This claim—like the one about Zelensky having left the country—might have had a dual use, i.e. to discredit Zelensky in the eyes of Ukrainians and to show the enemy commander-in-chief as flawed and weak. However, whereas the primary target audience for the fake information about Zelensky running away was clearly located in Ukraine, it would have been naïve to expect a Ukrainian audience to respond in some way to a two-year-old claim.

Russian propaganda continues to frame Zelensky as a puppet rather than as a real decision-maker. They do not claim that Kolomoisky is his puppeteer anymore, not after Zelensky signed a decree stripping Kolomoisky and several other political celebrities of Ukrainian citizenship (due to these people possessing other citizenships)[75] and, subsequently, nationalized his Ukrnafta and Ukrtatnafta companies, together with several other oligarchic enterprises.[76] Instead, Zelensky is presented in a contradictory manner; some claim he is a puppet of the West,[77] while others present him as an aggressive politician pushing the West for more radical measures in support of Ukraine, despite Western self-interest.[78]

Beyond demoralization, another important aim of Russian fake news campaigns has been to cover up war crimes. In April 2022, the Russian army was forced to leave northern Ukraine. The news accounts from the liberated towns of Kyiv oblast' were tragic; Russian soldiers had committed numerous war crimes against the locals, claiming many lives. Particularly notorious was the situation in the town Bucha. Russian propaganda was quick to create and promote an unsubstantiated conspiracy theory explaining these findings as being staged, and the bodies on the videos filmed by Ukrainians as being fake,[79] despite numerous subsequent investigations proving the allegations against the Russian army. Both the internal and the external need for this explanation is self-evident; domestically, Russia had to explain to its population that their side did nothing wrong, while externally, Russia had to counter the claims of war crimes conducted by its soldiers. Russia also expanded this information campaign to the "LNR" and "DNR" media which, in a matter of several days, produced dozens of news pieces claiming the Bucha tragedy to be faked.[80]

3.4. Propaganda outsourcing

One final important point to conclude the list of Russian propaganda escapades against Zelensky concerns propaganda outsourcing. Christo Grozev, Bellingcat's founder, and Matthew A. Lauder, a defense scientist, among others, argue that Russia outsources foreign influence to private actors.[81] Russian TikTok stars have been paid to spread pro-government propaganda,[82] and about 100 million rubles were reportedly spent to pay musicians on the *"Za Rossiiu"* (For Russia) tour.[83]

In other words, it is wrong to view Russian propaganda only through the lens of its traditional media or even major news portals; it can, and does, take more complicated forms.

These private contractors include hacker groups. The Ukrainian government has on multiple occasions warned that Russia might hack TV and radio broadcasts to claim that the government has capitulated. This, in particular, happened in March 2022, when the newsfeed of the *Ukraina 24* TV channel showed Zelensky's "capitulation" message.[84] In June, Russian hackers interfered with the broadcast of the decisive game between the national football teams of Wales and Ukraine on an online on-demand service; during the halftime break, messages about Ukrainian attacks on Donbas were broadcast.[85] In July, some radio broadcasts were hacked, transmitting a message claiming that Zelensky was seriously ill and in intensive care. Zelensky denied this claim in a video address.[86]

This outsourced propaganda can, of course, vary in quality and sometimes lead to absurdities. An attempted campaign consisting of Telegram posts in November 2022 called on Ukrainians to protest against the government over constant power outages (caused, in reality, by Russian missile and drone attacks on critical infrastructure). One of the images used in the campaign stated: "We just want light, and not to die in a war, started by the bloody clown in power!"[87] Ukrainian meme channels had already started referring to Zelensky ironically as "The Iron Clown" in early February,[88] even though this nickname did not gain much traction. In other words, an element of an actual Russian propaganda campaign was either consciously based on a Ukrainian meme or unironically employed a nickname that Ukrainians had used as an obvious joke. In either case, it indicates the contractor's lack of professionalism.

Then again, the Russian representative to the UN did claim that Ukraine had planned to use infected mosquitoes as a biological weapon against Russia.[89] Clearly absurd claims might be part of the aforementioned strategy of "censorship through noise"—and in the end, the consumer of Russian propaganda enters a worldview where, as Peter Pomerantsev correctly observed, "nothing is real and everything is possible."

4. Behind the media machine: the dynamics of the Russian and Ukrainian patronal systems

4.1. Zelensky's politics in a patronal democracy

Following the 2019 elections in Ukraine, Russia had initially expected Zelensky (or possibly Kolomoisky—depending on who they saw as Ukraine's real chief patron initially) to cave in to their demands. This did not happen—and the theory of patronalism might help us explain why.

Russia is categorized by Magyar and Madlovics as a consolidated "patronal autocracy." In this system, the chief patron—Putin—is the sole decision-maker, and the political system precludes the public from electing a different leader. He makes all the strategic decisions and wields "unconstrained informal power," particularly over media messaging, in addition to his formal competencies. His regime is consolidated; he does not have any realistic competitors, nor does he have any accountability before the public—aside from not overstepping some "stimulation threshold" that could lead to riots. (In fact, the latter is a very good explanation why Putin did not want to declare military mobilization until the autumn of 2022—despite Russian military bloggers calling for it from early on.)[90]

Putin's disdain for Ukrainian statehood is well-documented and evident from the article he wrote in 2021. Nevertheless, he might have expected to meet someone in a role homologous to his own; a person who could impose his own views on his country without any significant restrictions from the public. In other words, Putin may have considered Zelensky to be an acceptable person because he thought of Zelensky as a fellow patronal autocrat (or a figurehead in Kolomoisky's patronal autocracy). Consequently, Russian media were instructed not to criticize Zelensky too much in order to pull him towards a geopolitical deal auspicious for Russia.

The fact that Zelensky won the run-off of the 2019 presidential elections with 73% of the vote could have pushed Putin towards this line of thinking. In this scheme of things, the Ukrainian people were not a subject of decision-making, and Zelensky had the possibility to single-handedly change the ideology of the Ukrainian state to be more compatible with Russian goals.

This fits in well with the general line of Russian media messaging about democracies; Russian media not only speak from a position of substantive-rational legitimacy (i.e. one based on certain collectively-desired end goals) as opposed to legal-rational legitimacy, but paint other systems this way—i.e. where decisions in law-making and law-enforcement are actually politically driven and not independent. For the same reasons, Russian diplomats have also adopted the idea to constantly argue against the "Western" rules-based order in international relations, claiming that, in fact, these rules are written in a way that only benefits the West.[91] In fact, it is possible that this ideology adopted in the Russian media could have, in a loop, influenced Putin's thinking, as his advisors would most likely bring him those news reports (and analyses) which would invoke a positive reaction—and Western media have indeed reported that in recent years Putin has started to behave more like an ideological actor. This suggestion will be expanded upon towards the end of the chapter.

In reality, however, Zelensky was under public pressure to change his stance as president. His personal views from pre-election times, and indeed from 2019 and 2020, did seem more reconciliatory. However, in a patronal democracy such as

Ukraine, he did not have the necessary influence over the media and civil society to change the state narrative. Most Ukrainian media would have quickly turned on Zelensky had he opted for a bad deal with Russia—and that would have meant a threat to his political survival. To preclude this and to secure his future electoral prospects, Zelensky had to adopt a different ideological approach—and as late as 2021, it was clear that his policies, following popular demand, were directed strictly against Russia. An illustrative example was his decision to ban pro-Russian channels owned by Viktor Medvedchuk, which lead to a temporary increase in Zelensky's support in opinion polls.[92]

If a leader of a democracy—including a patronal democracy—steps too far over the "stimulation threshold," i.e. the manageable level of popular concern, they risk losing their office, in one way or another. For Zelensky, conducting elections in Donbas with Russian troops still in the area, and then reintegrating a region with a "special status" that could potentially extend to being able to play a blocking role in Ukraine's foreign policy would have been way beyond this threshold. So much so that this decision could have even led to a "color revolution" –and in any case, Zelensky would have not been reelected for a second term. For Putin, who had systematically neutralized all institutions that could have deprived him of power, this situation was foreign. This discrepancy between Putin's initial plans—to come to an agreement with Zelensky, based on the latter's conciliatory views, and reintegrate Donbas as an entity possessing a "special status" and eventual influence on Ukraine's foreign policy—and subsequent reality could have even been the final straw in his decision to invade. In any case, however, a shift in media messaging regarding Zelensky can surely be attributed to this discrepancy.

4.2. The goals of Russian information warfare

The monopolization of the media space in 2022 Russia marked a further shift from the pre-existing scheme of patronal autocracy towards dictatorship. The first model tends to tolerate a certain degree of dissent; as Magyar and Madlovics write, patronal autocracies limit "not content but outreach" and "trap critical voices in small circles where those who were already staunch opponents of the government merely converse among themselves." That is precisely what happened with media such as *Dozhd* and *Ekho Moskvy* in Putin's pre-2022 Russia—with the caveat that they had to compromise with the environment. However, in the present war—or as Russia continues to call it, the "special military operation"—even dissent in the small, mostly powerless circles of the liberal opposition is deemed unacceptable. The conditions within which the Russian media world had previously operated, as described by Pomerantsev and Gessen, now no longer exist and have been replaced by an even more homogenous and restricted environment.

Instead, information warfare has been amplified—in the full sense of the word "warfare." The aims of the Russian information operations against Zelensky and Ukraine can be summed up in three points:

1. creating dissent within Ukraine, thereby weakening the government;
2. solidifying the domestic pro-invasion consensus;
3. decreasing the foreign support for Ukraine.

The initial aim of this warfare was to facilitate the extremely ambitious goal to overtake Ukraine as quickly as possible and present the conquest as a fait accompli to the world. In this regard, the claims that Zelensky escaped Kyiv as Russian forces inched towards the capital served the same purpose as the special squads that the Ukrainian government alleges had been sent to assassinate the top politicians. If Ukrainians had believed that Zelensky had escaped or that he had been killed, the decapitation of Ukraine's political apparatus would have sowed chaos in the country. The subsequent messages about his "capitulation" served a similar goal.

On the other hand, as the frontline stabilized and it became clear that Ukraine would not collapse anytime soon, the nature of the fakes changed; now they were directed towards the second and third goals (i.e. solidifying the domestic pro-war consensus and decreasing foreign support for Ukraine). Moreover, the fakes have now penetrated non-Western governments (as with the story of Ukraine developing a biological weapon—amplified by China)[93] and Western extremists (the biological weapon story and the claims that Bucha was a fake—spread by the Western far-right).[94] It is likely that Russian propaganda will pursue these goals even more in the future, especially after seeing how outlets such as *Fox News* have made serious reports about Zelensky "waging war on Christianity"[95] because Ukrainian law enforcement has conducted searches in the Ukrainian Orthodox Church (Moscow Patriarchy). The latter is de facto controlled by the Russian Orthodox Church, has been used in hybrid warfare on many occasions,[96] and is only one of many Christian denominations in the country.[97]

4.3. The changing role of ideology in Russia

As for Russia itself, another sign of the most recent changes in the country is its use of ideology. While patronal autocracies normally use ideology as a façade (i.e., are ideology-applying rather than ideology-driven, according to Magyar and Madlovics's definitions), it seems[98] that in the case of Russia, the chief patron has indeed progressed to being ideological in his actions and motivations, and has selected ideologically similar people for his current inner circle. The systemic "liberal" technocrats (who generally do not support the war)[99] who had previously been an element of the patronal pyramid with access to the chief have now lost this access.

It may be that Putin, who once used propaganda to supply the ideology for his goals, eventually fell for this propaganda himself. At the very least, there was no sign of him being so strongly ideological before, whereas now he is. Journalists have traced this change to Putin's isolation during COVID and his desire to become a historical figure for Russia;[100] we should, however, add that in an autocracy, it is beneficial for subordinates to bring good news to their patron. This led to Putin having been severely misinformed at least in the preparations for and early stages of the war; and since the news accounts he received were ideologically filtered, so, too, the reader of these news accounts moved further towards this ideology. Putin's fascination with Ilyin did not help, nor did some of his imperialist subsidiaries marketing their ideas to him; this, for instance, applies to Vladislav Surkov. In this context, Aleksandr Dugin is frequently mentioned; and although his direct influence on Kremlin has always been limited,[101] his work *The Foundations of Geopolitics* has been mandatory reading for the Russian military elite for years, and has, therefore, shaped the minds of those reporting to Putin. Another factor here is Russia's legacy of power and its historical status as a civilizational core of Eastern Europe, which it is attempting to preserve.

In other words, Putin has apparently been caught in a propaganda loop. As he becomes more ideological, so, too, must the propagandists. The propagandists, however, do not necessarily believe what they spread; after all, it is well known that some of the most notorious Russian anti-Western propagandists have luxurious properties in the West—which they have lost access to due to personal sanctions. Marina Skabeeva, another notorious propagandist, recently uploaded video files with Putin's speeches to her official Telegram channel using peculiar file names, such as "Pynja" (a Russian derogatory nickname for Putin), "Puten," and "Putin_mobshiza" (from "mobilization" and "schizophrenia").[102] In a recent experiment, TikTok influencers showed a readiness to produce clearly fake videos (e.g. claiming that Zelensky's real surname is Bayraktar, like the name of Turkish military drones Ukraine uses) for money.[103] Nevertheless, what matters is that this propaganda works to create sufficient confusion in Russia resulting in people believing in either one or another propagandist version of reality. In any case, the government knows what it is doing and has reasons for this sort of intervention.

This change towards an ideological Russia has, in turn, influenced the functioning of the Ukrainian state. Whereas previously the use of ideological bywords could have been traced to electoral politics (see, for instance, Petro Poroshenko's 2019 campaign with the slogan "Army. Language. Faith"), now a cohesive ideology for Ukraine is immediately related to its survival. Therefore, the ideology is not only applied, but the regime is also driven by it—and constrained, since it is unlikely that Ukrainians will accept negotiations. However, this ideology is collectivist, and hence could be satisfyingly integrated into the patronal system without breaking it.[104] The recent debacles concerning the adoption of a law regarding the country's Constitution Court and the law favoring major property developers to the detriment of local communities[105] illustrate that Ukraine has still not moved away from patronalism. The "us and them" model of populism also naturally applies to the war environment for Ukraine; "in times of crisis, the people return by reflex to […] secure communities [including the nation – K.F.]."[106] There is no need to artificially construct "them" or make people lose empathy towards "them"—although some internal groups can be ascribed to the enemy's camp through propaganda. However, if "the "nation" is an emotionally binding community in the name of which sacrifice can be required,"[107] then there is a risk that the current government will continue speaking for the "nation" and eventually consolidate power in an authoritarian fashion.

However, there is a difference in the real-world case of Ukraine to the theoretical framework of the collectivist ideologies as proposed by Magyar and Madlovics. In Ukraine, the population has met with a real challenge which the state ideology has not created, but for which it only provides an interpretational framework. Instead of "collective egoism," an organic solidarity has arisen within the population. This differs from the situation in Russia, where there was no empirical reason for the "us" group (Russians) to mobilize against the "them" group (Ukrainians). Since the Ukraine did not attack Russia, it became necessary for the Russian purveyors of propaganda to construct an artificial case claiming that either (1) NATO or (2) Ukraine was going to unleash an attack on Donbas, Crimea, or Russia itself, or that (3) Ukraine was conducting genocide or (4) constructing a nuclear or (5) a biological weapon.

In describing the socio-ideological world of populism, Magyar and Madlovics point out that:

> The audience that views the world through the eyeglasses of the populist narrative will structure, interpret, and even supplement reality accordingly, with the help of real as well as non-real 'facts'—which, as they fit into their worldview, will be considered just as real as the true facts. The narrative creates its own reality: the news and facts, real or otherwise, are not the backbone of the narrative but it is the other way around, they are optionally changeable illustrations to pre-ordered judgments.[108]

This, together with the prevailing idea that Russia's leaders know what they are doing, is what allows the regime, on the one hand, to produce multiple mutually exclusive versions of reality, and for the people, on the other, to simply accept what the government does. It helps that the propaganda machine removes the moral constraints of society; according to a poll conducted in late 2022,[109] 46%

of Russians fully support strikes against Ukraine's energy infrastructure, while a further 17% somewhat support these actions. While Ukraine and the West can and should conduct countermeasures against Russian propaganda within their societies, it is necessary to understand that the problematic attitudes inside Russian society will continue to pose a challenge for peace and stability in Europe even when the war in Ukraine concludes.

Notes

1. Peter Pomerantsev, *Nothing is True and Everything is Possible: The Surreal Heart of the New Russia* (New York: Public Affairs, 2014).
2. Peter Pomerantsev, *This is Not Propaganda: Adventures in the War against Reality* (New York: Public Affairs, 2019).
3. Masha Gessen, *The Future Is History: How Totalitarianism Reclaimed Russia* (London: Penguin Publishing Group, 2017).
4. Olga Khvostunova, "A Brief History of the Russian Media," *The Interpreter*, December 6, 2013, https://www.interpretermag.com/a-brief-history-of-the-russian-media/.
5. Oleksiy Yarmolenko and Serhii Pyvovarov, "Putin Often Quotes the Philosopher Ivan Ilyin and General Anton Denikin. They Lived a Century Ago, Both Denied Ukraine's Independence and Advocated Dictatorial Rule," *Babel*, April 6, 2022, https://babel.ua/en/texts/77596-putin-often-quotes-the-philosopher-ivan-ilyin-and-general-anton-denikin-they-lived-a-century-ago-both-denied-ukraine-s-independence-and-advocated-dictatorial-rule-and-this-is-how-they-described.
6. The correct spelling of his surname in Latin, according to Ukrainian standards, would have been Zelens'kyi. However, the spelling "Zelensky" has solidified in Western media; hence its use in this chapter as well.
7. Peter Dickinson, "Переломный момент. Как революция в Украине изменила мир" [Breaking point: How the revolution in Ukraine has changed the world], *New Voice*, November 25, 2020, https://nv.ua/opinion/vladimir-putin-pochemu-oranzhevaya-revolyuciya-napugala-rossiyu-novosti-ukrainy-50126146.html.
8. "Від Майдану-табору до Майдану-січі: що змінилося?" [From Maidan-Camp to Maidan-Sich: What has changed?], Fond Demokratichni initsiatyvy imeni Ilka Kucheriva, February 6, 2014, https://dif.org.ua/article/vid-maydanu-taboru-do-maydanu-sichi-shcho-zminilosya.
9. Sonia Koshkina, *Майдан Нерозказана історія* [Maidan: The untold story] (Kyiv: Bright Books, 2015).
10. Andrei Avdeenkov and Elizaveta Shislakova, "Присоединение Крыма к Российской Федерации: контент-анализ российских печатных СМИ" [The annexation of the Crimea by the Russian Federation: an analysis of Russian print media], Moscow Higher School of Economics, March 3, 2016, https://www.hse.ru/data/2016/03/03/1125955854/%D0%90%D0%B2%D0%B4%D0%B5%D0%B5%D0%BD%D0%BA%D0%BE,%20%D0%A8%D0%B8%D1%88%D0%BB%D0%B0%D0%BA%D0%BE%D0%B2%D0%B0.pdf; John R. Haines, "Russia's Use of Disinformation in the Ukraine Conflict," Foreign Policy Research Institute, February 17, 2015, https://www.fpri.org/article/2015/02/russias-use-of-disinformation-in-the-ukraine-conflict/.
11. Nazar Chornyi, "ТОП-10 фейків про Петра Порошенка" [TOP 10 fakes about Petro Poroshenko], *Bukvy*, July 8, 2020, https://bykvu.com/ua/mysli/top-10-fejkov-o-petre-poroshenko/.
12. Zhanna Ulyanova et al., "'Шоколадный президент': как победил Петр Порошенко" ["Chocolate president": How Petro Poroshenko won], *RBK*, 25 May 2014, https://www.rbc.ru/politics/25/05/2014/57041d669a794761c0cea21a.
13. Kateryna Honcharova, "Звідки у ЗМІ з'явилася теза про 'Зеленського-наркомана'" [Where did the media claim about Zelensky as a drug addict come from], *Detector Media*, 26 April 2019, https://ms.detector.media/manipulyatsii/post/22796/2019-04-26-zvidky-u-zmi-zyavylasya-teza-pro-zelenskogo-narkomana/.
14. "Зеленський дав Порошенку 24 години: хоче дебатів на Олімпійському" [Zelensky gave Poroshenko 24 hours: Wants debates at the Olympic stadium], *Ukrainska Pravda*, 3 April 2019, https://www.pravda.com.ua/news/2019/04/3/7211209/.
15. Irina Pankevych, "Путін зник з України за одну ніч: Зеленський пояснив, що сталося" [Putin disappeared from Ukraine overnight: Zelensky explained what has happened], *Znaj.ua*, April 11, 2019, https://znaj.ua/politics/225350-putin-znik-z-ukrajini-za-odnu-nich-zelenskiy-poyasniv-shcho-stalosya.

16 Tereza Laschuk and Yuliana Skibitska, "Западные СМИ опасаются Коломойского, российские — выжидают: что пишут о победе Владимира Зеленского" [Western media are afraid of Kolomoisky, Russian media are waiting things out: What are they writing about Zelensky's victory], *Babel*, April 24, 2019, https://babel.ua/ru/texts/29173-zapadnye-smi-opasayutsya-kolomoyskogo-rossiyskie-vyzhidayut-chto-pishut-o-pobede-vladimira-zelenskogo; Kseniia Novikova, "'Проиграли идиоты из команды Порошенко.' Выборы в Украине глазами телевидения в России" [The idiots from team Poroshenko have lost: The elections in Ukraine in the eyes of Russian television], *Nastoiashcheie Vremia*, April 1, 2019, https://www.currenttime.tv/a/russian-tv-about-ukrain-election/29854365.html.

17 "Методологія дослідження ЗМІ в окупованих районів Донецької та Луганської областей" [Methodology of studying mass media of the occupied districts of the Donetsk and Luhansk oblasts], Instytut Masovoi Informatsii, September 24, 2019, https://imi.org.ua/monitorings/metodologiya-doslidzhennya-zmi-okupovanyh-rajoniv-donetskoyi-ta-luganskoyi-oblastej-i29725. Further confirmation is based on the research in a yet unpublished chapter for a collective project researching the unrecognized republics in the post-Soviet space: Kostiantyn Fedorenko, "Media and legitimization strategies of the de facto regimes," 2022.

18 "СБУ документує інформаційну агресію іноземних спецслужб в ОРДЛО" [The SBU documents the information aggression of foreign security services in the Russian-occupied territories], Sluzhba bezpeki Ukraini, May 25, 2020, https://web.archive.org/web/20200610125032/https://ssu.gov.ua/ua/news/1/category/21/view/7619#.9lapvhHf.dpbs.

19 "'Буду помогать': Коломойский о планах на Зеленского. Эксклюзив НТВ" ["I will help": Kolomoisky about his plans for Zelensky. NTV Exclusive], *NTV*, April 27, 2019, https://www.ntv.ru/novosti/2184066/; YuraSumy, "И все-таки — марионетка…" [A puppet, after all…], *NewsFront*, October 16, 2019, https://news-front.info/2019/10/16/i-vse-taki-marionetka/; Viktor Ukolov, "Зеленський – не клоун, а маріонетка – Уколов" [Zelensky is not a clown, he's a puppet], *Priamyi*, March 31, 2019, https://prm.ua/zelenskiy-ne-kloun-a-marionetka-ukolov/.

20 "Zelensky's New Year address: Everyone should answer the question: who am I?" *Unian*, January 1, 2020, https://www.unian.info/society/10816211-zelensky-s-new-year-address-everyone-should-answer-the-question-who-am-i.html.

21 Maksym Vikhrov, "'Зійтися десь посередині' не вийде: відчайдушна спроба втечі Зеленського приречена на фіаско" [It will not be possible to find a middle ground: Zelensky's desperate escape attempt is doomed to failure], *UAinfo*, January 11, 2020, https://uainfo.org/blognews/1578651393--ziytisya-des-poseredini-ne-viyde-vidchaydushna-sproba-vtechi.html; "Соцмережі про привітання Зеленського: 'правильна ідея' та 'ковбасна риторика'" [Social networks on Zelensky's address: "the right idea" and "salami rhetoric"], *BBC News Ukraina*, January 1, 2020, https://www.bbc.com/ukrainian/news-50964448.

22 "Зеленский в новогоднем поздравлении призвал украинцев к объединению" [Zelensky urged Ukrainians to unite in his New Year's address], *RIA Novosti*, January 1, 2020, https://ria.ru/20200101/1563055481.html.

23 "Поклонская прокомментировала новогоднее обращение Зеленского" [Poklonskaya commented on Zelensky's New Year address], *RIA Novosti*, January 2, 2020, https://ria.ru/20200102/1563080416.html.

24 Sofiia Sereda and Pavlo Kholodov, "'Та сторона.' Чому Зеленський уникає згадок про Росію, говорячи про війну на Донбасі?" ["That side": Why does Zelensky avoid mentioning Russia when talking about the war in Donbas?], *Radio Svoboda*, July 15, 2020, https://www.radiosvoboda.org/a/30728032.html.

25 Maite Fernández Simon and David L. Stern, "Who Is Viktor Medvedchuk, the Pro-Russia Mogul Arrested in Ukraine?" *Washington Post*, April 13, 2022, https://www.washingtonpost.com/world/2022/02/28/ukraine-russia-medvedchuck/.

26 Sereda and Kholodov, "'Ta storona.'"

27 Nicolaus von Twickel, *Events in the "People's Republics" of Eastern Ukraine*, Human Rights Monitoring in Eastern Ukraine, Annual Report 2019.

28 Liubko Petrenko, "Зеленський проти Медведчука" [Zelensky versus Medvedchuk], *Zaxid.net*, February 4, 2021, https://zaxid.net/zelenskiy_proti_medvedchuka_n1513956; Karl Volokh, "'Інколи й найпалкіший прихильник Оккама й Хенлона починає сумніватися...' - Карл Волох" [Sometimes even the most devoted fan of Occam and Hanlon starts to doubt... - Karl Volokh], *Spektr Novosti*, January 2, 2022, 2023, https://spektrnews.in.ua/news/nkoli-y-naypalkshiy-prihil-nik-okkama-y-henlona-pochina-sumn-vatisya---karl-voloh/126788#gsc.tab=0.

29 "Більшість українців не може оцінити 'формулу Штайнмаєра' – опитування" [The majority of Ukrainians cannot assess the Steinmeier formula], *TSN*, October 2, 2019, https://tsn.ua/ukrayina/bilshist-ukrayinciv-ne-mozhe-ociniti-formulu-shtaynmayera-opituvannya-1420476.html.

30 Dmytro Hordon, "Аваков про переговори в нормандському форматі: У Суркова здали нерви. Він кинув Єрмаку папери на стіл: мовляв, ми так не домовлялися!" [Avakov on the Normandy Format talks: Surkov had a nervous breakdown. He threw papers on the table towards Yermak: "That's not what we agreed on!"], *Gordonua.com*, December 10, 2019, https://gordonua.com/ukr/publications/-avakov-pro-peregovori-v-normandskomu-formati-u-surkova-zdali-nervi-vin-kinuv-jermaku-paperi-na-stil-movljav-mi-tak-ne-domovljalisja-1478666.html.

31 E.g. Kseniia Bogacheva, "Нормандская заморозка" [Normandy freeze-up], *Lenta.ru*, December 10, 2019, https://lenta.ru/articles/2019/12/10/norm_itogi/.

32 Iurii Vyshnevskyi, "Берлінський провал. Який порядок капітуляції висунув Путін Зеленському" [Berlin failure: Which order of capitulation did Putin announce to Zelensky], *DS News*, September 16, 2020, https://www.dsnews.ua/ukr/politics/berlinskiy-proval-kakoy-ultimatum-zelenskomu-vydvinul-putin-15092020-399191.

33 The concept "politolog" in the post-Soviet space differs from a "political scientist"; it usually describes either a media commentator of political events or a "political technologist" who works in campaign management and PR, or both.

34 A "tomos" is a document recognizing an Orthodox church as independent; the Orthodox Church of Ukraine received this status in 2019, with Poroshenko's staunch support, and with extreme criticism from both the Russian Orthodox Church and Russian politicians.

35 Dmitrii Bavyrin, "Россия загнала Зеленского в коронавирусную ловушку" [Russia has lured Zelensky into a coronavirus trap], *Vzglyad*, December 10, 2020, https://vz.ru/world/2020/12/10/1074902.html.

36 This refers to the previously mentioned conspiracy theory about Poroshenko's supposed alcoholism.

37 Rostislav Ishchenko, "Ничтожество в нормандском формате" [Null in the Normandy Format], *Ukraina.ru*, July 28, 2020, https://ukraina.ru/20200728/1028376708.html.

38 Anna Iuranets, "'Не икона, не идол': итоги года президентства Зеленского" [Not an icon, nor a leader: Results of Zelensky's year of presidency], *Gazeta.ru*, May 20, 2020, https://www.gazeta.ru/politics/2020/05/19_a_13089229.shtml.

39 Iurii Tkachev, "Год у власти" [A year in power], *Ogonek*, May 25, 2020, https://www.kommersant.ru/doc/4348154.

40 "Why is Billionaire George Soros a Bogeyman for the Hard Right?" *BBC*, September 7, 2019, https://www.bbc.com/news/stories-49584157.

41 Vasilii Stoiakin, "Зеленский начинает резко менять политический курс Украины" [Zelensky starts to radically change Ukraine's political direction], *Vzglyad*, March 23, 2020, https://vz.ru/world/2020/3/23/1030174.html.

42 Igor Shishkin, "Владимир Зеленский. Год зиц-президентства 'на отлично'" [Volodymyr Zelensky: Top marks for the sitting president's year], *Regnum*, May 3, 2020, https://regnum.ru/news/polit/2937406.html.

43 Vladimir Putin, "On the Historical Unity of Russians and Ukrainians," *Official Kremlin Website*, July 12, 2021, http://en.kremlin.ru/events/president/news/66181; for the original Russian ver-

sion, see Vladimir Putin, "Об историческом единстве русских и украинцев" [On the historical unity of Russians and Ukrainians], *Official Kremlin Website*, July 12, 2021, http://kremlin.ru/events/president/news/66181.

44 Viktor Nikolaiiev, "Путин: Запад пытается создать 'анти-Россию'" [Putin: The West is trying to create an anti-Russia], *Moskovskii Komsomolets*, March 3, 2022, https://www.mk.ru/politics/2022/03/03/putin-zapad-pytaetsya-sozdat-antirossiyu.html; "Путин: 'анти-Россия' на Украине — новое геополитическое оружие Запада" [Putin: An anti-Russia in Ukraine is the West's new geopolitical weapon], *News.ru*, April 27, 2022, https://news.ru/vlast/putin-ukrainskomu-narodu-ugotovlena-sudba-rashodnogo-materiala/.

45 "Путин призвал ВСУ сложить оружие и 'идти домой'" [Putin called on the AFU to lay down their arms and go home], *Lenta.ru*, February 24, 2022, https://lenta.ru/news/2022/02/24/vsu/.

46 Michael Schwirtz et al., "How Putin's War in Ukraine Became a Catastrophe for Russia," *New York Times*, December 16, 2022, https://www.nytimes.com/interactive/2022/12/16/world/europe/russia-putin-war-failures-ukraine.html.

47 Aleksandr Melman, "Клоун-президент и клоун-террорист: Зеленский проявил человечность" [Clown president and clown terrorist: Zelensky has demonstrated humanity], *Moskovskii Komsomolets*, July 28, 2020, https://www.mk.ru/social/2020/07/28/klounprezident-i-klounterrorist-zelenskiy-proyavil-chelovechnost.html.

48 Mykhaylo Zabrodskyi et al., "Preliminary Lessons in Conventional Warfighting from Russia's Invasion of Ukraine: February – July 2022," *Royal United Services Institute*, November 30, 2022, https://www.rusi.org/explore-our-research/publications/special-resources/preliminary-lessons-conventional-warfighting-russias-invasion-ukraine-february-july-2022.

49 Holly Bancroft, "'Nonsense': Russia Dismisses US Claims of False Flag Operation in Ukraine," *Independent*, February 4, 2022, https://www.independent.co.uk/news/world/europe/russia-us-ukraine-invasion-b2007598.html.

50 Calder Walton, "False-Flag Invasions Are a Russian Specialty," *Foreign Policy*, February 4, 2022, https://foreignpolicy.com/2022/02/04/false-flag-invasions-are-a-russian-specialty/.

51 Vladimir Putin, "Address by the President of the Russian Federation," Official Kremlin Website, February 24, 2022, http://en.kremlin.ru/events/president/news/67843; for the original Russian version, see Vladimir Putin, "Обращение Президента Российской Федерации" [Address by the President of the Russian Federation], *Official Kremlin Website*, February 24, 2022, http://kremlin.ru/events/president/news/67843.

52 "Фейк: В биолабораториях Украины проводили опыты с коронавирусом летучих мышей" [Fake: Tests using bat coronavirus were conducted in Ukrainian biological laboratories], StopFake.org, March 10, 2022, https://www.stopfake.org/ru/fejk-v-biolaboratoriyah-ukrainy-provodili-opyty-s-koronavirusom-letuchih-myshej/.

53 "China Pushes Conspiracy Theory about U.S. Labs in Ukraine," *Bloomberg*, March 8, 2022, https://www.bloomberg.com/news/articles/2022-03-08/china-pushes-russia-conspiracy-theory-about-u-s-labs-in-ukraine.

54 Jon Jackson, "QAnon Embraces Russia Conspiracy Theories on Ukraine Labs," *Newsweek*, March 10, 2022, https://www.newsweek.com/qanon-embraces-russia-conspiracy-theories-ukraine-labs-1686816.

55 Mariia Shchur and Robert Coalson, "Падіння літака рейсу MH17: одна трагедія, одна правда, безліч версій" [The fall of flight MH17: One tragedy, one truth, and an infinite number of versions], *Radio Svoboda*, July 17, 2015, https://www.radiosvoboda.org/a/27133581.html.

56 Bálint Magyar and Bálint Madlovics, *A Concise Field Guide to Post-Communist Regimes: Actors, Institutions and Dynamics* (Budapest – Vienna – New York: Central European University Press, 2022), 68

57 Peter Pomerantsev, quoted in Joshua Yaffa, "Is Russian Meddling as Dangerous as We Think?" *The New Yorker*, September 7, 2020, https://www.newyorker.com/magazine/2020/09/14/is-russian-meddling-as-dangerous-as-we-think.

58   Anatolii Kropivnitskii and Alia Denisenko, "'Мне с этим легче жить': почему факты не спасут от пропаганды" [It's easier for me to live with this: Why facts will not save us from propaganda], *Posle*, December 14, 2022, accessed January 16, https://posle.media/mne-s-etim-legche-zhit-pochemu-fakty-ne-spasut-ot-propagandy/.

59   "Вниманию российских средств массовой информации!" [Attention Russian media!], Roskomnadzor, March 27, 2022, https://rkn.gov.ru/news/rsoc/news74224.htm.

60   Elizaveta Goriacheva, "'Эхо Москвы' и 'Дождь' закрыты, но это не значит, что замолчали и их журналисты. Рассказываем, где их теперь смотреть, слушать и читать" [Echo of Moscow and Dozhd are now shut down, but this does not mean that their journalists have gone silent. We explain where they can be watched, listened to, and read], *Meduza*, March 27, 2022, https://meduza.io/slides/eho-moskvy-i-dozhd-zakryty-no-eto-ne-znachit-chto-zamolchali-i-ih-zhurnalisty-rasskazyvaem-gde-ih-teper-smotret-slushat-i-chitat.

61   "Роскомнадзор объяснил блокировку 'Медузы' и других СМИ 'лживой информацией о сущности военной операции' в Украине" [Roskomnadzor has explained the blocking of Meduza and other media with "fake information about the nature of the military operation" in Ukraine], *Meduza*, March 4, 2022, https://meduza.io/news/2022/03/04/roskomnadzor-ob-yasnil-blokirovku-meduzy-i-drugih-smi-rasprostraneniem-lzhivoy-informatsii-o-suschnosti-voennoy-operatsii-v-ukraine.

62   "Роскомнадзор ограничил доступ к изданию 'Новая газета. Европа'" [Roskomnadzor has restricted access to Novaia Gazeta. Evropa], *RIA Novosti*, April 29, 2022, https://ria.ru/20220429/dostup-1786120187.html.

63   William Andrews Evans, *The Anomaly of Ekho Moskvy: Adaptation Strategies for the Survival of Diversity of Viewpoints in Russian Media During the Putin Era*, master thesis, Department of Slavic and European Studies, Duke University, 2012, accessed January 16, 2023, https://dukespace.lib.duke.edu/dspace/bitstream/handle/10161/5519/Evans_duke_0066N_11445.pdf?sequence=1

64   Oksana Moroz, "Від 'хорошого' до 'корисного' один Крим. Як опозиційні росіяни підігрують пропаганді РФ. Дослідження" [From "good" to "useful" in one Crimea. How opposition-minded Russians play into the hands of Russian Federation propaganda], *Ukrainska Pravda*, November 9, 2022, https://www.pravda.com.ua/articles/2022/11/9/7375505/.

65   Based on data from Radiomap.eu.

66   Sergei Vysotskii, "ГУЛАГ от Донбасса до Владивостока: 'ЛДНР' поглотило Россию" [GULAG from Donbas to Vladivostok: The LDNR has swallowed up Russia], *Obozrevatel*, September 22, 2022, https://news.obozrevatel.com/russia/gulag-ot-donbassa-do-vladivostoka-ldnr-poglotilo-rossiyu.htm.

67   Marina Perevozkina, [Everyone has lost Zelensky], *Moskovskii Komsomolets*, February 25, 2022, https://www.mk.ru/politics/2022/02/25/zelenskogo-vse-poteryali.html.

68   "Володин сообщил, что Зеленский покинул Киев" [Volodin says that Zelensky feft Kyiv], *RIA Novosti*, February 26, 2022, https://ria.ru/20220226/zelenskiy-1775244614.html.

69   "Украинский депутат утверждает, что Зеленский давно сбежал из Киева" [Ukrainian MP claims Zelensky left Kyiv long ago], *RIA Novosti*, March 11, 2022, https://ria.ru/20220311/zelenskiy-1777702499.html.

70   "ФЕЙК: Владимир Зеленский сбежал из Украины после вторжения России" [FAKE: Volodymyr Zelensky escaped Ukraine after Russia's invasion], *Vox Ukraine*, March 11, 2022, https://voxukraine.org/ru/fejk-vladymyr-zelenskyj-sbezhal-yz-ukrayny-posle-vtorzhenyya-rossyy/.

71   Ani Kistauri, "Где записываются видеообращения Зеленского и что утверждают кремлевские СМИ?" [Where are Zelensky's addresses shot and what does the Kremlin media claim?], *Myth Detector*, October 17, 2022, https://mythdetector.ge/ru/gde-zapisyvayutsya-videoobrashheniya-zelenskogo-i-chto-utverzhdayut-kremlevskie-smi/.

72   "Фейк: Визит Зеленского в Бахмут – постановка" [Fake: Zelensky's visit to Bakhmut was staged], *Stopfake.org*, December 22, 2022, https://www.stopfake.org/ru/fejk-vizit-zelenskogo-v-bahmut-postanovka/.

73. Kateryna Honcharova, "Звідки у ЗМІ з'явилася теза про 'Зеленського-наркомана'" [Where did the media claim about Zelensky as a drug addict come from], *Detector Media*, 26 April 2019, https://ms.detector.media/manipulyatsii/post/22796/2019-04-26-zvidky-u-zmi-zyavylasya-teza-pro-zelenskogo-narkomana/.
74. David Gilbert, "The Kremlin Keeps Trying to Call Volodymyr Zelensky a Drug Addict," *Vice*, April 27, 2022, accessed January 18, 2023, https://www.vice.com/en/article/88gpd3/russia-zelenskyy-drug-addict.
75. "Указ президента про позбавлення громадянства Коломойського та Ко є, але засекречений – джерело ZN.UA в ОПУ" [There is a decree about stripping Kolomoisky and co. of Ukrainian citizenship, but it's a secret – ZN.UA source in the Presidential Office], *Dzerkalo Tyzhnia*, July 21, 2022, https://zn.ua/ukr/POLITICS/ukaz-prezidenta-pro-pozbavlennja-hromadjanstva-kolomojskoho-ta-ko-je-ale-zasekrechenij-dzherelo-dtua-v-opu.html.
76. Roman Kostiuchenko, "В Україні 'націоналізують,' 'Мотор Січ,' 'Укрнафту,' 'АвтоКрАЗ': Зеленський пояснив, навіщо" [In Ukraine, Motor Sich, Ukrnafta, and AvtoKrAz will be nationalized. Zelensky explained why], *Obozrevatel*, November 7, 2022, https://news.obozrevatel.com/ukr/economics/economy/v-ukraini-natsionalizuyut-motor-sich-ukrnaftu-avtokraz-zmi.htm.
77. Lusine Voskanyan, "Неделя с Владимиром Соловьевым: основные тезисы и манипуляции кремлевской пропаганды" [The week with Vladimir Soloviev: The main theses and manipulations of Kremlin propaganda], Fact Investigation Platform, May 13, 2022, https://fip.am/ru/19284.
78. Elena Leksina, "Эксперт: Зеленский шантажирует Запад разговорами о ядерном оружии" [Expert: Zelensky is blackmailing the West with talk about nuclear weapons], *Vzglyad*, February 20, 2022, 2023, https://vz.ru/news/2022/2/20/1144639.html; Mikhail Katkov, "Украине указали на место. Чем Зеленский разозлил Запад" [Ukraine was put in its place: How Zelensky angered the West], *RIA Novosti*, July 2, 2022, https://ria.ru/20220702/ukraina-1799511548.html.
79. Connor Perrett, "Russia is Promoting 'Outlandish and Ridiculous' Propaganda about the Killings in Bucha, Fact-Checkers Say," *Business Insider*, April 6, 2022, https://www.businessinsider.com/russia-promoting-outlandish-and-ridiculous-propaganda-about-bucha-killings-2022-4.
80. Based on research in a yet unpublished chapter for a collective project researching the unrecognized republics in the post-Soviet space: Kostiantyn Fedorenko, "Media and Legitimization Strategies of the De Facto Regimes," 2022.
81. Christo Grozev, "Russian Spying is Privatized and Competitive. Counterespionage Should Be Too," *Newsweek*, July 27, 2020, https://www.newsweek.com/russia-report-intelligence-trolls-interference-1520725; Matthew A. Lauder, "'Wolves of the Russian Spring': An Examination of the Night Wolves As a Proxy for the Russian Government – Analysis," *Canadian Military Journal* 18, no. 3 (2018), 5, http://www.journal.forces.gc.ca/vol18/no3/page5-eng.asp.
82. David Gilbert, "Russian TikTok Influencers Are Being Paid to Spread Kremlin Propaganda," *Vice*, March 11, 2022, https://www.vice.com/en/article/epxken/russian-tiktok-influencers-paid-propaganda.
83. IA Amitel, "Сколько заработали 'За Россию' спевшие перед барнаульцами Uma2rman и Сергей Бобунец" [How much did Uma2rman and Sergei Bobunets make to sing in Baranaul for Za Rossiyu], *Amic*, May 13, 2022, https://www.amic.ru/news/obschestvo/skolko-zarabotali-za-rossiyu-spevshie-pered-barnaulcami-uma2rman-i-sergey-bobunec.
84. Roman Petrenko, "В ефірі телеканалу вийшов текст 'капітуляції Зеленського,' президент відреагував" [Text of Zelensky's capitulation appeared live on TV, the president reacted], *Ukrainska Pravda*, March 16, 2022, https://www.pravda.com.ua/news/2022/03/16/7331861/.
85. Maksym Inshakov, "Російські хакери зламали трансляцію Україна – Уельс та замість футболу пустили пропаганду РФ" [Russian hackers hacked the Ukraine – Wales broadcast and broadcast Russian Federation propaganda instead of football], *Obozrevatel*, June 5, 2022, https://news.obozrevatel.com/ukr/sport/football/rosijski-hakeri-zlamali-translyatsiyu-ukraina-uels-ta-zamist-futbolu-pustili-propagandu-rf.htm.

86 Olena Kachurovska, "Зеленский прокомментировал фейк о своем здоровье" [Zelensky commented on the fake about his health], *Korrespondent*, July 21, 2022, https://korrespondent.net/ukraine/4497507-zelenskyi-prokommentyroval-feik-o-svoem-zdorove.

87 D7News | Demokratychna Sokyra, Telegram post, November 20, 2022, at 09:34, https://t.me/D7_channel/22330?single.

88 Persha Pryvatna Memarnia, Telegram post, February 1, 2022, at 16:58, https://t.me/privatnamemarnya/12943.

89 Alona Mazurenko, "'Combat Mosquitoes' Follow 'Dirty Bomb': Russian Representative to UN Tells More Frenzy Lies," *Ukrainska Pravda*, October 28, 2022, https://news.yahoo.com/combat-mosquitoes-dirty-bomb-russian-151700522.html.

90 Pjotr Sauer, "'We Have Already Lost': Far-Right Russian Bloggers Slam Military Failures," *The Guardian*, September 8, 2022, https://www.theguardian.com/world/2022/sep/08/we-have-already-lost-far-right-russian-bloggers-slam-kremlin-over-army-response.

91 Sarah Lain, "Russia and the West: Whose 'Rules-Based Order' Is It Anyway?" *Royal United Services Institute*, July 6, 2017, https://www.rusi.org/explore-our-research/publications/commentary/russia-and-west-whose-rules-based-order-it-anyway.

92 Volodymyr Fesenko, "Два тижні без 'каналів Медведчука': як змінився рейтинг Зеленського, Порошенка та кума Путіна?" [Two weeks without Medvedchuk's channels: How did the ratings for Zelensky, Poroshenko, and Putin's godfather change?], *24 Kanal*, February 16, 2021, https://24tv.ua/dva-tizhni-bez-kanaliv-medvedchuka-yak-zminivsya-novini-ukrayini_n1543831.

93 "China Pushes Conspiracy Theory About U.S. Labs in Ukraine," *Bloomberg*, March 8, 2022, https://www.bloomberg.com/news/articles/2022-03-08/china-pushes-russia-conspiracy-theory-about-u-s-labs-in-ukraine.

94 Sophie Lawton, "Far-Right Influencers Push Russian Propaganda to Claim the Reported Potential War Crimes in Bucha Are a False Flag," *Media Matters*, August 4, 2022, https://www.mediamatters.org/russias-invasion-ukraine/far-right-influencers-push-russian-propaganda-claim-reported-potential-war; Jon Jackson, "QAnon Embraces Russia Conspiracy Theories on Ukraine Labs," *Newsweek*, October 3, 2022, https://www.newsweek.com/qanon-embraces-russia-conspiracy-theories-ukraine-labs-1686816.

95 "Tucker Carlson Accuses Volodymyr Zelensky of Waging a 'War Against Christianity,'" *Media Matters*, December 21, 2022, https://www.mediamatters.org/fox-news/tucker-carlson-accuses-volodymyr-zelensky-waging-war-against-christianity.

96 E.g. Sonia Koshkina, "УПЦ (нібито не МП): Синод як вирок самим собі" [The UOC [the Ukrainian Orthodox Church] (allegedly not the MP [Moscow Patriarchy]): The synod as a sentence to itself], *LB.ua*, November 24, 2022, https://lb.ua/society/2022/11/24/536945_upts_nibito_mp_sinod_yak_virok.html; Liudmyla Zhukova, "Зрадники в рясах: у Мелітополі за російськими паспортами стоять священики УПЦ МП" (Traitors in robes: In Melitopol, priests of the Ukrainian Orthodox Church – Moscow Patriarchy are queuing for Russian passports], *RBC Ukraine*, July 21, 2022, https://styler.rbc.ua/ukr/zhizn/predateli-ryasah-melitopole-rossiyskimi-pasportami-1658392942.html.

97 On the role of the church in Ukraine, see the chapter by Tetiana Kalynychenko and Denis Brylov, "Ukraine's Religious Landscape: Between Repression and Pluralism," in *Ukraine's Patronal Democracy and the Russian Invasion*, 353–72.

98 Michael Schwirtz et al., "How Putin's War in Ukraine Became a Catastrophe for Russia."

99 Max Seddon and Polina Ivanova, "How Putin's Technocrats Saved the Economy to Fight a War They Opposed," *Financial Times*, December 16, 2022, https://www.ft.com/content/fe5fe0ed-e5d4-474e-bb5a-10c9657285d2.

100 Michael Schwirtz et al., "Putin's War: The Inside Story of a Catastrophe," *The New York Times*, December 17, 2022, sec. World, https://www.nytimes.com/interactive/2022/12/16/world/europe/russia-putin-war-failures-ukraine.html.

[101] Andreas Umland, "Aleksandr Dugin – A Russian Scarecrow," *New Eastern Europe*, March 20, 2017, https://neweasterneurope.eu/2017/03/20/alexander-dugin-a-russian-scarecrow/.
[102] @prof_preobr, Twitter post, November 15, 2022, at 12:59, https://twitter.com/prof_preobr/status/1592487545316995075.
[103] Anastasiia Pecheniuk, "Думали, что это для Кремля: тиктокеры из РФ за деньги озвучили пропагандистский бред (видео)" [They thought it was for the Kremlin: TikTok users from the Russian Federation voiced propaganda drivel for money], *Unian*, December 28, 2022, https://www.unian.net/russianworld/dumali-chto-eto-dlya-kremlya-tiktokery-iz-rf-za-dengi-ozvuchili-propagandistskiy-bred-video-12093204.html.
[104] Magyar and Madlovics, *A Concise Field Guide*, 152-54.
[105] Sofiia Mindzhotsa, "У ЄС розраховують, що Україна врахує рекомендації Венеційської комісії до закону про КСУ" [The EU expects Ukraine to consider the recommendations of the Venice Commission regarding the Constitutional Court of Ukraine bill], *24 Kanal*, December 23, 2022, https://24tv.ua/reforma-ksu-yes-napolyagayut-shhob-ukrayina-dosluhalasya-venetsiys-koyi_n2223097; Dasha Ptakhovska, "Законопроект №5655 нарушит права землевладельцев и уничтожит достижения децентрализации, – АГУ" [Bill 5655 would violate land owner rules, destroy the achievements of decentralization – Association of Ukrainian Cities], *24 Kanal*, December 13, 2022, https://24tv.ua/ru/chto-ne-tak-zakonoproektom-5655-agu-sdelali-zajavlenie_n2216924.
[106] Magyar and Madlovics, *A Concise Field Guide*, 156–57.
[107] Magyar and Madlovics, *A Concise Field Guide*, 156–57.
[108] Magyar and Madlovics, *A Concise Field Guide*, 161.
[109] "Моніторинг російського суспільства: Дзеркало Росії, листопад-грудень 2022 р," [Monitoring of Russian Society: Mirror of Russia, November-December 2022], ikar-thinktank.org, December 19, 2022, https://ikar-thinktank.org/ru/explorations/13.

Authoritarian Deflation: How Russia Lost the Information War against the West[1]
Péter Krekó and Boglárka Rédl

1. Introduction: the rise and fall of Russia's soft power

American "soft power," or the ability of the United States to win hearts and minds in the world and to serve as a model, has long been viewed with envy in Moscow. The Russian state has officially been paying more attention to soft power since the "color revolutions,"[2] primarily those in Ukraine and Georgia, which are perceived as success stories of Western soft power in initiating political change. The application of soft power by Russia, therefore, has been highly reactive from the very beginning. As one participant of the Valdai Club wrote in 2012: "Russia today is paying much more attention to soft power and intends to use it to restore its position in the world. And now—unlike in the 1990s or even the 2000s—this policy is backed by the appropriate financial resources."[3] President Putin has also talked about the importance of "soft power" several times publicly, both as a threat by the West and as a tool that Russia has to apply more cleverly in order to adapt to the changing demands and nature of public diplomacy. On February 11, 2013, when talking to Russian diplomats, he argued: "Competent use of 'soft power' methods is ever more of a priority. We need to boost the Russian language's position, be active in promoting a positive image of Russia abroad, and learn how to organically integrate ourselves into the global information flows."[4]

Russian soft power, obviously, has its limitations in persuading Western publics. Indeed, there seems to be an inverse correlation between how much Russia spends on winning the hearts and minds of the people and how popular it is perceived internationally. Of course, correlation is not equivalent to causation. The main reason for this inverse equivalence is that Russia begins spending more to persuade the international public usually *after* acknowledging its lost influence or outright ignoring the territorial integrity of other countries. *Russia Today* (RT), the propaganda channel of the Kremlin, for example, was established in 2005, one year after the Orange Revolution in Ukraine. Russky Mir, Moscow's version of the British Council or the Goethe Institute, was established in 2009, one year after the invasion of Georgia. RT significantly expanded after the 2014 annexation of Crimea as well.

The Crimean conflict seems to have been a turning point, after which the Russian state and other related actors started to invest immensely more in changing the image of Russia. As Matveeva argues, the 2014 crisis in Ukraine "brought greater consistency to Moscow's approach, which has become more strategic, mixing different elements in pursuit of foreign policy objectives."[5] At the same time, as we will see below, these attempts have proved rather unsuccessful in creating a more friendly image for the Kremlin.

On the other hand, before the full-scale invasion began in February 2022, Russia was successful in misleading and deceiving international public opinion about its intentions. Most experts, politicians, and the public in the Western world seemed to believe that Russia was only bluffing, and that the British and American secret services, which had warned well in advance about the possibility of an invasion, were just crying wolf and adding to the fog of disinformation. Thus, despite a military build-up taking place over many months, Russia was still able to surprise the Western public with the invasion.

This chapter aims to examine the extent of Russia's success in shaping public opinion following its invasion. By placing recent events within a broader international and temporal context, we can gain a better understanding of the effectiveness of Russia's persuasion tactics. The chapter's central claim is that Russia's soft power appeal has been severely undermined by the annexation of Crimea. However, Russia has maintained its ability to exert influence on political processes by engaging in "sharp power" tactics such as infiltrating the information and political spaces of Western countries. Additionally, Russia has used "authoritarian inflation" to create the appearance of being larger than life. Despite the continued popularity of some of its narratives in certain countries, Russia has largely failed in its information warfare against the West since the start of the invasion.

2. Russia's soft power and authoritarian inflation before 2022

2.1. The concept of soft power

Soft power, in its original meaning, is the ability of a country to persuade others to do what it wants without direct force or coercion, but solely through attraction.[6] In other words, it is the ability to change the behavior of others without using either the stick (military intervention) or the carrot (economic incentives). Soft power is about the "charm offensive": winning the hearts (and, to a smaller extent, the minds) of other nations via the "export" of values, culture, ideas, and attractive personalities. Soft power is about the role model status of a country with respect to other countries.

The advantage of the concept of soft power in trying to capture the nature of Russian influence is that it places the emphasis on the similarities between the Russian and Western toolkits, which is important for at least two reasons. First, as we argued before, Russia uses several soft power tools *because* they perceive that the West is using them successfully. Second, it better describes the nature of the influence, which is often much less centralized, more *ad hoc*, and network-like than as seen from the West.

In the following, a comparison of Russian and Western soft power will be carried out, highlighting the similarities and the differences.

2.2. Similarities of Russian and Western soft power

Even in the original description of soft power, the players are diverse: not only diplomats but universities, private companies, think tanks, and churches are involved as well.[7] Russia's attempt is aimed at "controlling chaos" while influencing Western political processes.[8] Besides the Russian foreign ministry and the secret services—mainly the Federal Security Service of the Russian Federation (FSB) and the Main Intelligence Directorate (GRU)—several other actors are also involved, such as oligarchs (like Konstantin Malofeev and Dmytro Firtash), think tanks (like the Valdai Club), the Russian Orthodox Church, government-organized non-governmental organizations (GONGOs), Russian politicians (not only from the United Russia party, but from Rodina and the Communist Party as well), ideologues (like Aleksandr Dugin and Ivan Ilyin), and financial institutions (like Vnyesekombank), who operate in a more or less coordinated, but not totally centralized manner, enjoying a degree of autonomy. This understanding of Russian soft power has pragmatic implications: the behavior of more decentralized, network-like organizational structures is more difficult to predict.

When it comes to foreign policy, the Kremlin often just "mimics" what they think the West is doing. The most obvious examples are the creation of think tanks, such as the Valdai Club, or the establishment of alternative human rights organizations, the Russian equivalents of Freedom House intended to influence political debates.[9] The "militarization" of soft power, to a certain extent, is also a result of this mimicking strategy. Half a year after the annexation of Crimea, in October 2014, Putin himself said this at a Security Council meeting:

> We need to take into account the risks and threats that exist in the information sphere. We see that some countries are attempting to use their dominance in the global information space to pursue not only economic but also military and political objectives. They make active use of information systems as an instrument of so-called "soft power" to achieve their goals.[10]

Another important example of this mimicking was when General Valery Gerasimov, the Chief of the General Staff, argued in his infamous article (wrongly taken as a "doctrine") for the need of a change in approach in the Russian armed forces, and for the development of more asymmetric tools. Gerasimov's main argument was that the West had demonstrated that they were using information and soft power in a more clever way not only during the "so-called colored revolutions" in the post-Soviet space, but also during the Arab Spring. Russia should meet this challenge, Gerasimov argued, exactly because the West is more successful.[11] The irony here is that the "doctrine," which is treated by many as the bible for non-linear war, is, in fact, Gerasimov's (conspiracy theory-based) description of how, in his opinion, the West and the United States use non-linear war against Russia and its allies. Another example of this open mimicking is the self-critical statement of the head of the Russkiy Mir Foundation, Vyacheslav Nikonov from 2013. In an interview, Nikonov said that Russia has a real deficit in the instruments of soft power:

> They include global mass media, that the Western countries have but that Russia practically lacks [...]. They also include nongovernmental organizations acting on the international arena. In the United States, there are about 15,000 such organizations. In Russia, at a maximum you would need the fingers on two hands to count them—and there are only a few major ones.[12]

The end goal of the Russian soft power-based foreign policy is similar to the foreign policy of other countries: to increase its international economic and political influence via long-term investments in culture, media, and NGOs in order to maximize long-term influence.[13]

2.3. The main distinctive features of Russian soft power

However, the similarities noted above do not mean that the soft power of Russia and the West are identical. Given that the term "soft power" was originally created to describe the nature of US foreign policy, it is obvious that the concept does not perfectly align with Russian influence efforts; the mimicking is never exact.

According to Marcel Van Herpen, probably the best observer of Russian soft power, the soft power of the Putin regime hardly even exists, constituting instead merely "hard power in velvet gloves."[14] He argues that the lines between soft and hard power are often blurred, especially in the context of international conflict. Russian support for extremist organizations, and the interventions in Georgia and Ukraine (the latter preceded by information warfare) are just a few examples of this principle.[15]

There are three important and distinctive features of Russian soft power attempts:

1. *Invention.* First, active measures and secret service operations play an important role in the Kremlin's soft power toolkit: this is the "invention" aspect of Russian soft power.[16] The intelligence services (especially the GRU, but to a certain extent the FSB and the SVR as well) are typically involved in running the soft power machine, even if, as mentioned above, But usually the Kremlin or security services do, or can, take control of its operations. A prime example is the above-mentioned Vyacheslav Nikonov, current leader of the Russkiy Mir Foundation, the "British Council of Russia," a GONGO created by Putin with a presidential decree in 2007. Nikonov was the former secretary to the head of the KGB and is the grandson of Vyacheslav Molotov, the Soviet foreign minister under Joseph Stalin. While the official goal of the foundation is to promote the Russian language and culture internationally (copying, again, the example of the British Council), it works in close cooperation with the Ministry of Foreign Affairs, the secret services, and the Russian Orthodox Church in exporting an ultraconservative, illiberal (neo-)Eurasianist ideology.[17] Another example might be Prigozhin's media empire and notorious "troll farm," which was created with the aid of the Kremlin and was immediately taken over by the security agencies of Russia after Prigozhin started his mutiny in June 2023.[18]

2. *Repulsion.* Second, in Russian soft power, creating "repulsion" between Russia and the West is at least as important as shaping attraction towards Russia itself. Russian soft power aims to discredit the West and make Russia more glorious by denigrating the image of the competitor. The way in which Russia and its president are made attractive is more indirect than direct—making Putin and Russia more "beautiful" by painting the West as "ugly." Depicting the liberal West as a liberal, valueless, nihilist community is essential in making Russia more attractive in comparison.[19]

3. *Confusion.* Third, the Kremlin's messaging is neither straight, linear, nor coherent (which is, obviously, not even technically possible in Western information environments). It aims to deliver several kinds of often contradictory messages, and pushes conflicting narratives in order to confuse the audience and create a world where "nothing is true and everything is possible."[20] This form of bizarre "postmodern dictatorship"[21] which Putin has built up in Russia is exported through the use of soft power tools. Supporting fringe forces on both sides and spreading conspiracy theories are essential and interrelated elements of this strategy.[22]

Of course, one can argue that in taking all these features together, "soft" power is an understatement, and applying it to the influence efforts of Russian actors might overstretch the limits of this term. An alternative to this term, one which has appeared recently in expert discourses, is "sharp power," which is mainly applied to the influence policies of authoritarian regimes such as Russia and China. These two countries see the West's soft power as an essential threat to their existence, and in turn, they elaborate less "soft" tools as a response.[23] Their tools are, in other words, sharp, as "they seek to 'pierce, penetrate, or perforate' the political and information environments of targeted countries."[24] As the inventors of this term, Christopher Walker and Jessica Ludwig argue, "this authoritarian influence is not principally about attraction or even persuasion; instead, it centers on distraction and manipulation."[25]

In the sections below, we will use both terms to grasp the nature and success of influence policies pursued by the Russian state and its proxies.

2.4. Authoritarian inflation: how Russia showed itself bigger than it was before the invasion

Surveys suggest that, in the last decade (and especially since 2014) Russia's soft power appeal has been anything but strong. Between 2010 and 2020, the share of citizens who viewed Putin's Russia favorably dropped from 49 to 19 percent in the United States, from 46 to 24 percent in the United Kingdom, and from 50 to 30 percent in Germany, according to a poll conducted by Pew Research.[26] In eight of the ten countries surveyed, Russia's popularity declined, showing an increase only in Italy. Yet despite its lack of likeability, Russia is seen as increasingly influential: across 25 countries surveyed by Pew, the share of respondents who believed Russia would play a more important global role than it had ten years ago was more than twice as high (42 percent) as the share who thought that Russia had grown less important (19 percent).

In short, while Russia is viewed with increasing antipathy and confidence in her leaders is low (especially in the democratic world), Russia was nonetheless seen as increasingly powerful prior to 2022. Russia has been remarkably more successful in employing sharp power than soft power, leading to a phenomenon that may be termed "authoritarian inflation."[27]

Authoritarian inflation is both a component and a byproduct of the sharp-power toolkit. In some cases, sharp-power activities may be specifically designed to pervade the information environments of democracies with narratives trumpeting the superiority of authoritarian models. In other cases, perceptions of authoritarian power may be a secondary effect of other operations, such as election-interference efforts that end up raising the profile of Putin's regime. Manipulating democratic institutions enables authoritarian superpowers not only to undermine the political systems of target countries, but also to create false impressions of their own near-omnipotence.

The success of authoritarian inflation lies in the public's perception of autocratic powers as stronger, richer, and more influential than they actually are. In Hungary, for instance, a survey conducted by the Political Capital Institute in 2018[28] revealed that the majority of the population had an inflated view of Russia's economic and military might. A staggering 80% of respondents overestimated Russia's significance in Hungary's trade relations, with half of them ranking it among Hungary's top six export partners, when in reality it was only the seventeenth largest. Similarly, 54% of respondents overestimated Russia's GDP relative to that of the much stronger UK and German economies. Furthermore, most Hungarians believe that Russia's military expenditures are higher than that of the US (which is ten times greater) or Beijing (which is three times greater), with two-thirds of them overestimating Russia's relative military spending. This phenomenon is not limited to Hungary: six out of nine Central and Eastern European countries polled by Globsec[29] showed that more people believed Russia to have the world's strongest military rather than the US.

For a long time, Kremlin messaging has focused on portraying Russia as economically strong and militarily threatening, with exaggerated claims of victory in hypothetical conflicts against NATO and veiled threats of nuclear war. Russian propaganda outlets, such as RT, have even gone so far as to suggest that Russia's GDP surpasses that of some G7 members, while other propaganda channels have tried, without evidence, to present Russian innovation as the driving force behind major technological advances such as Elon Musk's space shuttle and AstraZeneca's COVID-19 vaccine.[30] These efforts have failed to win over public opinion, but they have been successful in creating an illusion of Russian dominance over Western policy and politics, despite the country's relatively limited geopolitical reach.

One former Kremlin spin doctor, Gleb Pavlovsky, has observed that Russia can now simulate global power and influence by leaving its fingerprints on hacking and other influence operations, providing a theatrical performance for a global audience.[31] Nevertheless, before the 2022 invasion Russia had a real ability to engage selectively in geopolitical affairs and to "punch above its weight."

In sum, if we want to assess the success of Russian disinformation before the war, we have to identify what we understand by its goals. Focusing on the most important goals Russia wanted to achieve, three main points need to be mentioned with regards to the pre-invasion period:

1. *to be loved,* meaning the goal of increasing the popularity of Putin's Russia and his regime;

2. *to be feared*, meaning the goal of being seen as a superpower that is capable of reaching its goals;

3. *to be heard*, meaning the goal of selling the Russian narrative, including conspiracy theories, but also spreading a high number of contradictory narratives with the aim of "generating noise" to confuse the West and Western public opinion.

We can measure the success of these goals from a very pragmatic perspective: the extent to which they have been able to have some impact on public opinion and in altering political decisions. As the above data shows, since 2014 Russia's Western-directed attempts have been highly unsuccessful regarding point one ("to be loved"), while their efforts regarding points 2 and 3 ("to be feared" and "heard") have been only partially successful.

3. Authoritarian deflation: the crumbling image of a "strong Russia" in the West after the war

3.1. War propaganda: conspiracy theories and the spread of the Russian narrative in target countries

Dimitry Kiselyov, director general of Russia's state-controlled Rossiya Segodnya media conglomerate, once said: "Objectivity is a myth which is proposed and imposed on us."[32] This epistemological uncertainty might be one of the most successful propaganda exports of the Russian Federation. The receptivity to the relativizing message that all superpowers are lying and that we have to be suspicious in every direction goes well beyond the "fanbase" of Putin and Russia. In Political Capital's summer 2022 poll, one-third of the Hungarian population tended to agree with the statement: "Everyone lies and spreads fake news in this war." As Rand Waltzman argues, one of the main goals of Russian disinformation is to target audiences with multiple, conflicting narratives in order to sow seeds of distrust and doubt about the European Union (EU) as well as national governments.[33]

Conspiracy theories are very successful tools in spreading this epistemological uncertainty in a fashionable, entertaining, and seemingly revelatory way. In these kinds of narratives, one can see old Cold War-era KGB stories recycled and applied in a present-day context. For example, in the 1980s, the KGB started an operation with the title "Operation INFEKTION," which spread the message that it was the US government that created the HIV virus in labs and had then spread it all over the world. After 2022, Russian propaganda spread stories about secret US biolabs in Ukraine that were preparing viruses to selectively infect only Russians (!). This conspiracy theory, for example, was believed by 28 percent of the Hungarian public, with the figure rising to 45% (!) among the voters of Viktor Orbán's Fidesz.[34] A Globsec poll from 2022[35] indicated that public opinions in CEE are highly vulnerable to disinformation, with countries that have stronger historical, cultural or religious ties to Russia, such as Slovakia and Bulgaria, being the most prone to accept these theories (Figure 1).

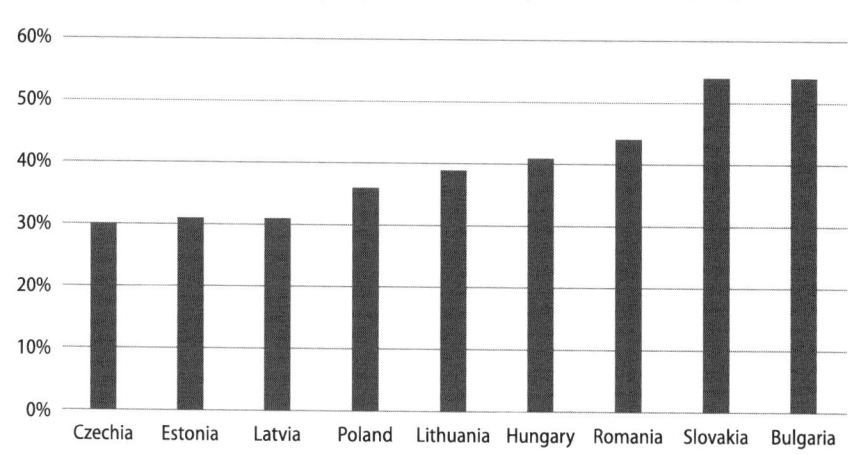

Figure 1. Average belief in three conspiracy theories and manipulative narratives (2022).

Country	Percentage
Czechia	30%
Estonia	31%
Latvia	31%
Poland	35%
Lithuania	38%
Hungary	40%
Romania	43%
Slovakia	53%
Bulgaria	53%

Source: Globsec.

Research conducted by Detector Media in June-October 2022 revealed narrative patterns of disinformation in 14 Central and Eastern European countries.[36] Unsurprisingly, the largest number of messages spreading narratives of Russian propaganda was recorded in Ukraine (almost 20% of all analyzed messages), but a high degree of propaganda was also found in other countries, such as the Baltic countries, Bulgaria, Hungary, and Poland. As for the content, most of the propaganda messaging was related to the events of the Russia-Ukraine war, with 55% suggesting that "Ukraine is losing the war" or "Ukrainians are targeting civilians and commit other war crimes"; the economic consequences of sanctions, with 17.7% claiming that "sanctions hurt the West more than Russia" or "the inflation and energy crises are caused by the false political approach of Europe and the US"; and military assistance to Ukraine, with 9.3% stating that "the West is using Ukraine to wage war against Russia" or "the war in Ukraine is not real/staged." Content was spread in both Russian and local languages, and also showed targeting with country-specific messages, such as "Poland should not help Ukraine due to their past historical conflicts."

A report from February 2023 found that "Russia's operational-level information campaigns aim either to set conditions for planned Russian operations or to mitigate Russian military failures," typically using the narrative that "Ukraine is incapable of defeating Russia because of inherent power disparities between the two states."[37] Regarding citizens of the target countries, it could be observed that Russian information sources feed into online extremist communities like European nationalists and American white supremacists on various social media platforms.[38]

The war against Ukraine has revitalized the "peace camp" in Europe. Calling for peace has become, in a bizarre manner, one of the most central arguments employed by pro-Kremlin voices all over Europe. Pro-Russian positions in this campaign often appear in the mask of the "peace" argument: If Europe wants peace, it should stay neutral and stop its support of Ukraine and sanctioning of Russia. In Hungary, after the start of the war, Fidesz's campaign messages repeated *ad nauseam* the following statement: War or peace? Those who want peace should choose the "national" side, while those who want war should side with the left. This rhetoric (amplified by Orbán's media machinery in the only informational autocracy in the EU),[39] is not unique to Hungary. In France, Marine Le Pen also structured her slogans on her constituents' fear of direct conflict. "I am obsessed with peace!" she stated during a political debate organized by TF1 television, and she went on saying: "I am afraid, sorry that I have to state it like this, that France possibly, against its will, has to join a war due to obligations forced by alliances."[40] Similar narratives are also prominent in other countries' populist parties. For example, during the Czech presidential elections that were held in January 2023, Andrej Babiš borrowed Fidesz's "pro-peace" disinformation narratives, though he was unsuccessful. In Italy, Matteo Salvini also tried to garner public support by questioning the effectiveness of sanctions against Russia.

3.2. Inefficiency on the political level: national and EU decisions to help Ukraine

While Russia seems successful in spreading conspiracy theories and other types of propaganda messages, this is not sufficient to achieve its specific objective of having an impact on political decision-making. For example, at the UN General Assembly meeting in March 2022, 141 countries voted against Russia (ordering the RF to abandon the territory of Ukraine), 35 abstained, and only a group of five—not so influential—countries voted against the resolution: Russia itself, Belarus, Eritrea, North Korea, and Syria.

The war between Russia and Ukraine in the EU's immediate vicinity has forced the EU and its member states to make a fundamental paradigm shift in their security and neighborhood policy.[41] The European "Ostpolitik," which emphasized an understanding and an open policy towards Russia, has become in many ways obsolete, as the war overturned the basic European foreign policy premise, which had sought to "pacify" the Soviet Union and then independent Russia through fruitful economic relations.

Russian threats that the supporters of Ukraine might themselves also become military targets has not dissuaded leaders from supporting Ukraine with weapons. As a sign of this change, 2022 has witnessed the shattering of a number of taboos, from German arms supplies ranging from helmets to Leopard 2 tanks to military training provided by the EU. After long hesitation, Ukraine will receive F16-s from its NATO allies. During the first year of the war, 17 EU member states, including typically hesitant nations like Germany and Sweden, have supplied Ukraine with heavy weapons, and even the EU has provided military aid. For the first time in its history, the EU authorized the transfer of lethal weapons to a third country. In one year, it has provided Ukraine with EUR 3.6 billion for arms purchases. Moreover, in November 2022 it launched a comprehensive training mission (EUMAM) with a two-year mandate for Ukrainian soldiers. This is the first EU mission to make a significant contribution to training soldiers from a non-EU country. The European countries (including the EU) allied with Ukraine have provided Ukraine with a total of nearly €15 billion in military assistance as of early 2023.

In early 2023, amid a potential Russian spring offensive, there was another significant leveling up: several member states, previously reluctant to take strong action against the Kremlin, such as Germany and France, offered modern heavy weapons from their active stockpiles. More recently, the international dialogue on the supply of fighter jets has also intensified. All this demonstrates a political commitment on the part of the EU's larger member states that is likely to shape the direction of EU foreign policy in the long term. At the same time, NATO appears unified in its response, with two more member states (Sweden and Finland) joining soon.

Lastly, in the space of just a few days the EU imposed economic sanctions of an unprecedented scale on Russia and has continued to enforce further restrictive measures since then. The European Council has passed a total of 10 sanctions packages prior to finishing this chapter, despite the reluctance of some member states (most notably Hungary), and some not-so-relevant steps to soften the sanctions (e.g., removing some oligarchs and Patriarch Kirill from the list as a result of Hungary's lobbying efforts).[42] According to estimates, the member states have taken in nearly 5 million Ukrainian refugees in total, and the EU has provided Ukraine with nearly EUR 30 billion in economic aid.

3.3. Inefficiency on the voter level: public opinion and elections

Opinion polls show that after one year, the majority of Europeans still support initiatives to help Ukraine. The data indicate a slight decrease in support for measures to help Ukraine compared to the months immediately following the outbreak of the war; nevertheless, a significant proportion of Europeans remain firmly in favor of supporting Ukraine. Although support for accepting refugees and imposing strict sanctions has fallen over the past year (by 9.1 percentage points on average), it remains well above 50% in most countries. Military and financial assistance have become slightly less popular. In Germany, the third biggest spender on military aid to Ukraine worldwide, the popularity of arms transfers has declined from 55% in March to 48% in December 2022.[43] However, this is anything but a dramatic change.

Last year, in March-April and November-December,[44] Ipsos asked questions about measures to support Ukraine in 28 countries, including 9 EU member states and the UK. The results show that, despite growing difficulties in making ends meet, a significant proportion of Europeans remain firmly supportive of the country defending itself against Russian aggression, albeit at a somewhat declining rate over time. Eurobarometer surveys show similar results.[45]

In the countries surveyed at the end of last year, there was still overwhelming support for measures to host Ukrainian refugees, even if this figure fell slightly: most notably in Germany and Belgium (by 14 percentage points), Hungary and France (by 10 percentage points), and in the UK by only 3 percentage points (Figure 2).

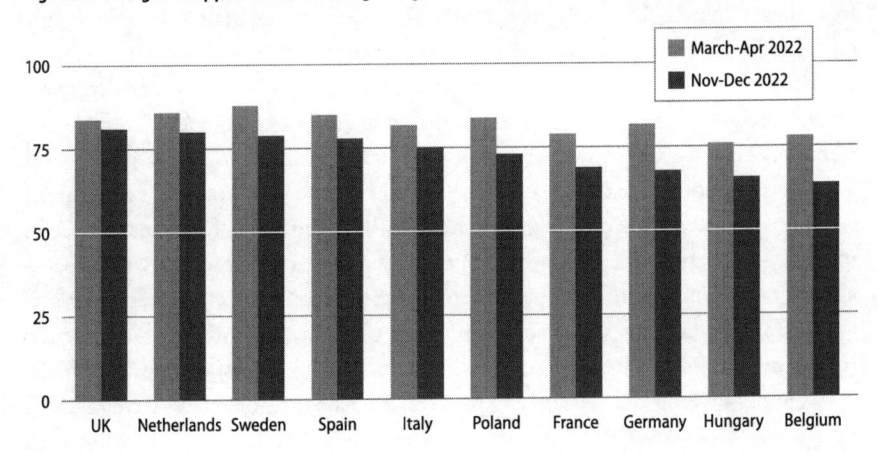

Figure 2. Change in support for welcoming refugees between March and December 2022 (%).

Source: Ipsos, Political Capital compilation.

There is also overwhelming support for sanctions in the European countries surveyed by Ipsos. After the outbreak of the war, the only country in which there was a minority (33%) in favor of tough sanctions against Russia was Hungary, while support for sanctions exceeded 60% in more than half of the countries surveyed. By the time of the second round of the survey, support for sanctions had already fallen in most countries (by more than 10 percentage points in the Netherlands, Germany and Poland) but still remained above 50% in eight out of the ten countries (Figure 3).

Figure 3. Change in the proportion of those calling for "the toughest possible sanctions" between March and December 2022 (%).

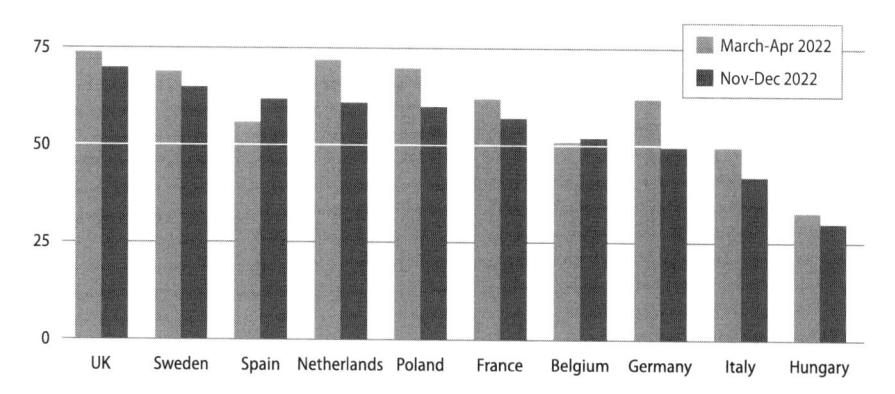

Source: Ipsos, Political Capital compilation.

As for the public perception of supporting Ukraine with weapons, the poll by Ipsos shows that it exceeds 50% in half of the countries surveyed. An important addition is that all countries surveyed by Ipsos, except Hungary, supply weapons to Ukraine (Figure 4). The level of support for arms transfers has not changed significantly in most countries over the past year: it has typically decreased but has increased in some countries, such as Spain, Poland, Belgium, and even Hungary. The latter is presumably due to the fact that it was a much hotter topic during the election campaign than at the time of the end-of-year survey. In Germany, the third biggest spender on military aid to Ukraine worldwide, public support for arms transfers fell by 7 percentage points, from 55% to 48%. Overall, therefore, Russia's strategy of deterring European countries and their leaders from supplying arms has not been successful.

Figure 4. Change in in support for policies calling for the transfer of weapons and/or air defense systems between March and December 2022 (%).

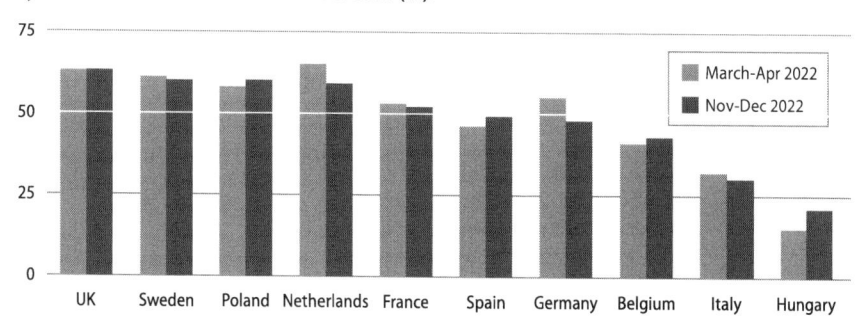

Source: Ipsos, Political Capital compilation.

Support for financial assistance lags behind that of arms transfers. In December 2022, the majority of eight out of the ten countries surveyed said that their country could not afford to provide financial assistance to Ukraine in the current economic crisis. Interestingly, the Poles, who are among the most unanimous supporters of Ukraine, are the least supportive of their government providing financial aid to Ukraine: 63% of Poles at the beginning of the war and 70% a year after rejected the possibility of financial aid. This figure is also indicative in the sense that public support for Ukraine is not a black-and-white question anywhere in Europe.

But even if the picture regarding public opinion on Ukraine is complex, elections during the past year are a powerful indicator of the persistent support for Ukraine and sections among the European public. With the exception of Hungary (and Italy, if we consider the stance of Lega and Forza Italia as junior coalition parties), no country has seen parties vocal against sanctions and helping Ukraine able to form a government in the past year. Although such campaign messages have emerged during almost all elections in Europe, parties campaigning with pro-Russian narratives, such as the French National Rally or Andrej Babiš's ANO 2011 in Czechia, have been, in most cases, defeated by candidates who were more supportive towards Ukraine. Even though there is a chance that candidates campaigning to curb support for Ukraine could come to power in Slovakia, and pro-Russian parties are gaining strength in Bulgaria, these developments are unlikely to have a lasting impact on the EU's foreign policy towards Ukraine.

The case of Sweden clearly shows that mainstream norms have changed substantially since the beginning of the invasion. The far-right-leaning Sweden Democrats party banned one of its members during the parliamentary elections after he had shared content on social media that questioned the Bucha massacre. One important reason for this may be changing attitudes of the electorate: according to a Pew Research Center study conducted in early 2022, even the attitudes of traditionally far-right, pro-Russian populist voters regarding Russia have significantly worsened compared to previous years.[46] Criticizing opponents for holding pro-Russian positions also proved to be a winning argument in many campaigns. The Swedish Social Democratic Party, for example, which was in power at the time and gained the most votes in the elections, stated that the nationalist Sweden Democrats party "poses a security threat for the country" due to their inability to choose between the US and Russia. Emmanuel Macron, in the second round of the French presidential election, called Marine Le Pen, whose previous election campaigns were indeed supported by the Kremlin, a "mercenary of Putin," and went on to win almost 60 percent of the votes.

3.4. The overall result: authoritarian deflation

As we discussed above, prior to the invasion Russia was already weak in soft power but strong in sharp power and authoritarian inflation: it was perceived as more powerful economically, militarily, and politically than it was in reality. The biggest failure of Russian information warfare during the invasion has been that this overblown image of a "strong Russia" has been blown apart. As a poll conducted by the European Council on Foreign Relations in 2023 shows, a relative majority of public opinion surveyed in 9 European countries sees Russia as weak – a stark contrast to the results of pre-invasion polls (Figure 5). The perception of a weak Russia is particularly strong in more hawkish countries such as Poland and Estonia, and somewhat weaker in more dovish countries such as Spain.

Figure 5. "Does the current conflict between Russia and Ukraine make you think Russia is stronger or weaker than you had previously thought?" (%).[47]

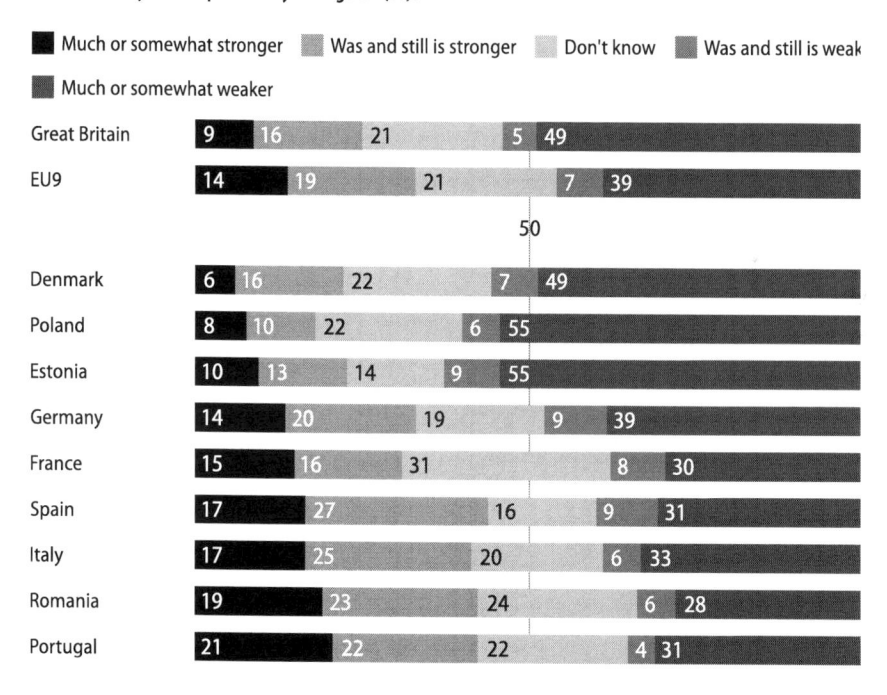

■ Much or somewhat stronger   ■ Was and still is stronger   ■ Don't know   ■ Was and still is weak
■ Much or somewhat weaker

Country	Much or somewhat stronger	Was and still is stronger	Don't know	Was and still is weak	Much or somewhat weaker
Great Britain	9	16	21	5	49
EU9	14	19	21	7	39
Denmark	6	16	22	7	49
Poland	8	10	22	6	55
Estonia	10	13	14	9	55
Germany	14	20	19	9	39
France	15	16	31	8	30
Spain	17	27	16	9	31
Italy	17	25	20	6	33
Romania	19	23	24	6	28
Portugal	21	22	22	4	31

Source: ECFR.

At the same time, the European Union is perceived to be stronger than before, according to the same poll, with a relative majority of the respondents saying that the EU is strong (Figure 6). It is also very important to note that the perceived weakness of Russia and strength of the EU seem to correlate with the support for Ukraine. The degree to which people perceive the EU as strong is closely linked to their support for Ukraine regaining its entire territory. In the nine EU countries surveyed, a majority (on average 54%) of those who view the EU as strong want Ukraine to regain all its territory, whereas only 25% prefer an immediate end to the war. On the other hand, those who see the EU as weaker have a more mixed opinion on this matter, with 38% preferring a quick end to the war, and 32% supporting Ukraine standing up to Russia.

Figure 6. "Does the current conflict between Russia and Ukraine make you think the EU is stronger or weaker than you had previously thought?" (%).

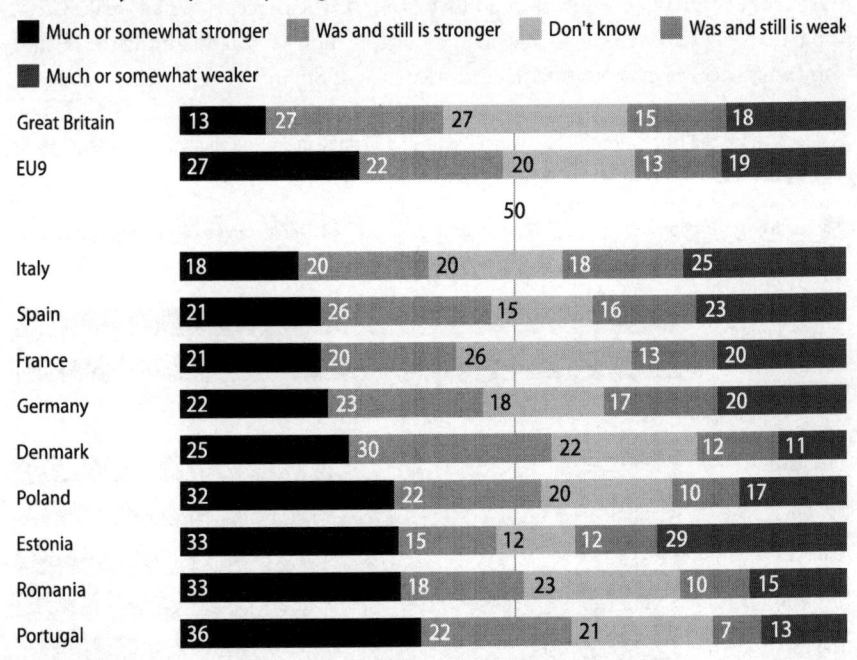

- Much or somewhat stronger
- Was and still is stronger
- Don't know
- Was and still is weak
- Much or somewhat weaker

Country	Much or somewhat stronger	Was and still is stronger	Don't know	Was and still is weaker	Much or somewhat weaker
Great Britain	13	27	27	15	18
EU9	27	22	20	13	19
Italy	18	20	20	18	25
Spain	21	26	15	16	23
France	21	20	26	13	20
Germany	22	23	18	17	20
Denmark	25	30	22	12	11
Poland	32	22	20	10	17
Estonia	33	15	12	12	29
Romania	33	18	23	10	15
Portugal	36	22	21	7	13

Source: ECFR.

4. Conclusion: why Russian disinformation proved to be so unsuccessful

In summary, it appears that while Russia made spectacular gains on the information front even after 2014 (mostly in being heard and being feared), it has been unable to achieve its strategic objectives in information warfare following the start of the invasion. Despite its efforts to sell its narrative to the Western world and undermine the EU's unity on sanctions, Russia has failed on both fronts. Moreover, Russia's once-scary reputation in the Western world has eroded, diminishing one of its last remaining assets.

One important question remains: why was Russia so unsuccessful in its information warfare in the Western world? We can think of at least four important reasons. The first one is the sanctions and strategic hit on the communications infrastructure of the Russian disinformation machine. In one of the earliest steps taken by the European Commission following the invasion, broadcasting of the Russian state-backed propaganda outlets *Russia Today* and *Sputnik* was halted in the territory of the EU, and their websites also became unavailable.[48] Major social media platforms, such as Twitter, Facebook, and YouTube, also suspended the profiles of these state-sponsored disinformation sources. As a result, the Kremlin could rely less on its traditional disinformation infrastructure than it did before.

Second, Russian information warfare lacks innovation. Rand Waltzman, an information expert with the Rand Corporation, mentioned in testimony back in 2017 that:

> At this point, Russian IO operators use relatively unsophisticated techniques systematically and on a large scale. This relative lack of sophistication leaves them open to detection. For example, existing technology can identify paid troll operations, bots, etc. The current apparent lack of technical sophistication of Russian IO techniques could derive from the fact that, so far, Russian IO has met with minimal resistance. However, if and when target forces start to counter these efforts and/or expose them on a large scale, the Russians are likely to accelerate the improvement of their techniques, leading to a cycle of counter-responses. In other words, an information warfare arms race is likely to ensue.[49]

Surprisingly, the war itself has not brought about any serious innovation in the disinformation domain—on either the technical or the narrative level. Classical counter-strategies against Russian disinformation (like switching off *RT* and *Sputnik*) therefore, proved to be highly efficient in pushing back the narratives of the Kremlin.

The third reason to be mentioned is political counter-messaging. In most Western countries, being openly pro-Russian and hostile towards Ukraine has become a stigmatized political position. Most governments have been pushing back against the central messages of the Kremlin, and have sided with Ukraine rhetorically (and action-wise). This mainstream position has weakened the impact of Russian disinformation. Russian conspiracy narratives have been able to become widespread and dominant only where they have gained notable support from mainstream governmental parties (like in Hungary).

Finally, we should note the possible boomerang effect of conspiracy theories as well. As Ilya Yablokov pointed out after the start of the full-scale invasion, Putin's regime started to believe in its own conspiracy theories (e.g. Ukraine as an oppressive, Nazi state) which it had spread for propaganda purposes.[50] Thus, Russian disinformation finally disclosed its greatest success in self-deception, having had a significantly greater impact on the leadership and the people of the Russian Federation than of the West.

Notes

1. This publication and the research was supported by the János Bolyai Research Fellowship of the Hungarian Academy of Sciences (recipient: Peter Kreko, research grant nr: BO/00686/20/2).
2. Alexander Sergunin and Leonid Karabeshkin, "Understanding Russia's Soft Power Strategy," *Politics* 35, no. 3–4 (2015): 347–63.
3. Aleksey Pilko, "What Is Soft Power and How Should Russia Use It?" Valdai Club, September 28, 2012, https://valdaiclub.com/a/highlights/what_is_soft_power_and_how_should_russia_use_it/.
4. "Meeting with Russian Foreign Ministry Staff," President of Russia, February 12, 2013, http://en.kremlin.ru/events/president/news/17490.
5. Anna Matveeva, "Russia's Power Projection after the Ukraine Crisis," *Europe-Asia Studies* 70, no. 5 (2018): 711–37.
6. Joseph S. Nye, *Soft Power: The Means to Success in World Politics* (New York: PublicAffairs, 2005); Joseph S. Nye, "Power and Foreign Policy," *Journal of Political Power* 4, no. 1 (2011): 9–24.
7. Nye, *Soft Power*.
8. Mark Galeotti, "Controlling Chaos: How Russia Manages Its Political War in Europe – European Council on Foreign Relations" (ECFR, September 1, 2017), https://ecfr.eu/publication/controlling_chaos_how_russia_manages_its_political_war_in_europe/.
9. Marcel H. Van Herpen, *Putin's Propaganda Machine: Soft Power and Russian Foreign Policy* (Lanham: Rowman & Littlefield Publishers, 2015).
10. "Security Council Meeting," President of Russia, October 7, 2014, http://en.kremlin.ru/events/president/news/46709.
11. Valery Gerasimov, "The Value of Science in Prediction," *Military-Industrial Courier*, July 6, 2014, https://inmoscowsshadows.wordpress.com/2014/07/06/the-gerasimov-doctrine-and-russian-non-linear-war/.
12. Vyacheslav Nikonov, "A Country's Image Primarily Depends on Its History," *Russkiy Mir*, February 12, 2013, https://russkiymir.ru/en/news/131104/.
13. Nerijus Maliukevičius, "(Re)Constructing Russian Soft Power in Post-Soviet Region," *Baltic Security and Defence Review* 15, no. 2 (2013): 70–97.
14. Herpen, *Putin's Propaganda Machine*.
15. Szabolcs Panyi, "Orbán Is a Tool in Putin's Information War against the West," *Index.Hu*, February 4, 2017, http://index.hu/kulfold/2017/02/04/orban_is_a_tool_for_putin_in_his_information_war_against_the_west/.
16. Herpen, *Putin's Propaganda Machine*; Mitchell A. Orenstein and Péter Krekó, "A Russian Spy in Brussels? The Case of 'KGBéla' — and What It Means for Europe," *Foreign Affairs*, May 29, 2014, https://www.foreignaffairs.com/articles/hungary/2014-05-29/russian-spy-brussels.
17. See for example Herpen, *Putin's Propaganda Machine*.
18. "'He lived by the troll, he dies by the troll': Putin takes on Prigozhin's business empire," *The Guardian*, July 5, 2023, https://www.theguardian.com/world/2023/jul/05/putin-takes-on-yevgeny-prigozhin-business-empire.
19. Ben Nimmo, "Anatomy of an Info-War: How Russia's Propaganda Machine Works, and How to Counter It," *StopFake*, May 19, 2015, https://www.stopfake.org/en/anatomy-of-an-info-war-how-russia-s-propaganda-machine-works-and-how-to-counter-it/.
20. Peter Pomerantsev, *Nothing Is True and Everything Is Possible* (New York: PublicAffairs, 2014).
21. Peter Pomerantsev and Michael Weiss, "The Menace of Unreality: How the Kremlin Weaponizes Information, Culture and Money" (New York: Institute of Modern Russia, 2014), http://www.interpretermag.com/wp-content/uploads/2014/11/The_Menace_of_Unreality_Final.pdf. See also our concept of "informational autocracy," applied to the case of Hungary in Péter Krekó, "The Birth of an Illiberal Informational Autocracy in Europe: A Case Study on Hungary," *Journal of Illiberalism Studies* 2, no. 1 (2022): 55–72.

22 Ilya Yablokov, "Conspiracy Theories as a Russian Public Diplomacy Tool: The Case of Russia Today (RT)," *Politics* 35, no. 3–4 (2015): 301–15.
23 Jeanne L. Wilson, "Russia and China Respond to Soft Power: Interpretation and Readaptation of a Western Construct," *Politics* 35, no. 3–4 (2015): 287–300.
24 Christopher Walker, "What Is 'Sharp Power'?" *Journal of Democracy* 29, no. 3 (2018): 9–23.
25 Christopher Walker and Jessica Ludwig, "From 'Soft Power' to 'Sharp Power': Rising Authoritarian Influence in the Democratic World," in *Sharp Power: Rising Authoritarian Influence* (National Endowment for Democracy, 2017), 6–25, https://www.ned.org/wp-content/uploads/2017/12/Introduction-Sharp-Power-Rising-Authoritarian-Influence.pdf.
26 Christine Huang, "Views of Russia and Putin Remain Negative across 14 Nations," *Pew Research Center* (blog), December 6, 2020, https://www.pewresearch.org/fact-tank/2020/12/16/views-of-russia-and-putin-remain-negative-across-14-nations/.
27 See Péter Krekó, "How Authoritarians Inflate Their Image," *Journal of Democracy* 32, no. 3 (2021): 109–23.
28 Péter Krekó, Csaba Molnár, and András Rácz, *Mystification and Demystification of Vladimir Putin's Russia* (Budapest: Political Capital Institute, March 2019), https://politicalcapital.hu/pc-admin/source/documents/pc_mystification_and_demystification_of_russia_eng_web_20190312.pdf.
29 Daniel Milo, *The Image of Russia in Central and Eastern Europe and the Western Balkans* (Bratislava: Globsec, 2021), www.globsec.org/wp-content/uploads/2021/04/Image-of-Russia-Mighty-Slavic-Brother-or-Hungry-Bear-Nextdoor.pdf.
30 "Disinfo: GDP of European Countries Like Great Britain, France or Italy Is Much Lower Than the Russia One," *EUvsDisinfo*, May 31, 2020, https://euvsdisinfo.eu/report/gdp-of-european-countries-like-great-britain-france-or-italy-is-much-lower-than-therussian-one; "Disinfo: The Space Shuttle of Elon Musk Is Probably Made in Russia, Moon Landing of the Americans Is in Doubt," *EUvsDisinfo*, May 31, 2020, https://euvsdisinfo.eu/report/space-shuttle-of-elon-musk-is-probably-made-in-russia-moon-landing-of-theamericans-is-in-doubt;
31 Cited by Peter Pomerantsev, *This is Not Propaganda: Adventures in the War against Reality* (New York: Public Affairs, 2019).
32 "Video of Dmitry Kiselyov's First Speech at RIA Novosti," *Interpreter mag*, December 13, 2013, https://www.interpretermag.com/video-of-dmitry-kiselyovs-first-speech-at-ria-novosti%e2%80%8f/.
33 Rand Waltzman, "The Weaponization of Information: The Need for Cognitive Security" (RAND Corporation, April 27, 2017), https://www.rand.org/pubs/testimonies/CT473.html.
34 Own calculations, based on the database of Political Capital Institute, from 2022. https://telex.hu/belfold/2022/06/29/oroszbaratsag-oltasellenesseg-kutatas-political-capital
35 "Globsec Trends," 2022, https://www.globsec.org/what-we-do/publications/globsec-trends-2022-central-and-eastern-europe-amid-war-ukraine.
36 "330 Shades of Russian Disinformation: Exploring the Media Landscape of Eastern Europe," Detector Media, December 30, 2022, https://en.detector.media/post/330-shades-of-russian-disinformation-exploring-the-media-landscape-of-eastern-europe?fbclid=IwAR1-xICYVZ6GAZq_95cKz3FX-KyoRTjWYWzfpcBfXGuZlGNSdDIZqN5a0yR4.
37 Kateryna Stepanenko and Frederick W. Kagan, "Russian Offensive Campaign Assessment, February 12, 2023," Institute for the Study of War, February 12, 2023, http://dev-isw.bivings.com/.
38 Rhys Leahy et al., "Connectivity Between Russian Information Sources and Extremist Communities Across Social Media Platforms," *Frontiers in Political Science* 4 (2022), https://www.frontiersin.org/articles/10.3389/fpos.2022.885362/full.
39 On the concept of "informational autocracy," see Krekó, "The Birth of an Illiberal Informational Autocracy in Europe."
40 "La France Face à la Guerre," *TF1*, March 14, 2022, https://www.tf1info.fr/replay-tf1/video-la-france-face-a-la-guerre-2213584.html.

41 "Russia's war in Ukraine – Predictions and Scenarios," Political Capital, February 23, 2023, https://politicalcapital.hu/events.php?article_id=3146.
42 See Bálint Madlovics and Bálint Magyar's chapter on Hungary's dubious loyalty in this volume.
43 "Europe: No Signs of Fatigue in the Support for Ukraine" (Political Capital, February 24, 2023), https://politicalcapital.hu/pc-admin/source/documents/pc_flash_report_one_year_after_the_invasion_2023.pdf.
44 "One year in, global public opinion about the war in Ukraine has remained remarkably stable," Ipsos, January 31, 2023, https://www.ipsos.com/en-th/war-in-ukraine-january-2023.
45 See for example "Spring Eurobarometer 2023," https://europa.eu/eurobarometer/surveys/detail/3052.
46 Moira Fagan and Laura Clancy, "Among European Right-Wing Populists, Favorable Views of Russia and Putin Are down Sharply," Pew Research Center, September 23, 2022, https://www.pewresearch.org/fact-tank/2022/09/23/among-european-right-wing-populists-favorable-views-of-russia-and-putin-are-down-sharply/.
47 "Fragile unity: Why Europeans are coming together on Ukraine (and what might drive them apart)," ECFR, March 16, 2023, https://ecfr.eu/publication/fragile-unity-why-europeans-are-coming-together-on-ukraine/.
48 "Ukraine: Sanctions on Kremlin-Backed Outlets," Text, European Commission, March 2, 2022, https://ec.europa.eu/commission/presscorner/detail/en/IP_22_1490.
49 Waltzman, "The Weaponization of Information."
50 Ilya Yablokov, "The Five Conspiracy Theories That Putin Has Weaponized," *The New York Times*, April 25, 2022, https://www.nytimes.com/2022/04/25/opinion/putin-russia-conspiracy-theories.html.

II.

Geopolitical Structures and the War: The Changing Position of Russia and Ukraine

In the Gravitational Tensions of East and West: The Systemic and Geopolitical Integration Patterns of Ukraine and Moldova

Kálmán Mizsei

1. Introduction

On February 24, 2022, Vladimir Putin launched a full-scale invasion of Ukraine, called in his propaganda "special military operation," having as its aim to eliminate forever the distinct Ukrainian identity and to absorb the territory of Ukraine. Ukraine has resisted in a way that it has surprised all analysts and political observers.

As one element of aid, the European Union lent moral support to Ukraine, and accepted its membership application.[1] On June 23, 2022, Ukraine and also neighboring Moldova were granted EU candidate status. This was a historic moment for the leadership and the population of the two countries. It was rightly perceived as overcoming a major hurdle towards full membership. For Ukraine, the momentous war and the perspective of membership in the EU, and possibly also in NATO, have created an entirely new situation for its evolution as a nation and state in a way that is now hard to predict. This chapter deals with this question from a systemic angle and concludes by formulating some policy guidance primarily for Ukraine's international supporters. Other chapters in this volume, and even more so in the first volume of this collection of studies (*Ukraine's Patronal Democracy and the Russian Invasion*), undertake to describe the systemic evolution of Ukraine; I take those findings as the starting point for my analysis.[2] This study, on the other hand, intends to provide input regarding the interaction between the international integration of these two countries and their systemic evolution. Since Ukraine and Moldova received candidate status to the European Union together, and because there are clear links between the geopolitical fates of the two countries, it is also logical to include Moldova in the discussion. While Ukraine's size and geopolitical significance is much greater than that of Moldova, there is still a significant degree of interaction between the trajectories of the two countries, not least of which being the unresolved Transnistrian conflict.

While Ukraine[3] aspires to membership in both powerful integrative organizations, the European Union and NATO, the main focus here will be on the EU. There are two major reasons for this. First, from a systemic perspective,

EU integration requires deeper harmonization and the accession process itself is more demanding; consequently, its transformational power is potentially, and most probably, greater than that of NATO.[4] The logical underpinning of this assertion is clear, but it also has some strong empirical underpinning if we look at the new NATO member states in the Western Balkans. Their membership certainly did not hurt and even provided them some useful democratic anchors, but from a long-term *developmental* perspective, the contribution of NATO membership on its own has been fairly marginal.

Second, for this very same reason, Russia's opposition to EU membership is actually greater than its opposition to NATO. Since the popular perception is the opposite, it is worth briefly exploring this assertion. Putin's Russia always vehemently argues that it is against NATO expansion, but its greatest fear, one which has also triggered aggressive actions, has been that the countries it regards as subordinate parts of its "world" may become prosperous and thus serve as an example to the Russian people about the power of freedom. Russia acted decisively when Ukraine decided to accept associate status in November 2013, ahead of the EU Vilnius summit. Conversely, Russia had almost no reaction at all to the announcement of Sweden and Finland that they intended to join NATO. This makes sense from Putin's perspective: Turkey, a NATO member, does not pose much of a systemic risk to Russia. While Turkey constitutes a competitor on the international arena, as seen in 2020 during the Nagorno-Karabakh war, it poses less of an irritant for Putin than the idea of a *developmentally* successful Ukraine.

In this chapter, I describe the path of Ukraine and Moldova to EU membership. The path, of course, starts with the collapse of the bipolar world order and the emergence of Putin's regime, which has exhibited expansionist characteristics and used blackmail and a wide range of coercive techniques for several years to prevent countries from escaping its "gravitational space." At the same time, these attempts—as we will see—were often counterproductive, and constituted a "push" towards the Western system of alliance, which in turn also had increasingly clear reasons to accept Ukraine and Moldova among its members. The path to EU membership has faced numerous difficulties, however, both on the part of the countries involved and on the part of the EU itself. I will describe the main pitfalls the EU must avoid in integrating these countries, while also explaining the systemic factors that may either support or hinder their integration.

2. Russia's imperialist instincts and attempts to preserve the cohesion of its civilizational gravitational space

2.1. The emergence of Putin's system and its expansionism

When in 1991 the bipolar global order collapsed, the world felt relief and rejoiced over the fact that it had crumbled rather peacefully. The Yugoslav crisis had terrible human consequences, but it was still easy to contain, exactly because Russia—temporarily, as it turned out—was too weak to exploit it. However, this changed when Russia revived economically. A well-noted factor in this revival was an oil boom which started right after Russia's 1998 financial crisis. Figure 1 shows the enormous good fortune Putin enjoyed with the oil price bonanza taking place right during the first years of his long reign. However, this was not the only factor; the much-criticized and therefore often disregarded market reforms of the 1990s also helped revive the Russian economy.

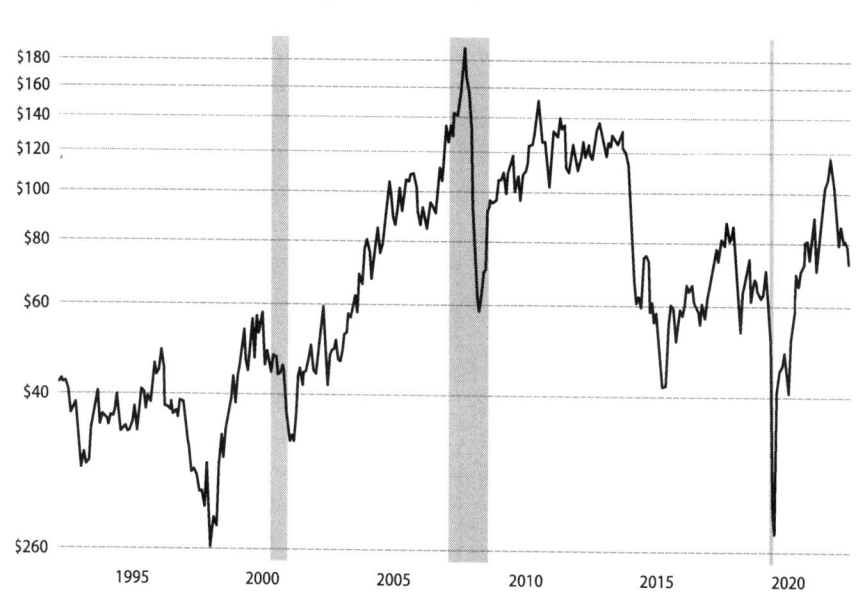

Figure 1. Long-term world market oil price (1990–2023).

Source: https://www.macrotrends.net/1369/crude-oil-price-history-chart.

Russia's efforts to keep the newly independent states in its fold started already with the signing of the Almaty Protocol in 1991,[5] and the establishment of the Commonwealth of Independent States (CIS). However, in terms of integration, this organization has not yielded much benefit to the participants. There are two main reasons for this. First, the CIS "united" one overwhelmingly dominant country (Russia) with many others which were much smaller in economic and security terms. Second, integration—unlike imperial subordination—requires a relatively high level of governance in each country, with the most critical issues being adherence to the rule of law and a judiciary independent from the executive branch of government. Clearly, these latter were absent, thus in the 1990s whatever these countries agreed to ended up unrealized. Less than 10% of the thousands of documents and resolutions adopted by CIS countries have actually been ratified by the member states.[6]

With great and prolonged effort, mainly on the part of Russia, where the reforms necessary for such a policy were, in relative terms, most advanced, a free trade agreement was sealed only in 2011. Clearly, besides purely economic purposes, Russia also intended to use this agreement to advance its revisionist political aims towards each member state, but particularly towards Ukraine, thus justifying the fear among member states of undue pressure from Russia. However, not all the participating members had even signed the agreement by the time Ukraine, the second largest CIS country in terms of population, had focused its attention on the Association Agreement with the European Union and its free trade component. Russia deemed the simultaneous integration of Ukraine in both blocs unfeasible, and tried to exert economic pressure on Ukraine even after the Revolution of Dignity. At the time it was the European Union which, hoping to foster a peaceful *de facto* shift on the part of Ukraine from its free trade agreement with the CIS towards the more ambitious arrangement with the European Union, allowed a one-year postponement in the application of its free trade agreement with Ukraine, until the beginning of 2016. Russia, however, was uninterested in finding a reconciliatory solution to the challenge of Ukraine having a free trade agreement with both blocs, and cancelled the bilateral provisions of the CIS free trade agreement (while Ukraine's free trade regime with other signatories of the CIS agreement remained in force). While in the long run, it is clear that participation in two economic integrations would have been feasible only if between the two blocks far-reaching trade agreements were established, in the short run reconciliation was not possible because Russia clearly wanted confrontation rather than reconciliation at this point.

In the 1990s, Russia still assumed a generally cooperative international posture towards the countries of the "developed West." This posture continued into the first years of the Putin regime. Most prominently, Russia strongly cooperated with the United States after 9/11. The picture is also blurred by the fact that among the CIS countries, the strongest economic reforms were initially undertaken by Russia, including the first years of Putin's presidency which, for instance, witnessed a very ambitious liberal tax reform. Among the countries of the former Soviet Union, the quality of these reforms was surpassed only by the radicalism of the economic reforms of the Baltic States.

The first decade of Putin's rule can be termed the decade of consumerism. The Russian consumer experienced a historically unprecedented consumer bonanza based on rapid economic growth, resulting in a huge increase in incomes and living standards. Given the inherently short time horizon of Russian behavior, economic growth was mostly translated into the kind of consumer boom that only post-communist societies, with years of pent-up hunger for consumption goods, can experience. The boom affected the Russian society in concentric circles: the primary beneficiaries were Muscovites, then St. Petersburg, other large cities and, finally, at the end of the pecking order, remote areas, particularly non-urban settlements.

Russian politics took a radical turn after the huge protests in Moscow and St. Petersburg in the winter of 2011–12. Cynics may say, in retrospect, that this was the moment when Russian politics returned to "normal."[7] The combination of a strongly regenerating economic might and the need to supply a surrogate for democratic politics, which was one of the basic expectations of the protestors of the winter of 2011–12, set Putin (and with him, Russian politics) on a strongly revisionist course internationally. Already then, insiders formulated that in his new presidential term Putin intended to achieve restoration of the "Russian World," that is, to subordinate the constituent parts of the former Soviet Union or the even earlier Russian Empire. In other words, Putin was set on re-colonizing the "near abroad."

However, this traditional Russian expansionism was implanted this time into a specific system of governance that evolved under Putin. This system was called the "party of crooks and thieves" *(Партия жуликов и воров)* by Alexei Navalny during the above-mentioned protests; the editors of this volume have termed it "patronal autocracy." In adopting imperial expansionism, the logical needs of ideology and patronal politics came together, as the regime had a great interest in repressing debate about being "crooks and thieves" and found a favorable theme in the old obsession of Russian expansion. Hence, Russia returned to its traditional expansionist reflexes.

As the Putin-regime consolidated, its internal reforms ceased and its international impact became more revisionist, it increasingly exerted a negative impact on the development of the CIS-countries' internal systems, trying to corrupt them into the direction of patronal autocracy. The three countries where it caused the most conflict, and had a very negative impact on economic development, were Ukraine, Moldova, and Georgia. In Georgia and Moldova, Russia fomented and nurtured conflict even before the onset of their independent existence. However, it would be inaccurate to say that around the time of the dissolution of the Soviet Union it was "the Russians" who generated those conflicts: the conflicts involved a much more diverse set of interests and actors but certainly the Soviet, and later Russian, secret services were a core part of this.

2.2. The techniques of forced integration: from "blackmail diplomacy" to the creation of conflict zones to ensure incompatibility with the West

Looking at the three decades behind us, Russia has tried several ways to reestablish the "integration," i.e., subordination, of these countries. The tools ranged from creating a nominally voluntary integration platform (first as the CIS and later as the Eurasian Economic Community), through the use of a variety of sticks and carrots (primarily through the corruption of target country elites), and finally by means of war (as in the case of Georgia and Ukraine). In the 1990s, Russia placed its main trust in the CIS. It was to some extent a voluntary enterprise, and was also legitimized by the more advanced economic reforms undertaken by Russia compared to that of its partners.

When, following the relatively liberal environment of the 1990s, Russia's "integration" repertoire widened with the use of increasingly coercive methods, it was assisted by the fact that it possessed vital energy resources that other countries needed. The energy infrastructure inherited from the Soviet Union greatly enhanced Russia's dominance through its partner countries' dependence on Russian energy, primarily oil and gas. Putin used this situation very consciously and fully to his own advantage by creating a number of giant energy companies with ownership, and thus decision-making, centralized under his control.

The most visible manifestations of using energy for blackmail purposes was the threatened—and at times actually implemented—shutting of the gas taps. This usually happened at the end of the year when energy contracts were due to be renegotiated or when Putin simply wanted to use any pretext possible to stop delivering primarily gas. It was also a convenient time as it occurred right before the bulk of the winter heating season. The primary target of such actions was Ukraine itself—as Ukraine had been the primary target of Russian revisionism overall. Even before its 2014 aggression, Russia had already resorted to cutting energy supplies to Ukraine twice, once in 2006 and again in 2009.[8]

The Russian "blackmail diplomacy" did not stop at the energy sector. Putin used phytosanitary pretexts to *ban imports* from countries targeted for blackmail, including Ukraine and Moldova.[9] In 2014, Russia introduced a range of punitive measures as part of its adopted confrontational line vis-à-vis Moldova, banning Moldovan exports of certain agricultural goods and food products.[10] However, such rather clear and naked attempts to force the elites of these countries to yield to Russian pressure and subordinate themselves to Moscow achieved, to some extent, the opposite result. The trust of Ukraine and Moldova in Russia decreased, although "pro-Russian" parties often campaigned—with decreasing success—on being more "friendly" towards Russia in order to secure energy imports and market access. These parties received diminishing electoral support, although in Moldova, due to the fragmentation of the pro-European parties, this has been a very slow and still tentative process.

Besides blackmail diplomacy, another tool used by Putin for forced integration and to prevent Russia's former colonies from escaping its gravitational field to the West has been to create *conflict as a spoiler and tool of blackmail*. During the struggle for independence, Soviet and later Russian force structures, particularly the KGB and then the FSB, fomented internal conflicts in some of the republics and later in the newly independent states, wherever ethnic animosities were suitable to foster separatist movements. Such included the Abkhazian and South Ossetian regions in Georgia as well as the Transnistrian region in Moldova. In the case of Abkhazia, massive ethnic cleansing supported by these Russian force structures during the period of active conflict helped secure a majority population for the ethnic Abkhaz people. In the case of Transnistria, a more complex fiction was used to legitimize the separation of the region since during the period of active conflict in 1991–92 a relative majority of the population (around 40%) was actually Moldovan. The political and economic elites, however, were not Moldovan but mostly Russian and Ukrainian. To this must be added the local Ukrainian population, whose fear of a pan-Romanian dynamic turned a large part of them against Moldovan independence. This conflict was also affected by the massive presence of Soviet, and later Russian, army structures, as the headquarters of the Soviet 14th Army was based in Tiraspol, the main town in the Transnistrian region.

The active stage of the conflict in Transnistria ended with a ceasefire in July 1992. Russia was able to create and legitimize a fictitious situation whereby Moldova and Transnistria were regarded by the international community as the "conflicting parties." Thus, any peace negotiations had to be between these two parties in a situation where Russia paraded in the role of peacekeeper in spite of being the strongest active party in the conflict. The actual truth was that it had been in Russia's interest to keep this conflict alive in order to pull Moldova firmly into its sphere of interest.

Since Russia is not a direct neighbor of Transnistria (and of Moldova in general), Ukraine ended up playing an important and initially largely pro-Russian role and has remained part of the formal "settlement negotiations" alongside the OSCE. Later, the European Union and the United States joined at the insistence of President Yushchenko of Ukraine. Russia had to yield to this development but its effort has always been directed at creating a situation whereby it would gain decisive influence over the country through the content and implementation mechanisms of any peace agreement. The most typical manifestation of this effort was the so-called Kozak Memorandum, named after the Russian presidential envoy Dmitry Kozak, whose secret diplomacy in 2003 created a settlement plan highly favorable to Russia via the planned constitutional role of Transnistria and also of Gagauzia, an autonomous Turkic enclave within Moldova.[11] The Kozak-trick finally ultimately failed due to resistance from the United States, the European Union, and other Western partners.[12] However, Russia's approach to the conflict which it itself initially created has remained the same: to use Transnistria to blackmail and trick Moldova into subordination.

This conflict then served as the model for the Donbas where Russia tried to use elements of the methodology employed in the case of Transnistria, namely, the pretention of a conflict between Ukraine and the people of the separatist regions with Russia as an outside peacemaking party. Here, however, more than two decades after Transnistria, Russia's direct involvement was even greater and more naked. In the case of the Crimea, Russia used a fake referendum to formally annex Ukraine's autonomous republic and gain a militarily strategic position in the Black Sea as a result. Similarly, Russia tried, and to some extent succeeded, in the so-called Minsk peace process, to legitimize the fiction of a conflict between Ukraine and the two Donbas "People's Republics" rather than between Ukraine and Russia. And when Ukraine did not yield to their demands, they launched a second phase of war, still camouflaged by naming it a "special operation" even though it constitutes the largest war on the European continent since World War II.

Russia's attitude towards its former colonies has changed together with its internal systemic evolution. In the case of the Transnistrian conflict, Russia in 1999, when still a democracy, had committed itself to remove all military personnel and equipment from both Moldova and Georgia by the end of 2002.[13] However, the interim saw Putin's emergence as Russia's leader in the wake of the second Chechen war, which proved immensely popular within Russia. Putin's internal consolidation of power and his external turn toward imperialist policies moved in parallel, and although Russia started the process of removing its military from Moldova and Georgia, it never finished it, thus breaching its obligations under the Istanbul Agreement. This was followed by a renewed diplomatic push by Russia to resolve the Transnistrian conflict in a way that would essentially secure Russian strategic control over Moldova, including legitimizing the stationing of Russian troops in the country for 25 years. The balance of power both internationally and locally in Moldova was such that the plan eventually failed, albeit by a very thin margin.

Since then, the influence of the European Union in Moldova in general and around the Transnistrian conflict in particular has markedly increased. In 2007, the EU established trade facilitation for Moldova, and then in 2013 it gave the country associate status along with signing a Deep and Comprehensive Free Trade Agreement. Finally, in the wake of the Russian aggression against Ukraine in 2022, Moldova also received EU candidate status. As for the Transnistrian conflict, the EU, together with the United States, has been part of the so-called 5+2 negotiating format since 2005 with strong influence as a major partner that is actually contributing to resolving the conflict, mainly within the framework of facilitating confidence building between Chisinau and Tiraspol.

3. Geopolitical reorientation: the result of Eastern "push" and Western "pull"

3.1. Western reorientation in trade and Russia's counterproductive attempts to prevent it

As we will see in this section, both Ukraine and Moldova have gradually implemented a cumulatively very significant (and in the case of Moldova, overwhelming) trade reorientation over the years of independence. It did not start with the Association Agreements but with the dissolution of the Soviet Union. One reason for this process is more than obvious: the European Union is the world's largest "trading bloc" and, in fact, to some extent, particularly in trade, it constitutes a supra-national organization. Trade in the Soviet Union was predetermined by the logic of political power. The various parts of the Soviet Union were directed to trade among themselves first of all, and with the other countries of the Soviet bloc secondly. Trading with the "West" was discouraged. When the Soviet empire dissolved, this forced trading geography immediately began to weaken. It did not disappear completely because from the start Russia continued to use its political weight to try to influence its former colonies to trade with it. However, Russia's primary tool was not trade but coercion. It used its "energy muscle" to blackmail countries into a geopolitical orientation towards it and not outwards. Additionally, it used corruption schemes, particularly in the gas trade, to link countries to itself politically.[14] Its ultimate goal was the restoration of the lost empire.

However, Russia's strategy did not work on two levels. First, the local businesspeople of the post-Soviet space, including the oligarchs, wanted to make profit and typically did not make their trading decisions on the basis of what the Russian political leaders preferred. Moreover, major business leaders and politicians alike, even seemingly pro-Russian ones, were not keen on allowing Putin's political influence to grow too large. Second, while there was—beyond geopolitical considerations—contempt as well towards the former colonies among Russian governing circles, Putin overestimated his potential to blackmail and to self-servingly hinder the post-communist states in establishing Western trade relations. Russian blackmail tactics backfired in terms of trade volumes: Georgian and Moldovan wines and agricultural products, among other things, found their way to more quality markets elsewhere.[15]

Russia's blackmail policy and eventual full-scale invasion pushed Ukraine completely towards the West as well. Every step undertaken trying to force Ukraine to submission, "kicking away" the country via retaliatory trade measures that had nothing to do with anything legitimate in WTO terms (although sometimes they were wrapped up into such language) has accelerated the gradual decrease of the disproportionate orientation of Ukraine's trade towards Russia and the CIS countries (Figures 2-3). When Russia's tactics seemingly succeeded, as in November 2013, when President Yanukovych refused to sign the EU-Ukraine Association

Agreement, the Ukrainian people reacted with mass protests and forced change of the regime. Needless to say, Russia's brutal invasion only contributed to this process, causing a dramatic decline in the country's trade with Ukraine. In other words, Russia has now placed all its trust in a coercive war. Predictably, this will make EU trade relations even more important, with one outcome already being Ukraine's full integration into the European electricity market.[16] The pressure of wartime emergency could achieve a similar outcome in the case of Moldova, where such integration has been clearly required for more than a decade. Access to natural gas via Romania has also become easier as of late. Thus, Russia's blackmailing potential in these areas has finally been significantly weakened. Russia will also most likely lose its favorable position as the primary foreign direct investor in Ukraine.

Figures 2-3. The trend in Ukraine's foreign trade during its period of independence according to main geographic partners (1996–2001).[17]

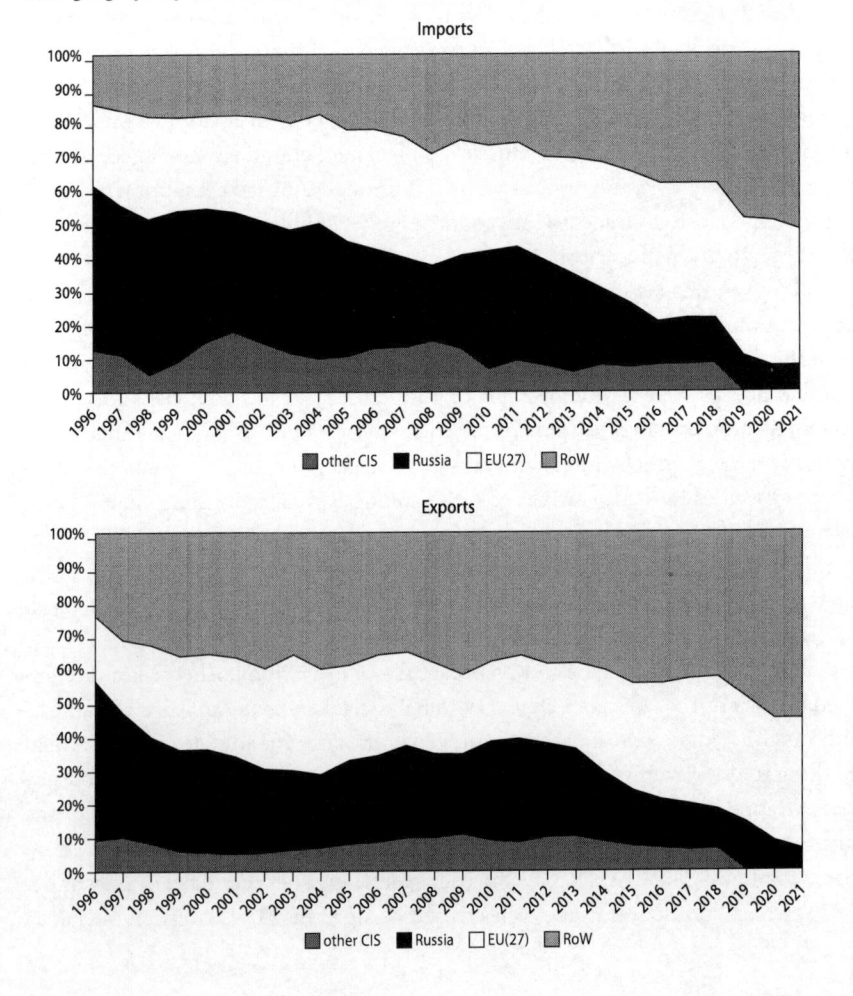

The Deep and Comprehensive Free Trade Agreement with the European Union, signed in 2014 and under this effect is tentative so far and not very large. This is primarily because Ukraine, being a larger country than Georgia and Moldova, has a larger export potential, with metals being a major product. Ukraine's trade reorientation towards Europe is also hindered to an extent by the country's systemic characteristics which, until recently, continued to place a disproportionate emphasis on heavy industry in the eastern part of the country. Here, too, Russia's share of trade has undergone natural erosion, accelerated later by its punitive trade measures and, in particular, its aggression in Crimea and the Donbas. While in 2013, Russia still accounted for 23.8% of Ukrainian exports, this figure had shrunk dramatically to 6.5% in 2019. Conversely, Europe's share of Ukraine's exports grew in the same period from 26.5% to 41.5% (Table 1). At the same time, this European trade orientation has also had an impact on systemic characteristics, leading to less corrupt practices in business, more decentralization, higher quality products, and the concomitant modernization of production processes.

Table 1. Ukraine's merchandise trade structure by country or region (2013 and 2019).

	2013				2019			
	Exports ($ mn)	Exports (%)	Imports ($ mn)	Imports (%)	Exports ($ mn)	Exports (%)	Imports ($ mn)	Imports (%)
EU	16,758	26.5	27,046	35.1	20,751	41.5	25.012	41.1
Russia	15.065	23.8	23,234	30.2	3,243	6.5	6,985	11,5
Other CIS	6,998	11.1	4,697	6.1	3,511	7.0	4,892	8.0
Other Europe	467	0.7	1,582	2.1	512	1.0	2,180	3.6
US	888	1.4	2,759	3.6	979	2.0	3,284	5.4
China	2,726	4.3	7,900	10.3	3,593	7.2	9,205	15.1
Rest of the world	20,407	32.2	9,743	12.7	17,466	34.9	9,242	15.2
Total	63,312	100.0	76.964	100.0	50,055	100.0	60,800	100.0

Source: State Statistics Service of Ukraine.

China's trade with Ukraine also grew robustly during this period, albeit from a lower base. Moreover, Ukraine's trade with China continued to grow until the war, with exports valued at USD 8 billion in 2021against imports worth USD 9.4 billion. This made China by far the largest trading partner of Ukraine (Figure 4). This dynamic also seems to indicate that, while the EU Free Trade agreement is important, it does not constitute an overwhelming factor yet in the direction of

European integration. Systemic characteristics can be (and, in case of Ukraine, they have been) an obstacle to economic reorientation. Low value-added exports of coal, steel, and other heavy industrial products find their way to China, and continued to be exported to Russia on a massive scale before the war. The effect of the war in this regard may be transformative because, paradoxically, Russia so far has destroyed industries and territories with which it had the strongest traditional economic ties. Hence, the emerging Ukrainian economy will, predictably, be much less centralized and concentrated, less oriented towards heavy industry, and more geared towards technology-intensive business.

Figure 4. Visualizing Ukraine's trade (2020).

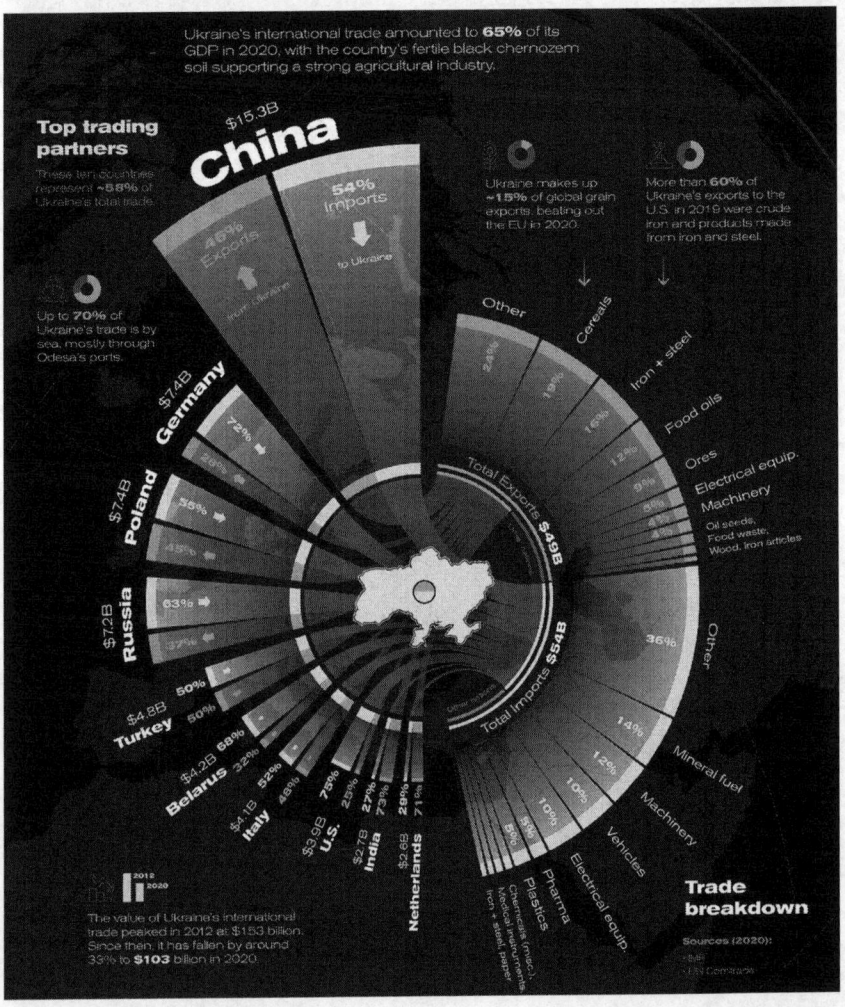

Source: Visual Capitalist.

The picture concerning foreign direct investments (FDI) is also not compelling. Both Ukraine and Moldova absorb much less FDI than more advanced countries in the region. Indeed, foreign investment early in the transition was an important contributor to success in those countries that have become member states of the European Union since 2004. This factor of integration into the EU is very much absent in Ukraine and Moldova.[18] The three most important reasons for this are geography (mostly distance accompanied by infrastructural disadvantages), political uncertainties caused by Russia's hostile behavior, and a high level of prohibitive corruption. Again, systemic characteristics have been an important obstacle to more intense integration into the European economy.

Moldova's trade integration with the European Union has advanced more clearly than Ukraine's over the last three decades. Figure 5 below, while somewhat counter-intuitively laid out, shows that Russia's share of Moldova's exports had already collapsed in the period preceding Moldova's Association Agreement with the European Union. While the process had its natural causes, since the earlier concentration on Soviet markets had been artificial and politically enforced, a reverse mechanism was also in play at this time. As was the case with Ukraine, Russia imposed politically motivated import bans on Moldovan agricultural products as a reaction to the country's European orientation in the expectation it could coerce Moldova into returning to the fold. Instead, these embargoes only accelerated Moldova's reorientation.

Table 2. The EU's share in Ukraine's merchandise trade (2013 to 2019).

Period	2014	2015	2016	2017	2018	2019
Total turnover	7,656	5,954	6,065	7,257	8,466	8,622
Turnover, EU	3,814	3,172	3,036	3,986	4,713	4,721
Growth (%)	5.7	-16.8	4.2	20.6	18.2	0.2
Share (%)	49.8	53.3	54.5	54.9	55.7	54.8
Total exports	2,340	1,967	2,045	2,425	2,706	2,779
Exports to the EU	1,246	1,218	1,332	1,597	1,862	1,831
Growth (%)	9.6	-2.2	9.4	19.9	16.6	-1.7
Share (%)	53.3	61.9	65.1	65.9	68.8	65.9
Total imports	5,317	3,987	4,020	4,831	5,760	5,842
Imports to the EU	2,586	1,954	1,974	2,389	2,851	2,890
Growth (%)	3.9	-23.9	1.0	21.0	19.3	1.4
Share (%)	48.3	49.0	49.1	49.5	49.5	49.5
Balance with the EU	-1,322	-736	-642	-792	-989	-1059

Source: Deepening EU-Moldova Relations: Updating and upgrading in the shadow of Covid-19, edited by Michael Emerson and Dionis Cenusa (London: CEPS, Brussels Expert-Group, Chișinău, Rowman& Littlefield International, 2021), 51.

This also had a positive externality insofar as the country had to upgrade the quality of its agricultural and food products and massively improve their phytosanitary parameters. Russia, in fact, against its own intentions, actively assisted in this process. Putin's retaliatory tactics arguably had perhaps an even greater trade reorienting effect than the Free Trade Agreement.

This trend continued, albeit at a somewhat slower pace, up to the most recent time (Figure 5). The political crisis of 2022 accelerated the pace of infrastructural investments and arrangements, making Moldova even less dependent on Russia. The war will probably separate Russia economically even more, with likely feedback consequences in the realm of politics. It is also probable that a more intensive focus on European partners and integration will help improve developmental conditions, as infrastructure investment will ease Moldova's geographic isolation, while neighboring Romania's economic growth is already providing a supportive factor for the Moldovan economy. However, tackling corruption and establishing a credible judiciary remain important tasks to be done.

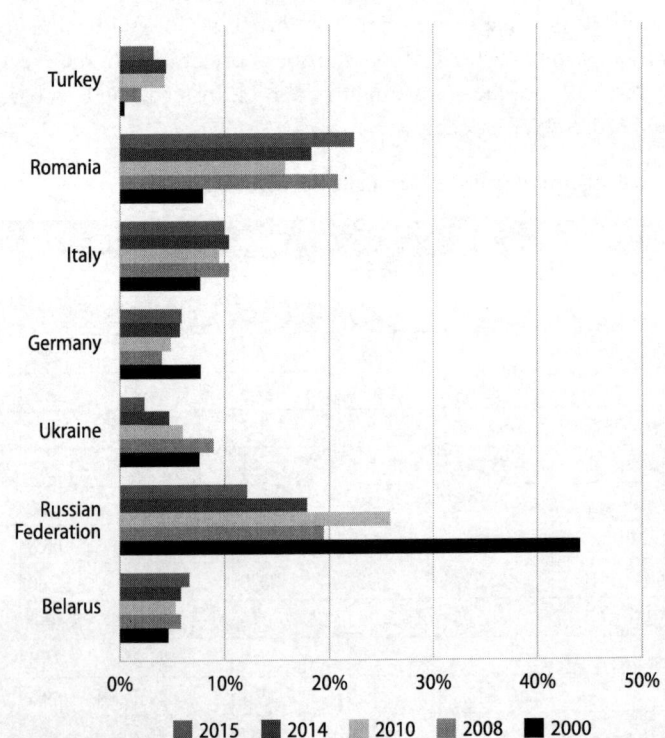

Figure 5. Changes in Moldova's main export destinations, 2000–2015.

Source: UN Economic Commission for Europe. Regulatory and Procedural Barriers to Trade in the Republic of Moldova: Needs Assessment. United Nations Publications, 2017.

3.2. Western reorientation in politics: the motives for joining the EU and the mixed attitudes of Western actors to Eastern partnership

Moving from trade to political reorientation, we should start by asking trivial-sounding questions: why is it important for these countries to join the European Union and, conversely, why are there obstacles? Also, what does the EU expect from its "Eastern neighbors"? Historically, the EU "neighborhood" mainly meant the Mediterranean countries. Socio-political and geopolitical processes in Eastern Europe and a rebalancing of interests within the EU have gradually changed this inherited *status quo*. Although Germany, one of the two most politically important member states, has arguably a more "natural" interest in Eastern Europe, as opposed to France whose main focus is the Mediterranean, it was thanks to two visionary foreign policy leaders from two smaller member states, Carl Bildt of Sweden and Radek Sikorski of Poland (both foreign ministers at the time), that the Eastern Partnership was created in May 2008.[19]

There are potentially three different motivations that could drive post-communist countries towards the main Western alliances, that is, NATO and the European Union. First, the deepest motivation is the *unity of societal values*. With the dissolution of the Soviet empire, many of the original elites of the newly liberated countries, those persons tasked with preparing and carrying out systemic changes, shared and were strongly committed to the values of *liberal democracy*, including free markets, unfettered political competition, and the rule-of-law. They were particularly strong advocates of the first two, and they felt that uniting with Western Europe—and with the North-Atlantic alliance more broadly—was a sort of "homecoming."

At the same time, two other issues were very much on their minds: to be part of the *rich and prosperous* free trade market, free trading alliance and also, in the case of NATO, *security* against a potentially future aggressive Russia. Today it is generally accepted that the elites of Eastern European societies assessed this latter risk much better than Western European politicians and societies. On this basis, nine former socialist bloc countries, including the three Baltic States of the former Soviet Union, joined the European Union (together with Cyprus) in 2004. Two more post-communist countries outside the former Soviet Union, Bulgaria and Romania, joined in 2007. NATO also accepted all of their candidacies, along with some of the countries of the former Yugoslavia.[20]

Extending EU integration further East, however, was a much more problematic proposition: the target societies themselves were divided about it, and the traditional members of the alliances were also reluctant to take on board Georgia and Ukraine in the case of NATO, and those two plus Moldova in the case of the European Union. First, they did not feel that those countries were ready in terms of governance characteristics, the latter sometimes mistakenly referred to as "capacities"—as if the issue concerned a lack of technical skills. Second, they did not want to alienate Russia which had adopted an increasingly threatening posture, emboldened also by EU and NATO hesitancy to respond with strength. Russians threats initially worked against Western European politicians, but they had a reverse effect in the case of the Eastern European countries, including their "already integrated" neighbors, particularly Poland and the Baltic countries, which assessed the Russian threats correctly. Indeed, paradoxically, Putin's Russia increasingly became the main driving force of both integrations. In other words, security concerns (plus financial incentives) have taken the place of the other above-mentioned motivations. Already in the case of the new Eastern European member states, various EU subsidies represent an enormous sum, altogether growing as high as 5% of the GDP for some of them.

The *promise* of EU membership for the Eastern European applicants, and to a lesser extent those in the Western Balkans, is obviously rather attractive in financial terms as well, as these countries are significantly poorer than the ones who joined the European Union earlier. Besides the possibility of joining the European free trade zone, the structural and cohesion funds of the EU also represent a fabulous treasure for the leaders of poor Eastern European countries. Even in the new member states, the EU cohesion funds, which were originally meant to be a temporary subsidy, have become a core budgetary supplement.

Conversely, for many countries, particularly those closer to the Atlantic, interest in the Eastern European countries has mainly been of—a minimalist—security nature. In their opinion, the Eastern Partnership should mainly serve to ensure stability in the region, so that unmanageable waves of migrants do not pose insurmountable challenges to their own countries. Moreover, smuggling needed to be contained, hence the emphasis on border management and, perhaps, with a much less systematic focus, the rule of law. At the same time, many countries further west and south-west operated on the assumption that they could maintain a fundamental relationship with Russia, while trying to negotiate a security arrangement for the "buffer" region mainly with them. It is needless to mention now how tragically and spectacularly wrong this approach proved to be on February 24, 2022.

I have emphasized the above in order to illustrate that the European *idea* in reality has very few active followers, either in the Western or in the Eastern European political space. It is yet to be seen whether Russia's war will shake us up. The idealist would wish that countries could enter into membership negotiations easier on the basis of the Amsterdam Treaty, but that the stipulations of the so-called Copenhagen Criteria[21] for joining would then be rigorously applied. In other words, this dichotomy would mean excluding no European country from applying for membership while ensuring the process for it remains very rigorous from the point of view of the sustainability of a liberal democratic regime involving a competitive market economy, rule of law, and a strongly democratic political order. This would be the optimal approach for countries like Ukraine who want to join the Western alliance system, while it would be rational for the EU as well, which could manage its enlargement this way by ensuring regime homogeneity (as opposed to regime heterogeneity, which could threaten the Union's internal stability, as we can observe today with eastern patronal member states).[22]

However, there has not been much of a following for this approach within the EU. Many member states did not think that EU membership for Eastern European countries was a particularly attractive idea at all. This was partly explained by the perception that moving the EU's center of gravity further east would mean empowering Germany in the alliance even more. The point is that while the process towards EU membership is partly technocratic (led by a legalistic European Commission bureaucracy), it is also partly an inherently political process. Many member states perceived that undue political pressure was applied (particularly from the UK) when deciding on the accession of the ten additional states in 2004, and even more so when Romania and Bulgaria were taken on board.

3.3. The case of Ukraine: revolutions and evolving international integration with the West

Ukraine's systemic evolution combined with an inevitable trade reorientation led to a gradual, logical, and necessary distancing from Russia under conditions of free economic choice. This distancing, however, has been far from even or smooth. It has been a process marked by periodically sharpening conflict, triggered by are nascent Russian imperial assertiveness, particularly since Putin's takeover. During this time, Russia made wide use of the "gas weapon" along with the method of corrupting willing parts of the Ukrainian elite in order to maneuver Ukraine into an economically as well as politically dependent status. Since Russia's initial reforms in the 1990s were of a markedly better quality than those in Ukraine, a significant gap opened up between the two countries' economic strengths, which helped Putin's efforts to subordinate Ukraine.

However, while Putin played politics well in Russia, he notoriously misjudged the political dynamic in the former colonies. Thus, in the case of Ukraine, the most important country for him by far, he involved himself deeply in the presidential elections in 2004 and triggered, via electoral fraud, resistance within Ukrainian society, which manifested itself in the Orange Revolution.[23]

EU membership only grew in significance when the door to NATO membership was closed to the countries of the Eastern Partnership, which were sandwiched between an increasingly resurgent Russian imperialism and the transatlantic community. In the case of Ukraine, both EU and NATO membership aspirations were ignored. For both integration processes, Russia's aggression against Georgia on August 8, 2008 was very consequential. Even prior to the aggression, President Bush made an effort to include Georgia and Ukraine in NATO's Membership Action Plan (MAP); the initiative, however, encountered diplomatic difficulties. Germany and France, predictably, did not agree to this, deeming it premature. NATO's failure to support the US initiative further encouraged Russia in its war against Georgia (which was also emboldened by the West's recognition of Kosovo's independence and the establishment of diplomatic relations with a number of Western countries).[24]

Following the Russian aggression against Georgia, the then French president, Nicolas Sarkozy, wanted to provide "at least" an impetus to the European integration of Ukraine. However, on September 9, 2008, the Ukraine–EU Summit in Spain vetoed EU candidate status for Ukraine.[25] Four years after the Orange Revolution, the country remained without robust international support for its integration into the main Western structures. At the same time, the *breakthrough in systemic reforms* expected after the Revolution failed to occur. While the overwhelming experience earlier was that the social system and attitudes changed the slowest, our evidence showed that society in this case "moved too far ahead."[26] The power elites were unable—and, indeed, unwilling—to institute radical systemic changes, as they were too busy replacing the previous actors with themselves within the same system, albeit in perhaps some milder forms and with fewer excesses than Yanukovych's adopted political family.[27]

The consequences of the lack of breakthrough reforms after the Orange Revolution and the systemic impact of Yanukovych's presidency in 2010 were such that Ukraine was thrown deeper into oligarchic order.[28] Russia's cultural influence in Ukraine still remained strong during the Yanukovych period, even if the economic role of the EU steadily increased. The Russian language was widely used, and even propagated by the "Donbas clan" which dominated so much of politics during this period. Russian-language television remained dominant with the additional impact that Russian, once almost exclusively spoken among the urban elites with the exception of Galicia, still retained its status as a mark of education, and, most of all, as a sign of "coolness."

While Yanukovych's role model was definitely Putin and the Russian system, he was never able to break free of the many pluralistic features of Ukrainian society. The oligarchic structure itself was pluralistic, unlike in Russia where Putin was able to create a tighter hierarchy; civil society in Ukraine remained robust and vocal. Paradoxically, however, another limiting factor for systemic transformation into a fully-fledged mafia state was Putin's Russia itself. Yanukovych, unlike other would-be dictators, was afraid to link his empire too closely to Putin; thus, he engaged in particular with the European Union, which also meant making certain commitments towards the rule of law. These commitments represented a limiting factor, inhibiting systemic transformation towards patronal autocracy. To view it from another angle: only Putin could build a strong, internally coherent single-pyramid order within Russia's orbit. Thus, paradoxically, Putin was one of the main obstacles for the leaders of the satellite countries who were trying to build their own autocracies. The ones in Central Asia and the Southern Caucasus who succeeded in creating various levels of autocracy or even dictatorship fended off full subordination to Putin. Belarus, then, is a partial exception as its pro-Russian platform combined with the fact that only Putin can protect it from its own, much more developed, civil society, has gradually reduced its room of maneuver. In addition, Belarus is more important for Putin than Central Asia.

Nevertheless, Putin's effort to subordinate Ukraine was always there and, as I mentioned above, it strengthened and became a fixation after the 2011–12 domestic political crisis. Putin's interference with Ukraine's European developmental choice in 2013 contributed in a fundamental way to the Revolution of Dignity, the second peaceful but revolutionary upheaval of Ukrainian society for the cause of dignity, but this time accentuating its pathway to European integration.[29] The Revolution of Dignity started with the clashes on November 21, 2013, triggered by Yanukovych's refusal to sign the Association Agreement with the European Union at the organization's Vilnius Summit. The brutal repression of the revolution forged the Ukrainian nation and further distanced it from the Russian world.

However, the aftermath of the Revolution of Dignity was similar to some extent to the aftermath of the Orange Revolution. Again, subsequent anti-patronal reforms were lukewarm and certainly did not represent a systemic breakthrough towards the liberal order. As we analyzed together with my co-authors, Vladimir Dubrovskiy, Mychajlo Wynnyckyj, and Kateryna Ivashchenko-Stadnik, the Revolution of Dignity failed to force through the critical mass of changes necessary in the Ukrainian socioeconomic system.[30] Neither leader of the post-revolution state (neither the president, nor the prime minister) proved to be nearly as committed to reforms as those leaders of the earlier successful Eastern European states. They largely pursued what they (wrongly, at least, in the case of President Poroshenko) believed to be their own personal interests. The presumption of the international community was that reforms, particularly of the rule of law and power organizations, would strengthen the state against possible Russian aggression. Those reforms, except for a rather marginal patrol police reform, essentially did not happen. Poroshenko could have led the nation towards such reforms but he did not have the imagination that some earlier Eastern European reformers clearly had. Internally, Ukraine was not ready at that time to formulate breakthrough reforms, let alone implement them.[31] Hence, the reforms again did not happen, even though the initial spark for the Revolution of Dignity was European integration.

The partial victory of the revolution, however, opened the doors for finalizing the Association Agreement. The Russians still remained at the figurative "negotiation table" in the sense that they could still vehemently object to the free trade agreement, claiming that it violated vital Russian commercial interests and therefore needed to be renegotiated. While they could not get their way in terms of renegotiation, they could delay the signing of the agreement. Eventually, in line with the above-analyzed Russian strategy, Putin interpreted the failure of the "voluntary" approach to integration as necessitating the use of force. Putin's initial retaliation for the Revolution of Dignity was to seize Crimea in February-March 2014 without any resistance from the deeply corrupted and demoralized state which President Yanukovych, himself immersed in criminal activity, left behind when he fled the country. Emboldened by this success, Putin went further and occupied roughly 7% of the large territory of Ukraine.[32] The 2022 invasion, however, apparently finalized the question as to which civilizational gravitational field Ukraine belonged: it received candidate status in the EU and now enjoys the full support of the Western countries, which finally (even if belatedly) recognized the Russian threat.

3.4. The case of Moldova: the attempt to consolidate a mafia state also failed

Broadly speaking, in Moldova we see a similar *drift towards the West*, albeit in a very different and highly complex way.[33] In the second half of 2009, popular pressure installed a coalition government with a declared European orientation. For the purposes of this chapter, what is particularly important to emphasize is that a declared European orientation does not necessarily imply such in practice. First, the Filat government (2009–2013) essentially failed to make use of the window of opportunity that such periods present in order to introduce *radical systemic reform*.[34] That such reform is possible has been demonstrated in many countries: in the Baltics, Poland, and to some extent Czechoslovakia and then the Czech Republic at the beginning of the transition. It was also possible to catch up with these initial, ground-breaking reforms at a later date, as the Dzurinda government in Slovakia in the period from 1998 to 2006 and the Saakashvili government in 2004–2011 showed.[35]

The Filat government was good at rhetoric but *significant* (let alone breakthrough) *systemic reforms* did not occur in practice. Moreover, the chief oligarch of the previous Voronin government, Vlad Plahotniuc not only positioned himself into the role of chief oligarch of the new regime but gradually gained the upper hand politically as well, above both Filat and the government in general. His method was devious: he advocated a European, and with it a concomitant Romanian, orientation yet tried to build his own patronal dominance over Moldova at the same time.

He even installed a socialist, "pro-Russian" politician as president, so that he could more effectively argue before Europe and Romania that he was the actual savior of Moldova's European orientation. That he succeeded represents a unique example of a (seemingly) European orientation combined with systemic deterioration. In this way he created a special type of patronal autocracy in Moldova in the period 2013–2019.

The most important element of Plahotniuc's success was that he concentrated more on mafia methods—controlling primarily the prosecution and the secret services—and relatively less on classic political fighting. He also needed international actors—less the European Union than the US and Romania—to play along with him and to buy into his "geopolitics" in place of systemic logic. This is of paramount importance to understand. For the European Union, however, it was much more consequential to pursue a rule of law agenda, having learned from its errors during the Filat government when Moldova, on the basis of pro-European rhetoric rather than deeds, was declared a "model student" and was offered association status in 2013 at the EU Vilnius Summit.[36]

However, Plahotniuc's dominance was not total, and he eventually had to flee the country in June 2019. Why was Plahotniuc ultimately unsuccessful in consolidating his power? We shall list a few factors. First, we need to recognize that Moldova, like Ukraine, has achieved considerable levels of pluralism over its short period of independence. Paradoxically enough, part of the reason for this pluralism is the differing geopolitical aspirations in both societies. In both countries, there was (and in Moldova, still is) a sizeable portion of society that would like to belong to the "Russian world" *(Русский Мир)*. In Moldova, there is a saying that the country has no *political* parties, only *geopolitical* ones. Of course, this saying contains a tremendous degree of oversimplification but it also contains some truth. In Moldova, the "left" means allegiance to Russia, while the "right" means commitment mainly to Romania but also broadly to the West or the European Union.

Another factor was that the oligarch, with his likely criminal background, was publicity-shy and thus unable to gain the kind of electoral legitimacy that some other "godfathers" (or chief patrons) in the region could. And when, on one occasion, Plahotniuc was close to bribing his way into the prime minister's position, the otherwise very unassuming president, Nicolae Timofti, refused to nominate him.

Thirdly, pluralism not only meant a stubborn diversity of political parties and actors, but also a significant civil society which, because Plahotniuc had cast his lot with the European Union and Romania, he could not easily eliminate. This civil society emerged in think tanks and, in particular, in media such as the popular news and talk show channel TV 7 (later reincarnated as TV 8), which exposed the nature of his system through investigative journalism and critical interviews. Moreover, the EU, after the disappointment with the Filat government, learned its lesson in taking a principled stance on the rule of law instead of satisfying itself with declarations of Europeanness. Lastly, and again paradoxically, Plahotniuc got into trouble with powerful interests in Russia. There are many allegations about how exactly he did this, but it is a fact that during governmental crisis in the spring of 2019, the Russians pushed President Dodon, *de facto* head of the pro-Russian Socialist Party, *not* to establish a coalition with Plahotniuc—even though the numbers were there for forming a government together and there was evidently an unspoken arrangement between the two.

The events in early Summer of 2019 that led to the escape of Plahotniuc and formation of a coalition between Maia Sandu's Party of Action and Solidarity (PAS) and Igor Dodon's Socialist Party were partly the result of strong civil society and pro-European party political activism but partly also that of the unique temporary coincidence of interests of the European Union and Russia—even if the calculations and expectations of the two were wildly differing. Sandu's presidential victory in 2020 and her party's victory in the 2021 parliamentary election has created a unique political situation insofar not only was presidency and parliament in the same hands but the victory of PAS was overwhelming.

Unfortunately, the lack of an astute understanding of the nature of breakthrough reforms combined with the gas crisis and subsequent war in Ukraine have meant that this unique opportunity of a reformist president supported by a large parliamentary majority has not been utilized for breakthrough reforms.[37] As analyst Adrian Lupusor stated at a conference, this was meant to be a reformist government but it became a good crisis-management government instead. Since the fall of 2021, the government has first had to manage the gas crisis and then the refugee crisis, both within a sharply deteriorating regional security environment. It has managed this situation rather well and used the opportunity presented when the EU offered candidate status to Ukraine in the face of Russian aggression in order to negotiate candidate status for Moldova as well. It was also greatly helped by the Romanian voice within the European Union. (It should be noted that Georgia has not been fully included in this offer. In its case the EU has been deliberately ambiguous, understandable given the poor political record of the Georgian government as of late, not to mention its backsliding on the radical reforms of the Saakashvilli era.)

When the EU handed candidate status to the two countries, it also engaged in a good balancing act: Moldova's institutional preparedness at that moment was no weaker than Ukraine's. The latter, however, lobbied heavily to be the only one from the Eastern Partnership to get this status as they felt the EU needed to emphasize strongly their heroic commitment to European values. At the beginning of the conflict, they also expressed some hard feelings towards Moldova as the latter was only providing moral support and solidarity but had failed to join the EU sanctions regime. Moldova at that point felt too vulnerable to Russia's gas blackmail and to the possibility of Russian military aggression and thus displayed a measured attitude, condemning the aggression but not joining the sanctions regime. While Ukraine had a valid point, the EU decision-makers were correct in not making this the sole consideration. Thus, on balance, they judged rightly that both countries should be given candidate status.

The central obstacle to the rapid process of EU integration of Ukraine and Moldova is the governance deficit in both countries, just as it has been in the Western Balkans, which provides a cautionary tale. The Balkan countries as a group were offered the famous "European perspective" at the EU summit in Thessaloniki in 2003 which enabled them to apply for EU candidate status.[38] And yet, it is now two full decades later and none of these countries have progressed in a convincing manner towards maturity in governance sufficient for EU membership. North Macedonia has been a candidate country for 17 years as it was granted this status in 2005. Montenegro was subsequently granted candidate status in 2010, Serbia in 2012, and Albania in 2014. This process has been characterized by mutual frustration as the countries involved have not achieved any breakthrough progress in this long period of 8 to 17 years, and thus are no closer to being granted membership in the Union.[39] Domestic politics have failed to facilitate the attainment of this goal, and the European Union has yet to figure out how to incentivize these countries to effect the necessary reforms, even though there is much less geopolitical competition here with Russia (or any other country) than in the case of Ukraine and Moldova.[40]

It is customary to believe that since the countries of the Western Balkans have remained candidates for the European Union for a very long time,[41] with neither their institutional development nor opinion-makers in the countries themselves presaging an early entry into the Union, a similar trajectory thus awaits the Eastern Partnership countries that recently joined the club. It is also often mentioned, not without reason, that Ukraine and Moldova obtained their status largely on political grounds and not because they qualified in terms of institutional maturity or adherence to the rule-of-law. At the moment, enthusiasm remains strong in these new candidate countries, but it would be important to harness it. Rapid progress is not impossible if cooperation between the European Union, particularly the Commission, and the candidate states is very close. What the Balkan experience tells us is that there will be two critical issues for Ukraine and Moldova on the complex road towards EU membership. First, there must be a strong political elite commitment similar to that which the earlier post-socialist accession countries clearly had. Second, the European Union must find a way to incentivize effectively adequate reforms. This leads us to the next section on the difficulties of Western integration.

4. The difficulties of Western integration: how to work together on reforms complying with European standards

4.1. Three common pitfalls: the need to see the essence of the rule of law, reform priorities, and the local context

If Ukraine is able to maintain its independence, at least for a generation, it will become a country hostile to Russia and Russians, as a consequence of the incredible brutality of Russia's war against the Ukrainian people. This makes Ukraine's integration with the European Union likely even more than economic determinants. It should also be underlined that the money for reconstruction is to be found mainly in the European Union. China also has significant financial resources but public opinion will almost certainly favor using European funds, although the costs of reconstruction will be so great that they may still leave room for Chinese investments. This issue is of crucial importance because foreign investors tend to bring with them their corporate culture, which, in turn, depends strongly on their home country's political economy.

In Ukraine, presidents and their presidential teams typically try to build up their own patronal empires. Even if a president has no inclination to do so, his entourage will certainly expect him to do that and will push him in that direction.[42] While there is no reason to doubt the current president's personal decency, the logic of the system he has inherited and the reflexes and expectations of the participants of political and economic life are such that they pose a strong pull factor. Moreover, a war always triggers centralization of power and a war of this magnitude even more so. This war is so disruptive that the likelihood of major changes in the systemic characteristics of the country has definitely increased. Funds for both the war and the post-war reconstruction are and will be enormous. The temptation will inevitably be great for those around the president to build their own economic empire based on this situation. The countervailing forces are, on the one hand, Ukraine's international supporters, none of which want to spend taxpayers' money on enriching new oligarchs, and, on the other, Ukraine's civil society. As the recent scandal around military food procurements shows, the enormously strengthened civil society is such that political actors need to take into account.[43]

As Vladimir Dubrovskiy describes in the first volume, some of the oligarchs have weakened during the Zelensky presidency in Ukraine. The question is whether this means a weakening of the oligarchic (albeit pluralistic) system as such or whether it will be reproduced with different participants or, finally, whether the war will open the door to a more monolithic patronal regime. As Dubrovskiy rightly concludes, the motivations for Ukraine's anti-oligarchy law were more about weakening politically-competing business clans than about establishing the rule of law, something which the presidential team knows little about in the first place.

Moreover, recent experience about virtually all the institutions of justice point to a bumpy road ahead for the most crucial issues concerning what is necessary to transform Ukraine into a country suitable for membership in the European Union.

The above may sound harsh in the face of the enormous heroism Ukraine has displayed in this genocidal war launched against it, but these are two different things. NATO accession would probably be a less demanding exercise and if it occurs it could also contribute to anchoring Ukraine to European values. A further, bumpy road ahead may also mean a longer process of joining. It is in the vital existential interests of the European Union to be very strict on rule of law standards, and this holds true with respect to countries within the Union as well, such as Hungary and Poland. Political compromises in this area are not the right approach. However, what is vital is that the European Union develops the necessary institutional intelligence on the relevant developmental issues so that it is able conduct an intelligent and consequential dialogue with the Ukrainian authorities on crucial systemic challenges. These are beyond human rights and democracy issues and I assume that the criteria here are straightforward, and the EU will be able to have a meaningful and result-oriented dialogue. In three areas, however, it has historically not been as effective:

1. The first issue is the *essence* of the rule of law. The overwhelming routine of the European machinery in integrating countries is for them to adopt the *acquis communautaire*, that is, the accumulated legislation, legal acts, and court decisions that constitute the body of European Union law since 1993. This strategy, broadly speaking, worked when the community was made up of six countries, and later also when countries which had similar rule of law standards joined the initial core members. But even then there were significant challenges in many places, the most visible being the difficulty with modernizing the Italian *Mezzogiorno*[44] and the weaknesses of Greek integration, which became particularly evident during the protracted Greek debt crisis of 2009–2012.[45]

    New difficulties came with the dilemma that, while the European project's historical success was the function of the rules-based liberal order of its participants, that very success increased the pressure on other countries with fewer such credentials to join. In particular, the EU needed to cope effectively with the challenge that in some of its new member states the culture of *informality* was so intense that the written law was only a loose influencer of their business and governmental practices. As we move further into the Balkans and into Eastern Europe, the problem becomes more acute. Establishing a rules-based liberal order requires much more than adopting the *acquis communautaire* as the European Union gradually recognized. Thus, Bulgaria and Romania, upon joining the EU, were obliged to adhere to the Cooperation and Verification Mechanism (CVM),[46] an annual mechanism to monitor and evaluate progress in the area of justice. However, the European Union needs to acquire a much deeper understanding, closer to the decision-making level, to be able to guide the process of sustainable rule of law reform.[47] And one of the key things to monitor is the *implementation* of the written law and, ultimately, the establishment of a strongly independent and professional judiciary. It may take time for such an institutional situation to take root, but there is no other way: shortcuts here are simply not prudent.

The EU should also avoid what I call the fallacy of the anti-corruption drive. Often, and this includes Ukraine and Moldova, thorough, deep, and complex reforms towards establishing the rule of law have been replaced by something much narrower: the drive to eradicate corruption through exclusively repressive tools.[48] The problem here concerns three issues. First, establishing the rule of law is much broader as it involves building institutions. Second, anti-corruption campaigns look impressive both to the public and to external friends, but upon closer scrutiny their main purpose all too often is to clamp down on political or oligarchic opponents.[49] Third, and crucially, corruption should not be "fought" exclusively, or even predominantly, with repressive tools. Equally, or even more important, is the creation of the appropriate positive incentives in the form of supporting honest civil service and eliminating the usually enormous administrative blockages to doing business.[50]

2. The second issue is the *number of priorities*. The EU accession process is too mechanical and bureaucratic. Of course, this legalistic approach had its advantages, as at the time of accession-enthusiasm was depicted by Heather Grabbe.[51] This view proved to be overoptimistic even for the then new member states, and it is certainly inadequate now. The European Union negotiates 35 chapters of the EU *acquis*, each of which details a number of simultaneous priorities, and then clicks the boxes. This approach to systemic transformation is very inadequate, and does not consider the importance of a *strategy* for change. In other words, it does not ask the question which reforms have a breakthrough effect and may trigger cascading changes or at least make other changes easier. The EU needs to be able to enforce a sense of priorities over its bureaucratic routine of negotiating everything. For this, the EU needs to establish strategies for breakthrough reforms through the inclusion of local experts who have an intimate knowledge of the local specifics. When the Revolution of Dignity occurred in Ukraine, a unique coalition of NGOs spontaneously emerged, called the Reanimation Package of Reforms (RPR). This uniquely qualified group of experts eventually broke up partly because of financing issues and partly over organizational disagreements. However, many exceptionally good experts became visible there whose expertise should be

employed in the process of reforms for EU accession. Of course, one can still negotiate different chapters, and there are some minor changes that would be useful in the absence of the breakthrough ones. But operationally speaking, the view on priorities needs to be enforced, and these need to be less "politically correct" than real in the sense of their contributions to the overall success in establishing liberal democracy.

3. The third and final issue is that the EU needs to learn how to account for *the local context*. Bureaucratic capacities in the two candidate countries are inadequate, not to mention the overall level of corruption which poses an additional hindrance to bureaucratic efficiency. It is not only that in such circumstances prioritization is important, as I mentioned in the previous paragraph, but that some of the regulatory solutions applicable to countries that have high bureaucratic capacity may not be "optimal but bearable" but can be outright dysfunctional in the member states as well as the candidate countries. The EU needs to identify these areas and to reconcile with a transition period where sudden institutional change is not feasible. Ukraine and Moldova may well have to work with lower regulatory barriers and with simplified variants relative to the body of EU regulations during the period before accession in order to arrive at a state compatible with EU membership. This approach would be new to the EU's bureaucratic routine, yet *it is vital for systemic reform in the two candidate states, particularly in Ukraine.*

Overall, it will be important to form teams from among the EU and candidate countries' experts who can work together and bridge the gap between outside expertise on EU expectations in different fields and how these can be interpreted and implemented in the local context.

4.2. The dangers of derailment: Moldova's bumpy (but promising) road to the EU and the importance of transparent reconstruction in post-war Ukraine

Since I concluded that EU accession should preferably be a longer process, it is justified to ask about the risks that may derail it. Indeed, the risks in the two countries are asymmetrical. The Moldovan process may be easier in three ways. First, as we saw, the country's economic integration with the EU is more advanced than that of Ukraine (although the separation from the Russian economy is essentially completed in the latter, too, not least because of Russia's suicidal aggressive posture itself). Second, Moldova's EU path is to some extent assisted by Romania. Third, Moldova is small, does not have very large oligarchs, and the EU's policy influence, if applied skillfully, could be greater and easier to materialize than in the case of Ukraine.

The sense in which there is a greater risk in Moldova than in Ukraine is based on the fact that the war has made drawing close to Russia politically unfeasible for Ukraine (unless Russia is able to establish a puppet regime there, but this would require the occupation of Kyiv which does not look realistic). In the case of Moldova, there is still a sizeable and politically influential constituency for either a pro-Russian or a neutral, equidistant stance. It is beyond the task of this chapter to explain the motivations for such a—perhaps surprising—situation. In brief, this is the combined effect of different factors. First, Russian speakers (both Ukrainians and Gagauz) are afraid of losing their linguistic identities, as both speak predominantly Russian. In the case of the Gagauz, they are also worried about losing their "autonomy" status. Some also cultivate a historical narrative with negative connotations regarding the Romanian period between the two world wars. Additionally, pro-European governments have brought intense disappointments. This is particularly true of the Filat government after 2009 until the arrival of the Socialists in power. The government that is still remembered as the most effective is that of President Voronin between 2001 and 2009. The missed reform opportunity of the current period is also a challenge for the pro-European constituency, although it is mitigated by the horrifying deeds of the Russian army in neighboring Ukraine. However, politics tends to be local in Moldova as well and the failure of the current government to fulfill its promise of cleaning up the public administration and justice has put a serious dent in its popularity. The Moldovan public is generally disillusioned, and it is difficult to predict where this will lead. The greatest risk, obviously, is that a government with a firmly pro-Russian intent may lock the country in.

One specific problem for Moldova's EU integration is the unresolved Transnistrian conflict. However, 2023 may offer an opportunity for the breakaway region's reunification with the rest of the country. Politically speaking, not all the relevant players would necessarily be in favor of it and for three reasons. One reflects a political calculus: some may worry that combining the country with a "brainwashed" region could shift the electorate towards the pro-Russian opposition. Second, others may worry that, along with Transnistria, Moldova may import the kind of oligarchic system that it barely managed to get rid of in 2019. Third, many simply believe that "they are different from us," and are quite reluctant to take on board what is perceived as a culturally different population. Incidentally, fears exist on the Transnistrian side, too, as a large part of the population is concerned (1) that their currently cheap household energy, ultimately subsidized by Russia, may give way to energy prices many times higher; (2) that the status of properties acquired during the existence of the illegal statelet would be uncertain, and (3) that the Russian language, now official and factually monopolistic in Transnistria, will be officially delegitimized. These fears would also have to be addressed if a settlement to this 31-year-old conflict is to be successful and sustainable.

However, Moldova's joining the EU will not necessarily be made dependent on resolving the Transnistrian conflict. Overall, in the case of Moldova, it is more likely that the EU accession process will not only be successful but will ultimately turn the country into a liberal democracy. But even in their case the road will be thorny and full of risks. Moldova is small and poor, and while its political culture is generally non-violent it is still a complex society without the kind of governance and behavioral traditions that would support such a process. And so far the country's two pro-European governments have both failed to deliver breakthrough reforms that could be deemed credible by the public.

The case of Ukraine is even more complicated. The country has a strong tradition of patronal democracy, most of the time with a lively display of democratic political competition.[52] The EU should embrace a tough and potentially long process of guiding Ukraine toward the kind of state that is compatible with EU accession. Again, this is not to undermine in any way the current leadership's mighty and heroic stance in its existential struggle against a heinous aggressor. However, for the European Union, it is an equally existential issue not to allow its own rule of law standards to be undermined. As mentioned before, EU accession is also traditionally motivated by the amount of cohesion and structural funds available. This legitimate consideration should not hasten the pace of EU accession. Indeed, for many years Ukraine's reconstruction needs will surpass manifold the theoretical available structural funds should Ukraine be an EU member. The EU should remain ready to take the lead in financing Ukraine's reconstruction, and also in setting up procedural expectations as to funds' disbursement.

The European Union will be the main supporter of Ukraine's post-war reconstruction, which will require hundreds of billions of euros. The way in which the reconstruction process and related spending will be organized will have a fundamental influence on Ukraine's systemic characteristics. Given the vast amount of large-scale public projects required, it will obviously be difficult to establish fair market conditions and to avoid the kind of oligarchic concentration of economic and political power so characteristic of much of the post-Soviet environment. Undoubtedly, the oligarchs of the previous period have been weakened during the Russian invasion. In this sense, the war has had a disruptive effect on the patronal democracy of the earlier period in two senses: the traditional oligarchs have been weakened, while, at the same time, the necessary war-time concentration of political power may challenge some of the democratic credentials. The question is whether the old oligarchs will be able to regain their power and whether new ones will emerge or not. What the European Union can do at the very least is to manage the process of Ukraine's reconstruction with strong, meaningful transparency imposed on the receiving end.

At the same time, the EU should embrace Ukraine and Moldova as much as possible during the process, inviting them to observe and participate in almost all institutions. We do not yet know how French President Macron's initiative for a European Political Community will develop, and to what extent it will satisfy the expectations of countries eager to join the European Union.[53] So far, it is my impression that it will be very difficult and perhaps impossible to do that insofar as candidate countries require three things: (1) the financial strength of the European Union; (2) security guarantees against future Russian aggression; and (3) participation in key decisions affecting the allocation of money and power within Europe. The two key institutions seem to remain the European Union and NATO.

The question may arise: will maintaining due process in EU integration not weaken Ukraine's international security? I do not think this will be the case. Candidate status has already given an enormous moral boost to the country. Now due process needs to be maintained. At the same time, NATO accession remains a legitimate aspiration, as NATO is the main potential guarantor of Ukraine's security. At the same time, should NATO accession become a reality, this in itself will present a supportive environment for Ukraine's democratic aspirations and progress in the rule of law. It is important to use different integration formations what they are meant for. In the meantime, it remains to be seen how well the European Political Community can meet the security concerns of Ukraine and Moldova.

5. Conclusion

Ukraine and Moldova have had a difficult start to their independent lives. Under the towering shadow of Russian colonial revisionism, they had to confront mostly artificially generated conflicts, corrupt governance, and all the problems of patronal societies. They have sunk in this post-Soviet situation to become the poorest countries of Europe. However, they have established an independent life, have generally maintained democracy, and have developed a new, ambitious middle class which aspires to embrace a European future.

After the dissolution of the perverse economic system of the Soviet Union, trade relations between Ukraine and Moldova almost inevitably became more balanced, leading to the crumbling of Russia's central role. The decline was more accentuated in their exports and happened more slowly in their imports where Russian energy remained difficult to replace or at least to reduce significantly. This natural process was accelerated by opposing forces pushing and pulling from the East and the West, respectively. Russia's imperialism and the closing of its markets to exports from these countries forced them to turn to other markets, which fostered quality improvements, whereas Russia's threatening behavior and energy boycotts made Ukrainian and Moldovan elites and a growing proportion of their respective societies inclined to see their future in the Western community. Meanwhile, the European Union, besides fairness, also offered the prospect of large-scale and long-term financial support. In the case of Ukraine, the Russian war against the country has also gradually shifted public opinion towards the desire for NATO-membership.[54] Moldovan public opinion is split on the issue, particularly among Russian speakers for whom the traditional distrust of NATO as the archenemy from Soviet times maintains a strong influence. A majority of Moldovan society still sees safety in neutrality—an opinion, however, that is gradually changing, and I expect will continue to change in the direction of a desire to find shelter under the NATO umbrella.

Russia's full-scale invasion of 2022 has brought the question of the integration pattern to the fore. It has become an existential question: given the terrible experiences of the war and Russia's desire to destroy Ukrainian identity, the only way forward for Ukraine now is Western integration. The most secure shelter would be NATO and, in the view of the author of this chapter, this will actually happen at some point. However, the question remains if and when the North Atlantic alliance will accept Ukraine's application.

Given the uncertainty about Ukraine's accession to NATO, which has provided large-scale support in the country's defense, there is a strong emphasis on the country joining the European Union. Ukraine and Moldova have both earned candidate status; however, accession should not be unduly hastened. The European Union functions well if it has some core homogenous (or nearly homogenous) shared values and systemic characteristics. The kind of reforms that create a liberal competitive economy and the rule of law take time. As past experience shows, the leverage of the European Union is at its greatest while candidate countries are trying to fulfill membership conditions. Thereafter this leverage radically weakens. Moreover, reform reversal[55] in new EU member states makes the EU particularly attentive to opening the doors to new members only if their reforms appear largely irreversible in the political and the economic system.

EU accession is a very formidable challenge, not only for Ukraine but also for the EU. On the one hand, this project should not be approached cynically: Ukraine genuinely deserves an enormous effort to allow it a process that offers a realistic chance of success. However, the intellectual and organizational preparedness of the EU is what needs to improve. It needs to have a scientifically well-analyzed and educated understanding of which *breakthrough reforms* have a chance of transforming Ukraine so that it can safely enter the European Union. It will definitely not be a two-year process, but it should also not follow the example of Turkey or the Western Balkans either. Again, this means identifying the breakthrough areas and *strongly* prioritizing them instead of approaching all 35 chapters simultaneously with equal weight. At the same time, Ukraine's postwar reconstruction process should be harmonized with the need to create breakthrough reforms. This will not be easy at all, since reconstruction will involve hundreds of billions of euros, mainly from public sources. The amount of funds will be so overwhelming for both sides that the temptation will be very high to ignore this principle, especially in Ukraine, and to avoid applying the strictest professional and transparency criteria set by EU institutions. But the stakes are very high not to allow this process to feed corruption and oligarchy (even if it means new oligarchs) because this will cause enormous delays in EU accession and will foster the kind of disappointment and cynicism that we know all too well from the Western Balkans. This is a once in a lifetime opportunity to get Ukraine onto a good systemic and developmental trajectory and it should not be squandered.

Moldova's situation contains elements that are similar and also ones that are dissimilar from that of Ukraine. Moldova has managed to avoid the war for now. Nevertheless, the country faces the same challenges as Ukraine regarding long-run reforms. Moldova is much smaller than Ukraine, both in territory and in population. Furthermore, Moldova has a strong advocate within the European Union in the form of Romania. Having such an ally can be powerful, as the example of Cyprus has demonstrated. While the relationship is complex, it could ultimately be a great blessing in making both the EU and Moldova focus on advancing the accession agenda.

The example of the Western Balkans countries shows that it is easy to lose focus in this complex endeavor. The success of the accession process depends most critically on very deep reforms relative to the countries' historical trajectories. These reforms will not come automatically; they will necessitate both a reformist government that knows what reforms to introduce and how to manage them, and a dedicated and focused European Union. It will be a tall order for both candidate countries and for the European Union itself. In Moldova, the current government's lack of popularity (I do not differentiate between the previous government of Natalia Gavrilita and the current one of Dorin Recean but regard them both as "the government of Maia Sandu") in itself represents a major short- and perhaps medium-term challenge. Of course, in the ideal case, Russia's influence will be pushed back and the "political pendulum" will stop. In this respect, resolving the Transnistrian conflict "in a European way" could well add a powerful incentive for a long-term breakthrough systemic reform.

In the case of Ukraine, there are three structural factors that may improve its chances of systemic evolution towards the maturity of European Union membership. The first is the dramatic social change that has taken place since the Revolution of Dignity, which has accelerated in some important respects since

Russia's full-scale invasion.[56] Ukraine's population, significantly larger than that of Moldova, is now firmly pro-EU and pro-NATO. In this sense, Ukraine will not experience the same political uncertainties that Moldova may go though over the next few years. Second, Ukraine also has a supporter within the EU, in some ways even more powerful, even if less unambiguous: Poland. Third, Ukraine's oligarchy has, as discussed above, been severely weakened. The challenge now is not to return to patronal democracy but to create something more resembling a liberal, freely competitive economic and political order. It will require all the wisdom and determination Ukraine's international friends can assemble to make this transition successful, and thus clear the path to membership in the European Union. It is clear that the systemic development of both Ukraine and Moldova are closely intertwined with their integration patterns, especially towards the European Union, but also towards NATO.

Notes

1. "European Council Meeting (23 and 24 June 2022) – Conclusions" (Brussels: European Council, June 24, 2022), https://www.consilium.europa.eu/media/57442/2022-06-2324-euco-conclusions-en.pdf.
2. This is especially so since one of the authors in this volume is my co-author in Vladimir Dubrovskiy et al., "Six Years of the Revolution of Dignity: What Has Changed?" (Kyiv: CASE Ukraine, June 2020), https://case-ukraine.com.ua/content/uploads/2020/06/6-years-of-the-Revolution-of-Dignity_v-02_06.pdf.See also the two editors' recent volume, which provides a system analysis which was instrumental to framing this chapter: Bálint Magyar and Bálint Madlovics, *A Concise Field Guide to Post-Communist Regimes: Actors, Institutions, and Dynamics* (Budapest–Vienna–New York: CEU Press, 2022).
3. Moldova's case is different as it has neutrality enshrined in its constitution. Of course, this war, which holds many implications for Moldova, may change perspectives and the security equation.
4. This fact is challenged by Dimitry Kochenov and Ronald Janse, "Admitting Ukraine to the EU: Article 49 TEU Is the 'Special Procedure,'" SSRN Scholarly Paper (Rochester, NY, April 13, 2022), https://papers.ssrn.com/abstract=4083111.
5. "USSR Ceases to Exist, 11 Republics Forming CIS," accessed March 5, 2023, https://interfax.com/newsroom/top-stories/73424/.
6. Andrej Krickovic, "Imperial Nostalgia or Prudent Geopolitics? Russia's Efforts to Reintegrate the Post-Soviet Space in Geopolitical Perspective," *Post-Soviet Affairs* 30, no. 6 (2014): 503–28.
7. As the former Russian prime minister, Viktor Chernomyrdin, once put it: "*Хотели чтобы было лучше, а получилось как всегда*," that is, "we intended the best, but it turned out as always."
8. Przemyslaw Furgacz, "The Russian-Ukrainian Economic War," *Ante Portas–Studia Nad Bezpieczeństwem* 5, no. 2 (2015): 115–30.
9. The history of using this pretext by Russia to pressure Moldova is very rich. For an early example, see "Russia Intends to Stop Importing Agricultural Products from Moldova," Moldova.org, May 17, 2005, https://www.moldova.org/en/russia-intends-to-stop-importing-agricultural-products-from-moldova-2671-eng/. For selective use of the tool, see "Rosselhoznadzor Allowes 43 Moldovan Companies to Supply Fruit to Russia," Infotag.md, July 26, 2016, http://www.infotag.md/economics-en/228433/. And, for a recent application, see "Russia to Ban Imports of Crop Products from 31 Districts of Moldova as of Aug 15," Interfax, August 10, 2022, https://interfax.com/newsroom/top-stories/82092/. In each of these cases, as well as other ones, the phytosanitary argument was a thinly veiled pretext and the real purpose was political pressuring.
10. Denis Cenusa et al., "Russia's Punitive Trade Policy Measures towards Ukraine, Moldova and Georgia," CEPS Working Document, September 25, 2014, https://www.ceps.eu/ceps-publications/russias-punitive-trade-policy-measures-towards-ukraine-moldova-and-georgia/.
11. For a detailed description of the story of the Kozak Memorandum and its failure, see William H. Hill, *Russia, the Near Abroad, and the West: Lessons from the Moldova-Transdniestria Conflict* (Washington, D.C.: Woodrow Wilson Center Press, 2013).
12. See John Löwenhardt, "The OSCE, Moldova and Russian Diplomacy in 2003," *Journal of Communist Studies and Transition Politics* 20, no. 4 (2004): 103–12; Hill, *Russia, the Near Abroad, and the West*.
13. "The 1999 OCSE Istanbul Summit Decisions on Moldova and Georgia: Prospects for Implementation," Wilson Center, October 24, 2002, https://www.wilsoncenter.org/event/the-1999-ocse-istanbul-summit-decisions-moldova-and-georgia-prospects-for-implementation; Vladimir Socor, "Russian Troops in Moldova – Main Remaining Obstacle to CFE Treaty Ratification," *EuroJournal.Org - Journal of Foreign Policy of Moldova*, no. 3 (2007), https://www.ceeol.com/search/article-detail?id=27348.
14. Alexei Pikulik, "Belarus, Russia, and Ukraine as Post-Soviet Rent-Seeking Regimes," in *Stubborn Structures: Reconceptualizing Post-Communist Regimes*, ed. Bálint Magyar (Budapest–New York: CEU Press, 2019), 489–505.

[15] Also, it is clear in retrospect that Putin and his inner circle have never fully counted on the power of trade and have ultimately relied on the power of brute force instead; so, if trade blackmail did not work, they always had in the back of their minds that they could do what they did first in Georgia in 2008, and then in Ukraine in 2014, and what revealed its true face in February 2022.

[16] See Dymtro Tuzhansky, "Ukraine's Energy Sovereignty in Time of War: Russia Lost Influence, but the Oligarchs Did Not," in *Ukraine's Patronal Democracy and the Russian Invasion*, eds. Bálint Madlovics and Bálint Magyar (Budapest–Vienna–New York: CEU Press, 2023), 193–220.

[17] Computation by Vladimir Dubrovskiy. An earlier version of this table is in Dubrovskiy et al., "Six Years of the Revolution of Dignity."

[18] See "Foreign Direct Investment in Ukraine: War and Peace," Dnipropetrovsk Regional Council, accessed March 5, 2023, https://oblrada.dp.gov.ua/en/investors/foreign-direct-investment-in-ukraine-war-and-peace/. It also shows that a large proportion of FDI comes from tax havens, usually of Ukrainian or Russian origin.

[19] "Eastern Partnership," European Council, January 20, 2023, https://www.consilium.europa.eu/en/policies/eastern-partnership/.

[20] Thomas E. Ricks, "7 Former Communist Countries Join NATO," *The Washington Post*, March 30, 2004, https://www.washingtonpost.com/archive/politics/2004/03/30/7-former-communist-countries-join-nato/476d93dc-e4bd-4f05-9a15-5b66d322d0e6/.

[21] "Conditions for Membership," European Commission, June 6, 2012, https://neighbourhood-enlargement.ec.europa.eu/enlargement-policy/conditions-membership_en.

[22] On the case of Hungary, see Bálint Madlovics and Bálint Magyar's chapter in this volume.

[23] In fact, even earlier, the Kuchmagate scandal may well have been a Russian "special operation" to discredit the then Ukrainian president, according to the well-researched book by Taras Kuzio, *Ukraine: Democratization, Corruption, and the New Russian Imperialism* (Santa Barbara, California: Praeger, 2015). See also Patrick E. Tyler, "New Tapes Appear With Threats by Ukraine's President," *The New York Times*, February 19, 2001, sec. World, https://www.nytimes.com/2001/02/19/world/new-tapes-appear-with-threats-by-ukraine-s-president.html.

[24] For a good discussion of the international law aspect of Kosovo's declaration of independence, see Christopher J. Borgen, "Kosovo's Declaration of Independence: Self-Determination, Secession and Recognition," *American Society of International Law* 12, no. 2 (2008), https://www.tjsl.edu/slomansonb/2.4_KosSecession.pdf.

[25] The Summit declared that the next step in the relations would be an Association Agreement. "EU-Ukraine Summit" (Paris: Council of the European Union, September 9, 2008), https://www.consilium.europa.eu/uedocs/cms_data/docs/pressdata/en/er/102633.pdf.

[26] Dubrovskiy et al., "Six Years of the Revolution of Dignity."

[27] Although anecdotal evidence also points to "inefficiencies" in corruption during the Poroshenko–Yatseniuk regime: whereas in the previous period illegal favors were allegedly well-oiled and the tariffs well established, after the revolution people stopped knowing whom to bribe and with how much. By some accounts "transaction costs" actually increased in the less certain power situation following the Revolution of Dignity.

[28] See Vladimir Dubrovsky's chapter on the chances of anti-patronal transformation in *Ukraine's Patronal Democracy and the Russian Invasion: The Russia-Ukraine War, Volume One*, edited by Bálint Madlovics and Bálint Magyar (Budapest–Vienna–New York: CEU Press, 2023).

[29] At that point NATO accession was not on the agenda and, in fact, did not enjoy majority support from Ukrainian society. Only Putin's renewed aggression led to an almost unanimous preference for NATO.

[30] Dubrovskiy et al., "Six Years of the Revolution of Dignity."

[31] The author's Blue Ribbon Committee, instituted while working as a regional director of the United Nations Development Program, was initiated specifically in order to establish a joint effort in this direction. (See Ian Traynor, "Ukraine Must Reform Fast, UN Team Says," *The Guardian*, January 13,

2005, sec. World news, https://www.theguardian.com/world/2005/jan/13/ukraine.iantraynor.) However, the then prime minister, Yulia Timoshenko, was not ready to sacrifice her perceived (indeed, misperceived) political interests at the altar of breakthrough reforms. The final report of the Commission, with the hindsight of later experience, also contained weaknesses. In particular, the approach to the rule of law was not ambitious and concrete enough.

32 Ukraine is the largest country located entirely within Europe.

33 I analyzed this process in some detail in Kálmán Mizsei, "The New East European Patronal States and the Rule-of-Law," in *Stubborn Structures: Reconceptualizing Post-Communist Regimes*, ed. Bálint Magyar (Budapest–New York: CEU Press, 2019), 531–610.

34 Leszek Balcerowicz, "Poland: Stabilization and Reforms under Extraordinary and Normal Politics," in *The Great Rebirth: Lessons from the Victory of Capitalism over Communism*, ed. Anders Åslund and Simeon Djankov (Washington, DC: Peterson Institute for International Economics, 2014), 17–38.

35 Sadly, both examples demonstrate that we still do not know how to ensure that such reformist governments are not followed by anti-reformist ones: in both cases eight years of deep and comprehensive reforms were followed by a serious backlash which, while not wiping out all the reforms, certainly eroded much of their impact.

36 "Eastern Partnership: The Way Ahead," Joint Declaration of the Eastern Partnership Summit (Vilnius: The Council of the European Union, November 29, 2013), https://www.consilium.europa.eu/media/31799/2013_eap-11-28-joint-declaration.pdf.

37 For a thorough and critical review of the missed reforms, see Elena Vitanova, "Деолигархизация с молдавской спецификой. Инна Шупак о борьбе с клептократией и упущенных возможностях PAS [Deoligarchization with a Moldovan specificity. Inna Shupak on the fight against kleptocracy and missed opportunities of PAS]," NewsMaker, December 9, 2022, https://newsmaker.md/rus/novosti/deoligarkhizatsiya-s-moldavskoj-spetsifikoj/.

38 "EU-Western Balkans Summit - Declaration" (Thessaloniki, June 21, 2003), 5, https://www.consilium.europa.eu/uedocs/cms_data/docs/pressdata/en/misc/76291.pdf.

39 Their integrational vacuum has been filled, however, by NATO membership in the case of Albania, Montenegro, and North Macedonia.

40 See in the extensive literature on the subject in John O'Brennan, "Enlargement Fatigue and Its Impact on the Enlargement Process in the Western Balkans," LSE IDEAS Special Report on EU Enlargement (London School of Economics and Political Science, September 2013), https://www.academia.edu/12882126/Enlargement_Fatigue_and_its_impact_on_the_Enlargement_Process_in_the_Western_Balkans_.

41 Not to speak about Turkey's candidate status that dates to 1999. See "Candidate Countries - Enlargement - Environment - European Commission," European Commission, accessed March 5, 2023, https://ec.europa.eu/environment/enlarg/candidates.htm.

42 See Mikhail Minakov's chapter on Zelensky and patronal politics in *Ukraine's Patronal Democracy and the Russian Invasion: The Russia-Ukraine War, Volume One,* edited by Bálint Madlovics and Bálint Magyar, 141-65.

43 Christopher Miller, "Anatomy of a Scandal: Why Zelenskyy Launched a Corruption Crackdown in Ukraine," *Financial Times*, January 27, 2023.

44 Carlo Trigilia, "Why the Italian Mezzogiorno Did Not Achieve a Sustainable Growth: Social Capital and Political Constraints," *Cambio. Rivista Sulle Trasformazioni Sociali* 2, no. 4 (2012): 137–48.

45 Dina Abdel Moneim Rady, "Greece Debt Crisis: Causes, Implications and Policy Options," *Academy of Accounting and Financial Studies Journal* 16 (2012): 87.

46 "Mechanism Report on Romania," European Commission, accessed March 5, 2023, https://ec.europa.eu/commission/presscorner/detail/en/qanda_21_2882.

47 Backlash is inevitable in post-communist transitions but its extent and nature is important. One should avoid the kind of chronic rule of law setbacks that are experienced in some member states as well as the very slow progress from low levels that are experienced in some others.

48 Already in 2007, Vladimir Dubrovskiy argued as follows: "Yet another closely related example is anti-corruption policies aimed at increasing the risk of being punished in cases of corruption. Given that under the 'soft' rule of law the legislation is very often difficult to implement, and therefore corruption is a normal practice, catching and jailing of selected scapegoats does not, in fact, significantly reduce the overall level of corruption. However, as long as enforcement remains selective, the anti-corruption persecution is used mostly as a tool in the political, bureaucratic or business wars against rivals, not necessarily the most corrupted persons. Their punishment is respectively (and for the most part fairly) perceived as a result of their bad luck or inability to concord with those in power, rather than as fair consequence of their corrupt behavior. On the other hand, the increasing risk of corrupted deals further solidifies the networks of favors, both at the nexus between business and bureaucracy (reputation is needed to give a bribe, otherwise the bribe-taker risks too much), and within the bureaucracy (in order to protect her/himself from being selected as a scapegoat, a corrupted bureaucrat has to establish and maintain good connections with upper authorities and law enforcement officers). Both effects, in turn, lead to further limitation of access through increased barriers of entry due to higher bribe taxes and direct obstacles for those who are less involved in networks of favors." In Vladimir Dubrovskiy et al., "Institutional Harmonization in the Context of Relations between the EU and Its Eastern Neighbours: Costs and Benefits and Methodologies of Their Measurement," CASE Network Reports (Warsaw: CASE – Center for Social and Economic Research, 2007), 33, https://www.econstor.eu/bitstream/10419/87584/1/555598454.pdf.

49 Oksana Huss, *How Corruption and Anti-Corruption Policies Sustain Hybrid Regimes: Strategies of Political Domination Under Ukraine's Presidents in 1994–2014* (ibidem Press, 2020).

50 "Success of Reforms Is Key to Stability in Ukraine According to Mizsei," Central European University, March 26, 2015, https://www.ceu.edu/article/2015-03-26/success-reforms-key-stability-ukraine-according-mizsei.

51 Heather Grabbe, *The EU's Transformative Power: Europeanization Through Conditionality in Central and Eastern Europe* (Basingstoke: Palgrave Macmillan, 2006).

52 See Bálint Madlovics and Bálint Magyar's introductory chapter in *Ukraine's Patronal Democracy and the Russian Invasion: The Russia-Ukraine War, Volume One*.

53 Branislav Stanicek, "'Beyond Enlargement': European Political Community and Enlargement Policy Reform," At a Glance (European Parliamentary Research Service, November 2022), https://www.europarl.europa.eu/RegData/etudes/ATAG/2022/739209/EPRS_ATA(2022)739209_EN.pdf.

54 See the chapter of Evgenii Golovakha and his colleagues "From Patronalism to Civic Belonging: The Changing Dynamics of the National-Civic Identity in Ukraine," in *Ukraine's Patronal Democracy and the Russian Invasion: The Russia-Ukraine War, Volume One*, 297-329.

55 István P. Székely and Melanie E. Ward-Warmedinger, "Reform Reversal in Former Transition Economies (FTEs) of the European Union: Areas, Circumstances and Motivations," IZA Policy Paper (Institute of Labor Economics, 2018), https://www.iza.org/publications/pp/142/reform-reversal-in-former-transition-economies-ftes-of-the-european-union-areas-circumstances-and-motivations.

56 See, among others, Dubrovskiy et al., "Six Years of the Revolution of Dignity"; "How the War Changed Me and the Country. Summary of the Year," Comprehensive research (Rating Group, February 2023), https://ratinggroup.ua/en/research/ukraine/kompleksne_dosl_dzhennya_yak_v_yna_zm_nila_mene_ta_kra_nu_p_dsumki_roku.html.

Neo-Backwardness and Prospects for Long-Term Growth: The Effects of Western Sanctions on Russia and the Changing Embeddedness of Ukraine in the World Economy
Dóra Győrffy

1. Introduction

Following Vladimir Putin's unjustified aggression against Ukraine, NATO members and their allies immediately imposed harsh sanctions on Russia. Initially there were hopes that the sanctions would immediately cripple the Russian economy, but these hopes did not materialize, and the Russian economy proved to be more resilient than many had expected. Russian propaganda insists that the sanctions are not working and are hurting the sanctioning countries more than Russia. Furthermore, there is little question that the war has had devastating consequences for the Ukrainian economy. However, short-term economic outcomes should not be confused with future development prospects.

This chapter examines the long-term economic impact of the war on Russia and Ukraine relying on various theories of economic growth. It is argued that while the destruction of the war has been disastrous for the Ukrainian economy, over the longer-term Russia will become a neo-backward country and is facing economic ruin, while Ukraine has the opportunity to dismantle its patronal structures, integrate into the Western alliance, and embark on the path of dynamic economic development.

The chapter proceeds as follows. The first part will analyze the sanctions against Russia from a theoretical and practical perspective focusing on their immediate effects. The second part of the chapter will compare the long-term economic prospects for Russia and Ukraine based on theories of economic growth.

2. Sanctions: theoretical considerations and pre-2022 sanctions against Russia

International sanctions represent a middle way between doing nothing and military intervention in influencing another government's decision-making. Such coercive tools—ranging from trade, financial, military, and travel restrictions to individual asset freezes—have become increasingly important during the post-Cold War period.[1] The most frequent sanctioning country is the US, followed by the EU countries as a group, with the latter compensating for their military weakness.[2] In many cases sanctions are demonstrations of resolve when the costs of inaction would be too high, while in others they aim to deter further objectionable acts or signal the defense of national interests to domestic audiences.[3]

Whether sanctions are successful or not depends strongly on the specific objective pursued. According to the extensive overview of Hufbauer et al. only 34% of the 174 sanctions cases they studied from the period since World War I can be considered at least partially successful. More specifically, those with modest goals such as the release of prisoners had a 51% success rate, while those with more ambitious targets such as regime change or the disruption of military adventures had success rates of 31% and a 21%, respectively.[4] Gerald Schneider and Patrick M. Weber found somewhat better results with threats of sanctions alongside actual sanctions increasing the success rate to 57.5%.[5] In the broader literature several factors have been identified which predict the chances for success: positive correlation with the effectiveness of sanctions was found for factors such as economic weakness, political instability, democracy in the target country as well as the strength of pre-sanction relations, while third party assistance to the target and the duration of the sanctions have negative impact.[6]

Russia has been facing various international sanctions since 2012. The first sanctions regime was the Sergei Magnitsky Rule of Law Accountability Act, which aimed to punish those Russian officials who were responsible for the death of the 38-year-old Russian lawyer Sergei Magnitsky in a Russian prison in November 2009.[7] The law allows for visa restrictions and asset freezes to be imposed on the perpetrators, which meant that Putin could no longer guarantee impunity for his collaborators, something which Magyar and Madlovics call the Achilles' heel of the mafia state.[8] Reversing this law was probably one of the main reasons why Putin interfered in the 2016 US presidential elections.[9] The economic sanctions against Russia were broadened in 2014 following the occupation of Crimea and the Donbas, and then again in 2017 after Russia's inference in the US elections became evident. Business dealings with the occupied areas were prohibited, and individuals involved in either the occupation or the election interference were personally sanctioned. The EU and Canada also joined the US in sanctioning Russia. In his 2021 evaluation of the impact of sanctions, Anders Åslund argued that although the sanctions did not lead to the withdrawal of Russian forces from the occupied territories, they succeeded in cutting Russian GDP growth by around 2.5 to 3% per year.[10]

Despite the presence of various sanctions against the occupied territories, business between Russia and the EU did not stop. In September 2015, just after the occupation of the Crimea, the Nord Stream 2 pipeline project was signed by Gazprom and five European companies—Wintershall, Uniper, E.ON, OMV, and Shell. It was already well-known already then that Russia was using energy as a geopolitical tool and the pipeline would only increase Europe's energy dependency on Russia.[11] This project ultimately became the symbol of European reluctance to address the security threat posed by Russia, something which was also reinforced by trade statistics. In 2021 trade between the EU and Russia[12] amounted to €257.5bn. Russia was the fifth most important trading partner for the EU with a 5.8% share of total trade, primarily in mineral fuels (62% of imports). For Russia the EU was its top trading partner responsible for 36.5% of its imports and 37.9% of its exports. Beyond trade relations pre-war financial relations between Russia and the West were also significant. In 2019, the EU was the largest investor in Russia with foreign direct investment (FDI) outward stock in Russia amounting to EUR 311.4 billion, while Russia's FDI stock in the EU was estimated at €136 billion.

Besides trade and FDI relationships, Russians also held large amounts of wealth in both the European Union and the US. According to the calculations of Anders Åslund and Julia Friedlander, dark Russian money has flooded the West and amounted to around USD USD 1 trillion by 2020 with one quarter of this money belonging to Putin personally, while the rest belonged to his associates.[13] While some of this money has been used to enjoy the lifestyle opportunities provided by the West, another more important function for these funds has been to conduct influence operations against Western governments, such as carrying out Russian propaganda, corrupting decision-makers, and building up extremist parties.[14] This network has also helped Putin to arouse distrust and fragmentation within Western societies, which not only undermines their political systems, but also hinders a unified stance against Russian aggression.

3. Sanctions in response to Russian aggression against Ukraine in 2022

When the decision was made to attack Ukraine, the Russians counted on a feeble Western response due to the corrupt ties that had been established over the previous decades. This was most explicitly elaborated by Dmitry Medvedev, Chairman of the Russian Security Council, at a Security Council meeting on February 21, 2022. Recalling the 2008 invasion of Georgia, Medvedev claimed:

> I emphasize, I think we have learned how to do this under the leadership of the President—the *tension that is now vibrating around our country will subside one way or another*. Not quickly, not all at once, but this is how human history works: sooner or later, they will get tired of this situation and will themselves ask us to resume discussions and talks on all issues of ensuring strategic security.
>
> Here, you know, it is like that line from the famous book by Bulgakov: *never ask for anything, they will come to you themselves and offer everything*. This is about how developments

unfolded in 2008–2009. They came to us and suggested resuming relations across the board. *Let us face it, Russia means a lot more than Ukraine for the international community and **our friends in the United States and the European Union**, and everyone understands this, including the Ukrainians.*[15] (emphasis added)

Fortunately, Medvedev's assessment proved to be wrong. Immediately after the invasion, Russia was hit by an unprecedented number of sanctions, which continued to increase as the war progressed.[16] Figure 1 shows the number of sanctions against Russia and other sanctioned states as of November 30, 2022.

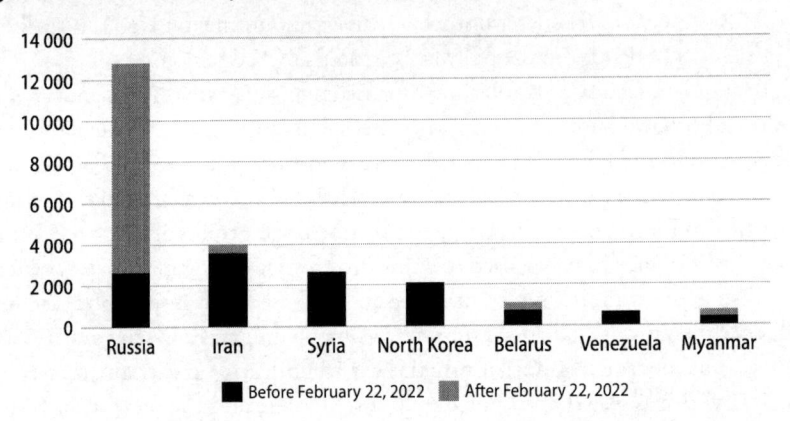

Figure 1. Number of sanctions placed worldwide by target country.

Source: Castellum.AI.

The main types of sanctions have been the following:[17]
- individual sanctions (travel bans and asset freezes) against Russian political, military, media, and economic leaders;
- financial sanctions restricting access to the Western financial system and freezing Russian central bank reserves (~USD 300 bn out of total ~630 bn);
- transport sanctions closing access to Western airspace, ports, and roads to Russian-owned vehicles as well as restricting exports related to this sector;
- energy sanctions restricting imports of Russian oil and coal and banning exports of goods as well as investments related to the Russian energy sector;
- defense sanctions banning the export of weapons and dual-use technologies;
- trade sanctions banning exports of luxury goods as well as imports of steel, iron, wood, seafood, spirits, cosmetics, gold, and jewelry;
- bans on services including engineering, IT, and legal services;
- suspension of state-owned propaganda media including *Sputnik* and *Russia Today*.

Despite the extensive sanctions, Russia did not stop the aggression; meanwhile, average household electricity and gas prices rose 15% and 34%, respectively, in the EU during the first half of 2022.[18] In the EU, soaring energy prices have contributed to inflation, while for Russia they have meant enormous revenues as the country registered a record USD 70bn current account surplus in the second quarter of 2022.[19] This windfall revenue could further finance Russia's war machine and contribute to rebuilding the country's frozen reserves. These developments have also contributed to fueling the Russian narrative, which insists that sanctions do not work and hurt the West more than Russia.[20] However, a deeper look beyond the surface reveals that sanctions do work and that the Russian economy is in much greater trouble than the Kremlin propaganda machine wants to admit.

The first comprehensive overview of the impact of the sanctions was written by Jeffrey Sonnenveld et al. in July 2022. Their main findings can be summarized as follows:[21]

- Russia has irretrievably lost its largest export market for energy, the European Union. While oil exports could be redirected towards Asia, it is with significantly greater transport costs and at discount prices (USD 35/barrel below Brent oil), as most existing gas pipelines are oriented towards Europe with the majority going through Ukraine. With few pipelines running towards China and limited LNG capacities, Russia will face significant hurdles to reorient its gas exports, 83% of which used to go to Europe. As 60% of government revenues come from energy exports, these developments represent a serious blow to future revenue prospects.
- Imports declined by 50%, which has led to severe shortages in crucial raw materials and components for the domestic economy.
- The collapse in trade has been accompanied by the flight of over 1000 Western companies, whose total investments accounted for 40% of Russian GDP.
- By summer 2022 over 500,000 Russians had left the country—50% of them highly educated. Some 15,000 ultra-high net worth individuals also left, which meant at least USD 70bn in capital flight.
- Putin was able to keep the Russian economy afloat during 2022 only with the help of unsustainable monetary and fiscal support, which drew on the National Wealth Fund—consequently, Russian reserves declined by USD 75bn during the first half of 2022.
- Russia is on its way to economic oblivion, and there is no way to avoid it.

In a December 2022 paper, Heli Simola examined whether Russia would be able to adapt to its isolation.[22] Her findings support the earlier analysis of Sonnenveld et al.:

- While oil was redirected to Asia, further redirection—in response to the EU price cap imposed in December 2022—will pose a significant challenge for Russia because of a lack of shipping capacity. Given the missing pipelines to Asia, gas can be redirected from Europe to an even lesser extent, and Russian gas exports have already declined by about 45% during 2022.
- Imports have recovered somewhat since the first half of 2022, but they are still 30% below the pre-war level (Figure 2). A major reorientation has taken place towards China, Turkey, and Kazakhstan, but these countries cannot substitute for the Western technology lost due to the sanctions.

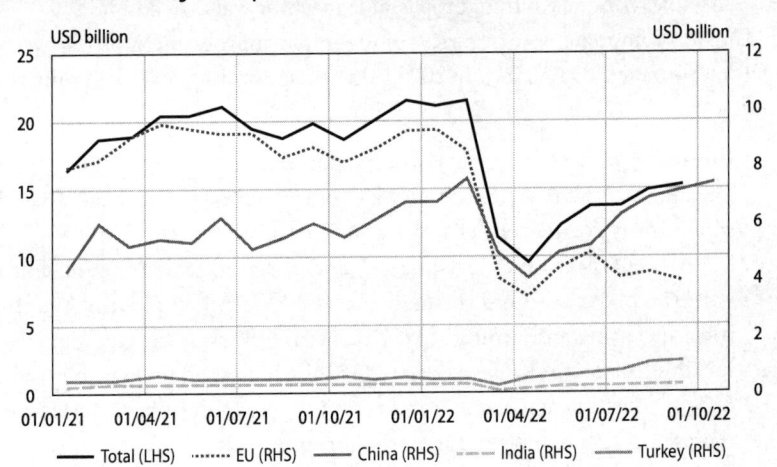

Figure 2. Value of Russia goods imports 2021–2022 (USD billion).

Source: Simola, Can Russia Reorient Its Trade?, 14.

While most analyses focus on the immediate impact of sanctions, assessing the long-term prospects for a country requires a more extensive analysis of various factors of economic growth. In the following section the main theories of economic growth will first be introduced and then applied in a comparative analysis of the economic prospects of Russia and Ukraine.

4. The long-term consequences of the war for growth in Russia and Ukraine

4.1. The causes of economic growth: a theoretical background

Modern theories of economic growth rely on the Solow model,[23] which argues that growth is dependent on capital, labor, and the efficiency of their use, which is determined by technology. The latter factor is considered an exogenous variable, which ultimately drives growth. Based on this model, growth can be induced by increasing the amount of capital, increasing the quantity and quality of the labor force, or increasing the level of technology.

While technology has remained a critical element of growth models, productivity has become a crucial variable in assessing the efficiency of resource use. As stated by Nobel laureate Paul Krugman: "Productivity isn't everything, but in the long run it is almost everything."[24] This implies the need to raise output per worker. Raising productivity is an extremely broad concept and involves areas such as high-quality infrastructure, education, and research, as well as competition in the markets for goods, labor, capital, and services. These factors are measured by various indices, such as the World Economic Forum Global Competitiveness Index.

A key element in competitiveness is the quality of formal institutions, which represent the "rules of the game" for economic activity.[25] The ability of the state to protect property rights and enforce contracts provides the foundation for economic activity according to institutional economists. By the 2000s this idea had become widely accepted as it was shown that the quality of formal institutions predominated over both geography and openness to trade as an explanatory factor for economic growth.[26] Acemoglu and Robinson have also emphasized that inclusive institutions, which provide access to public goods for the whole society, are more advantageous for growth than extractive institutions, which only serve the interests of elite groups.[27]

However, even institutions might not be the final cause of economic growth. McCloskey argues[28] that periods of growth explosions in history cannot be explained by more labor, capital, or trade, or by a somewhat better institutional framework—which she considers material factors—but rather by ideas assigning dignity and liberty to ordinary people. Freedom is the ultimate basis for creativity and innovation, which in turn drives economic growth.

In assessing future growth prospects in the following section, I will review the main determinants of growth first in Russia and then in Ukraine, assessing the quantity and quality of capital and labor, access to technology, the role of the state, and the prospects for the dominance of liberal ideas.

4.2. Neo-backwardness in Russia: the impact of the war on long-term growth

In 2022 the decline in Russian GDP is expected to be only 3.4% followed by another decline of 2.3% in 2023 according to the IMF.[29] Considering the extent of the sanctions, this appears to be a moderate reduction. There are multiple reasons for this muted response to the sanctions: (a) energy sanctions came too late, resulting in a revenue windfall from increased prices; (2) loose monetary and fiscal policies cushioned the blow of sanctions; and (3) the share of military industrial production increased from 1–2% to 4-5% of all industrial production.[30] However, the long-term determinants of growth paint a bleaker picture for Russia.

Russia has lost access to Western capital markets due to the sanctions and, as noted in the previous section, over 1000 foreign firms have left the country and are unlikely to return. The collapse of the Russian capital market is indicated by the over 50% fall in the Russian stock market index (MOEX) as shown by Figure 3.

Figure 3. Russian stock market index (MOEX) 2018-2022.

Source: Yahoo Finance.

Furthermore, it is not only foreign capital which is fleeing, there is also a collapse in domestic lending—the combination of economic recession and mobilization has increased loan arrears by 19% for cars and 35% for mortgages, while new loan issuance has declined sharply due to excessive uncertainty. The financing of future investments will depend strongly on China, which, however, does not have an interest in modernizing the Russian economy. As argued by Gabuev, China instead aims to increase its leverage for its own interests—acquiring sophisticated weapons and their designs, gaining preferential access to the Arctic, ensuring accommodation of its security interests in Central Asia, and obtaining support for its positions on global and regional issues at the UN.[31]

Labor trends also paint a bleak picture for the future. Since the start of the invasion, more than one million Russians have fled their country, making this the largest wave of emigration since the Bolshevik revolution in 1917. Some 300,000 had left by mid-March and at least 500,000 by September, with another 400,000 leaving by early October—after the mobilization.[32] Most of them are men who wanted to avoid the draft. It is estimated that around 30% of all IT engineers have left the country.[33] As long as the war continues, they have little incentive to return as they might immediately be called up to the army. Even after the war they might stay away for several reasons, including fear of punishment for evading the draft, the bleak social, economic, and political prospects in Russia, and better living conditions elsewhere. Their absence undermines the Russian economy as it becomes increasingly isolated from the developed world. It also contributes to exacerbating the demographic decline of the country as annual birth rates are at their lowest level in modern history with 1.2 million births per year against annual deaths of around 2 million.[34]

Access to Western technology has been hampered both by sanctions and by the exit of multinational companies. While imports represent only 20% of GDP, Russia is nevertheless dependent on foreign technologies both for intermediate products and for final consumer goods. This dependence is especially severe in high-tech sectors such as computers and electronics (35% foreign inputs), motor vehicles and other transport (27%), as well as machinery and equipment (26%).[35] One of the hardest hit sectors has been car production, which was down 80% in September.[36] While increased imports from East Asia may substitute for Western imports in certain sectors, this proves more difficult in high-tech sectors; Taiwan and South Korea, the dominant players in semiconductors, have joined the sanctions regime, while non-sanctioning countries such as China have cause for concern about secondary sanctions and thus do not export substitute goods.[37] The collapse of imports has led to the emergence of smugglers or "import-export specialists," who use their creative energies to find loopholes in the sanctions regime and get sanctioned goods through customs.[38] This activity is reminiscent of Soviet times, when stealing technology was an important objective of agents operating abroad, and Vladimir Putin was probably one such official in Dresden.[39] However, it did not help the Soviet system either, which fell significantly behind the capitalist countries in innovation.[40] The drop in intellectual input in the Russian economy is likely to lead to "retarded adaptation"—the forced innovation[41] of substituting Western technology with domestic inputs—or altering the product and leaving the missing input out. The car industry offers some early signs of this process: following the sanctions, Russian authorities eased regulations on safety and air pollution standards, as a result of which the Lada Granta is currently sold without airbags.[42]

As a patronal autocracy with Putin the chief patron since 2003—the year of his second presidential election victory and the takeover of Mikhail Khodorkovsky's Yukos oil company[43]—institutional conditions have hardly been ideal for market-based innovation or development. Putin's return to the presidency in 2013 started a new period of oppression aimed at neutralizing discontent with the suppression of independent civil society, media, and entrepreneurs.[44] As structural change in the economy did not take place and development stalled,[45] nationalist sentiments were cultivated by the occupation of the Crimea and through prestige projects such as the Sochi Winter Olympics in 2014 and the World Cup in 2018. The integration of organized criminal groups under state control for Putin's specific purposes such as killing opponents[46] implies weak property rights, an unaccountable state, and scarce incentive for economic success. The invasion of Ukraine implies a further deterioration of institutional conditions. One aspect has been repressive adaptation, which means that the authorities need to increase the use of force to make people and companies comply with increasingly unpopular decisions, such as mobilization of the economy and the population for the purposes of war. Konstantin Sonin underlines three factors which are inherently ruining the Russian economy: (1) the war, which has immediately led to greater state involvement in the economy, especially in the war-related industries, thus stifling private initiative; (2) mass mobilization, which forces companies to negotiate with various regional and national groups in order to preserve their workforce; and (3) the establishment of private armies and regional volunteer armies, which will likely lead to the return of decentralized corruption and roaming violent groups threatening businesses like in the 1990s.[47] Under such conditions, economic activity has little chance to thrive.

Table 1. Neo-backwardness: sanctions-driven recession.

		Cyclical recession	Sanctions-driven recession
GDP drop		+	+
Lost access to Western financial system (public and private)		−	+
Intellectual input declining due to…	Banned high-tech "dual use" goods	−	+
	Departing enterprises	−	+
	Departing high quality workers	−	+
Retarded adaptation ("forced innovation")		−	+
Repressive adaptation (political suppression)		−	+
Modified trend line of economic development		−	+

If we accept that economic growth is ultimately the outcome of an ideational setting where innovation, creativity, and entrepreneurship are appreciated and liberty is protected, it is easy to see why the Russian economy is facing long-term ruin. As the war increases totalitarian control, any ingenuity is likely to focus on smuggling missing inputs and dealing with rival criminal groups rather than competitiveness in global markets.

Although the widespread sanctions did not cause the immediate collapse of the Russian economy, the war has undermined every factor of long-term growth in the country, including capital, labor, and access to technology, institutions, and ideas. This implies that the Russian economic recession cannot be compared to the normal cyclical fluctuations of the business cycle in Western economies. While a 3–4% recession occasionally occurs among the latter as well, it is not accompanied by the loss of all access to Western capital—if a country is shut out of the financial markets, it can turn to the IMF, which ensures the country's financing until it can return to private capital markets. Such a country also does not experience a decline in intellectual inputs, and the exit of multinationals and highly educated people as a result of sanctions. It follows that there is no need either for forced innovation due to missing inputs or for increasing repression. Once the crisis passes, the country can usually return to its trend line of economic development especially if the structural reforms, which are usually included in an IMF stand-by arrangement (SBA), are implemented. In contrast, Russia faces a modified trend line of economic development as the fundamentals of its former model have radically changed due to its illegal war against Ukraine. Becoming asymmetrically dependent on China for its imports and exports can hardly be expected to lead to economic prosperity. Although Ukraine has suffered devastating losses during of the war, its prospects are much brighter.

4.3. Economic prospects in Ukraine

The Ukrainian economy is set to decline by 35% in 2022.[48] Its critical infrastructure providing housing, electricity, heating, and water has been severely damaged through large-scale shelling by Russian forces. Demographically, 16.1 million people left the country after the start of the invasion, although 8.3 million have already returned.[49] The role of the state in the Ukrainian economy has grown enormously, rising from 40% to 78% of GDP as it has taken on the responsibilities for military spending and social assistance, in addition to becoming the main employer of the population.[50] This is clearly reflected in the growth of budgetary expenditures after the start of the invasion, which has also resulted in high budget deficits (Figure 4). Five strategic companies have been nationalized from major oligarchs,[51] further increasing the power of the state.

Figure 4. Changes in expenditure and revenue of the Ukrainian central government (2021–2023, billion UAH).

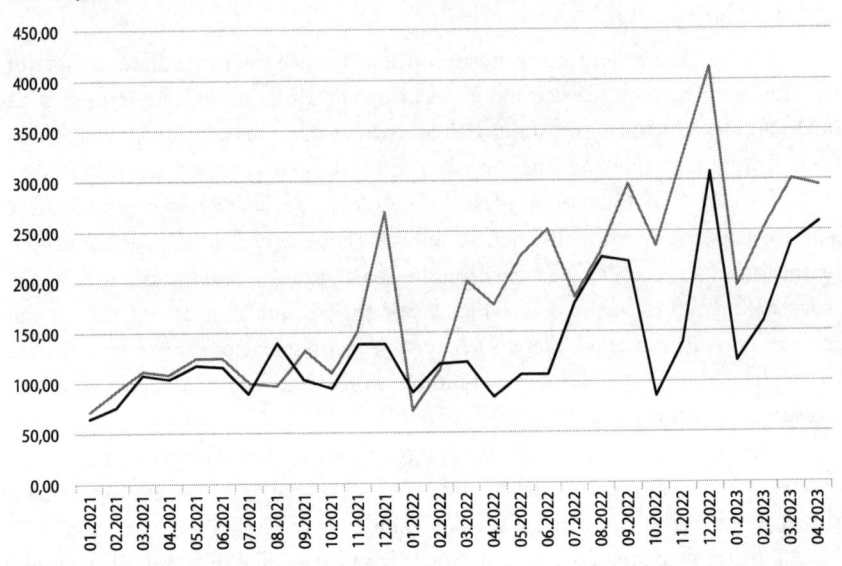

Source: National Bank of Ukraine.

In a comprehensive damage and needs assessment, the World Bank estimated the total bill for reconstruction at USD 349 billion as of June 1, 2022,[52] which grew to USD 500–600 billion by December.[53] Russia should bear most of this sum but whether the USD 300 billion in frozen central bank reserves and private wealth could be used for this is a question for the future.[54]

While the end of the war may bring about a post-war economic miracle up until the pre-war trend is reached,[55] a large sample of wars shows that GDP per capita returns to trend levels within five years only in one third of the cases, while in close to half of all cases GDP remains below trend even 25 years after a violent conflict.[56] Recovery is thus far from certain and cannot be taken for granted.

The prospects for Ukraine are also subject to enormous uncertainty regarding the success of regaining the country's territorial integrity and establishing lasting peace. The decisive defeat of Russia is a necessary factor for such an outcome. Preparations for post-war reconstruction have already started and Ukraine has a window of opportunity following the war for the construction of a Western-style economic system to ensure development and long-term growth.

In December 2022, a major report on the rebuilding of Ukraine after the war was published as a collaborative effort between Ukrainian scholars and practitioners and leading Western economists, such as Gérard Roland, Kenneth Rogoff, and Barry Eichengreen.[57] The report envisions a future Ukraine in the transatlantic alliance as a member of the EU and NATO. It recognizes that the pre-war Ukraine should not be rebuilt but rather a new Ukraine should be constructed in its place. The report also suggests that the destruction brought on by the war provides the window of opportunity for this endeavor. The main pillars this new Ukraine are democracy, robust institutions ensuring the rule of law, a strong economy and education, and a strong defense sector. The report concludes that the war has strengthened Ukrainian national cohesion, produced a vibrant civil sector, and generated a moral clarity about shared national objectives, which, together with strong Western support, provide a robust foundation for a hopeful future.

Table 2. Different post-war prospects for Russia and Ukraine.

	Russia	Ukraine
Labor	Emigration of young and able, mainly men, especially after mobilization—unlikely to return	Women and their children left Ukraine, strong potential for returning home to their partners
Capital	Cut off from international capital markets, assets frozen in the West, but potential financial sources from China	Constant flow of economic assistance from the West; reconstruction attracts further funds (possibly from confiscated Russian assets as reparation payments). Later business investments can be expected into the country.
Technology	Cut off from Western technology, strong reliance on China	Steady access to Western technology
Institutions	Patronal autocracy with increasingly totalitarian tendencies. Returning armed groups could lead to the revival of mafia-style security companies endangering physical security, discouraging investment and wealth accumulation	War has broken up patronal structures. Western integration and help in building governance structures, which move the country toward democracy and rule of law will ultimately provide a favorable context for investment
Ideas	Liberalism and independent thinking persecuted, innovation and creativity stifled, entrepreneurship discouraged	A role model of defending freedom for the entire world. Cohesive national identity forged during the war, rejection of the Soviet past, strong Western orientation. An emerging national identity similar to the Baltics—a very good basis for wealth creation though possible clash with security state.

Once the war ends and reconstruction starts, Ukrainian possibilities for long-term development are significantly better than for Russia. The different prospects of the two countries are summarized by Table 2. In the Ukraine's case, the vast majority of refugees, mainly women and children, want to return to home.[58] Capital inflows will be ensured first by development assistance, and then by the inflow of Western FDI. This will guarantee that Ukraine has access to leading Western technology, augmenting the digitalization of the government and the economy already fostered by the war with the help of SpaceX Starlink.[59] The greatest challenge for Ukraine will be the building of resilient institutions under the rule of law and rooting out patronal networks. The war has already fostered the de-oligarchization process as elaborated by Mikhail Mihankov.[60] The strong commitment to Western ideals will help the process in a similar way as it helped in the Baltic States in the 1990s. In terms of valuing the idea of freedom, Ukraine is already a role model for the entire world, reminding even a complacent West that "democracy is a value for which an elected official—or a citizen, for that matter—might choose to live or die."[61] Institutionalizing the ideals of liberty and creative thinking might clash with a strong security regime, but the Baltic experience provides a way to reconcile the two.

5. Conclusions

Although Western sanctions imposed on Russia did not immediately cripple the Russian economy, this does not mean they are ineffective. Russia has lost its most pros-perous markets in the EU for its energy products, while trade reorientation towards Asia faces major obstacles given the limitations of transport capacities such as gas pipelines or shipping. The outlook is even worse for its long-term growth prospects. The sanctions and the war have undermined all major factors of growth including access to capital and technology, the available quantity and quality of labor, the institutional system, and freedom. The war has made Russia a neo-backward country.

The relative certainty of the long-term decline of Russia stands in contrast to the uncertainties surrounding the prospects of post-war Ukraine. While success is far from guaranteed, Ukraine has a window of opportunity to leave its post-Soviet patronal structures behind, and build a resilient democracy, rule of law, and a strong market economy with Western support. The return of refugees, the inflow of Western capital for reconstruction, access to technology, assistance in institution building, and a strong social commitment to the idea of freedom provide a strong foundation for a new Ukraine embedded in the transatlantic alliance. Achieving this vision is the shared hope and responsibility of Ukraine and the West in their fight against autocracies.

Notes

1. William H. Kaempfer and Anton D. Lowenberg, "The Political Economy of Economic Sanctions," in *Handbook of Defense Economics*, vol. 2, eds. Todd Sandler and Keith Hartley (Amsterdam: Elsevier, 2007), 869.
2. Gerald Schneider and Patrick M. Weber, "Biased, But Surprisingly Effective: Economic Coercion after the Cold War," *CESifo Forum* 20, no. 4 (2019), 12.
3. Gary C. Hufbauer, Jeffrey J. Schott, Kimberly A. Elliott, and Barbara Oegg, *Economic Sanctions Reconsidered*, 3rd ed., (Washington, DC: Peterson Institute for international Economics, 2008), 5-6.
4. Hufbauer et al., *Economic Sanctions*, 159.
5. Scheider and Weber, "Biased but Surprisingly Effective," 12.
6. See the review of the literature by Kaempfer and Lowenberg, "The Political Economy of Economic Sanctions," 896–97.
7. On the tragic story of Sergei Magnitsky, the workings of the Russian criminal state, and the fight for accountability, see Bill Browder, *Red Notice: How I Became Putin's No. 1. Enemy* (London: Transworld Publishers, 2015).
8. Bálint Magyar and Bálint Madlovics, *A Concise Field Guide to Post-Communist Regimes: Actors, Institutions, and Dynamics* (Budapest—Vienna—New York: CEU Press, 2022), 172.
9. The Magnitsky sanctions bill was the main topic of the infamous Trump tower meeting between the Trump campaign and Russian government attorney, Natalia Veselnitskaya. See Robert Müller, *Report on the Investigation into Russian Interference in the 2016 Presidential Election* (Washington, DC: US Department of Justice, 2019), 118-130.
10. Anders Åslund and Maria Snegovaya, *The Impact of Western Sanctions on Russia and How They Can Be Made Even More Effective* (Washington, DC: Atlantic Council, 2021).
11. Antto Vihma and Mikael Wigell, "Unclear and Present Danger: Russia's Geoeconomics and the Nord Stream II Pipeline," *Global Affairs* 2, no. 4 (2016), 382-83.
12. The source for the following numbers is: European Commission, "EU Trade Relations with Russia: Facts, Figures and Latest Developments," accessed December 3, 2022, https://policy.trade.ec.europa.eu/eu-trade-relationships-country-and-region/countries-and-regions/russia_en.
13. Anders Åslund and Julia Friedlander, *Defending the United States against Russian Dark Money* (Washington DC: Atlantic Council, 2020), 2.
14. See Cathrine Belton, *Putin's People: How the KGB Took Back Russia and Then Took on the West* (London: Williams Collins, 2020), Chapter 13.
15. For a transcript of the speech, see "Security Council Meeting," President of Russia, February 21, 2002, http://en.kremlin.ru/events/president/news/67825.
16. For a comprehensive timeline of the sanctions against Russia, see Chad P. Brown, "Russia's War on Ukraine: A Sanctions Timeline," Peterson Institute for International Economics, May 8, 2023 (updated), accessed December 3, 2022, https://www.piie.com/blogs/realtime-economics/russias-war-ukraine-sanctions-timeline.
17. The presented summary of sanctions is based on "EU Sanctions Against Russia Explained," European Council, accessed December 3, 2022, https://www.consilium.europa.eu/en/policies/sanctions/restrictive-measures-against-russia-over-ukraine/sanctions-against-russia-explained/.
18. In the first half of 2022, average household electricity prices in the EU increased from EUR 22.0 per 100 kWh in 2021 to EUR 25.3 per 100 kWh in 2022. Average gas prices compared with the same period rose from EUR 6.4 per 100 kWh to EUR 8.6 per 100 kWh. Source: "Electricity and Gas Prices in the First Half of 2022," Eurostat, October 31, 2022, https://ec.europa.eu/eurostat/web/products-eurostat-news/-/ddn-20221031-1
19. Data source: Bank of Russia, Russia's Balance of Payments – Information and Analytical Commentary, No. 1-2 (11), 2022 Q2, https://www.cbr.ru/Collection/Collection/File/42212/Balance_of_Payments_2022-1-2_11_e.pdf.

[20] For an overview about these narratives and their reception in Central Europe, see Ukraine Monitor, *Energy Security and the 'Harsh Winter' in Extremist Discourse about the Russian Invasion of Ukraine*, accessed 3 December, 2022, https://www.politicalcapital.hu/pc admin/source/documents/Zinc_XFR%20Disinfo_Report_Energy_221006.pdf
[21] Jeffrey Sonnenfeld, Steven Tian, Franek Sokolowski, Michal Wyrebkowski, and Mateusz Kasprowicz, *Business Retreats and Sanctions Are Crippling the Russian Economy*, July 20, 2022, https://ssrn.com/abstract=4167193.
[22] Heli Simola, *Can Russia Reorient its Trade and Financial Flows?*, BOFIT Policy Brief No. 7 (2022).
[23] Robert Solow, "A Contribution to the Theory of Economic Growth," *The Quarterly Journal of Economics*, 70, no. 1 (1956), 65–94.
[24] Paul Krugman, *The Age of Diminished Expectations: US Economic Policy in the 1990s* (Cambridge, MA: MIT Press, 1994), 11.
[25] Douglass North, *Institutions, Institutional Change and Economic Performance* (Cambridge: Cambridge University Press, 1990).
[26] Dani Rodrik, Arvind Subramanian, and Francesco Trebbi. "Institutions Rule: The Primacy of Institutions over Geography and Integration in Economic Development," *Journal of Economic Growth* 9 (2004), 131–65.
[27] Daron Acemoglu and James Robinson, *Why Nations Fail: The Origins of Power, Prosperity and Poverty* (New York: Crown Business, 2012).
[28] Deirdre McCloskey, *Bourgeois Dignity: Why Economics Can't Explain the Modern World* (Chicago: University of Chicago, 2010).
[29] "The World Economic Outlook Database," International Monetary Fund, accessed December 3, 2022, https://www.imf.org/en/Publications/WEO/weo-database/2022/October.
[30] This summary is based on the information in Boris Grozovski, "Russia's Economy at the End of 2022: Deeper Troubles," Wilson Center, November 23, 2022, https://www.wilsoncenter.org/blog-post/russias-economy-end-2022-deeper-troubles.
[31] Alexander Gabuev, "China's New Vassal," *Foreign Affairs*, August 9, 2022. https://www.foreignaffairs.com/china/chinas-new-vassal.
[32] Georgi Gotev, "The Brief — The Demographics of War," *Euractiv*, December 19, 2022, https://www.euractiv.com/section/global-europe/opinion/the-brief-the-demographics-of-war/.
[33] Grozovski, "Russia's Economy"
[34] Gotev, "The Brief – The Demographics of War"
[35] Aino Röyskö and Heli Simola, *Russia's Technology Imports from East Asia*, BOFIT Policy Brief No. 6, (2022), 4.
[36] Polina Ivanova and May Seddon, "Russia's Wartime Economy: Learning to Live without Imports," *Financial Times*, December 14, 2022.
[37] Röyskö and Simola, *Russia's Technology Imports*, 13-14.
[38] Ivanova and Seddon, "Russia's Wartime Economy"
[39] Belton, *Putin's People*, Chapter 1.
[40] The reasons for this reversion include the lack of competition, a system of financing helping the diffusion of the new technology, and the lack of social recognition of innovators. See János Kornai, "Innovation and Dynamism: Interaction Between Systems and Technical Progress," *Economics of Transition* 18, no. 4 (2010), 642.
[41] Mihály Laki, "Kényszerített innováció," *Szociológia* (1984-1985, 1-2), 45–53.
[42] Gregory Kantchev and Nick Kostov, "Where Are the Air Bags? Russia's Hobbled Auto Industry Struggles to Reboot," October 30, 2022, https://www.wsj.com/articles/russia-auto-cars-lada-reboot-air-bags-11667141126.
[43] See Magyar and Madlovics, *A Concise Field Guide*, 223-24.
[44] Magyar and Madlovics, *A Concise Field Guide*, 224.

45. Russia remained "Kuwait with nuclear weapons" as aptly put by László Csaba, *Válság-Gazdaság-Világ* [Crisis-Economy-World] (Budapest: Éghajlat Könyvkiadó, 2018), 216–219.
46. See Anders Åslund, *Russia's Crony Capitalism: The Path from Market Economy to Kleptocracy* (New Haven and London: Yale University Press, 2018), Chapter 5.
47. Konstantin Sonin, "Russia's Road to Economic Ruin," *Foreign Affairs*, November 15, 2022, https://www.foreignaffairs.com/russian-federation/russias-road-economic-ruin.
48. IMF, *The World Economic Outlook*
49. "Monthly Macroeconomic and Monetary Review," December 2022," National Bank of Ukraine, https://bank.gov.ua/en/news/all/makroekonomichniy-ta-monetarniy-oglyad-gruden-2022-roku, 20.
50. Andrii Ianitskyi, "State Becomes Main Player in Ukrainian Economy," Institute for War and Peace Reporting, December 22, 2022, https://iwpr.net/global-voices/state-becomes-main-player-ukrainian-economy.
51. The companies are: Motor Sich, one of the world's largest aircraft turbine manufacturers; Zaporizh-transformator, a manufacturer of power transformers and electric reactors; AutoKrAZ, a truck and special purpose vehicles producer; Ukrnafta, a natural gas company; and Ukrtatnafta, an oil refinery company. Source: Ianitskyi, "State Becomes Main Player."
52. World Bank, *Ukraine – Rapid Damage and Needs Assessment*, accessed December 22, 2022. https://documents1.worldbank.org/curated/en/099445209072239810/pdf/P17884304837910630b-9c6040ac12428d5c.pdf.
53. "Die Entwicklung von 15 Jahren ist ausgelöscht" [Fifteen years of development has been erased], *Die Presse*, December 6, 2022, https://www.diepresse.com/6223189/ukraine-die-entwicklung-von-15-jahren-ist-ausgeloescht.
54. Sam Fleming and Henry Foy, "EU Wants to Use Frozen Russian Assets to Fund Ukraine Reconstruction," *Financial Times*, November 30, 2022, https://www.ft.com/content/a96c3e66-39ab-45d2-a7ff-b6302b1c9284.
55. Ferenc Jánossy, *The End of the Economic Miracle: Appearance and Reality in Economic Development* (White Plains, NY: International Arts and Sciences Press, 1971).
56. Zsoka Koczan and Maxim Chupilkin, "The Economics of Post-War Recoveries and Reconstructions," CEPR, November 22, 2022, https://cepr.org/voxeu/columns/economics-post-war-recoveries-and-reconstructions.
57. Yuriy Gorodnichenko, Ilona Sologoub, and Beatrice Weder di Mauro, eds., *Rebuilding Ukraine: Principles and Policies* (London: CEPR Press, 2022).
58. National Bank of Ukraine, Monthly Macroeconomic and Monetary Review, 20.
59. Mike Wall, "What's Going On with Elon Musk, SpaceX's Starlink and Ukraine?" *Space.com*, October 19, 2022, https://www.space.com/spacex-starlink-elon-musk-ukraine-explainer.
60. See Mikhail Minakov, "War, De-oligarchization, and the Possibility of Anti-Patronal Transformation in Ukraine," in *Ukraine's Patronal Democracy and the Russian Invasion,* eds. Madlovics and Magyar, 141–65.
61. Timothy Snyder, "Ukraine Holds the Future: The War between Democracy and Nihilism," *Foreign Affairs* 101, no. 5 (2022), 133.

From Partner to Pariah: The Changing Position of Russia in Terms of International Law

Tamás Lattmann

The morning of February 24, 2022 saw Russia launch a military offensive against Ukraine, turning a low intensity conflict into an all-out war. This also meant that Russia's aggression, pursued since 2014, could no longer be "hidden" by the Kremlin, and all states, organizations and other political actors had to face the fact of a blatant violation of international law and order.

This study aims to examine the implications of this tragic step. Does it make the political positions of Russia stronger or weaker? Does it aid the resilience of international organizations or is a step like this liable to strike a mortal blow against the current international order as we know it? The focus is on Russia's global (United Nations) and regional (Council of Europe) environment and on possible institutional developments in international criminal law (International Criminal Court).

1. Before the full-scale invasion

In February and March 2014, Russia not only contributed to various tensions on the territory of Ukraine but also infiltrated and subsequently annexed the Crimean Peninsula and other parts of the country, mainly in the Luhansk and Donetsk oblasts. These actions already revealed Russia's serious intention to change the status quo, essentially indicating the first steps towards a wider war—even if most commentators and state leaders carefully tried to avoid talking about it at that time.

Regardless, these events can already be qualified as an act of aggression. The annexation was formalized on March 18, 2014, when Vladimir Putin signed the treaty of accession (annexation) with local leaders flown in to Moscow. This happened after local referenda, the legitimacy of which was heavily criticized not only by states but by legal experts[1] and even bodies like the Venice Commission.[2]

The annexation was deemed illegal under international law, and reactions quickly followed accordingly. The United Nations General Assembly adopted a condemnatory resolution,[3] and it has consistently upheld its position of not recognizing the annexation as legitimate, referring to Russia as an "occupying power" in its later resolutions.[4]

Additionally, Russia was suspended from the G8 and subsequently declared its final withdrawal, after several G7 members rejected then-US President Trump's suggestion to reaccept Russia as a member. Russian Foreign Minister Lavrov later stated that the Russian Federation had no interest in rejoining the political forum.

Many state actors also decided to impose sanctions on Russia. These were aimed at supporting the sovereignty and territorial integrity of Ukraine, led by the United States and member states of the European Union. As a reaction, Russia accused these states of funding and directing the earlier Ukrainian revolution (Euromaidan or, as the Ukrainians refer to it, the "Revolution of Dignity"), and chose to retaliate against these sanctions by imposing its own without any serious implications. The only countries to support the annexation of Crimea have been Cuba, Nicaragua, Venezuela, Syria, Afghanistan, and North Korea, all of whom owe Russia for previously shielding them from international political pressure on various issues.[5]

Already during this period, it could be seen that Russia's foreign policy actions related to Ukraine had resulted not only in criticism but also in a serious loss of influence and international support. This process only accelerated after Russia embarked upon its military invasion in February 2022.

2. Russia within the United Nations

2.1. The central role of the General Assembly

Right from the moment Russia began its open aggression against Ukraine, the tone of the UN changed, especially compared to the style it had employed at the time of Russia's initial military actions related to the Crimean Peninsula in 2014. Already from the very beginning of the military operation starting in February 2022, the organs of the UN have considered it to be a violation of the territorial integrity and sovereignty of Ukraine, an unlawful use of force, a violation of the prohibition against the use of force, and as contrary to the principles of the Charter of the United Nations, adopted in 1945, forming the basis of the world order since the end of World War II.[6]

And it has not only been words, as actions have also followed to give weight to these political positions. A new assistant secretary-general, Amin Awad, was appointed to serve as the United Nations Crisis Coordinator for Ukraine, and numerous resolutions have been adopted by the relevant organs of the organization.[7] In parallel, the Security Council has started to steadily lose influence as Russian threats to use its veto has made it abundantly clear that this body is not going to play a crucial role in the situation. This, of course, is a problem, as according to the Charter, the Security Council bears the primary responsibility for maintaining international peace and security. Russia, however, made it clear very early on, already during the initial phase of the conflict, that it was willing to use its veto power to try to evade responsibility.[8] As a result, the General Assembly of the United Nations has grown to be a central player in the situation, reviving its 1950 "Uniting for Peace" resolution,[9] and claiming a dominant political position for itself—a move which has not met serious resistance from the member states as of yet. Thus, the Russian aggression against Ukraine has created a seemingly new situation in international relations, the end result of which is still to be seen.

What is also worthy of mention here is that this new situation provides support for other international organizations as well, those whose activities in other situations are often criticized with great intensity. For example, the February 28 statement of the prosecutor of the International Criminal Court (ICC) about opening an investigation into Russia's war crimes and crimes against humanity was met with an unusual amount of support from the international community (more about this in the next part). Similarly, a later decision of the ICC on March 16 ordering Russia to immediately suspend its military operations in Ukraine[10] met very similar reactions, even if the somewhat expansive interpretation of the relevant rules could also have attracted criticism.

2.2. Becoming a pariah: UN resolutions adopted against Russia after February 2022

The United Nations General Assembly and the international community, including the majority of G20 countries (Table 1), have repeatedly taken a stance against Russia's invasion and in favor of Ukraine's self-defense.[11] One of the first signs of this steadfastness was the resolution adopted in the General Assembly on March 2. The resolution deplored the Russian "aggression" against Ukraine,[12] and was supported by 141 countries, with only 5 voting against and 35 abstentions, thus showing an overwhelming amount of support among the 193 members of the General Assembly. Moreover, the UN Human Rights Council also made its voice heard: it adopted a resolution on March 4 calling for the "swift and verifiable" withdrawal of Russian armed forces from the entire territory of Ukraine with 32 of the 47 countries on the Council voting in favor of the resolution proposed by Ukraine. The only member states voting against were Russia and Eritrea, while 13 other member states abstained. It may be worth noting that since its inception in 2006, the Human Rights Council (just like its predecessor, the UN Commission on Human Rights) has often been criticized for being politically biased and influenced by states like Russia.[13] Clearly, such criticism would be unwarranted this time. Additionally, the Human Rights Council decided on March 5 to establish an independent international commission of inquiry related to human rights violations in the situation following the Russian aggression against Ukraine, leaving no doubt about the position of the majority of its member states.[14]

Table 1. G-20 members in the United Nations vote on supporting Ukraine.

Country	Suspending Russia's membership in the UN Human Rights Council	Calling for international legal consequences for Russia	Condemning Russia's aggression against Ukraine	Expressing concern at the humanitarian consequences	Condemning the Russian annexation of four Ukrainian regions	Urging a comprehensive, just, and lasting peace for Ukraine
Argentina	Yes	Yes	Yes	Yes	Yes	Yes
Australia	Yes	Yes	Yes	Yes	Yes	Yes
Canada	Yes	Yes	Yes	Yes	Yes	Yes
France	Yes	Yes	Yes	Yes	Yes	Yes
Germany	Yes	Yes	Yes	Yes	Yes	Yes
Italy	Yes	Yes	Yes	Yes	Yes	Yes
Japan	Yes	Yes	Yes	Yes	Yes	Yes
South Korea	Yes	Yes	Yes	Yes	Yes	Yes
Turkey	Yes	Yes	Yes	Yes	Yes	Yes
United Kingdom	Yes	Yes	Yes	Yes	Yes	Yes
United States	Yes	Yes	Yes	Yes	Yes	Yes
Mexico	Abstained	Yes	Yes	Yes	Yes	Yes
Brazil	Abstained	Abstained	Yes	Yes	Yes	Yes
Indonesia	Abstained	Abstained	Yes	Yes	Yes	Yes
Saudi Arabia	Abstained	Abstained	Yes	Yes	Yes	Yes
India	Abstained	Abstained	Abstained	Abstained	Abstained	Abstained
South Africa	Abstained	Abstained	Abstained	Abstained	Abstained	Abstained
China	No	No	Abstained	Abstained	Abstained	Abstained
Russia	No	No	No	No	No	No

Source: United Nations / The Washington Post.

On March 24, the General Assembly adopted another resolution, again with an overwhelming majority, demanding civilian protection and humanitarian access to victims in Ukraine, while also criticizing Russia for creating a "dire" humanitarian situation.[15] The resolution was passed with 140 votes in favor, only 5 against, and 38 abstentions. A few days later, the UN appointed a body of three human rights experts to investigate violations of international law committed during the conflict, after more and more reports began to surface about the horrific crimes committed against the civilian population in places like the town of Bucha. Images of mass graves and of dead civilians with their hands tied behind their backs have had a destructive effect on the credibility of the Russian leadership and its political positions at the UN.

A clear sign of this was Russia losing its seat on the Human Rights Council, something which had happened earlier only to Libya in 2011.[16] On April 7, the UN General Assembly voted on Russia being suspended from the body,[17] and once again, the resolution generated overwhelming support, receiving more than the necessary two-thirds majority of those voting (minus abstentions). Some 93 states voted in favor of the resolution, agreeing with the position that Russia was responsible for "committing gross and systematic violations of human rights," and that this constituted grounds for excluding a member state. The 24 states that voted against the resolution included Russia, its usual allies (Cuba, North Korea, Iran, Syria, Vietnam), and China, which has generally tried to avoid setting dangerous precedents in bodies like the Human Rights Council.[18] The 58 countries that abstained from the vote included India, Brazil, South Africa, Mexico, Egypt, Saudi Arabia, United Arab Emirates, Jordan, Qatar, Kuwait, Iraq, Pakistan, Singapore, Thailand, Malaysia, Indonesia, and Cambodia, some of which have developed economically beneficial ties with Russia, in recent years, but this was not enough to render it support in the UN.

After losing its seat on the Human Rights Council, Russia tried to save face, with its UN representative suddenly announcing that Russia had already decided to leave the Human Rights Council, claiming that the Council was "monopolized by a group of States" who use it "for their short-term aims."[19] As this claim had not been raised earlier by Russia, it was fairly clear this was nothing more than a desperate attempt at political messaging—very similar to what happened with the Council of Europe (see the relevant part below).

Losing its seat on the UN Human Rights Council is a serious—although far from fatal—blow to Russian capabilities at the level of international relations, not only in the ongoing conflict but also in general. It may be worth adding that this development may at the same time help the Human Rights Council, which has been struggling with credibility issues since its creation in 2006. Later, on May 12, the Council adopted a resolution at its special session on Ukraine to begin an investigation into atrocities committed by Russian occupation troops.[20] At that point, Russia could no longer block this resolution.

2.3. The changing position of the Security Council

April 26, 2022 saw the adoption of a novel UN General Assembly resolution which called on the five permanent members of the UN Security Council to justify the use of their veto power. This came after Russia had used its veto to block a resolution in the Council the day after its invasion of Ukraine.[21] The proposed Security Council resolution called for Russia's immediate and unconditional withdrawal from Ukraine, but the Russian veto paralyzed the Council. As indicated earlier,[22] this was not the first time that Russia has used this means to evade responsibility, but it is clear the vast majority of states have decided not to let Russia get away with it so easily. Apart from the overwhelming support for adopting the resolution, the proposal itself had 83 co-sponsors, which suggests that the veto power wielded by permanent members of the UN Security Council may come under concentrated attack by members of the international community. This, combined with the fact that the Security Council has been continually circumvented by the General Assembly during the Russia-Ukraine war, indicates that fundamental changes are taking place in international politics, the end result of which is currently difficult to predict or foresee.

This change led to the first instance in which the Security Council was finally able to adopt anything related to the war—a statement issued on May 6, 2022 expressing "strong support" for the efforts of the Secretary-General to achieve a peaceful solution in Ukraine.[23] Of course, the careful drafting of the text indicates that a temporary consensus among permanent powers not to put the blame on any one party in the situation was the deciding factor—but it is hard to ignore the fact that dissatisfaction among other member states had a strong effect on this development. At this point, it is not only Russia that has to face the threat of their veto power becoming irrelevant; as a result, other permanent members may also be interested in more consensus-based activities in the Security Council.

Another very important political blow was leveled against Russia on and after September 29, 2022, when the UN Secretary-General stated that the Russian plan to annex the occupied regions of Ukraine would qualify as a violation of international law and should not be recognized by states but rather condemned.[24] The next day, Russia had to use its veto power once again, when the Security Council wanted to adopt a resolution condemning Russia's attempted annexation of the aforementioned regions. On October 12, the issue was placed on the agenda of the UN General Assembly, which passed a resolution calling on all member states not to recognize the annexation of these regions, regardless of the results of the referenda held in September.[25] It is important to add that these referenda have been commonly used by Russia as "legitimization tools," as was the case in Crimea earlier, and have even involved the efficient use of Russia's European political allies (e.g., members of the European Parliament) as "observers" to legitimize Russia's territorial gains.[26] The voting proportions in this case were once again quite convincing: 143 member states voted in favor of the resolution, while 5 voted against and 35 abstained, thus sending a clear message about the lack of support for Russia's actions.

More General Assembly resolutions were adopted later on various aspects of the war, none of them helping the case or supporting the position of Russia, indicating a clear loss of support. The resolution of November 14, for example, which called for Russia to pay war reparations to Ukraine, was passed with the support of 94 states, with only 14 states voting against and 73 abstaining.[27] The resolution adopted on February 23, 2023 called for ending the war and demanded Russia's immediate withdrawal from Ukraine, making it very clear that this was a violation of the UN Charter.[28]

At the same time, the Security Council has still not been able to make any substantial decisions on the matter, while the question of possible criminal responsibility for Russia's aggression (including crimes against humanity and war crimes) has gradually started being raised among states and has also appeared in public discourse. During the meeting of the Security Council on February 24, Ukraine's Minister for Foreign Affairs indicated the need for the creation of a special criminal tribunal with jurisdiction over the crime of aggression, the possibility of which is still an open question today.[29]

In conclusion, we can see that Russia has lost valuable positions in the United Nations and its bodies, and the full-scale invasion has even led to serious institutional changes or at least rearrangements of political influence. The Security Council's loss of relevance has never been so obvious before, which may have long-lasting implications for the structure of international law as we know it.

3. Russia and the Council of Europe

3.1. Losing membership in the Council

Russia's membership in the Council of Europe (CoE), the most relevant European regional organization, has always been somewhat problematic. While Russia upheld its membership as an important element of its continental relevance, it sometimes used its membership as a tool to get involved in and even cause confusion in European or EU-related matters. One example of this was Russia's activities related to Protocol 14 of the European Convention on Human Rights.[30] Indeed, Russia slowly developed a tense relationship with the organization and some of its bodies, most notably with the Strasbourg-based European Court of Human Rights (ECHR), which had already taken a very active approach to the examination of human rights violations by Russia, with the occupation of Crimea and other Ukrainian territories feeding it more and more new cases. This intensifying engagement was not welcomed by Putin and his government, but it was not until the open aggression against Ukraine on February 24 that an open break between

Russia and the CoE took place. Problems no longer needed to be hidden under the carpet as the new situation made it possible to bring these tensions to the surface.

On March 16, 2022, the Committee of Ministers, the main decision-making body of the CoE, adopted a decision by which the Russian Federation ceased to be a member of the Council of Europe after 26 years of membership.[31] This was directly preceded by a statement of the Russian government on March 15, 2022, in which it informed the Secretary General of its withdrawal from the Council of Europe in accordance with the Statute of the Council of Europe. It also expressed its intention to denounce the European Convention on Human Rights, essentially removing itself from the jurisdiction of the European Court of Human Rights.[32]

The Committee of Ministers based its decision to exclude Russia on the procedure launched under Article 8 of the Statute of the Council of Europe. Clearly, the Russian government wanted to avoid the embarrassing situation of being "expelled," but even so this is no longer relevant now. The question of Russia leaving on its own accord or being thrown out of the organization may have had relevance only until the end of 2022. After this period of time the legal effects of these two pathways were identical: Russian membership was terminated, and Russia lost all institutional influence it ever had in the most relevant continental organization.

3.2. Detachment from the European Court of Human Rights

The break with the European Court of Human Rights has been a longer process, deeply rooted in the bilateral relationship of the Court and Russia. The final shot came on June 7, 2022, when the Russian Duma passed a pair of bills terminating the jurisdiction of the Court with respect to Russia,[33] thus formally breaking their ties. Their relationship, however, had been very troubled for a long time, with the relationship between European Court and the Russian Constitutional Court being a topic of discussion and professional and human rights-related concerns over recent years.[34] In 2015, a draft amendment to the Russian Constitution expanded the jurisdiction of the Russian Constitutional Court to consider petitions asserting a "discovered contradiction" between the Russian Constitution and any judgment of the Strasbourg-based Court.[35] This unprecedented law, never seen in any other member state of the CoE, made it possible for the Russian Constitutional Court to forbid compliance with a given judgment if a case of "contradiction" was found. This gave a clear possibility for the Russian government to ignore its human rights obligations under the European Convention on Human Rights, a possibility it subsequently took advantage of numerous times.[36]

The June 7 decision of the Russian parliament merely put the final seal on this sad process of Russia leaving not only the most relevant European political community but also the set of human rights values it enshrined. Of course, values are somewhat subjective, as Vyacheslav Volodin, speaker of the Russian parliament's lower house stated in reference to the European Court: "Some of its decisions were in direct contradiction to the Russian constitution, our values and our traditions."[37] Still, there is no doubt that this is not so much a question of values but of trying to maintain political space for maneuvering clear of human rights-related obstacles.

Russia's departure from the Council of Europe, and especially from the continent's leading human rights organ, has been condemned by all relevant actors, most notably by human rights groups concerned about the impact on victims and the probable lowering of protection measures with respect to present and future human rights abuses in Russia.[38] With this in mind, the decision of CoE member states to push Russia out of the organization can also be criticized, even though it can be seen that Russia would likely have made the same step itself.

Russia's leaving the structure not only carries symbolic weight, it also has concrete consequences. Since the European Convention on Human Rights now ceases to apply to Russia, victims of human rights violations by the Russian government (including any persons living in the Russian-occupied territories of Ukraine) will no longer be able to turn to the European Court of Human Rights for defense, making it harder to hold Russia accountable for its violations. At the same time, it should be stressed that the mere fact of leaving the Court (and the CoE) does not relieve Russia of all of its human rights obligations, while it does negate all possibility for Russia to directly influence regional decisions.

4. Russia and the International Criminal Court

The relationship between Russia and the International Criminal Court (ICC) has never been easy. These relations had already worsened prior to February 2022, after the Court had published its decision to initiate preliminary examinations related to the ongoing Russia-Ukraine tensions years earlier.[39] In November 2016, Russia announced it was withdrawing its signature from the Rome Statute, the founding treaty of the ICC. Russian foreign minister Sergey Lavrov argued that the court "did not live up to the hopes associated with it and did not become truly independent."[40] This argument was nothing new: it is often iterated by states and political actors seeking the attention of the Court. In the case of Russia, this controversial step followed the publication of a report by the prosecutor of the ICC at that time, Fatou Bensouda,[41] which included some strong statements and legal points which the Russian government found disturbing and which were already at odds with Russia's claims at that time. The report stated for the first time that the armed conflict on the territory of Ukraine amounted to an international armed conflict between Russia and Ukraine, and that the situation regarding Crimea qualified as "an on-going state of occupation." It also addressed other issues such as the MH17 incident.

These statements by the ICC even then were already in very clear contradiction to the Russian official narrative, according to which Russia did not have any troops in Ukraine and that Crimea had joined Russia voluntarily as the express will of its population via a free and fair referendum (see the criticism of this in the previous part). The image constructed by Russia at that time was somewhat similar to the one constructed during and after the full-scale invasion of February 2022, denying the existence of a "war" in general, while trying not to endanger another image Russia had made for itself as a protector of multilateralism and international peace.[42]

The picture has become somewhat clearer after Russia's open aggression of February 2022. Since neither Russia nor Ukraine were state parties to the founding international treaty of the ICC, the so-called Rome Statute, the Court required a specific linking element to provide it with operational jurisdiction.

According to the Statute, this may have been possible via a UN Security Council referral: the Council would have to refer the situation to the Court, which would logically require either the consent or at least the abstention of the Russian Federation; however, there was never any doubt that the country would use its veto to block this. Indeed, such an example was seen a few years ago, when the idea to create a special tribunal to examine possible responsibility for the tragedy of flight MH17 was raised.[43] Even if it had not been politically unfeasible, some concerns related to this possibility can be raised. As I have analyzed earlier, this kind of referral has not proven to be an effective method in past years and conflicts.[44]

However, such a technique was not required in the current situation, as Ukraine had already accepted the jurisdiction of the ICC in 2014-2015 through unilateral declarations according to the relevant provisions of the Statute.[45] Based on these, the Office of the Prosecutor had already been conducting preliminary examinations leading to Russia withdrawing from the ICC in 2016, meaning Russia withdrawing its signature from the founding statute instead of concluding the ratification procedure.[46] This means that the Court has jurisdiction over any war crimes committed on the territory of Ukraine since the very beginning of the war, regardless of the nationality of the perpetrator. Based on this, the Prosecutor stated very early on that he plans to initiate investigations that may lead to actual charges.[47]

It is interesting to note that there was a bit of a twist in the question regarding jurisdiction. In his statement, the Prosecutor called upon the states party to the ICC to refer the situation in Ukraine to the Court according to Article 14 of the Statute, whereas based on Article 15, he could have initiated investigations and, if need be, press charges simply *proprio motu*, that is, in his own right, based on

Ukraine's abovementioned declarations. Many state parties responded to this call very quickly, but this may lead to some questions. Up to now, states party to the Statute have only referred to situations occurring on their own territory, never on the territory of another state party and especially not on the territory of a state not party to the Statute. The only situation resembling this related to Venezuela and resulted in the state itself finally consenting by making the referral itself,[48] Logically speaking, by doing this the Prosecutor intended to circumvent the pretrial procedure which is needed when implementing Article 15, which states that if the Prosecutor initiates investigations *proprio motu*, he needs permission from the Court. Implementation of Article 14, that is, referral by a state party, does not require this and investigations can be initiated immediately.

Obviously, the goal of the Prosecutor was to save time and to apply political pressure on Russia as soon as possible. Interestingly, one of the main arguments of the US against the ICC from the very beginning has centered on the question of limiting the powers of the Prosecutor in case they attempt to overstep the rules.[49] The solution to this problem was the pre-trial procedure, which now seems to have been circumvented by the Prosecutor. The problem is mostly of a theoretical nature, since any practical questions that may possibly arise are still ahead of us, e.g., whether a state party can refer a situation to the Court based on Article 14, if that state itself lacks jurisdiction over that situation (the referral practice so far has been compatible with the principle of complementarity and the general provisions of international law). As of now, the fact is that the Prosecutor of the ICC immediately gained the needed support from states party to the Rome Statute, which indicates a weak position for Russia with respect to possible criminal responsibility for war crimes and crimes against humanity.

On March 17, 2023, the first arrest warrants were issued by the Court. The Pre-Trial Chamber issued arrest warrants for Vladimir Putin, Sergey Lavrov, and others in connection with alleged war crimes concerning the deportation and "illegal transfer" of children from the occupied territories of Ukraine.[50] The Russian political leaders are accused of being directly involved in or having facilitated the war crimes in question, with reasonable grounds to believe they committed the criminal acts directly, in addition to working with others. With Putin, there is the additional accusation that he failed to use his presidential powers to stop children being deported from Ukrainian territories.

There is a clear connection between this development and the events of the previous day, that is, March 16, 2023, when the UN Commission of Inquiry on Ukraine released its first report to the Human Rights Council, stating the responsibility of the Russian authorities for a wide range of violations of international humanitarian law and human rights in various regions of Ukraine.[51] These allegations had already been raised by many actors, and various states have committed themselves to provide assistance and to help shed light on atrocities committed during the conflict.

Not surprisingly, the Russian government has denied the allegations and has described the warrants as "outrageous," arguing also that they are "null and void" as Russia does not recognize the jurisdiction of the ICC, is not a state party to it, and has no obligation to cooperate with it.[52] As I have explained earlier, the ICC has jurisdiction over the territory of Ukraine, so these arguments are irrelevant. And even if President Putin (or any other Russian individual) currently has no fear of being brought before the Court, the existence of the arrest warrants does have an effect on Russia's foreign policy. They can limit the international travel of their subjects, as there is the danger that those states which are party to the Rome Statute will be obliged to arrest anyone wanted by the Court if said persons enter their territory.

5. Conclusions: raising the price for violating the international order

Many have feared that Russia's open aggression will mark the end of the current and longstanding international legal order as we know it. Although these fears are well-founded, it is still too early to take a position on this issue, as it is not easy to foresee future developments and all the possible implications of Russia's destructive actions.

However, what we can see now is that the current international system is seemingly not that "easy to kill" and has plenty of ways and means to fight back against the actor attacking it. This is not a unique or novel phenomenon in international relations: every country has always had to pay the political price when their unilateral actions have approached or transcended the boundaries of the current framework of the international legal order. This includes the United States losing political support and influence over its actions in Iraq,[53] or, in an even more fitting case, Kosovo's separation from Serbia, which has served as a political precedent for Russia's actions towards other states in the post-Soviet space.[54] Other, smaller-scale, systematic violations or cases of disregarding international law by states such as Israel (in relation to the Palestinian situation) and their consequences can be seen as further examples.[55] These raise the political costs of state actions and must be factored in before making foreign policy decisions.

For the sake of both the future and the current legal order, we can only hope that states realize this, and they are unwilling to pay a high price in the future for wrong decisions today. Let this war be one of the last of its kind.

Notes

1. Thomas D. Grant, "Annexation of Crimea," *American Journal of International Law* 109, no. 1 (2015): 68–95.
2. See European Commission for Democracy through Law (Venice Commission), Opinion on "Whether the Decision Taken by the Supreme Council of the Autonomous Republic of Crimea in Ukraine to Organise a Referendum on Becoming a Constituent Territory of the Russian Federation or Restoring Crimea's 1992 Constitution Is Compatible with Constitutional Principles," Doc. No. CDL-AD (2014)002, para. 15 (Mar. 21, 2014), http://www.venice.coe.int/webforms/documents/default.aspx?pdffile=CDL-AD(2014)002-e.
3. "UN General Assembly Resolution 68/262" (United Nations, March 27, 2014), https://undocs.org/A/RES/68/262.
4. See, for example "UN General Assembly Resolution 71/205" (United Nations, December 19, 2016), https://undocs.org/A/RES/71/205.
5. Jeremy Bender, "These Are the 6 Countries on Board with Russia's Illegal Annexation of Crimea," *Business Insider*, May 31, 2016, https://www.businessinsider.com/six-countries-okay-with-russias-annexation-of-crimea-2016-5.
6. See "Principles of the Charter of the United Nations Underlying a Comprehensive, Just and Lasting Peace in Ukraine: UN General Assembly Resolution ES-11/L.7," March 2, 2023, https://digitallibrary.un.org/record/4004933?ln=en.
7. "Secretary-General Appoints Amin Awad of Sudan United Nations Crisis Coordinator for Ukraine," *UN Press*, February 25, 2022, https://press.un.org/en/2022/sga2102.doc.htm.
8. See Tamás Lattmann, "The Case against Russia for the Attack on Flight MH17," International Law Reflection (Prague: Institute of International Relations, May 27, 2016), https://www.iir.cz/the-case-against-russia-for-the-attack-on-flight-mh17.
9. See "'Uniting for Peace': UN General Assembly Resolution 377(V)" (United Nations, November 3, 1950), https://www.refworld.org/docid/3b00f08d78.html.
10. "Order of 16 March 2022. Allegations of Genocide Under the Convention on the Prevention and Punishment of the Crime of Genocide (Ukraine v. Russian Federation)" (International Court of Justice, 2022), https://www.icj-cij.org/public/files/case-related/182/182-20220316-ORD-01-00-EN.pdf.
11. Michael O'Hanlon, Constanze Stelzenmüller, and David Wessel, "What 6 Data Points Tell Us about the Status of the War in Ukraine," *Washington Post*, April 26, 2023, https://www.washingtonpost.com/opinions/interactive/2023/ukraine-war-status-resources-brookings/.
12. "UN General Assembly Resolution ES-11/2" (United Nations, March 24, 2022), https://digitallibrary.un.org/record/3966630?ln=en.
13. Rosa Freedman and Ruth Houghton, "Two Steps Forward, One Step Back: Politicisation of the Human Rights Council," *Human Rights Law Review* 17, no. 4 (2017): 753–69.
14. "Human Rights Council Establishes an Independent International Commission of Inquiry to Investigate All Alleged Violations of Human Rights in the Context of the Russian Federation's Aggression against Ukraine," OHCHR, March 4, 2022, https://www.ohchr.org/en/press-releases/2022/03/human-rights-council-establishes-independent-international-commission.
15. "UN General Assembly Resolution ES-11/2."
16. See "UN General Assembly Resolution 65/265" (United Nations, March 1, 2011), https://digitallibrary.un.org/record/698967?ln=zh_CN.
17. "UN General Assembly Votes to Suspend Russia from the Human Rights Council," *UN News*, April 7, 2022, https://news.un.org/en/story/2022/04/1115782.
18. On China, see Gyula Krajczár's chapter in this volume.
19. "UN General Assembly Votes to Suspend Russia from the Human Rights Council."
20. "Human Rights Council Adopts Resolution on the Deteriorating Human Rights Situation in Ukraine and Closes Special Session," OHCHR, May 12, 2022, https://www.ohchr.org/en/press-releases/2022/05/human-rights-council-adopts-resolution-deteriorating-human-rights-situation.

21 "UN General Assembly Resolution 76/262" (United Nations, April 26, 2022), https://digitallibrary.un.org/record/3969448.

22 See Lattmann, "The Case against Russia for the Attack on Flight MH17." It is worth adding that the incident is currently being examined by both the International Court of Justice and the European Court of Human Rights, so the veto has not produced a long-lasting result for Russia.

23 "Security Council Presidential Statement Expresses Strong Support for Efforts by Secretary-General in Seeking Peaceful Solution to Ukraine Conflict," *UN Press*, May 6, 2022, https://press.un.org/en/2022/sc14884.doc.htm.

24 "Ukraine: UN Secretary-General Condemns Russia Annexation Plan," *UN News*, September 29, 2022, https://news.un.org/en/story/2022/09/1129047.

25 "UN General Assembly Resolution ES-11/4" (United Nations, October 12, 2022), https://undocs.org/A/RES/ES-11/4.

26 Alisher Faizullaev and Jérémie Cornut, "Narrative Practice in International Politics and Diplomacy: The Case of the Crimean Crisis," *Journal of International Relations and Development* 20, no. 3 (2017): 578–604.

27 "UN General Assembly Resolution ES-11/5" (United Nations, November 14, 2022), https://undocs.org/A/RES/ES-11/5.

28 "Principles of the Charter of the United Nations Underlying a Comprehensive, Just and Lasting Peace in Ukraine: UN General Assembly Resolution ES-11/L.7."

29 "Statement by H.E. Mr. Dmytro Kuleba, Minister of Foreign Affairs of Ukraine, at the UN Security Council Meeting," Ministry of Foreign Affairs of Ukraine, February 24, 2023, https://mfa.gov.ua/en/news/statement-he-mr-dmytro-kuleba-minister-foreign-affairs-ukraine-un-security-council-meeting.

30 William E. Pomeranz, "Uneasy Partners: Russia and the European Court of Human Rights," *Human Rights Brief* 19, no. 3 (2011): 17–21.

31 "Resolution CM/Res(2022)2 on the Cessation of the Membership of the Russian Federation to the Council of Europe" (Committee of Ministers, March 16, 2022).

32 "The Russian Federation Is Excluded from the Council of Europe," Council of Europe, March 16, 2022, https://www.coe.int/en/web/portal/-/the-russian-federation-is-excluded-from-the-council-of-europe.

33 "Russian State Duma Votes To Quit European Court Of Human Rights," *Radio Free Europe/Radio Liberty*, June 7, 2022, https://www.rferl.org/a/russian-duma-votes-to-quit-european-court-human-rights/31887853.html.

34 Pomeranz, "Uneasy Partners."

35 Federal Constitutional Law No. 7-FKZ "On Amendments to the Federal Constitutional Law 'On the Constitutional Court of the Russian Federation,'" December 15, 2015.

36 Jeffrey Kahn, "The Relationship between the European Court of Human Rights and the Constitutional Court of the Russian Federation: Conflicting Conceptions of Sovereignty in Strasbourg and St Petersburg," *European Journal of International Law* 30, no. 3 (2019): 933–59.

37 "Russian MPs Vote to Quit European Court of Human Rights," *Al Jazeera*, June 7, 2022, https://www.aljazeera.com/news/2022/6/7/russia-exits-european-court-of-human-rights-jurisdiction.

38 "Russia's Withdrawal from Council of Europe a Tragedy for Victims of Kremlin's Abuses," Amnesty International, March 15, 2022, https://www.amnesty.org/en/latest/news/2022/03/russias-withdrawal-from-council-of-europe-a-tragedy-for-victims-of-kremlins-abuses/; Priyanka Shankar, "What Does Russia Leaving the Council of Europe Mean?," *DW.com*, March 17, 2022, https://www.dw.com/en/what-does-russia-leaving-the-council-of-europe-mean/a-61164543.

39 "The Prosecutor of the International Criminal Court, Fatou Bensouda, Opens a Preliminary Examination in Ukraine," International Criminal Court, April 25, 2014, https://www.icc-cpi.int/news/prosecutor-international-criminal-court-fatou-bensouda-opens-preliminary-examination-ukraine.

40 "Russia Formally Withdraws From Hague Criminal Court," *Radio Free Europe/Radio Liberty*, November 16, 2016, https://www.rferl.org/a/russia-withdraws-icc-international-criminal-court/28120789.html.

41 "Report on Preliminary Examination Activities (2016)" (International Criminal Court, November 14, 2016), https://www.icc-cpi.int/sites/default/files/iccdocs/otp/161114-otp-rep-PE_ENG.pdf.

42 On Russia's self-image, see the chapters of András Rácz and Zoltán Sz. Bíró in this volume.

43 Tamás Lattmann, "All's Wrong That Starts Wrong: Withdrawals from the International Criminal Court," International Law Reflection (Prague: Institute of International Relations, February 22, 2017), https://www.iir.cz/the-case-against-russia-for-the-attack-on-flight-mh17.

44 Tamás Lattmann, "Situations Referred to the International Criminal Court by the United Nations Security Council: 'Ad Hoc Tribunalisation' of the Court and Its Dangers," *Pécs Journal of International and European Law* 2 (2016): 68–78.

45 "Ukraine Accepts ICC Jurisdiction over Alleged Crimes Committed since 20 February 2014," International Criminal Court, September 8, 2015, https://www.icc-cpi.int/news/ukraine-accepts-icc-jurisdiction-over-alleged-crimes-committed-20-february-2014.

46 Lattmann, "All's Wrong That Starts Wrong."

47 "Statement of ICC Prosecutor, Karim A.A. Khan QC, on the Situation in Ukraine," International Criminal Court, February 28, 2022, https://www.icc-cpi.int/news/statement-icc-prosecutor-karim-aa-khan-qc-situation-ukraine-i-have-decided-proceed-opening.

48 "ICC Prosecutor, Mr Karim A.A. Khan QC, opens an investigation into the Situation in Venezuela and concludes Memorandum of Understanding with the Government," Press Release: 5 November 2021, ICC-OTP-20211105-PR1625.

49 See "US Sanctions on the International Criminal Court," Human Rights Watch, December 14, 2020, https://www.hrw.org/news/2020/12/14/us-sanctions-international-criminal-court.

50 "Russia: International Criminal Court Issues Arrest Warrant for Putin," *UN News*, March 17, 2023, https://news.un.org/en/story/2023/03/1134732.

51 "Report A/HRC/52/62" (Independent International Commission of Inquiry on Ukraine, March 15, 2023), https://reliefweb.int/report/ukraine/report-independent-international-commission-inquiry-ukraine-ahrc5262enruuk-advance-unedited-version.

52 "Kremlin: ICC Warrants Outrageous and Unacceptable, but Null and Void for Us," *Reuters*, March 17, 2023, sec. Europe, https://www.reuters.com/world/europe/russia-warrant-against-putin-meaningless-russia-does-not-belong-icc-2023-03-17/.

53 See Mina Al-Oraibi, "American Influence After Iraq," *Foreign Affairs*, March 24, 2023, https://www.foreignaffairs.com/united-states/american-influence-after-iraq.

54 See Valur Ingimundarson, "The 'Kosovo Precedent': Russia's Justification of Military Interventions and Territorial Revisions in Georgia and Ukraine," LSE IDEAS Strategic Update, July 13, 2022, https://lseideas.medium.com/the-kosovo-precedent-russia-s-justification-of-military-interventions-and-territorial-revisions-14ad7ff894e6.

55 See Patrick Kingsley, "U.N. Investigator Accuses Israel of Apartheid, Citing Permanence of Occupation," *The New York Times*, March 23, 2022, https://www.nytimes.com/2022/03/23/world/middleeast/israel-apatheid-un.html.

Forced Displacement of Ukrainians during the War: Patterns of Internal and External Migration (2014–2022)

Oksana Mikheieva, Viktoriya Sereda, Lidia Kuzemska

1. Introduction

Ukraine is faced with the phenomenon of forced migration in the context of Russian aggression. Millions of Ukrainian people have been forced to leave their homes for a variety of war-related reasons, and have relocated both within the country (internal forced migration) and abroad (external forced migration). The first wave of massive displacement happened after the Russian occupation of Crimea and parts of Donetsk and Luhansk *oblasts* in 2014. This wave was mostly contained within the country, and therefore the people affected can be considered as internally displaced persons (IDP). The second, much bigger, wave was directed both inside and outside, and was caused by the full-scale Russian invasion on February 24, 2022.

This chapter offers an overview and analysis of the factors, figures, and types of migration with respect to Ukrainians forced to flee due to the war and the circumstances it has created, in addition to the active kidnapping carried out by the Russian authorities. In the first section, we discuss the peculiarities of internal displacement in Ukraine. In the second section, we describe cross-border flows since 2014, and compare the governance response patterns to migration in neighboring countries. The final part discusses the situation of war-displaced Ukrainian citizens in Russia as a separate case requiring special attention.

2. Internal migration: the two waves of Ukrainian internal displacement

2.1. An overview of internal displacement figures and context

Internal displacement is "internal" because it takes place within one country. This refers specifically to migrants who are forced to leave their homes but do not cross state borders, and thus remain citizens of their state. This has resulted in the perception that internal forced migration is less problematic, and thus does not merit as much attention as refugeeism, making IDPs to a certain extent invisible.[1]

In reality, however, the situation for IDPs can be much more problematic than in the case of external refugees. Obtaining refugee status provides a person with protection under international law and international agencies, while agencies seeking to help persons "who have not crossed a border require permission from the very political authorities who may be responsible for the displacement."[2] In situations of internal displacement, people face a range of constraints due to different opportunities in the areas of political rights, property, access to health services, and attitudes toward IDPs in society in general.[3] All of this activates one of the principles of assistance and protection for IDPs, namely "sovereignty as responsibility." As Weiss and Korn explain, this idea has "two essential parts: governments are responsible for the human rights of their citizens as part of the essence of statehood; when they are unwilling or unable to provide for the security and well-being of their citizens, an international responsibility arises to protect vulnerable individuals."[4] In the process of protecting the rights of IDPs, their own agency will also play an important role.[5]

According to the *Global Report on Internal Displacement 2022*, the number of internally displaced persons is steadily increasing. In 1998, the number of IDPs was 17 million; by the end of 2021, there were 59.1 million internally displaced persons across the world (53.2 million as a result of conflict and violence, and 5.9 million as a result of disasters).[6] This increase in the figures has brought increased attention to the phenomenon. In the *World Migration Report 2022*, Ukraine was ranked among the top 20 countries with the highest number of internally displaced persons,[7] which puts it in second place among European countries, according to the *Global Report on Internal Displacement 2022*.[8] (It should be noted that these figures do not take into account the situation after the full-scale Russian invasion, and the data given in this report does not match the numbers of officially registered IDPs in Ukraine.) The scope and specificities of internal displacement in Ukraine, as well as the state and societal response to the problem, have considerable heuristic potential. In this respect, the Ukrainian experience should be taken into consideration when trying to find ways to address the problem globally as well.

The massive internal displacement in Ukraine associated with the start of the Russian aggression in 2014 created many challenges for Ukrainian statehood. The main features of this first wave can be summarized in the following points:

- *It took place in two phases,* which differed significantly in context. The first phase was the so-called "soft" (i.e., without the use of weapons) occupation of the Crimean Peninsula with its further annexation and incorporation into the Russian Federation as a separate federal district. The second phase followed the Russian hybrid invasion and occupation of parts of the Donetsk and Luhansk *oblasts* with the further establishment of the quasi-state formations of the "DPR" and the "LPR" which were essentially collaborationist governments in the occupied territories.

- *The flows of internal migrants had different preferences and levels of cohesion* based on the phase in which they were forced to migrate. While the situation with the occupation of the Crimean Peninsula was one of social tension and hostility towards people with a pro-Ukrainian stance, in parts of the Donetsk and Luhansk regions people were forced to leave due to military action and direct threats to their lives. This context conditioned the political preferences of the IDP groups. The IDPs from Crimea were more homogeneous in their pro-Ukrainian stance, and were more cohesive, therefore, as a group. The people who left the Donetsk and Luhansk oblasts due to the outbreak of hostilities constituted a much more heterogeneous group in their views, and consequently had a much lower level of social cohesion. This difference has largely shaped the subsequent actions of different segments of IDPs and their ability to recognize themselves as a social group with specific needs and political agendas.

- *It involved forced internal displacement on a large scale*, although the exact extent of it is unknown. During the initial phase of external aggression, around 2 million people were displaced from their places of permanent residence. Subsequently, and before the full-scale invasion of Ukraine by the Russian Federation, the number of registered IDPs averaged 1.5 million. These figures do not accurately represent the full scale of internal migration as some of the IDPs refused to register officially. This was due partly to the reluctance of IDPs to transfer their own problems onto the state, and partly to the stigmatizing nature of the status and the specific perception of IDPs by Ukrainian society in the initial phase of Russian aggression. Nevertheless, we are talking about a situation in which more than 1.5 million people simultaneously started to turn to the state system with certain requests.

- *Internal forced displacement was dispersed rather than concentrated* in nature. Much of the international academic literature related to the study of internal migration centers on cases where migrants find themselves in compact settlements, often in refugee camps, as a result of forced displacement. However, in the Ukrainian case, most of the forced displacement took place at the individual level or through the work of volunteer groups.[9] In 2014, there was no centralized evacuation of the population from war zones organized by the state. This also determined the nature of the resettlement of IDPs. In most cases, people chose their new location on their own, and relied on their previous experiences and contacts. These included family ties or professional contacts, employment opportunities, or more accessible housing prices.

- *It was primarily "urban"* as people mostly moved to the major cities. As a result, a large group of IDPs became almost immediately invisible, dissolving into the urban space. This made it difficult to provide assistance to IDPs, and prompted a search for new models of support and integration for people who did not have everyday sustainable connections with each other. It is also important to bear in mind that a significant proportion of IDPs tried to settle close to the demarcation line. This was partly due to people's desire not to move too far from home, to be able to check on the condition of their homes from time to time, and to support their relatives.

- *The majority of those registered as IDPs were of retirement age* in government-controlled parts of Donetsk and Luhansk *oblasts*.[10] A large proportion of these people actually lived in the occupied territories, and entered Ukrainian government-controlled areas occasionally to undergo identification procedures and receive pensions (this is also confirmed by the scale of the demarcation line crossings: before COVID-19-related restrictions, between one and two million people passed through entry-exit checkpoints each month).[11] In this case, the specifics of state policy towards the occupied territories placed people of retirement age in difficult circumstances, limiting their right to receive pensions under the solidarity pension system of Ukraine, and depriving people with limited mobility of this right entirely. A study of involuntary immobility is important for a critical understanding of forced migration in general.[12] On the other hand, the same policy created conditions in which it became problematic to count the number of IDPs who were not only registered in Ukrainian-controlled territory but who had actually relocated and required appropriate government assistance policies as well as assistance in integrating into their local host communities.

The lack of a clear understanding of the actual number of IDPs permanently residing in Ukrainian government-controlled areas, rather than just formally registered in Ukraine, has been one of the factors hindering a number of IDP support projects (including those that could have been supported by foreign donors). The key problems at this stage of displacement were, and still are, the problems of housing and employment. The housing problem was linked to the lack of social housing and relevant state policies on this issue in Ukraine, as well as to the prevalence of shady rental housing practices, which left both parties to the informal transaction unprotected and led to an accumulation of negative experiences. Problems with employment were often linked to regional differences in the structure of the economy, the local unemployment rate, and the need to pursue requalification and change careers. State assistance provided to IDPs was insufficient even for basic survival: the amount of state aid for persons with disabilities and unable to work was UAH 1000 (EUR 36) monthly before 2022, and UAH 442 (EUR 16) monthly for those able to work.[13] Consequently, IDPs could only live in Ukrainian government-controlled territory if they were employed and had a salary that allowed them to rent an apartment.

The second wave of forced internal migration is linked to Russia's full-scale aggression against Ukraine, which began on February 24, 2022. The war changed the scale and nature of internal displacement significantly. According to the International Organization for Migration (IOM), almost a third of Ukraine's total population has been forced to leave their places of permanent residence for at least some period of time. As of October 2022, 6.2 million Ukrainians remained IDPs as a result of the war. Of these, 41% were male and 59% were female; 25% of the total numbers of IDPs were children (1.1% infants, 4.7% children under the age of 5, and 19.4% children from 5 to 17).[14]

The complexity of dealing with both the numbers and the consequences of forced internal displacement stems from the dynamic nature of displacement, in particular its procedural character. People are constantly migrating depending on the scope and outcome of hostilities. As of October 2022, there were 6,036,000 returnees (21% of whom had returned from abroad). Consequently, in this context we should not only talk about the number of those forcibly displaced, but also about the duration of this displacement. Thus, the average duration of internal displacement as of October 27, 2022 was 168 days, with 79% of IDPs away from home for 3 months or more, and more than half of IDPs away for more than 6 months.[15] Moreover, of those IDPs surveyed in October 2022, 46% of households had members 60 years of age or older, 44% had children aged 5 to 17, 38% included chronically ill persons, 26% had members with disabilities, 14% had children aged 1 to 5, and 6% indicated there were pregnant women in the household.[16] The key motives for returning were family reunification, moving back into their own home (financially cheaper than renting), and returning to work. Factors preventing people from returning home primarily involved security issues. However, over time, additional motives for not returning home have emerged, including employment in the new location or enrollment of children in school.

This second wave of forced internal displacement has been significantly more massive in number than the first wave. Its specificity is that it has occurred in the context of Russia's ongoing full-scale invasion of Ukraine. This has made all regions of the country problematic in terms of security and living conditions. The systematic targeting of infrastructure by the Russian regime has created additional hardship for the population at large, and has increased the problematic nature of the IDPs situation. The geography of displacement has also changed considerably: while in 2014 most displaced persons settled close to the line of contact, under the conditions of the full-scale invasion people have sought to move further away from the armed conflict. According to IOM data, the highest number of IDPs in October 2022 were in the Kharkiv (431,793), Dnipropetrovsk (342,228) and Kyiv regions (329,756). The cities with the highest number of IDPs were Kyiv, Dnipro, Zaporizhzhia, Kryvyi Rih, and Odesa. The majority of IDPs, on the other hand, were residents of Donetsk, Kharkiv, and Luhansk *oblasts*.[17]

2.2. The transformational potential of forced internal displacement

War and forced displacement have been catalysts for change in Ukrainian society. An important point in understanding this situation is that a significant number of IDPs, both consciously and unconsciously, have also become agents of change. The Ukrainian state system in 2014 was faced with a one-time resettlement of around 2 million people[18] who had to deal with their own problems in their new surroundings. The mass and systematic nature of appeals to state structures created the grounds for necessary changes.

For example, the situation of massive internal displacement has contributed to reforms in the medical field. These changes have resulted in: (1) the independence of service provision from the potential patient's place of registration; (2) a new system of family doctors with whom people can contract for care; and (3) the emergence in the public discourse of discussions related to the development of a system of care, not only for physical but also for mental health.[19] All these changes have significantly improved health care, making it accessible to those people who previously could not receive it due to lack of registration at their actual place of residence. The activism of IDPs in asserting their political rights led to their right to vote and be elected in local elections, which they had lost 2014, to be restored in 2020.[20] In this case, it was not only the result that was important, but also the process of fighting for political and other human rights and drawing attention to a situation where citizens of one country faced different types of inequality, which made the nature of citizenship unequal and undermined social justice. The involuntary resettlement situation also raised questions in society about the shadow nature of rental housing and the lack of an adequate state policy for the provision of social housing. This issue is important not only for IDPs but also for a number of other social groups who cannot afford to own their own housing and have to pay significant amounts in rent. Unfortunately, this problem remains unresolved in Ukraine even today.

In all reports on the situation of IDPs in Ukraine, people of retirement age have received an enormous amount of attention. The payment of pensions has been particularly problematic. In the solidarity model that exists in Ukraine today, pensions should be linked to citizenship, not to local budgets and social assistance. However, pensions in 2014 were tied to local budgets. In the first wave of displacement, people of retirement age faced the need to register in Ukrainian government-controlled territory and undergo humiliating identification procedures every few months. This policy especially affected elderly people with limited mobility who ended up being completely denied access to pension provision. It has been estimated that the number of such people unable to receive a pension in 2014-2015 was over half a million.[21]

In the second wave, which started with the full-scale Russian invasion, the scope of the occupied territories has increased. Today, it is no longer just a problem of Ukrainian citizens living under occupation in the Crimean Peninsula, and in parts of Donetsk and Luhansk *oblasts*. It is now also a problem for residents of parts of Kherson, Kharkiv, and Zaporizhzhia *oblasts*. While the procedure for accruing pensions has been simplified (it is automatically extended and money can be transferred to an account by bank card) the problem for pensioners in the occupied territories remains the inability to receive the money. The Russian Federation blocks Ukrainian mobile communications and restricts access to Ukrainian websites and services via the internet for residents of the occupied territories. Even if residents of the occupied territories have a bank card with money transferred to it, there is no place to cash it, and it is not possible to pay with it in shops.

As of today, heated discussions about the possibility of paying pensions to so-called "collaborators" seem to have subsided. The Ukrainian state demonstrates maximum loyalty in the accrual of pensions for those who have earned it according to the solidarity pension system in Ukraine, wherever these people are located. After earlier ambiguous statements about the population of the occupied territories, government officials now clearly articulate the people as the state's primary interest. The current policy of the Ukrainian state and society towards the victims of the full-scale Russian invasion, considerably more humane and less discriminatory in nature, was the result of the struggle for their rights by the first IDPs along with extensive public debates.

2.3. *The agency of internally displaced persons*

In response to the onset of Russian aggression in 2014 and the situation of mass displacement, international humanitarian organizations and Ukrainian civil society activists began to intensify their activities in Ukraine. In this context, Ukrainian IDPs have not remained at the level of aid recipients, but have themselves become involved in various activities aimed at addressing the problems of IDPs and the population of the "grey zone," as well as those who have remained in the occupied territories. A key element in the formation of Ukrainian IDP agency has been the support of international organizations which have not only provided humanitarian aid but also helped shape experiences and practices of civic engagement. Another area of activity for Ukrainian civil society has been support for the army and participation in volunteer military formations.

International organizations were ready to support civilian peace initiatives aimed at assisting different categories of the population affected by the military conflict. However, the idea of supporting the state army and supplying military units was obviously not supported by said organizations and foundations. Consequently, in parallel with the internationally supported development of the civil sector in Ukrainian society, NGOs and volunteer groups began to develop as they sought and found domestic resources for activities aimed at solving problems of defending state sovereignty. Going beyond the normal boundaries of civic voluntary activity, involvement in security issues and defending the territorial integrity and sovereignty of the state are specific features of Ukrainian volunteering. The Russian aggression and forced displacement in 2014 intensified the process of creating informal coalitions and networks of interaction which resulted in the formation of "weak" ties[22] or what has been defined as "bridging" capital.[23] Participation in such coalitions, collaborations, and logistical aid schemes became a tool for overcoming mistrust and a mechanism for building social capital through the formation of ties between representatives of different social and status groups.

All of this has played an important role in building trust and a new level of interaction, both between state structures and organized civil society and within civil society itself. "Compared with the Western model that was replicated in Ukraine before 2013, the emerging Ukrainian model is less formal, more activist and has a strong political dimension. Much like their Western counterparts, volunteers in Ukraine provide services to those in need. At the same time, a volunteer in the country is more than just a service provider. He or she also has a potential to play an active role in state- and nation building. The volunteer is an advocate of democracy."[24] All this was an important factor in the resilience of Ukrainian statehood in the face of full-scale Russian aggression. The end result was that national NGO s and volunteer groups were able to respond to the 2022 invasion immediately, whereas international organizations acted with apparent delay. As has been noted, "With a few exceptions, even the international agencies with prior presence inside Ukraine needed at least five weeks to re-enter and ramp up before they began any aid delivery."[25]

3. External migration: the two waves of displacement in Western and Eastern directions

3.1. The EU direction before the full-scale invasion: refugees conflated with labor migrants

The most general criterion for distinguishing Ukrainian IDPs who decided to move abroad is their direction: whether they relocated to the West (to EU countries) or to the East (to Russia). However, we also need to distinguish between refugees and labor migrants, and between the first wave of external migration (after the occupation of Crimea) and the second wave (starting in 2022). Regarding the first wave of external migration, the number of asylum applications filed by Ukrainian citizens in European countries in 2015 grew 20 times when compared to the pre-conflict numbers and exceeded 22,000.[26] Of these, only 415 applicants were granted Geneva Convention asylum status within the EU space (28 countries) in 2015, and another 475 in 2016 (or approximately 2 percent of those who applied). In subsequent years, when the conflict deescalated and a temporary ceasefire was achieved after the Minsk I and Minsk II Agreements, the number of asylum applications gradually decreased by half, and the number of successful applications increased because in many cases it took a long time to reach a decision in a particular case.[27] An analysis of labor migration flows also shows an unsurprising picture: for a long time, Russia was the top destination country for Ukrainian labor migrants, but after the Russian aggression against Ukraine the situation changed and migration outflow turned westward.[28] A visa-free regime agreement signed in 2017 between the EU and Ukraine (allowing Ukrainian citizens visa-free entry to the Schengen-zone countries for a period of 90 days within any 180-day period) further facilitated this shift in Ukrainians' international mobility flows.[29]

However, what needs to be seen, and is underlined by recent studies on global migration governance, is that transborder migration is increasingly politicized by states due to its scale and its social-economic and political implications.[30] Although based on universal treaties, the politics of cross-border migration is characterized by a fundamental power asymmetry that constitutes what Stephen Castles describes as "hierarchies of citizenship."[31] States preserve a significant degree of autonomy in determining their migration policies which enables them to maximize the benefits and minimize the costs of mobility. The aimed benefits are not always or exclusively economic, and may also be related to security, development, human rights, and peace-building efforts[32]—or, on the contrary, be linked to a form of transborder nationalism.[33]

The provision of refugee protection is ideologically constructed as a global public good which states should collectively value and support. However, in reality states have little incentive to assume the role of providers because of the non-excludable nature of the humanitarian and security benefits of protection, and those that do assume the role of host subject asylum seekers to policies advocating ever more restrictive measures.[34] Jaeeun Kim[35] introduces the concept of "migration-facilitating capital," the uneven distribution of which produces material and symbolic stratification on local, national, and global levels. It can be applied to show how in the current debate about the "refugee crisis" various state and non-state actors mobilize diverse and competing views on the "salvability" of irregular migrants and transform them into refugees. Therefore, in exploiting existing legal and ethical frameworks for international humanitarian and human rights, states may pursue their own interests, using media or political campaigns to "explain" why one particular category of migrants is deemed "worthy of rescue" or declared a priority while another is not.

The Ukrainian IDPs who decided to move abroad can be used as an interesting case study in examining the practices and rhetoric that neighboring states employ for the management of this conflict-related migration. Moreover, their situation can also be used to show how the discourse on the politics of humanitarianism ("saving Ukrainian refugees") can be used for political purposes of "influence seeking,"[36] perceived economic benefits, "managing otherness" within national borders,[37] or even as a pretext for launching a war (as in the case of Russia, where this was one of the arguments used to justify the invasion of Ukraine in February 2022). The Ukrainian case can also shed some light on the restrictive policies and selection criteria used by neighboring countries to control the mass influx of refugees from protracted conflicts, and what challenges they pose to the global refugee governance regime.

In the following, we focus on three countries: Poland and Hungary, which are Ukraine's immediate neighbors, and Germany, which is a close neighbor and important destination for Ukrainian asylum seekers. Even though all three countries lie in close proximity and belong to the EU, their migration and refugee policies often represent different political and migration regimes. It should be noted, however, that the first inflow of Ukrainian migrants to these countries coincided with another conflict-induced forced migration wave, namely, the unfolding refugee crisis in Europe caused by refugees and undocumented migrants fleeing war-affected countries of the Global South (mostly from Syria).

Poland and Hungary before 2022 provide a good example of how the universal discourse on refugee support and the responsibility to protect can be transformed by state politicization of "salvability" based on hierarchical preferences and desired economic benefits when bestowing citizenship. Almost simultaneously with the above-mentioned 2017 visa-free regime agreement, Poland liberalized its employment and legalization procedures, extended the validity of temporary residence permits, and signed a bilateral social security agreement with Ukraine. Hungary and the Czech Republic followed Poland's example. As a result, Poland became the primary EU destination for Ukrainian migration, including temporary workers, students, and permanent labor migrants. The estimated number of Ukrainian migrants in Poland almost tripled by 2017, reaching 507,000.[38] According to a survey conducted in 2018 among Ukrainian migrants in Poland,[39] over 70 percent of those surveyed held different types of long-term permits, while only 4.2 percent claimed to be undocumented. However, only 5 percent of those labor migrants surveyed in 2017 had come from the Eastern regions of Ukraine (the Donbas and Kharkiv *oblast*).

At the same time, Polish authorities, in contravention of the legal status of Ukrainian migrants, tried to present them as asylum-seeking refugees, using this as an argument against accepting the EU-mandated quota of Syrian refugees. In 2016, the Polish prime minister, Beata Szydlo, rejected the Syrian refugee quota assignment, and told the European Parliament that Poland had taken instead "a million Ukrainian refugees." In reality, only eight Ukrainians were granted asylum in Poland by that time.[40] In a similar way, when Hungary faced a labor shortage, the government of Prime Minister Viktor Orbán granted privileges to Ukrainian labor migrants and citizenship to Ukrainian citizens of Hungarian ethnicity, but refused to accept Syrian refugees.[41] Hungary subsequently moved into the top five EU destination countries for Ukrainian labor migration. Like Poland, Orbán's Hungary used "the Ukrainian refugees" card, representing labor migrants as valid refugees. However, according to UNHCR data, there were only 19 UNHCR-mandated refugees in Hungary in 2016, in addition to five official asylum seekers.[42] The Polish and Hungarian cases both show that even democratic EU states use the discourse of humanitarianism ("saving Ukrainian refugees") for political purposes of influence seeking (granting passports to the Hungarian minority in Ukrainian Transcarpathia), economic benefits (limiting accessibility to asylum status and redirecting potential asylum-seekers to labor migration), and managing otherness within national borders (trying to avoid "unwanted" migrant and refugee flows).

According to UNHCR[43] and Eurostat data, Germany was among the top EU countries for Ukrainian asylum applications between 2015 and 2020 (4570 in 2015, 2390 in 2016, 1090 in 2017, and 460 in 2020).[44] Interviewed respondents, who arrived in Germany or Poland from the temporarily occupied territories of Crimea and parts of Donets and Luhansk *oblasts*, explained that they were told that refugee applications from Ukrainian citizens were almost automatically rejected on the grounds that major parts of Ukraine lay outside the conflict zone, and that preference was given to refugees from other countries. As a result, many dislocated Ukrainians were not sure about their rights and procedures. The absolute majority of respondents, therefore, chose the path of documented or undocumented labor migration, education, marriage strategies, or a combination of these as a way of migrating instead of applying for refugee status. In those isolated cases where migrants had applied for refugee status and had been rejected, the respondents struggled to renegotiate their status to avoid deportation.

An analysis of the main trends of cross-border displacement in 2014–2021 caused by the annexation of Crimea and the military conflict in parts of Donetsk and Luhansk *oblasts* shows that citizenship was an important marker in social hierarchization and othering. Displaced persons were subjected to uneven citizenship and hierarchization in local host communities, with their experiences framed by borders, laws and administrative practices, and the state's symbolic power of nomination and categorization. They became part of the fabric of transnational hierarchies of citizenship, politicized debates on "salvability," and politics of humanitarianism used for the political purpose of limiting access for unwanted migrants.

3.2. The EU's position after the full-scale invasion: the specificities of refugee reception in Germany and Poland

After February 2022, the character of Ukrainian migration to the EU radically changed. If the previous wave of displacement was mostly contained within the country, this new wave was actively directed towards the outside of the country. Nobody predicted the real scale of the refugee crisis, which turned to be the largest European population displacement since the end of World War II, with close to 50,000 crossing the border during some peak days. This time the EU and many countries around the world demonstrated their highest level of support by adopting fast and efficient admission policies. The visa-free regime, in combination with simplified procedures for admission, allowing war refugees from Ukraine to skip lengthy asylum application processes and granting temporary protection in the EU for up to three years, opened new possibilities for Ukrainian refugees.

By November 2022, UNHCR had recorded 7,867,219 refugees from Ukraine across Europe, with 4,751,065 refugees registered for the EU's Temporary Protection program or similar national protection schemes. Over the same period, more than 7 million people had crossed the Ukrainian border in the opposite direction (this figure reflects cross-border movements and not individuals).[45]

However, due to country-based differences in the implementation of the Temporary Protection program and other factors, such as the level of civil society support, the size of the Ukrainian labor migration, and cultural proximity, some countries have become primarily transition spaces (Hungary, for instance, with 2,933,815 border crossings by July 2023 but only 36,315 refugees registered for Temporary Protection) or serve as only minor destinations (Liechtenstein, with only 640, and Bosnia and Herzegovina, with 75 refugees who applied for national protection schemes). Other countries, such as Poland and Germany, have become real refugee hubs. According to UNHCR data, from the beginning of the Russian aggression until the end of July 2023, over 12,724,955 Ukrainian nationals crossed the Polish-Ukrainian border and 1,618,785 applied for Temporary Protection. It is much more challenging to estimate the number of Ukrainians who stayed in Poland. In April 2022, the registration of Ukrainians in Poland according to the PESEL system began. This electronic registration system assigns identifying numbers to Ukrainian war refugees, affording them access to free public services, such as medical assistance, health care, and schools, as well as employment. There are now over one million Ukrainians voluntarily registered in PESEL. Another way to determine the number of Ukrainians in Poland is to count those legally able to work in the country. Such individuals are required to pay into the ZUS, the Polish social security system, which registered over 500,000 Ukrainians in 2022 alone. In December 2022, there were over 766,000 Ukrainians officially employed in Poland, although this number included both labor migrants and newly arrived refugees.[46]

According to the latest UN data report (UNHCR 2023),[47] Germany hosts the second largest number of displaced Ukrainians with a total of 1,072,705 people, of which those registered for the Temporary Protection program number 958,590. However, the number of arrivals might be over-reported due to the slow procedure of deregistering cases. Germany also experienced a rapid surge of arrivals during early March and April 2022 which required intensive civil society support including meeting refugees and migrants at train stations and other points of entry, doing translating, providing food, clothing, and shelter, and offering medical and psychological support, legal assistance, and other necessary support. Despite the rapid surge it was still not as rapid and intensive as in Poland because the Ukrainians first had to get to Poland and then continue their travels later, meaning they gradually accumulated. As in Poland, civil society, volunteer organizations, and self-aid networks were the first to respond, with state and local administration structures joining later on. Again, as in Poland, Ukrainian refugees gravitated towards the country's primary cities, which eventually had to declare that they were closing their doors to newcomers. By September 2022, 12 of Germany's 16 states reported that they were at their breaking point, according to the Federal Interior Ministry.[48] In comparison to Poland, Ukrainian refugees in Germany have had a difficult time finding employment. By October 2022, some 423,000 Ukrainians had registered as looking for employment, with only 51,000 employed full-time and an additional 17,000 having part-time jobs. These figures do not include self-employed individuals as they were not included in the statistics at that time.[49] Our study[50] shows that this lag in employment may be explained by the slower bureaucracy in Germany, extended waiting periods for school and kindergarten placements, and requirements for language proficiency. In addition, Ukrainian refugees in Germany whose German is insufficient must take six months of language courses, which also delays their entrance to the job market.

Many observers also stress the distinctive character of this wave of forced external migration both in terms of the number of displaced within a brief period of time and also due to its social-demographic characteristics. It is a war-induced mass displacement, with a distinct socio-demographic profile compared to previous European refugee waves since the late 1990s. This is especially the case when compared to previous large waves of refugees from the wars in Syria, Libya, and Afghanistan which were predominately defined by young males.[51] In contrast, due to wartime regulations in Ukraine, men are not allowed to leave the country, so most of the war migrants and refugees have been women and children, in most cases crossing the Ukrainian border with their relatives. A UNHCR survey of Ukrainian refugees conducted in nine European countries between May and November 2022 involving 43,571 respondents the generalized respondents' profile indicates total dominance of woman (85%) mostly young (only 13% were aged over 60) with higher level of education—47% higher and 29% vocational, 73% of whom were previously employed in wide variety of spheres—mostly in retail (15%), education (14%), healthcare (9%). Women and children represent 87% of all family members that left Ukraine.[52] This demographic profile of fleeing displaced people, mostly young women accompanied by several children and older adults requiring additional assistance, created novel circumstances.

This new wave of war-induced migration from Ukraine and its predominantly female character elicited a rise in solidarity and spontaneous aid initiatives for refugees in all neighboring countries.[53] Refugees crossing Ukraine's borders received various forms of support, as mentioned above. Social surveys during this time reveal a radical change in views on accepting refugees, with only 3% in Poland and 4% in Germany stating that no Ukrainians should be allowed in.[54]

With a temporary stabilization of the front line beginning in May 2022, border crossings in and out of the country almost approached a 1:1 ratio. UNHCR data show a gap of nearly 3.3 million persons between the number of border-crossings to Europe and the number of refugees from Ukraine registered for Temporary Protection or similar national protection schemes there. This difference in numbers may be partially explained by Ukrainian refugees incorporating seasonal labor migration patterns into their own migration strategies; specifically, this refers to people using their 90-day visa-free stay in the EU and then returning to their families for another 90 days. After their initial stage of legalization and adaptation, many war refugees and migrants returned to visit their families (husbands or elderly who could not or refused to move). Such a strategy may also become an additional restraining factor in the speedy and full integration of war migrants and refugees into local job markets and in accessing social benefits in the receiving countries because it often presupposes the voluntary rejection of Temporary Protection status. However, the recent large-scale destruction of critical infrastructure and power plants by Russia might provoke a new wave of refugees seeking shelter from their dark, cold, and destroyed cities.

In discussing migration from Ukraine, we should not leave aside the impact the 2022 invasion has had on the approximately 400,000 immigrants in Ukraine who represent a diversified population: dissidents from other post-Soviet countries, such as Kazakhstan, Belarus, and Russia; persons displaced by other conflicts in the region—Georgia, Chechnya, and Azerbaijan; refugees from the global south; and international students. Policy responses to their displacement, both within the country and in neighboring EU states, led to some controversies regarding this issue. During the first weeks of massive displacement following the February 2022 invasion, there were reported cases of racial discrimination in prioritizing those who could leave the country, as well as in the refusal of their admittance by neighboring countries. The latter was based on the argument that these persons were nationals of countries that did not have a visa-free regime with the EU and that Ukrainian residency permits did not suffice. There were also cases in which admission or registration was refused to Ukrainian Roma fleeing the war.

On the other hand, some critical voices pointed to the preferential treatment afforded Ukrainians as both white and Christian in contrast to the previous waves of refugee migration. Such an approach creates a simplified picture of Ukrainian refugees as a single group, and does not consider the ethnic and religious diversity of Ukraine's population. Moreover, it also overlooks the nature of the war which has elicited feelings of solidarity as well as the long history of citizenship hierarchization, discrimination, and othering towards Ukrainian nationals within the European space.

3.3. War-displaced Ukrainian citizens in Russia: data uncertainty and the procedures for the deportation and silencing of Ukrainian identity

The situation facing displaced Ukrainian nationals in the Russian aggressor state is difficult, as they have limited institutional support other than from the Russian state or state-controlled organizations. Unlike in any other country, Ukrainians in Russia cannot rely on support from their diplomats in defending their rights or receiving state services abroad, as Ukraine broke diplomatic ties with the aggressor on the first day of the invasion. Ukrainian bank cards, SIM-cards and e-documents do not function in Russia, so communication and support from abroad is virtually impossible. There are also limitations on the legal exchange of Ukrainian hryvnias to Russian rubles, which restricts Ukrainians in their daily life and in making future plans. Moreover, the operations of those international organizations that would traditionally provide assistance in situations of mass refugee influx, such as the UNHCR, IOM, and the ICRC, are also limited in Russia. Using the metaphor of a chokehold, Magyar and Madlovics argue that the Russian domestic political system is built on the elimination of autonomous action and "a permanent framework of the possibility [(and use!) – LK] of repression,"[55] which prevents and punishes most organized independent initiatives. In addition, with the launching of the full-scale invasion against Ukraine, Russia has transformed further into a "criminal state with a central project of a crime against humanity,"[56] with Ukraine and Ukrainians being its target, as this section will illustrate.

As of October 3, 2022, UNHCR has recorded 2,852,395 border crossings from Ukraine to Russia since the start of the full-scale invasion on February 24. A further 105,000 people crossed to the Russian Federation from the previously occupied territories of Donetsk and Luhansk *oblasts* (ORDLO) between February 18 and 23 after the occupying authorities announced a so called "evacuation." The total estimated number of Ukrainian refugees in Russia currently stands at 2.8 million.[57]

UNHCR statistics, however, have several limitations. First, they come mainly from governmental sources of the respective states, so the trustworthiness of border crossings provided by Russia is difficult to verify. Ukrainian and Russian official sources give vastly different figures for the number of displaced Ukrainians in Russia—1.6 million[58] versus 4.7 million[59] in October 2022—both figures significantly different from the UNHCR number. Second, UNHCR uses the term "refugees" generically for all persons who have had to flee war irrespective of their legal status in the country of destination. In the case of war-displaced Ukrainian citizens in Russia, the term "refugee" is misleading because the majority of them are not given either national or international protection status in Russia. Instead, Ukrainians are pressured into applying for Russian citizenship if they need to stay in Russia longer—actions which constitute a continuation of the previous policy of forced passportization in the occupied territories of Donbas and Crimea.[60]

Figure 1. Dynamics of the War Displacement from Ukraine to Russia (February-October 2022).

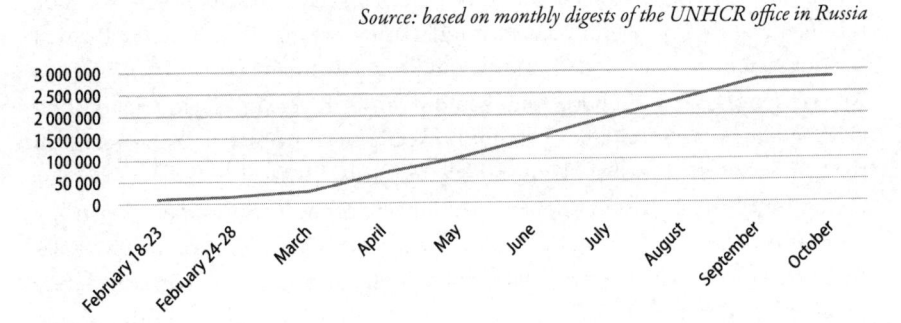

Source: based on monthly digests of the UNHCR office in Russia

(https://www.unhcr.org/ru/monthlydigest).

We also need to consider the nature of planned actions taken by the aggressor state towards civilians in Ukraine. Reports on the deportation of civilians from the occupied territories to Russia started to circulate from the second half of March 2022, especially from occupied Mariupol.[61] Soon after, the Ministry of Reintegration of the Temporarily Occupied Territories issued instructions on how to behave in case of deportation to Russia or ORDLO.[62] Some 27 thousand civilians who wanted to leave the territory of active military operations were required to undergo "filtration" procedures (as of April 19, 2022) since Russia blocked humanitarian corridors to Ukrainian-controlled territory.[63] Ukrainian human rights organizations announced that civilians who remained behind under occupation and who lacked the financial or other means to allow them to leave should be supported and not condemned.[64] In the end, the Ukrainian government called on its citizens to use any means to leave the occupied territories, even if it required traveling via Russia or receiving Russian travel documents, reassuring them that they would not face legal prosecution for this later.[65] In a situation where local inhabitants have no choice about the route of escape from an active war zone, we can talk about the deportation of a significant number of Ukrainian citizens from the occupied territories. The Ministry of Reintegration of the Occupied Territories has reported that Ukrainian nationals who also hold Russian passports have been prevented from leaving Russia on their way to Estonia and Latvia, making them effectively hostages.[66] Overall, "deportees" or "forcefully displaced civilians" would be more accurate terms to use than "refugees."[67]

Another problem with UNHCR statistics is that they do not account for the secondary movements of people. Thousands of Ukrainian citizens who had to transit via Russian territory to other states (either to the EU/EEA, the Caucasus, and even Central Asia) are still included in the 2.8 million border crossings recorded by UNHCR. For instance, by the end of 2022, Georgia recorded 25,204 Ukrainian refugees, Azerbaijan almost 4,000, Armenia 360, and Kazakhstan around 3,000.[68] These figures do not account for those Ukrainian citizens who transited via these countries. For example, a report by the UNHCR and World Vision Georgia indicate that at least half of Ukrainian refugees in the country entered from Russia and originated from Donetsk and Kherson oblasts.[69] Moreover, there is no data on the number of Ukrainians who crossed back to Ukraine from Russia or crossed the border multiple times.[70]

The Ukrainian Parliament has recognized the forcible transfer of civilians, especially children, to Russia as part of the ongoing genocide against Ukrainians.[71] Human Rights Watch[72] and Amnesty International[73] have both issued reports documenting severe human rights violations and war crimes committed by Russia, including: the punitive and abusive mass illegal collection of biometric data, body searches, searches of personal belongings and phones, questioning about political views and relations with the Ukrainian armed forces, interment, the refusal to return documents, arbitrary detention, tortures, pressure to testify about alleged war crimes of the Ukrainian armed forces, and disappearances. The horrors of the filtration camps became one of the bases for Russian war crimes investigations.[74]

Once in Russia, forcibly displaced Ukrainians have few options depending on their social ties, available resources, and socio-demographic characteristics. Those who have relatives or friends in Russia, have sufficient financial means, or wish to avoid increased surveillance can try evading state-ordained pathways of being mandatorily distributed across the Russian regions according to governmental quotas[75] and settled into one of the Temporary Accommodation Points (TAPs). As of October 24, 2022, the Russian Ministry for Emergencies reported that there were 807 TAPs in 58 regions accommodating 40,680 persons, including 12,470 children.[76] Unaccompanied, separated, or orphaned children, older people, and people with disabilities from Ukraine are the most vulnerable when it comes to having no choice about their destination and subsequent stay in Russia.[77] Ukrainian human rights activists argue that approximately 50,000 children from the occupied territories were deported to the Russian Federation between February and October 2022.[78] The Russian, Commissioner for Children's Rights, Maria Lvova-Belova, confirmed that between 1.5 and 2.5 thousand children from ORDLO stayed in Russian TAPs throughout 2022, and that "only 380 of them had been placed in Russian foster care families."[79] The UNHCR office in Russia has reportedly urged Lvova-Belova to help with the family tracing of separated children and the re-establishment of family links back in Ukraine.[80] The fate of children placed under foster care in Russia remains on both the national and international agenda,[81] but only 125 of them had returned to Ukraine by the end of 2022.[82]

UNHCR does not work directly with Ukrainians (or rather is not allowed to do so by the Russian state), apart from occasional joint monitoring visits to the TAPs together with Russian officials. Instead, it relies on its partnerships with a few local organizations, such as the Civic Assistance Committee, the charitable foundation "Health and Life," the SILSILA Foundation, and, most importantly, with the Russian Red Cross, which operates across the country in close cooperation with the state authorities in the provision of basic needs assistance (food, clothing, medicine, and counseling) for war-displaced civilians.[83] Another major provider of humanitarian assistance and shelter across the country is the Russian Orthodox Church, which is supported by the Presidential Grants Foundation.[84]

Based on its monitoring missions, UNHCR reports[85] that most frequently ask questions by Ukrainians in the TAPs include how to apply for refugee status in Russia, accommodation options, arrivals to and departures from Russia, receiving humanitarian assistance and medical care, exchanging currency, the replacement of lost or destroyed documents, receiving financial help from the government (RUB 10,000), finding a job, accessing pensions and bank accounts in Ukraine, accessing social benefits in Russia, and compensation for lost properties in Ukraine. Many reportedly expressed hopes of returning to Ukraine, yet still applied for temporary protection or citizenship in Russia for the time being.[86]

War-displaced Ukrainians living outside the government-run TAP system face numerous everyday challenges as well. In the absence of state supervision and official humanitarian aid providers, they rely predominantly on the assistance of acquaintances, volunteers, and fellow displaced persons in Russia in navigating the complex bureaucratic procedures and shifting legal provisions regarding the multiple legal statuses they can apply for in Russia. Considering the staggering, although disputed, figure of 2.8 million border crossings from Ukraine into Russia during 2022, the following statistics on the legalization of Ukrainians in Russia are telling.

According to a report by the Civic Assistance Committee based on statistics of the Russian Ministry of the Interior, as of September 30, 2022 only 28 Ukrainians had obtained refugee status while 88,658 persons had received "temporary protection" status.[87] At the same time, some 266,250 Ukrainian nationals received Russian citizenship during the first nine months of 2022.[88]

According to Svetlana Gannushkina, the head of above-mentioned committee based in Moscow, Ukrainian citizens in Russia struggle to gain access to public services (education, healthcare, financial and social support) without first legalizing their stay in Russia, which often takes three to six months.[89] Bureaucratic delays, missing or destroyed documents due to the war, difficulties in obtaining necessary documentation in Russia, such as residence registration, medical examination reports, and official translations of Ukrainian documents, place people in financially precarious positions. Official employment and long-term renting require legal status in Russia. Elderly people, people with disabilities, and those wounded due to the war cannot access the necessary social support and medical care. While waiting for their documentation, many forcibly displaced Ukrainians in Russia take on precarious informal jobs and live in extremely strenuous conditions. Some are forced to rely on volunteer donations of basic food and non-food items, toiletries, bedding, basic furniture, stationery for children, and second-hand computer devices for studying and working online. Besides the political and moral dilemmas Ukrainians face when forced to rely on charity in the aggressor state (the primary cause of their displacement), cases of discrimination and school bullying have also started to emerge.[90]

What awaits forcibly displaced Ukrainians in Russia? Analyzing previous Russian state policy towards those displaced from the ORDLO since 2014, Irina Kuznetsova noted: "Russia has a selective refugee policy, based on nationalistic narratives of Slavic brotherhood and a contemporary geopolitical situation in which Russia is attempting to win back lost influence [in its perceived geopolitical neighborhood]."[91] Kuznetsova situates this policy under the "manual control" of President Putin, citing Schenk who refers to this as "'a technique of authoritarian rule employed by Russian political elites that uses personal intervention in policymaking in order to maintain popular legitimacy for the regime and shore up the vertical of power.'"[92] Already in 2014-2021, those Ukrainians who had resettled to Russia found few opportunities to preserve their language and culture as their Ukrainian identity was effectively silenced.[93] At the same time, they were actively encouraged to apply for the Russian compatriot program as a fast track to citizenship. An estimated 1.4 million Ukrainian citizens from the occupied territories of Donbas received Russian nationality between 2014 and 2021.[94] As media interest in the displaced waned quickly by 2017, state support was minimized and the displaced could only rely on themselves, volunteer support groups, and a few NGOs.[95] We can expect the Russian authorities to likely follow a similar approach with the current wave of the forcibly displaced, albeit with a greater emphasis on ensuring they do not pose any "security threat" to Russia.

Why would some Ukrainian citizens prefer to remain in Russia (at least for now) despite all the challenges they face? According to Lida Moniava, director of the Lighthouse Charitable Foundation, which provides support to some 7,000 war-displaced persons from Ukraine in Moscow and the Moscow region,[96] there are three common reasons for this.[97] First, people are afraid of the unknowns they will face elsewhere, especially if they do not speak foreign languages and have had no previous experience of international travel. Second, many are exhausted by war, forced displacement, and everyday struggles, so want to settle down, at least for the time being. Moreover, those with elderly persons or people who require immediate medical help cannot travel further. Finally, people have hopes: they hope they can reunite with family members or relatives in Russia; they hope they can rely on friends and support networks which they might not have in other countries, and; they hope they can return home some day and wish to remain close by.

Those Ukrainian citizens who want to leave Russia rely on volunteer networks, e.g. Rubikus.helpUA, which can help them leave the country or organize travel on their own. Since December 2022, the State Migration Office of Ukraine has issued return permits to those displaced persons whose Ukrainian travel documents have been lost, destroyed, or taken away by the Russian authorities. These permits allow the holder to return to Ukraine and are valid for three months.[98] However, it is not clear how these return permits will be delivered to their owners currently on Russian territory. Ukrainians who have already left Russian territory and are currently staying in other countries (e.g. Estonia, Georgia, Kazakhstan, Turkey, and Latvia) should receive help from the local Ukrainian embassies in renewing their documents and returning home.[99]

3. Conclusion and future dilemmas

In this chapter, we discussed the various forms and specificities of forced migration, external and internal, of Ukrainian people as a result of Russian aggression. One of the ways to summarize the two waves of displacement (after 2014 and 2022, respectively) is by analyzing whether forced refugees have been able to freely select their route of escape and their destination, and whether their movement to that destination has been facilitated by state and/or private institutions. Table 1 summarizes the main features of the first and second waves of internal and external migration from this perspective.

Table 1. The two waves of internal and external migration of Ukrainians according to freedom and facilitation in the selection of migration destination (activity of relevant actors).

	Internal migration		External migration	
	activity of the state	*activity of civil society*	*activity of EU countries*	*activity of Russia*
First wave (from 2014)	unprepared state apparatus	active volunteer movement	migration allowed but politicized	Ukrainian identity silenced, passportization
Second wave (from 2022)	transformed state services	continued activism	supported by EU countries (e.g. Poland and Germany)	no protection status granted, mass deportation, passportization

The process of forced migration raises a number of dilemmas. With respect to internal migration, the Ukrainian state will face several problems to be solved in the future. Given the possible protracted nature of military action, further responses and policies to the situation of internal displacement need to be developed; the problem of burnout among active representatives of civil society, who work in the sphere of minimizing the impact of war on people's lives, needs to be addressed; and the practical problem of how long a person has to live with internally displaced status (i.e., how to determine the termination of such status) requires a solution. In addition, civic activism raises a question for both policy makers and sociologists: Is there a prospect for the institutionalization of volunteering in Ukraine, or is institutional "weakness" its value and strength? Future discussion needs to tackle these issues to be able to handle the increasing problem of IDPs in Ukraine in the most effective way.

As an ongoing process, a number of issues related to the current wave of Ukrainian people fleeing to EU countries need to be the focus of future research. First, from the perspective of the receiving countries, there is the visible discrepancy between the high demand for employment and the high level of human capital in terms of education and skills of the arriving Ukrainian refugees and the ability of the local job markets of many countries to fulfil these needs without pushing the new arrivals into the sector of low-paid unskilled jobs. Second, from the perspective of Ukraine, the issue of the drain of human capital is rightly raised in the context in which Ukrainian refugee children gradually join the local education systems and the elderly gain access to medical services, both of which can easily become new anchoring factors. Third, the role of Temporary Protection status needs to be addressed, as it gives more flexibility to Ukrainian refugees in terms of mobility and access to the job market but does not provide long-term legal status and can be withdrawn any time. Finally, if the war lasts for some time and Ukrainian refugees end up being absorbed by the local job markets, how will the economies of the receiving communities react if the refugees start returning home?

Lastly, the difficult situation of war-displaced (and forcibly deported) Ukrainians in Russia poses several questions that will require policy actions from Ukraine and its international allies. The most urgent question concerns the improvement of mechanisms to prevent the deportation or forcible transfer of civilians, especially those most vulnerable (children, the elderly, people with disabilities) in a war situation, as well as enabling their safe return or resettlement. What instruments and actors can Ukraine and international organizations mobilize in order to support Ukrainians currently on the territory of the Russian Federation or to facilitate their transit to other countries? Then, there is the unresolved issue of the return and reintegration policy of Ukraine towards war-displaced Ukrainian citizens in Russia, and in particular whether it should be the same as towards Ukrainian refugees returning from other countries. And as a final, and difficult, topic, the de facto dual citizenship of many war-displaced Ukrainians as a result of forced passportization along with potential cases of collaboration with the aggressor state will be an area where the Ukrainian state must develop a policy by the end of the war.

Notes

1. Barbara Harrell-Bond and Eftinia Voutira, "In Search of "Invisible" Actors: Barriers to Access in Refugee Research," *Journal of Refugee Studies* 20, no. 2 (2007): 281–98.
2. Thomas G. Weiss and David A. Korn, *Internal Displacement: Conceptualization and its Consequences* (Abingdon: Routledge, 2006), 1.
3. See, for example, Tania Bulakh, "'Strangers among Ours': State and Civil Responses to the Phenomenon of Internal Displacement in Ukraine," in *Migration and the Ukraine Crisis. A Two-Country Perspective*, eds. Agnieszka Pikulicka-Wilczewska and Greta Uehling (Bristol: E-International Relations Publishing, 2017), 49–61; Kateryna Ivashchenko-Stadnik, "The Social Challenge of Internal Displacement in Ukraine: The Host Community's Perspective," in *Migration and the Ukraine Crisis. A Two-Country Perspective*, eds. Agnieszka Pikulicka-Wilczewska and Greta Uehling (Bristol: E-International Relations Publishing, 2017), 25–48; Dorota Woroniecka-Krzyzanowska and Nika Palaguta, "Internally Displaced Persons and Elections under Military Conflict in Ukraine," *Journal of Refugee Studies* 30 no. 1 (2017): 27–46; Tetyana Durnyeva, H.H. Jepsen, and Hannah Roberts, "IDP's Electoral Participation Gap," *Journal of Internal Displacement* 9, no. 1 (2019): 5–35; Irina Kuznetsova and Oksana Mikheieva, "Forced Displacement from Ukraine's War-Torn Territories: Intersectionality and Power Geometry," *Nationalities Papers* 48, no. 4 (2020): 690-706; Viktoriya Sereda, "'Social Distancing'and Hierarchies of Belonging: The Case of Displaced Population from Donbas and Crimea," *Europe-Asia Studies* 72, no. 3 (2020): 404-431; Viktoriya, Sereda, *Displacement in War-Torn Ukraine: State, Displacement and Belonging* (Cambridge: Cambridge University Press, 2023).
4. Weiss and Korn, *Internal displacement*, 3.
5. Greta Uehling, "A Hybrid Deportation: Internally Displaced from Crimea in Ukraine," in *Migration and the Ukraine Crisis. A Two-Country Perspective*, eds. Agnieszka Pikulicka-Wilczewska and Greta Uehling (Bristol: E-International Relations Publishing, 2017), 62–77; Greta Uehling, "Three Rationalities for Making Sense of Internal Displacement in Ukraine," *Migration Studies* 9, no. 3 (2020): 1536–1559; Olga Novikova, "Трансформация проблем переселенцев Донбасса: от социальной защиты к ресурсу развития" [Transformation of the problems of the Donbas migrants: From social protection to a resource for development], *Ekonomichnyj visnyk Donbasu* 48, no. 2 (2017): 4–14.
6. Internal Displacement Monitoring Center (IDCM), *GRID 2022: Children and Youth in Internal Displacement*, https://www.internal-displacement.org/sites/default/files/publications/documents/IDMC_GRID_2022_LR.pdf, 12.
7. International Organization of Migration (IOM)-UN Migration, *World Migration Report 2022*, https://publications.iom.int/system/files/pdf/WMR-2022_0.pdf, 51.
8. IDMC, *Global Report*, 82.
9. On volunteer groups, see Csilla Fedinec's "The Ukrainian Civil Volunteer Movement during Wartime (2014–2022)," in *Ukraine's Patronal Democracy and the Russian Invasion*, eds. Madlovics and Magyar, 331–52.
10. United Nations High Commissioner for Refugees (UNHCR), "Ukraine: Internally Displaced People – 23 March 2015," ReliefWeb, March 27, 2015, https://reliefweb.int/map/ukraine/ukraine-internally-displaced-people-23-mar-2015.
11. State Border Guard Service of Ukraine, "Контрольні пункти в'їзду-виїзду (КПВВ): помісячний перетин лінії розмежування" [Control points for entry and exit (KPBB): monthly crossings of the demarcation line], accessed December 10, 2022, https://app.powerbi.com/view?r=eyJrIjoiO-TU4ODVjYTktNjk3ZC00N2E5LTlkNTQtYzk3ZTYzNzliYjk4IiwidCI6IjdhNTE3MDMzL-TE1ZGYtNDQ1MC04ZjMyLWE5ODJmZTBhYTEyNSIsImMiOjh9.
12. Stephen C. Lubkemann, "Involuntary Immobility: On a Theoretical Invisibility in Forced Migration Studies," *Journal of Refugee Studies* 21, no. 4 (2008): 454–75.

13. Cabinet of Ministers of Ukraine, "Постанова від 1 жовтня 2014 р. № 505 Про надання щомісячної адресної допомоги внутрішньо переміщеним особам для покриття витрат на проживання, в тому числі на оплату житлово-комунальних послуг" [Decree of October 1, 2014 No. 505 On the monthly targeted support for IDPs to cover their housing expenses], Verkhovna Rada of Ukraine, https://zakon.rada.gov.ua/laws/show/505-2014-%D0%BF#Text.
14. IOM-UN Migration, "Ukraine Internal Displacement Report. General Population Survey Round 10 (17 – 27 October 2022)," 6-7, https://displacement.iom.int/reports/ukraine-internal-displacement-report-general-population-survey-round-10-17-27-october-2022.
15. IOM-UN Migration, "Звіт про статистику про повернення українців #1 (Вересень 2022 року)" [Ukraine – Report on statistics of the return of Ukrainians #1 (September 2022)], https://displacement.iom.int/reports/ukraina-zvit-pro-statistiku-povernennya-ukrainciv-1-veresen-2022-roku
16. IOM-UN Migration, "Ukraine Internal Displacement Report," 7.
17. IOM-UN Migration, Ukraine Displacement Report. Area Baseline Report (Raion level). Round 14 (3–16 October 2022), https://displacement.iom.int/reports/ukraine-displacement-report-area-baseline-report-raion-level-round-14.
18. The exact number of IDPs is not known for several reasons (people not being registered; returning home and migrating back to Ukrainian-controlled areas; having undetermined status in the grey zone, resulting in irregular registration of IDPs, etc.).
19. Irina Kuznetsova, Oksana Mikheieva, Jon Catling, John Round, and Svitlana Babenko, "The Mental Health of Internally Displaced People and the General Population in Ukraine," University of Birmingham and Ukrainian Catholic University (January 2019), https://www.humanitarianresponse.info/sites/www.humanitarianresponse.info/files/documents/files/mental_health_of_idps_and_general_population_in_ukraine.pdf.
20. Durnyeva, Jepsen, and Roberts, "IDP's Electoral Participation Gap," 5–35.
21. Kuznetsova and Mikheieva, "Forced Displacement from Ukraine's War-Torn Territories," 690-706.
22. See Mark Granovetter, "The Strength of Weak Ties: A Network Theory Revisited," *Sociological Theory* 1 (1983): 201-233.
23. See Richard D. Putnam, "Bowling Alone: America's Declining Social Capital," *Journal of Democracy* 6, no.1 (1995): 65-78.
24. Anton Oleinik, "Volunteers in Ukraine: From Provision of Services to State- and Nation-Nuilding," *Journal of Civil Society* 14, no.4 (2018): 381.
25. Abby Shoddard, Paul Harvey, Nigel Timmins, Varvara Pakhomenko, Meriah-Jo Breckenridge, and Monica Czwarno, "Enabling the Local Response: Emerging Humanitarian Priorities in Ukraine March-May 2022, *Humanitarian Outcomes*, June 2022, 10, https://www.humanitarianoutcomes.org/sites/default/files/publications/ukraine_review_2022.pdf.
26. IOM Ukraine, "Міграція в Україні. цифри і факти, 2021" [Migration in Ukraine. Facts and figures, 2021], accessed July 4, 2023, https://ukraine.iom.int/sites/g/files/tmzbdl1861/files/documents/migration_in_ukraine_facts_and_figures_2021-ukr_web.pdf
27. Eurostat Data Browser, *Asylum applicants by type of applicant, citizenship, age and sex - annual aggregated data (rounded)*, accessed September 4, 2021, https://ec.europa.eu/eurostat/databrowser/explore/all/popul?lang=en%20%5B&subtheme=migr&display=list&sort=category.
28. Olena Malynovska, "International Migration of the Ukrainian Population since Independence," in *Migration from the Newly Independent States. Societies and Political Orders in Transition*, ed. Mikhail Denisenko, Salvatore Strozza, and Matthew Light (Springer, 2020), 169–85.
29. "Ukrainians Can Now Travel to EU Member States without a Visa," SchengenVisa, June 11, 2017, https://www.schengenvisainfo.com/news/ukrainians-can-now-travel-to-eu-member-states-without-visa/
30. See, for instance, Alexander Betts, *Global Migration Governance* (Oxford: Oxford University Press, 2011); Zeynep Şahin Mencütek, *Refugee Governance: State and Politics in the Middle East* (Routledge Global Cooperation Series, 2018).

31. Stephen Castles, "Nation and Empire: Hierarchies of Citizenship in the New Global Order," *International Politics* 42 (June 1, 2005): 203–24.
32. Alexander Betts, "North–South Relations in the Global Refugee Regime: The Role of Linkages," *Global Governance* 14, no. 2 (2008): 157–78
33. Rogers Brubaker, "Migration, Membership, and the Modern Nation-State: Internal and External Dimensions of the Politics of Belonging," *Journal of Interdisciplinary History* 41, no.1 (2010): 61–78.
34. See, for example, Alexander Betts, "Public Goods Theory and the Provision of Refugee Protection: The Role of the Joint-Product Model in Burden-Sharing Theory," *Journal of Refugee Studies* 16, no. 3 (2003): 274–96; Hans de Haas, Katharina Natter, and Stefano Vezzoli, "Growing Restrictiveness or Changing Selection? The Nature and Evolution of Migration Policies," *International Migration Review* 52, no. 2 (2016): 324–67.
35. Jaeeun Kim, "Migration-Facilitating Capital: A Bourdieusian Theory of International Migration," *Sociological Theory* 36, no. 3 (2011): 262–88.
36. Tetyana Malyarenko and Stefan Wolff, "The Logic of Competitive Influence-Seeking: Russia, Ukraine, and the Conflict in Donbas," *Post-Soviet Affairs* 34, no. 4 (2018): 191–212.
37. Michael Skey, "'How Do You Think I Feel? It's My Country': Belonging, Entitlement and the Politics of Immigration," *The Political Quarterly* 85, no. 3 (2014): 326–32.
38. Hanna Vakhitova and Agnieszka Fihel, "International Migration from Ukraine: Will Trends Increase or Go into Reverse?" *Central and Eastern European Migration Review* 9, no. 2 (2020): 125–41.
39. *Challenges of modern migration. Ukrainian community in Poland. Report* [in Ukrainian], ed. Oksana Mikheieva and Viktor Susak (Lviv: Ukrainian Catholic University, 2019), https://www.researchgate.net/publication/357311060_VIKLIKI_SUCASNOI_MIGRACII_UKRAINSKA_SPILNOTA_V_POLSI_Analiticnij_zvit_Za_zag_red_O_Miheevoi_V_Susaka.
40. "Szydło w PE o milionie ukraińskich uchodźców w Polsce. 'W 2015 r. było ich dwóch'" [Szydło in the EP about the million Ukrainian refugees in Poland. There were two of them in 2015], *Gazeta Prawna*, January 20, 2016, http://www.gazetaprawna.pl/wiadomosci/artykuly/918747,szydlo-milion-ukrainskich-uchodzcow-w-polsce.html.
41. Cecilia Marrinan "The Hypocrisy of Hungary's Refugee Crisis Response," *GRC*, June 1, 2022, accessed July 4, 2023, https://insights.grcglobalgroup.com/the-hypocrisy-of-hungarys-refugee-crisis-response/
42. UNCHR, Refugee Data Finder, accessed September 2, 2021, https://www.unhcr.org/refugee-statistics/download/?url=zkHE09.
43. UNHCR, Refugees and Asylum-Seekers from Ukraine, accessed September 4, 2021, https://unhcr-web.github.io/refugee-statistics/0001-Vis-PoCs/Ukrainians.html
44. Eurostat Data Browser, "*Asylum applicants*", accessed July 4, 2023, https://ec.europa.eu/eurostat/databrowser/explore/all/popul?lang=en%20%5B&subtheme=migr&display=list&sort=category
45. UNHCR, Ukraine Refugee Situation. Operational Data Portal, accessed November 30, 2022, https://data.unhcr.org/en/situations/ukraine/location.
46. Patrycja Otto and Paulina Nowosielska, "Ukraińcy na rynku pracy radzą sobie dobrze. Ale mogliby lepiej" [Ukrainians are doing well in the labor market. But it could be better], *Gazeta Prawna*, December 22, 2022, https://praca.gazetaprawna.pl/artykuly/8618086,zatrudnienie-rynek-pracy-pracownicy-z-ukrainy.html.
47. UNHCR, Ukraine Refugee Situation. Operational Data Portal, accessed July 4, 2023, https://data.unhcr.org/en/situations/ukraine/location.
48. William Noah Glucroft, "Ukrainian Refugees Push German Cities to Their Limits," *DW*, October 29, 2022, https://www.dw.com/en/ukrainian-refugees-push-german-cities-to-their-limits/a-63582661.

49 Bundesagentur für Arbeit, "Auswirkungen der Fluchtmigration aus der Ukraine auf den Arbeitsmarkt und die Grundsicherung für Arbeitsuchende" [The effects of refugee migration from Ukraine on the labor market and basic security for job seekers], Berichte: Arbeitsmarkt kompakt, May 2023, https://statistik.arbeitsagentur.de/DE/Statischer-Content/Statistiken/Themen-im-Fokus/Ukraine-Krieg/Generische-Publikationen/AM-kompakt-Auswirkungen-Fluchtmigration-Ukraine-Arbeitsmarkt.pdf?__blob=publicationFile&v=6&fbclid=IwAR1Gx0EM0gqDnOynz_ckBhgiEe5Mm302l1XprPQ8GSnEqF8GrQgu6fyDpc8

50 Josephine Andrews, Jakub Isański, Marek Nowak, Victoriya Sereda, Alexandra Vacroux, Hanna Vakhitova, "Feminized forced migration: Ukrainian war refugees," *Women's Studies International Forum* 99 (2023).

51 Sabrina Juran and P. Niclas Broer, "A Profile of Germany's Refugee Populations," *Population and Development Review* 43, no.1 (2017): 149–57.

52 UNHCR, Regional Protection Profiling and Monitoring Factsheet. Refugees and Asylum Seekers from Ukraine. Profiles, Needs and Intentions of Refugees from Ukraine. December 2022. Access July 4, 2023. https://app.powerbi.com/view?r=eyJrIjoiMWU3NjkzYmEtNDYzMC00M2EyLTkwMjctMGIwZTA0MTQwMjU5IiwidCI6ImU1YzM3OTgxLTY2NjQtNDEzNC04YTBjLTY1NDNkMmFmODBiZSIsImMiOjh9&pageName=ReportSectionb9333061a0a2e93930ea.

53 See, for instance, Jakub Isański, Marek Nowak, Michał Michalski, Viktoriya Sereda, and Hanna Vakhitova, eds., *Social Reception and Inclusion of Refugees from Ukraine*, UKREF Research report 1, May 11, 2022, https://www.researchgate.net/publication/360541536_SOCIAL_RECEPTION_AND_INCLUSION_OF_REFUGEES_FROM_UKRAINE_Edited_by; UNHCR, Refugees and Asylum-Seekers from Ukraine, accessed December 13, 2022, https://unhcr-web.github.io/refugee-statistics/0001-Vis-PoCs/Ukrainians.html.

54 Lenka Dražanová and Andrew Geddes, "Europeans Welcome Ukrainian Refugees but Governments Need to Show They Can Manage," *MPC Blog*, Debate Migration, June 20, 2022, https://blogs.eui.eu/migrationpolicycentre/attitudes-towards-ukrainian-refugees-and-the-responses-of-european-governments/.

55 Bálint Magyar and Bálint Madlovics, *A Concise Field Guide to Post-Communist Regimes: Actors, Institutions, and Dynamics* (Budapest: Central European University Press, 2022), 143.

56 Magyar and Madlovics, *A Concice Fuild Guide*, 225.

57 UNHCR, Ukraine Refugee Situation.

58 Volodymyr Zelensky, "We Need Your Support to Bring Back Peace Faster – Address by the President to the Participants of the Session of the General Assembly of the Organization of American States, Which is Ongoing in Lima," President of Ukraine, Official website, October 6, 2022, https://www.president.gov.ua/news/nam-potribna-vasha-pidtrimka-shob-priskoriti-nastannya-miru-78305.

59 "Число прибывших в РФ с территории Украины и Донбасса беженцев превысило 4,7 млн человек" [The number of persons coming from Ukraine and Donbas to Russia reached 4.7mln people], *TASS*, November 2, 2022, https://tass.ru/obschestvo/16223423

60 Fabian Burkhardt, Maryna Rabinovych, Cindy Wittke, and Elia Bescotti, "Passportization, Diminished Citizenship Rights, and the Donbas Vote in Russia's 2021 Duma Elections," HURI, January 19, 2022, 2022, https://huri.harvard.edu/news/new-tcup-report-passportization-diminished-citizenship-rights-and-donbas-vote-russia's

61 Petro Andriushchenko (andriyshTime), "Маріуполь. Вперше можемо побачити, як відбувається депортація" [Mariupol. It is the first time we can see how the deportation is taking place], Telegram, May 21, 2022, https://t.me/andriyshTime/984.

62 "Як діяти, якщо вас насильно депортують до росії?" [What should you do if you are being forcefully deported to Russia?], Ministry of Reintegration of the Temporarily Occupied Territories of Ukraine, April 3, 2022, https://minre.gov.ua/2022/04/03/yak-diyaty-yakshho-vas-nasylno-deportuyut-do-rosiyi/.

63 Sergiy Kyslytsya, "Statement by Ambassador Sergiy Kyslytsya, Permanent Representative of Ukraine to the UN at the UN Security Council Meeting on 'Maintenance of Peace and Security of Ukraine,'" Facebook, April 19, 2022, https://www.facebook.com/sergiy.grau/posts/pfbid0agX-T4QLEK1NMjyWUsjHati6pxMciXTTPwnFXGxNFuBqj7UrJo8Yv1b4ygy2RtJoZl.

64 Coalition of Ukrainian NGOs, "Не всі можуть поїхати: влада повинна допомогти виїхати людям з окупації, а не засуджувати їх' [Not everyone can leave: the government should help people to leave, not blame them], *Zmina.ua*, June 3, 2022, https://zmina.ua/statements/ne-vsi-hto-ho-tily-poyihaly-vlada-ma ye-dopomogty-vyyihaty-lyudyam-z-okupacziyi-a-ne-zasudzhuvaty-yih/.

65 See, for instance, Kateryna Tyshchenko, "Верещук закликала мешканців Херсонщини виїжджати через окупований Крим" [Vereshchuk called on residents of Kherson region to evacuate through the occupied Crimea], *Ukrajinska Pravda*, June 20, 2022, https://www.pravda.com.ua/news/2022/06/20/7353708/; "Вимушений виїзд з ТОТ до росії під час війни – не злочин" [Forced exit from TOT (Temporary Occupied Territories) to Russia during war is not a crime], Ministry of Reintegration of the Temporarily Occupied Territories of Ukraine, June 14, 2022,https://minre.gov.ua/2022/06/14/vymushenyj-vyyizd-z-tot-do-rosiyi-pid-chas-vijny-ne-zlochyn-2/.

66 "ФСБ не випускає із росії українців з російськими паспортами" [FSB is not letting Ukrainians with Russian passports out of the country"], Ministry of Reintegration of the Temporarily Occupied Territories of Ukraine, October 6, 2022, https://minre.gov.ua/2022/10/06/fsb-ne-vypuska-ye-iz-rosii-ukrayincziv-z-rosijskymy-pasportamy/.

67 Note the difference between deportation and forced displacement/transfer. Deportation entails forced transfer to Russian territory (within its internationally recognized borders), whereas coercive relocation within the occupied territory should be called forced displacement. See more: Ombudsman of Ukraine, "Special Report of the Ukrainian Parliament Commissioner for Human Rights on the Observance of the Rights of Persons Affected by the Armed Aggression of the Russian Federation against Ukraine (for the period February 24 – October 31, 2022), https://ombudsman.gov.ua/storage/app/media/Доповіді/ДоповідьАнгл.pdf.

68 Iryna Vereshchuk, "Велике інтерв'ю Ірини Верещук каналу 'Ми – Україна'" [Major interview with Iryna Vereshchuk on the channel We are Ukraine], Youtube video, 38:13, October 17, 2022, https://www.youtube.com/watch?v=gYMZFA0Xe8w.

69 UNHCR and World Vision Georgia, "Ukrainian refugees in Georgia: Profile, Intentions and Needs," November 2022, https://data.unhcr.org/en/documents/details/97675.

70 In September, approximately 22 thousand people left the occupied territory of Kharkiv region to the neighboring Russian region of Belgorod and then further on to Voronezh and Kursk regions fleeing intensified military actions. It is not clear how many of them returned. In November 2022, based on Decree No. 756, the Russian occupying administration forced around 115,000 persons to leave Kherson and the Kherson region. We don't know how many people returned following the Ukrainian recapture of these territories. See more: President of the Russian Federation, "Указ Президента Российской Федерации от 19.10.2022 г. № 756 О введении военного положения на территориях Донецкой Народной Республики, Луганской Народной Республики, Запорожской и Херсонской областей" [Decree of the President of the Russian Federation No. 756 about the introduction of martial law on the territories of DNR, LNR, Zaporozhye and Kherson regions], Official Publication of Legal Acts website, October 19, 2022, http://publication.pravo.gov.ru/Document/View/0001202210190002; " Сальдо: из Херсона с февраля уехали более 150 тыс. Человек" [Saldo: More than 150 thousand people left Kherson since February], *Kommersant*, December 21, 2022,https://www.kommersant.ru/doc/5735376.

71 "Про Заяву Верховної Ради України 'Про вчинення Російською Федерацією геноциду в Україні'" [On the declaration of the Verkhovna Rada of Ukraine, On genocide committed by the Russian Federation in Ukraine], Verkhovna Rada of Ukraine, April 14, 2022, https://zakon.rada.gov.ua/laws/show/2188-20#Text.

72 "'We Had No Choice.' 'Filtration' and the Crime of Forcibly Transferring Ukrainian Civilians to Russia," *Human Rights Watch*, September 1, 2022, https://www.hrw.org/report/2022/09/01/we-had-no-choice/filtration-and-crime-forcibly-transferring-ukrainian-civilians.

73 "'Like a Prison Convoy': Russia's Unlawful Transfer and Abuse of Civilians in Ukraine During 'Filtration,'" Amnesty International, November 10, 2022, https://www.amnesty.org/en/documents/eur50/6136/2022/en/.

74 See more: Oleksandr Kliuzhev and Oleksandr Neberykut, "Окуповані. Як українців пропускають через фільтраційні табори" [Occupied. How Ukrainians are being processed in filtration camps], *Dzerkalo Tyzhnia*, July 4, 2022, https://zn.ua/ukr/internal/okupovani-jak-ukrajintsiv-propuskajut-cherez-filtratsijni-tabori.html.

75 Government of the Russian Federation, "Постановление Правительства Российской Федерации от 12.03.2022 № 349 «О распределении по субъектам Российской Федерации граждан Российской Федерации, Украины, Донецкой Народной Республики, Луганской Народной Республики и лиц без гражданства, постоянно проживающих на территориях Украины, Донецкой Народной Республики, Луганской Народной Республики, вынужденно покинувших территории Украины, Донецкой Народной Республики, Луганской Народной Республики и прибывших на территорию Российской Федерации в экстренном массовом порядке" [Resolution of the Government of the Russian Federation No, 349 from March 12, 2022 about the distribution across the regions of the Russian Federation of citizens of the Russian Federation, Ukraine, DNR, LNR and stateless persons permanently residing on the territories of Ukraine, DNR, LNR, who were forced to leave the territory of Ukraine, DNR, LNR and are coming to the territory of the Russian Federation urgently and en masse], Official Publication of Legal Acts website, March 12, 2022, http://www.publication.pravo.gov.ru/Document/View/0001202203120005

76 "Число ПВР для беженцев в России достигло 807" [The number of TAPs for refugees in Russia has reached 807], *RIA*, October 24, 2022, https://ria.ru/20221024/bezhentsy-1826256366.html.

77 Amnesty International, "'Like a Prison Convoy.'"

78 Media Center Ukraine-Odesa (mcu_odesa), "Аналітичний звіт «Примусова депортація дітей до рф», наданий ГО «Східна правозахисна група»" [Analytical report. Forcible deportation of children to the Russian Federation, provided by the NGO Eastern Human Rights Group], Telegram, https://t.me/mcu_odesa/239.

79 Veronika Shevtsova, "Как детей из новых регионов устраивают в российские семьи и как возвращают родственникам, рассказали в пресс-службе уполномоченного при президенте РФ по правам ребенка" [How children from the new regions are accommodated in Russian families and how they are returned back to families – child ombudsman interview], *Miloserdie.ru*, November 11, 2022, https://www.miloserdie.ru/news/kak-detej-iz-novyh-regionov-ustraivayut-v-rossijskie-semi-i-kak-vozvrashhayut-rodstvennikam-rasskazali-v-press-sluzhbe-upolnomochennogo-pri-prezidente-rf-po-pravam-rebenka/.

80 UNHCR Russia, Monthly Digest. Russian Federation, October 2022," https://www.unhcr.org/ru/wp-content/uploads/sites/73/2022/12/UNHCR-monthly-digest_Russia_October-2022_EN.pdf.

81 Kateryna Rashevska, "How Russia Is Destroying the Identity of Ukrainian Children", *PassBlue*, December 26, 2022, https://www.passblue.com/2022/12/26/how-russia-is-destroying-the-identity-of-ukrainian-children/?highlight=2022.

82 Child Ombudswoman of Ukraine, Children of War Platform, accessed December 28, 2022, https://childrenofwar.gov.ua/en/.

83 UNHCR Russia, "Куда можно обратиться за помощью лицам, прибывающим на территорию РФ в связи с конфликтом в Украине?" [Where can people coming to the territory of the RF due to conflict in Ukraine receive help?], accessed December 20, 2022, https://www.unhcr.org/ru/28617-helpforukrref.html.

[84] For more information and monthly reports on types of help, see "Церковная помощь беженцам и пострадавшим мирным жителям" [Church help for refugees and civilian victims], Social Service Department of the Russian Orthodox Church, accessed December 20, 2022, https://помочьвбеде.рф/#reports; "Церковная помощь беженцам" [Church help for refugees]", Presidential Grants Foundation, accessed December 20, 2022, https://президентскиегранты.рф/public/application/item?id=5e9ab0ab-7ecd-43a4-a033-d82aca925056.

[85] UNHCR Russia, "Monthly Digest. Russian Federation. July 2022," https://www.unhcr.org/ru/wp-content/uploads/sites/73/2022/09/UNHCR-monthly-digest_Russia_July-2022_EN.pdf.

[86] UNHCR Russia, "Monthly Digest. Russian Federation. July 2022."

[87] 'Civic Assistance Committee, "Ministry of Internal Affairs of Russia Published Migration Statistics for 3rd Quarter of 2022," *Refugee.ru*, December 12, 2022, https://refugee.ru/en/dokladyi/stats-third-q-2022/.

[88] Based on the combined figures from the Civic Assistance Committee, "Их осталось триста. Статистика МВД: в России еще никогда не было так мало людей с официальным статусом «беженец»" [There remains 300 of them. Ministry of Interior Statistics: there have never been so few people with the official 'refugee' status in Russia], *Refugee.ru*, September 19, 2022, https://refugee.ru/dokladyi/six-month-stats-2022/; and Civic Assistance Committee, "Ministry of Internal Affairs of Russia."

[89] "Деньги получают только 'правильные украинцы': Светлана Ганнушкина о ситуации с беженцами в России [Only 'good Ukrainians' receive money': Svietlana Gannushkina about the situation of refugees in Russia], *Cherta*, June 20, 2022, https://cherta.media/interview/gannushkina-interview-bezhentsy/.

[90] Vera Chelishcheva and Zoya Svietova, "Lida Moniava: 'It is important to name things as they are'" [in Russian], *Novaya.media*, November 4, 2022, accessed December 28, 2022, https://novaya.media/articles/2022/11/04/lida-moniava-vazhno-nazyvat-veshchi-svoimi-imenami

[91] Irina Kuznetsova, "To Help 'Brotherly People'? Russian Policy towards Ukrainian Refugees," *Europe-Asia Studies* 72, no. 3 (2020): 509.

[92] Caress Schenk, "Controlling Immigration Manually: Lessons from Moscow (Russia)," *Europe-Asia Studies* 65, no. 7 (2013): 1446.

[93] Kuznetsova, "To Help 'Brotherly People'?" 512-513.

[94] 'Civic Assistance' Committee, "Refugee for 0.04% of world refugees: Russian migration statistics for 2021 and its analysis" [in Russian], *Refugee.ru*, June 27, 2022, accessed December 28, 2022, https://refugee.ru/news/russia-asylum-for-the-few-2021/

[95] Vladimir Mukomel, "Migration of Ukrainians to Russia in 2014–2015. Discourses and Perceptions of the Local Population", in *Migration and the Ukraine Crisis. A Two-Country Perspective*, eds. Agnieszka Pikulicka-Wilczewska and Greta Uehling (Bristol: E-International Relations Publishing, 2017), 105-115.

[96] Lighthouse Foundation, "Отчёт о работе Фонда помощи беженцам «Дом с маяком» в октябре — ноябре 2022 года" [Report on the activity of the Lighthouse charitable foundation from October-November 2022]", *Mayak.fund*, https://mayak.fund/about/reports/7.

[97] Lida Moniava (lidamoniava), "Пока я не начала заниматься помощью беженцам …" [Until I started to help refugees …], Telegram, May 13, 2022, https://t.me/lidamoniava/788; Lida Moniava (lidamoniava), "Я получаю очень много хейта из-за помощи беженцам." [I receive a lot of hatred because of helping refugees], Telegram, June 28, 2022, https://t.me/lidamoniava/898; Olga Allenova, "Им сдали квадратные метры на кухне без спального места" [They have been rented a few square meters in the kitchen without a sleeping place], *Kommersant*, October 10, 2022, https://www.kommersant.ru/amp/5606886.

[98] "Набрала чинності постанова, яка допоможе насильно вивезеним до рф українцям повернутися додому" [Decree allowing Ukrainians forcefully deported to Russia to return home enters into force], State Migration Service of Ukraine, November 14, 2022, https://dmsu.gov.ua/news/dms/13331.html

[99] "Формалізовано роботу координаційного штабу, який допомагатиме у поверненні з ТОТ і рф через треті країни українців, – рішення Уряду" [The government has created a coordination body that will help Ukrainians returning from the TOT and through the third countries], Ministry of Reintegration of the Temporarily Occupied Territories of Ukraine, October 18, 2022, https://minre.gov.ua/news/formalizovano-robotu-koordynaciynogo-shtabu-yakyy-dopomagatyme-u-povernenni-z-tot-i-rf-cherez.

# III.

The International Community: Patronal and Non-Patronal Responses to the War

Crescent Rising? The Baltic, Romanian, and "V3" Reaction to the 2022 Russia-Ukraine War[1]

Zsombor Zeöld

> *"The most serious threat is the neo-imperial policy of the authorities of the Russian Federation, pursued also by means of military force."*
> *(National Security Strategy of Poland, 2020)[2]*

1. Introduction

This chapter aims at providing an international angle to the responses various Central and Eastern European states (in particular the Baltic states, the Czech Republic, Poland, Romania, and Slovakia) have given to the 2022 Russian aggression against Ukraine. These states have opted for continuous, strong support for Ukraine, and their stance can be easily explained as being a (national) security-driven approach. However, the aim of at least some of these countries goes beyond altruism, and can be seen as a regional response to processes, challenges, and developments originating both in the European Union (EU) and in the United States (US).

For these countries, what is at stake is both simple and difficult at the same time: they need to find answers to a new role that the European (EU and NATO) semi-periphery plays in shaping the international system. This extends to issues concerning alliance-forming and rivalry *within* the same semi-periphery—where size, political, and economic power will be the defining factors.

Accelerated by the renewed war of 2022, the main question of this chapter is whether these processes will become permanent—thus, solidifying a more prominent international role for the countries in question. This new role and responsibility is closely connected to the circumstances by which the war may be ended, and affects not only the individual countries' national *room for maneuver*, but the future of regional cooperation formats as well.

2. The geopolitical context: the war that started in 2014

We must look back almost a decade in order to assess the processes that formed not only the above-mentioned Central and Eastern European countries' approach to the 2022 Russia-Ukraine war, but are also likely to shape their future steps as well. The responses these countries gave to regional, external threats cannot be detached from their wider international environment—and must be seen as regional reactions to a complex problem that extends not only to Russia (or Ukraine), but to the stances of the European Union and the Transatlantic alliance as well.

For most of the above-mentioned countries, this war did not start in 2022, but in 2014. The illegal annexation of the Crimean Peninsula by the Russian Federation sparked strong reactions mainly from the Baltic countries, Poland, and Romania, and fueled long-term, strategic thinking on Russia, and the role of those states situated on the semi-periphery of NATO and/or the EU.[3]

Coalition-building (classic diplomacy) and country size are key in the second half of the 2010s, the above-mentioned five countries opted for obtaining wider international support for their policies on Russia. These years were characterized by pathfinding, and efforts to take advantage of events unfolding in both the EU and the US.

2.1. The EU in the 2010s: an eastward-shifting political center

For decades, the effective functioning of the EU depended mainly on the quality and depth of Franco-German cooperation, in addition to the countervailing actions Great Britain. In this regard, London saw some of the Central and Eastern European states as natural partners for providing more counterweight against Paris and Berlin. Brexit, however, not only ended the issue-based cooperation between Great Britain and certain CEE countries, but—from the latter's perspective—posed additional challenges regarding the region's future political influence in the EU. Brexit also caused a shift in the EU's political center towards the "2004 newcomers" in the east, triggered political reactions mainly from Germany, and likely led to the desire for intensified cooperation among the Visegrád Cooperation (V4), a low-level institutionalized group of the Czech Republic, Hungary, Poland, and Slovakia.[4]

Regarding effective power projection within larger international frameworks, the CEE region has always faced two key problems: the region is not only fragmented politically, its constituent countries also differ significantly from one other in terms of their size and population as well. To achieve an effective representation of regional political interests, regional actors can follow two mains strategies: either (a group of) CEE countries can unite themselves utilizing a regional framework, or they can seek larger frameworks which may accommodate their strategies. Both strategies can "ruffle the feathers" of non-regional actors, however.

Concerning the region, one external factor posing a threat to achieving more political leverage inside the EU has come from Germany: for example, instead of agreeing to a joint V4-Germany meeting hosted by Budapest, Berlin agreed to a joint meeting of the Slovak V4 Presidency in the second half of 2017—successfully (and visibly) dividing the Group into two (Poland and Hungary; the Czech Republic and Slovakia).

Due to fundamental differences present within the group, the V4 failed to realize a permanent role in cementing a shift of power inside the EU. Having in mind to capitalize on a post-Brexit intra-EU power vacuum, larger—thus more influential—CEE countries opted to pursue the same goal by utilizing various frameworks, and tried to gain the support of smaller regional states for these projects. In the mid-2010s, an opportunity arose to present regional interests in a wider international environment as a way to successfully attract support originating from outside the CEE region. Some Central and Eastern European politicians reached out to the other side of the Atlantic.

2.2. Prince Charming on a white horse: US policy towards the CEE and regional responses between 2016 and 2020

In 2016–17, a fundamental change occurred in the US: the newly elected presidential administration, led by Donald J. Trump, adopted a foreign policy that broke sharply with the principles of its predecessor. The Trump administration operated on the premise of slowly diminishing US influence, and that Washington should engage its main competitors (the Russian Federation and China) at the same time, worldwide, and with the help of select partners. (Theoretically speaking, the US dusted off Sir Halford John Mackinder's *Heartland* theory,[5] and adapted it to meet the challenges of the past decade.) For Washington, great power competition became the foundation of a new foreign policy era.[6] In terms of Europe, Washington envisioned a more prominent role for Central and Eastern Europe in achieving its foreign policy goals.

This policy was supported by both economic tools (the gradually growing amount of US liquefied natural gas exported to Europe) and political initiatives. Concerning the latter, the main difference for the CEE manifested itself in a shift in US-German relations. Under the Obama administration, Washington "outsourced" the maintenance of US-CEE political relations to Berlin. In contrast, the Trump administration opted for direct engagement with CEE countries at the expense of Berlin's diminishing importance in Washington.

CEE countries made use these changes, and came up with additional ideas in support of the above-mentioned core US foreign policy goals. One of these ideas was the so-called Three Seas Initiative (3SI), originally a joint Polish-Croatian framework that aimed at countering malign Russian and Chinese influences in three fields: energy security and digital and physical infrastructure. The 3SI's goal was to unite twelve CEE countries (the Baltic States, the countries of the Visegrád Group, Austria, Bulgaria, Croatia, Romania, and Slovenia) in order to provide a counterweight to both the Russian presence and goals in the EU's energy mix, and the China-led *Belt and Road Initiative*. Until the 2022 Rīga 3SI Summit, however, it was never publicly acknowledged that the project was at its core primarily military in nature, aimed at facilitating inter- and intra-regional military mobility using rail and road networks on NATO territory.[7]

The main problems concerning the 3SI involved both internal and external factors. The Initiative's staunchest supporter, Poland, neither succeeded in uniting other members for the cause, nor fostered sufficient financial backing to support the goals of the Initiative. An additional problem (one that was never acknowledged publicly) concerned internal rivalry between the twelve countries. After the illegal annexation of Crimea, perception of the Russian threat expanded from the Baltic Sea to the Black Sea region. Romania, keen on capitalizing on this, stirred up Romanian-Polish relations and fueled the latter's fears of its own diminishing importance. (Bucharest's approach and fear of further Russian aggression, however, was well-founded, especially in light of the 2022 Snake Island campaign).[8] Regarding external factors, a non-unified region's project which the US treated as European simply could not harness enough financial support from the other side of the Atlantic to guarantee its success. Washington treated its own financial contribution as *complementary* to that of its European partners. This led to a stalemate, finally broken during the 2020 Munich Security Conference, when then Secretary of State Mike Pompeo *tentatively* pledged up to USD 1 billion[9] for the Initiative. Despite the fact that the 3SI was supported by other US initiatives, such as the Department of Energy's P–TEC[10] (Partnership for Transatlantic Energy Cooperation) platform, this financial pledge came too late.

US political changes aside, the Department of Defense started working on scenarios that predicted a shift away from the theoretical option of engaging in a two-front confrontation. These were built on the assumption that the US would be unable to fight two adversaries at once, therefore Washington needed to prioritize the main threat. Scenarios formulated in 2020 by A. Wess Mitchell, one of the key shapers behind the Trumpian foreign policy, extended to redefining conceptual tools, dealing with credibility loss among former allies, and the need to maintain a certain degree of attention towards de-prioritized geographical areas.[11]

The proposed options[12] (buying time with the long-term threat; consolidation with the secondary rival; exclusive focus on the main threat; the use of active alliances against the main threat) have already started to be put into play by Washington, and are likely to be implemented in the forthcoming years. One of the key questions that remains open is whether these strategies will overlap with one another, but the unilateral intention to change US strategy will likely affect Central European countries—mainly in the domain of alliance-building.

2.3. Murky roads ahead: the Biden administration's policy towards Russia and the CEE

The Biden administration swiftly returned to the idea of a greater role for Germany and to an initially undefined policy on Russia (the 2021 Interim National Security Strategic Guidance[13] mentions Russia 6 times, while China appears 22 times).

PR worked just fine: Washington rebranded the Trump administration's "great power competition" as "strategic competition." A significant shift occurred in naming China as *the* main competitor for the US ("this agenda will strengthen our enduring advantages, and allow us to prevail in strategic competition with China or any other nation")[14] and in opting for another reset-like situation with Russia. For Central Europe, these policies resulted in (1) the Biden administration waving sanctions over the Russian energy project *Nord Stream 2*[15] (with a possible explanation being to prevent China from obtaining more natural gas); and (2) a turning away from Europe—and thus, the hollowing out of such regional formats as the Three Seas Initiative. Reducing the potential financial contribution to 3SI down to USD 600 million and adding renewables to the now renamed P–TECC (Partnership for Transatlantic Energy and Climate Cooperation)[16] elicited changes in the CEE countries' approaches towards Washington, and resulted in both a rise of political tensions, as well as individual states opting to pursue closer bilateral (financial) cooperation with Washington. The former was Poland's experience, which even went so far as publicly attacking[17] the then US ambassador-nominee Mark Brzezinski, while the latter was the road taken by Lithuania, which cut diplomatic ties with China, invited Taiwanese capital into the country, and secured a USD 600 million trade deal with the US in November 2021.[18] Three months later, Russia attacked Ukraine once again, causing US policies on Russia to be upended, making military issues *the* main shaper of US-CEE relations, and triggering a revamped national security strategy which (at least) acknowledged the threat Russia posed:

> Out-Competing China and Constraining Russia [...] The PRC and Russia are increasingly aligned with each other but the challenges they pose are, in important ways, distinct. We will prioritize maintaining an enduring competitive edge over the PRC while constraining a still profoundly dangerous Russia.[19]

By the time of the 2022 Russian aggression, the above-mentioned processes (fighting a power vacuum in Europe, and the ability of the Central European region to draw attention to itself) had been put back on the table once again. With the exception of Hungary, CEE regional states opted to provide enhanced support to Ukraine.

3. The full-scale invasion and the CEE crescent: a not (entirely) altruistic response

The regional states' responses go beyond the issue of Ukraine, but the support they have given Kyiv is a good litmus test for assessing the pursuit of strategic-level goals. Derived from their history and experiences of an imperialist Russia, these countries are well aware of the difference between "sphere of influence" and "sphere of interest." Hence, they have acted almost collectively to support Ukraine—even at the expense of a significant reduction in their own defense capabilities (Figure 1).[20] Contrary to common belief, the response of the CEE countries to the 2022 Russian invasion of Ukraine was not entirely altruistic, but was also rational and calculated in nature (as early as February 25, 2022, a Polish economic portal wrote about the possible consequences of the war for the Polish economy).[21]

The war has brought back a strong realist approach to conducting diplomacy, where the four main determining factors are geographical size, geographical location, population, and economic size. The region is, naturally, divided along all these factors, but given the presence of an existential, external threat, the smaller countries have begun gravitating towards Poland, which is the largest regional country by landmass, economy, and population. Polish diplomacy has successfully managed to rally Central European states in support of Ukraine, and has capitalized on the lack of classic (non-military) diplomacy on the part of the US and Western Europe with respect to Russia. As a result of this, smaller regional states (like the Baltic States) have started to use Warsaw as a vehicle to channel their own national interests, aiming to occupy a more influential position at the international level.

The 2022 Russian invasion of Ukraine brought about a situation where the credibility of Central European states has grown. It is not only that their approach of continuously regarding Russia as an aggressive actor turned out to be valid; their large-scale support for Ukraine has also reinforced their trustworthiness. In early 2023, one of the most pressing issues looming over the political fate of Central European countries was whether they could remain *credible* international partners inside both the EU and NATO. This credibility is closely associated with the ability to utilize an intelligent combination of classic, military, and cultural diplomacy—all of which extends to the ability to build and maintain coalitions. As the countries in question are limited by the small size of their diplomatic corps, this requires a careful selection of not only (regional) initiatives, but the utilization of bilateral relations as well. As the region has never been (and never will be) completely independent from processes originating from outside Central Europe, the countries of this region need to plan ahead, having both a Transatlantic and an EU perspective in mind. As a result, coalition-building will likely remain important—both among the countries within the region, and with countries outside of it.

It should be mentioned that not all these regional countries' populations share the same view on Russia and its aggression as do their political elites: some societies, such as those of Slovakia[22] or, to a lesser degree, Romania,[23] are divided. From an international perspective, however, the posture of the elites is more important *at the present moment*, but should changes in government take place in certain countries, a change in this approach—and a change in the *current* Central European regional coalition supporting Ukraine—cannot be ruled out, even after the reelection of Estonian Prime Minister Kaja Kallas in early March 2023.[24] Ultimately, since

Polish society and its respective political elite are united in their views regarding Russia and the war, this societal factor reinforces Poland's position and aspirations to become and remain a key regional partner—both to Ukraine and inside NATO.

Figure 1. Data visualization on the transfer of heavy military equipment to Ukraine.

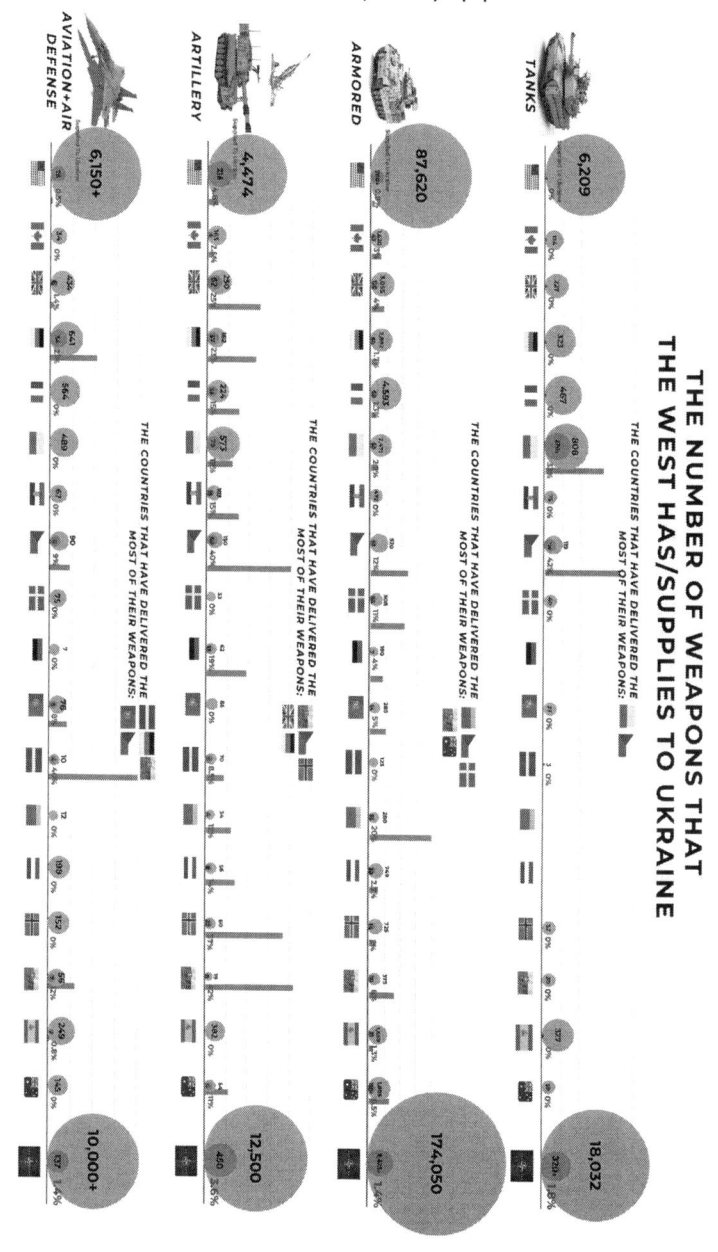

Source: Volodymyr Dacenko's visualization, Twitter.

4. Poland: the center of regional gravity

In order to determine possible future approaches to be taken by the Central European region, we need to look deeper into the Polish case, taking the above-mentioned factors into consideration. In early 2023, Warsaw's main goal was to make the attention now paid to this region permanent. A window of opportunity of roughly 5 to 8 years will likely exist in which Poland (and other regional states) can aim at making the above-mentioned intra-EU political alignment a prolonged reality for the region.

Despite the efforts of most regional states to rally around Poland, the Central European countries supporting Ukraine are also in competition with one another to secure a better position for themselves at the international level. One of the most pressing issues in the region is the looming competition between Poland and Romania inside NATO; a competition that concerns the relative importance of the Baltic and the Black Sea regions for the NATO Alliance. (As a result of the Russian fleet's actions in the latter area, some US analytical circles are advocating for a permanent strategy for the Black Sea,[25] a policy which would herald a key role for Bucharest, while simultaneously hampering Warsaw's goal to remain *the* most influential Russia-focused NATO partner on the Eastern Flank.) These policy intentions regarding the Black Sea are well-known, and—based on a January 2023 interview[26] conducted with the former head of the international bureau of the Polish Presidential Office—are likely to be mitigated by Poland. (It is likely that this desire to mitigate, and to make the security cooperation closer between the two countries, manifested in the 2023 summer nomination of Paweł Soloch, the former head of the Polish President's National Security office as the next Polish ambassador to Romania.)[27]

Based on the above, in order to continue supporting Ukraine (politically, economically, and militarily), Poland is likely to expand the policy tools at its disposal in four main areas in the coming years:

- taking the non-regional international environment into consideration when deciding on strategic planning;
- utilizing regional cooperation formats to support initiatives;
- enhancing the importance of bilateral cooperation as a tool of Polish foreign and trade policy;
- conducting economic and trade policy in support of these goals.

Some of these policy tools go beyond Ukraine and the support being provided Kyiv.

Based on the steps undertaken by the Biden administration early on (e.g. waving the sanctions on Nord Steam 2; expanding the US military alliance system in the Pacific),[28] it is likely that elements of the above-mentioned Mitchell report—

temporary appeasement with Russia, prioritizing China, coalition-building to counter Beijing[29]— have already been put into practice. As this strategy is comprehensive enough, and given the Central European region's dependency on external factors, the Mitchell document bears the promise of serving as a good foundation for the realization of these factors.

4.1. We are not (?) alone: isolationism vs. internationalism in the sphere of national security

Although there were some (fringe) voices in Poland that spoke in favor of resurgent isolationism,[30] the steps undertaken by the current Polish government point in the completely opposite direction.

The focal point in this sense is the relationship between NATO and Poland, and—to a lesser degree—the relationship between the US and the European NATO members. During his February 2023 visit to Poland, President Biden stated that

> [t]he truth of the matter is: The United States needs Poland and NATO as much as NATO needs the United States, because [...] for our ability to operate anywhere else in the world, and our responsibilities extend beyond Europe, we have to have security in Europe. It's that basic, that simple, that consequential.[31]

If we interpret the presidential statement in the context of the 2022 Russia-Ukraine war and the strategic competition between the US and China, it is likely that the long-term US goal is to make the European NATO partners *solely* responsible for the military security of not only the continent, but its borderlands as well—the latter extending not only to the Arctic, but to North Africa too. The core goal of this policy is to keep Russia "at bay"—a task that should be effected by a regional coalition which extends beyond NATO to Ukraine as well. In order to maintain a key regional role, Poland needs to consider four main issues:

- *Time limitations for conducting a more active foreign and security policy.* Once Germany finds its "new voice" after the medium term implementation of the *Zeitenwende*[32] policy shift, the Polish *room for maneuver* will likely shrink. In this sense, Warsaw's efforts to put more pressure on Berlin (demanding the supply of Leopard main battle tanks to Ukraine, for example) can be interpreted as an attempt to hamper these German plans. In order to prolong the timeframe at Warsaw's disposal, it needs to maintain a larger coalition—and this is likely to be problematic inside the EU. As of April 2023, discussions were still ongoing in the EU *vis-à-vis* the future of consensual decision-making in foreign policy, and the threat of growing differences of opinion persists.[33] Another issue is the future of Ukraine's EU prospects—if the EU makes positive recommendations, Kyiv will be closer to securing EU financial resources in the near term, although these same funds might be missing from other regions such as the Western Balkans.

- *How may Warsaw maintain its extensive support of Kyiv, especially if a post-war heavily armed and vengeful Ukraine remains a viable prospect?* As the November 2022 missile explosion[34] near the Polish-Ukrainian border and the shelving of the late December 2022 (opposition-backed) attempt[35] to pass a new bill[36] to eradicate criminal liability for those Poles fighting in Ukraine both showed, there are limits to the support that may be extended to Ukraine. Poland is first and foremost a NATO member, and should therefore minimize any possible negative consequences the Alliance might encounter. Meanwhile, as Beijing's importance continues to grow, it will likely be harder to maintain interest in Ukraine once the current level of hostilities subsides. (In making use of military aid packages that are also aimed at the long-term, the US is already preparing Ukraine for a moment when Washington will no longer need to provide Kyiv military support). As of July 2023, the possibility of a prolonged war cannot be completely excluded, and thus the exact location of Ukraine's future borders presents an unresolved issue. An additional issue stemming from this is whether Ukraine will decide to launch a larger-scale operation in the forthcoming years to regain (some) of the territories that Russia has unlawfully occupied. In sum, military operations in 2023 will most likely determine whether we will see the appearance of a temporarily frozen conflict.

- *What role, if any, may Poland play in shaping and executing a NATO Arctic and/or North African command?* As of April 2023, Washington had not made any apparent decision in naming the "key" state(s) for this role; however, some reports from late 2022 point towards Polish willingness to provide the required air capabilities[37] which, in theory, may serve as the core force for out-of-area NATO operations. (It should be noted, however, that the Polish army has been significantly expanding its territorial defense capabilities as well—pointing towards a more robust task for Warsaw in containing Russia, without significant US involvement.)[38] (On the road to NATO's July 2023 Vilnius Summit, however, sporadic information appearing in the media—concerning a Nordic air defense integration[39] and a Dutch-German land force merger[40]—suggested both a growing importance of bloc politics and a preliminary solution as to divide the areas of responsibilities between NATO Eastern Flank countries.)

- *How may Warsaw mitigate the shift in attention from the Baltic to the Black Sea?* Poland and Romania are not the only countries competing for influence. In particular, Turkey's growing importance is also something Warsaw needs to take into consideration. Although a trilateral Polish-Romanian-Turkish consultation forum exists, the relative difference in size between Turkey and Poland, combined with a Russian-occupied Crimea, is also likely to limit Polish *room for maneuver*.

These issues taken together point towards the likelihood of a divided European semi-periphery based on bloc politics. Any attempts to conduct regional cooperation should reflect both on this possibility, and on the need to conduct diversified and goal-oriented bilateral diplomacy.

In his speech before the Polish Parliament on April 13, 2023, Foreign Minister Zbigniew Rau addressed[41] some of the issues mentioned in points a)–d). Siding with EU foreign policy unanimity,[42] Rau pointed out the importance of coalition-building between Poland, Turkey, and Romania.[43] Concerning the latter, for economic and military security reasons, April 2023 was key in showing the need to bolster the bilateral Polish-Romanian cooperation.[44]

The minister was very straightforward: understanding the importance of its own size and by acting as a voice for the region, the

> closest neighbourhood—Central and Eastern Europe—is the key point of reference for Poland's foreign policy;[45]

and by

> ensur[ing] that the region's countries can collectively exert the strongest possible impact on shaping the policies of the free world, democratic Europe, and the North Atlantic Alliance,[46]

> Poland must derive political potential from its activity in the region [...] [and] must pursue policy initiatives that integrate interests, values, and political experiences with nations we share a past with and with whom we want to and will build [a] future together.[47]

The key to the success of these goals is whether Warsaw manages to combine its cultural diplomacy tools with other diplomatic instruments.

4.2. Regional cooperation: the historic importance of Polish-Ukrainian reconciliation

The Polish attitude towards regional cooperation began to change in 2021[48] when a more security-focused approach gained ground in response to growing threats (a precursor to hybrid warfare originating from Belarus, and the growing pressure on Ukraine, for example). This process became absolute after February 2022: for Warsaw—and most Central European states—regional cooperation efforts only matter when they extend to military defense, and when they are focused enough to provide effective tools for solving certain economic or security issues.

For Poland, the changing threat environment resulted in a significant altering of its former approach vis-à-vis regional cooperation. Since Hungary viewed the issue of the war through a completely different lens than the other three states of the Visegrád Group,[49] interest in maintaining the pre-2022 level of commitment towards the V4 dwindled.

The changed international environment affected the Three Seas Initiative as well. On the one hand, its military nature became apparent and was put into effect;[50] on the other hand, the 3SI's shortcomings became more evident. The Initiative covers a large region where unity on common issues can only be partially achieved. Russian aggression, however, catalyzed many of the original goals of the Initiative, placing additional pressure on the participating countries to secure external funding in order to achieve their goals. Although the 2022 Rīga Summit mentioned both increased support for Ukraine and the welcoming of Japan, among others, as a like-minded global partner,[51] *bilateral* trade agreements—as opposed to Initiative-wide arrangements—have become more important over the past one to one and a half years. A particularly heavy blow for the sustainability of the Initiative was Lithuania's November 2021 trade deal with the US which was on par financially with what Washington agreed to with the entire Initiative. Since then, Vilnius has also managed to secure Taiwanese investments in high added-value industries,[52] and has also worked towards intensifying its trade relations with Australia,[53] demonstrating among other things that Asian capital can flow into the region from other counties than China.

Reports from the autumn of 2022 concerning the creation of a formalized network[54] of Initiative researchers under the auspices of the Warsaw-based Polish Academy of Sciences (Polska Akademia Nauk; PAN) can be interpreted as an attempt to "unburden" the Polish Ministry of Foreign Affairs from dealing with the Initiative, thus allowing the ministry to concentrate more on bilateral (trade) relations.[55] It is likely that in making use of the information provided by PAN and other Polish think-tanks, a support network for the Polish Ministry of Foreign Affairs is being created, which may also be able to provide input concerning regional trade as well.

In 2021, Ukraine, Lithuania, and Poland decided on the creation of a new regional initiative called the Lublin Triangle. Since then, this new regional initiative has seen two high-level meetings. During the latter meeting, organized in January 2023, something unprecedented occurred: the participants jointly acknowledged their shared historical-cultural ties, in which Poland played the decisive role.[56] It should be kept in mind that one of the issues hindering the swift realization of the Three Seas Initiative in the mid-2010s was concern over the revival of the assertive Polish foreign policy of the interwar era, foreshadowing a secondary role for other Initiative members such as Lithuania. However, the combination of

Polish diplomatic efforts and the 2022 Russian aggression bore fruit even in the short-term, leading to the 2023 meeting and the start of a historical reconciliation between Ukrainian and Polish societies and key members of their respective political elites. The importance of this reconciliation can hardly be exaggerated; its historical significance with respect to Eastern Europe is on par with that of the Franco-German reconciliation process in Western Europe following World War II, which was a prerequisite for the foundation of the EU. The attitude of Ukrainian society towards Poles and Lithuanians is likely to be used in fostering closer economic and trade relations, as data from a recent survey suggests (Figure 2).[57]

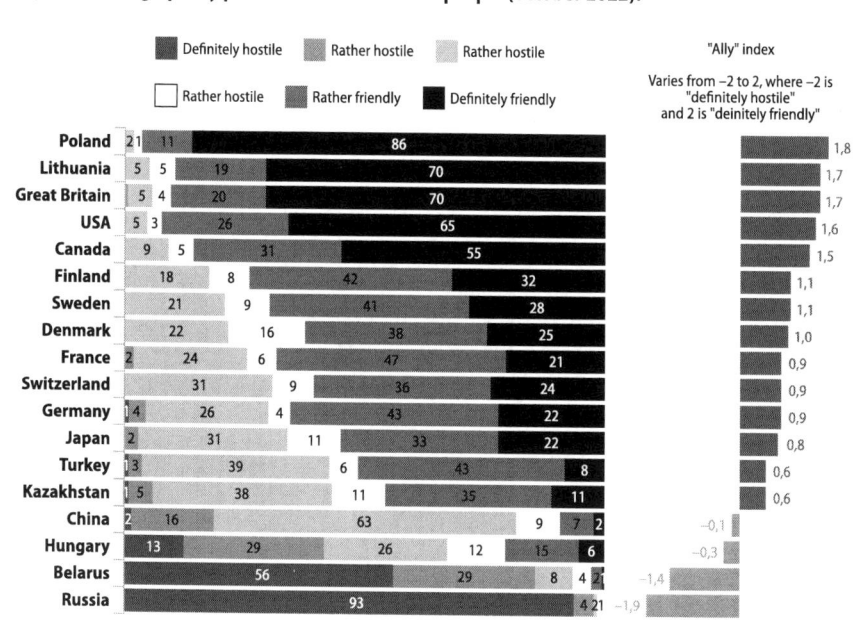

Figure 2. Foreign policy preferences of Ukrainian people (October 2022).

Country	Definitely hostile	Rather hostile	Rather hostile	Rather hostile	Rather friendly	Definitely friendly	"Ally" index
Poland	2	1	1	1		86	1,8
Lithuania	5	5	19			70	1,7
Great Britain	5	4	20			70	1,7
USA	5	3	26			65	1,6
Canada	9	5	31			55	1,5
Finland		18	8	42		32	1,1
Sweden		21	9	41		28	1,1
Denmark		22	16	38		25	1,0
France	2	24	6	47		21	0,9
Switzerland		31	9	36		24	0,9
Germany	4	26	4	43		22	0,9
Japan	2	31	11	33		22	0,8
Turkey	3	39	6	43		8	0,6
Kazakhstan	5	38	11	35		11	0,6
China	2	16	63	9	7	2	−0,1
Hungary	13	29	26	12	15	6	−0,3
Belarus	56		29	8	4	2	−1,4
Russia	93				4	2 1	−1,9

"Ally" index varies from −2 to 2, where −2 is "definitely hostile" and 2 is "definitely friendly"

Source: Rating Group.

4.3. At the intersection of societal sympathy and economic and trade policy

In providing extensive support to Ukraine, the Polish state sees an opportunity that is *mutually beneficial* for both countries. Since the summer of 2022, Warsaw has been keen on initiating a series of bilateral agreements aimed at developing economic and transport cooperation, among other things, and whose first fruits may appear as early as 2023 with the completion of a European standard gauge railroad between Warsaw and Lviv.[58]

Economic factors play a part in other areas as well, such as defense cooperation[59] and the welcoming of Ukrainian refugees to Poland. By providing ID documents to those fleeing Ukraine and paving the way towards their (future) employment in Poland,[60] the Polish government also aims at solving domestic issues such as structural unemployment, and providing opportunities to Polish companies to maintain their pre-2022 production levels as well.[61]

The above-mentioned, mutually beneficial elements extend to efforts aimed at strengthening the connections between Polish and Ukrainian SMEs. Back in January 2015, the then-Civic Platform-led government initiated a EUR 100 million program aimed at helping Polish companies entering the Ukrainian market and at strengthening bilateral trade and economic relations between the two countries.[62] As information about the program and its results quickly disappeared that same year, it is likely that problems related to structural differences—such as corruption—affected the realization of the stated goals.

Russia's 2022 aggression also proved that the Polish state and state actors did not have an unrealistic view on what can be expected from Ukrainian economic actors concerning business practices. Warsaw hopes the war and the steps the Ukrainian authorities have undertaken to curb corruption and to initiate changes in the Ukrainian legislative system will have positive effects and will provide opportunities for Polish companies in the post-war reconstruction of the war-torn country.

In 2022, the Polish Development Bank (Bank Gospodarstwa Krajowego; BGK) and the Polish Investment and Trade Agency (Polska Agencja Inwestycji i Handlu; PAIH) started linking SMEs together. Sporadic open source information points towards significant interest on the part of Polish companies with the PAIH mentioning[63] 1750 businesses interested in participation by late February 2023. Not surprisingly, preparing Polish companies for the specificities of the Ukrainian legal system—rules concerning public procurement, for example—became a dedicated goal.[64]

Strictly from an economic point of view, strengthened cooperation between Polish and Ukrainian SMEs and Warsaw's participation in the rebuilding of Ukraine are likely to be used to prepare Poland for when the country becomes a net contributor to the EU budget. It is not unlikely that the current tension between Poland and the EU also reflects this—adding another reason why it is actually in the interests of the Warsaw government to find a solution to long-standing disagreements. Relations with the EU, however, involve yet another (very) problematic issue: the future of relations with Germany and France, and whether Poland can utilize the Weimar Triangle as a vehicle in which to showcase itself a responsible international actor.

Any possible, large-scale economic involvement in the reconstruction of a post-war Ukraine, however, has one major precondition: the presence and enforceability of international security guarantees for Ukraine backed by influential actors. As of July 2023, given the current state of hostilities and the unfulfilled nature of both combatants' minimal conditions for ending the active phase of the war, the international community is far from providing anything approaching this.

4.4. Economic and trade policy: Ukraine as a tool, and not a goal

One of the main economic concerns looming over the European countries supporting Ukraine is the financial future of the European Union. It is natural that Russia's 2022 aggression has led to a massive rise in military expenditures and procurement in which the issue of timely deliveries *in sufficient quantity* is important. This puts European arms producers in a disadvantageous situation, resulting in the growing possibility (and threat) that European military procurements will contribute to non-EU countries' economic growth.[65]

One way to offset this is to intensify bilateral economic and trade cooperation with regional partners (such as Ukraine) as well as non-regional states. It is likely that political limitations will gain more ground in this field. Once countries such as Japan, the Republic of Korea, and Australia make changes in their security arrangements in response to the growing threat of China, CEE regional states are likely to find long-term political-economic partners in them.

In theory, Polish aims and intentions to achieve the above-mentioned goals could still be derailed should the Polish political elite lose the support of a significant part of Polish society. Besides the financial cost of hosting refugees, another source of existing tensions within Polish society concerning Ukrainians (and *not* Ukraine as a country) has a historical-cultural basis and is connected to fundamentally different manner in which Stepan Bandera[66] is remembered in the two countries. In late 2022–early 2023, the Polish intelligentsia and media pointed out how the Bandera cult started to grow after 2014 and how Russia could take advantage of subsequent Polish-Ukrainian tensions. The late 2023 Polish general election, and the campaign leading up to it, will likely be good indicators as to the future importance of historical remembrance.

5. Going beyond Poland: regional conclusions

Poland's response to Russia's ongoing aggression against Ukraine has been largely shared by other regional states such as the Baltic States, the Czech Republic, Romania, and Slovakia.[67] The ruling political elites in these countries have focused on strategies aimed at securing the *room for maneuver* for their *countries*, and not for themselves personally. A salient example of this has been the attitude of the Slovak political elite which—despite facing domestic backlash—has continued to pursue a pro-Ukrainian course, extending to the provision of lethal weapons to the defending party.

The goal (and likely, strategy) of these states is to avoid the reintroduction of spheres of influences, a notion extending to the unilateral use of military force—a force that the EU, as an organization, has failed to develop and efficiently use. The steps undertaken by these countries, therefore, can be seen as an attempt to pre-serve the importance of the EU at the international level.[68]

This all points to developments that, as of the April 2023 Polish understanding, lead to the reemergence of bloc politics. Concerning the European subcontinent, the issue of how successful the unification of the so-called semi-periphery (referring to countries on *both sides* of EU and NATO borders) can be remains an open question. Due to its geographical location and sheer size, Ukraine remains key. From the perspective of NATO's Eastern Flank, the most important issue remains an open question: how cooperation versus rivalry will unfold between Poland, Romania, and Turkey—three states that are sizeable enough to claim an important role in shaping policies, vis-à-vis both Ukraine and Russia.

From the standpoint of the international system, however, a problem arises: the issues concerning Ukraine and the European semi-periphery cannot be divorced from the problem of Moscow itself. Bloc politics by definition need to take potential adversaries into account. In the Russian case, the international community has to address a country that is likely to become exceedingly closed, and a country that aims at exercising more and more control over Belarus. The issue of Belarus touches Poland especially, as Belarusian authorities since the summer of 2022 have singled out the Polish community living in the country, and have been systematically destroying cultural sites[69] and references[70]—in addition to repressing the Polish minority leadership.[71]

As far as bloc politics and the West are concerned, two factors must be mentioned. First, the CEE countries in question will very likely continue to regard the US and NATO as their key military partners and security guarantors. Second, the approach Washington has taken concerning China and the threat Beijing poses to the US-led world order will not change.

At the intersection of these two factors are the steps which the CEE counties could (or should) undertake to address the Chinese threat. Following the example of bilateral cooperation with Washington set by Lithuania (a radical shift away from China, and later on securing a trade deal with the US) and Romania's declaration that it will exclude Chinese companies from public infrastructure contracts,[72] the question arises whether these countries should largely or entirely adopt the US approach towards China—or, if not fully, to what extent? Using the example of the 2022 Russian aggression, the aforementioned CEE countries have made significant steps in securitizing[73] the issue of foreign, systematic threats—could this securitization "spill over" to their Chinese relations?[74] Between 2024 and 2026, these countries will likely update their national security strategies; the resulting strategic documents are likely to provide answers to these questions.

Transformative power, the desire to affect another state's policies, is present and is employed in bilateral relations between the aforementioned regional states and Ukraine. Two approaches can be seen in this respect. On the one hand, Warsaw, making use of its support for Kyiv, uses an economic-societal, non-coercive approach that aims at eliminating bilateral trade barriers, while also aiming at settling historical differences. However, since the Ukrainian state is also focused on cracking down on corruption,[75] the Poles might be knocking on open doors. Romania, on the other hand, another key regional state, is taking an approach that extends to coercion, and utilizing international organizations[76] to resolve the issue of the Romanian minority in Ukraine.[77] On the basis of information[78] published by the Ukrainian Institute for Central European Strategy, the efficacy of the Polish approach is likely to be higher.

Regardless of whether the non-coercive, the coercive, or a one that uses elements of both will prevail, under no circumstances should coercion extend to hampering the strategic Ukrainian goal of achieving closer integration with Euro-Atlantic structures.

Regarding the CEE region and the role Poland wants to play within, one of the key questions concerns the openness of other states to accept Polish (economic) goals, an objective that has been lately emphasized by President Andrzej Duda as well.[79] According to the media, Germany has backed off from opening a Poland-based repair center serving weaponry handed over to Ukraine.[80] In his 2023 speech, Foreign Minister Rau was very open in stating that Poland aims at utilizing the Three Seas Initiative for the reconstruction of Ukraine[81]—it is likely that the ambassadorial nomination[82] of the head of the Polish Development Bank, Beata Daszyńska-Muzyczka aims at providing the necessary diplomatic background. Acting as the voice for 11 other states as well, a unilateral desire of this magnitude will need answers from CEE states.

Notes

1. The author would like to thank the Warsaw-based Wacław Felczak Institute for providing financial support to conduct a series of background talks during Autumn 2022, whose findings are incorporated in this chapter.
2. Biuro Bezpieczeństwa Narodowego. *National Security Strategy of Poland*. 2020. 6. https://www.bbn.gov.pl/ftp/dokumenty/National_Security_Strategy_of_the_Republic_of_Poland_2020.pdf
3. The NATO and EU semi-periphery is not limited to CEE countries exclusively: similar processes have also been initiated in Sweden and Finland, for example. The annexation of the Crimean Peninsula resulted in debates concerning the demilitarization of Gotland and the Åland Islands—see e.g. Justyna Gotkowska and Piotr Szymański, "Gotland and Åland on the Baltic Chessboard – Swedish and Finnish Concerns," Centre for Eastern Studies, October 26, 2016, https://www.osw.waw.pl/en/publikacje/analyses/2016-10-26/gotland-and-aland-baltic-chessboard-swedish-and-finnish-concerns.
4. However, it is true that the Group's importance first grew as a response to the 2016 illegal mass migration flow into Europe. I see this event as a political struggle for influence over shaping EU policies between the V4 and Germany, and the subsequent V4 proposition concerning dual quality food products as an attempt to capitalize on the growing political capital.
5. See e.g. Adnan Kapo, "Mackinder: Who Rules Eastern Europe Rules the World," Institute for Geopolitics, Economy and Security, February 8, 2021, https://iges.ba/en/geopolitics/mackinder-who-rules-eastern-europe-rules-the-world/.
6. The White House, *National Security Strategy of the United States of America*, December 2017, https://trumpwhitehouse.archives.gov/wp-content/uploads/2017/12/NSS-Final-12-18-2017-0905.pdf.
7. TIMELINE right now, "[ENG] Right Now - Brief by the Presidents of Levits, Duda & Iohannis at the 3 Seas Initiative Summit," June 20, 2022, YouTube video, 11:10–11:35, https://www.youtube.com/watch?v=AUxroZCS7aQ.
8. The main Russian goal behind capturing the island was to gain additional A2AD (Anti-access/area denial) capabilities in the Black Sea region—this time significantly closer to NATO borders than before. A successful Russian operation could have meant the permanent presence of Russian reconnaissance and air defense capabilities which would have been able, *inter alia*, to monitor the airspace over NATO members.
9. U.S. Mission Luxembourg, "Secretary Pompeo and Secretary Esper Speak at Munich Security Conference 2020," U.S. Embassy in Luxembourg, February 19, 2020, https://lu.usembassy.gov/secretary-pompeo-and-secretary-esper-speak-at-munich-security-conference-2020/.
10. U.S. Mission Romania, "U.S. Secretary of Energy Rick Perry at the Three Seas Initiative Business Forum," U.S. Embassy in Romania, September 20, 2018, https://ro.usembassy.gov/secretary-of-energy-rick-perry-at-the-three-seas-initiative-business-forum/.
11. A. Wess Mitchell, "Strategic Sequencing: How Great Powers Avoid Multi-Front War," Marathon Initiative Working Paper, 2020, 67–73.
12. Mitchell, "Strategic Sequencing," 81–82.
13. The White House, *Interim National Security Strategic Guidance*, March 2021, https://www.whitehouse.gov/wp-content/uploads/2021/03/NSC-1v2.pdf.
14. Ibid. 19.
15. Andrea Shalal, Timothy Gardner, and Steve Holland, "U.S. Waives Sanctions on Nord Stream 2 as Biden Seeks to Mend Europe ties," *Reuters*, May 19, 2021, https://www.reuters.com/business/energy/us-waive-sanctions-firm-ceo-behind-russias-nord-stream-2-pipeline-source-2021-05-19/.
16. Office of International Affairs, "The Partnership for Transatlantic Energy and Climate Cooperation (P-TECC)" Department of Energy, https://www.energy.gov/ia/partnership-transatlantic-energy-and-climate-cooperation-p-tecc.

17 Barbara Bodalska. "Pat ws. nowego ambasadora USA w Polsce?" [A stalemate regarding the new US ambassador to Poland?], *Euractiv,* July 14, 2021, https://www.euractiv.pl/section/demokracja/news/ambasador-usa-brzezinski-obywatelstwo/.

18 "A contract for guarantees for bilateral business development worth 600 million dollars signed with the U.S.," Ministry of Foreign Affairs of the Republic of Lithuania, November 24, 2021, https://jp.mfa.lt/default/en/news/a-contract-for-guarantees-for-bilateral-business-development-worth-600-million-dollars-signed-with-the-us.

19 The White House, *National Security Strategy,* October 2022, 23, https://www.whitehouse.gov/wp-content/uploads/2022/10/Biden-Harris-Administrations-National-Security-Strategy-10.2022.pdf,

20 Volodymyr Dacenko (@Volodymyr_D_) "The number of weapons that the West has/supplies to Ukraine How many Western countries have weapons and how many of these weapons were transferred to Ukraine during the 8 months of the war? 1/17," Twitter, November 3, 2022, 10:29 pm. https://twitter.com/Volodymyr_D_/status/1588282311937732609/.

21 "Wojna w Ukrainie. Co piąta polska firma musiała ograniczyć działalność" [War in Ukraine. Every fifth Polish company has had to limit it activities], *Money.pl,* February 25, 2022, https://www.money.pl/gospodarka/wojna-w-ukrainie-co-piata-polska-firma-musiala-ograniczyc-dzialalnosc-6750264914602816a.html.

22 Łukasz Lewkowicz, "Słowacja wobec agresji Rosji na Ukrainę: kontekst społeczny" [Slovakia and Russia's aggression against Ukraine. The social context], Instytut Europy Środkowej, 2023, https://ies.lublin.pl/komentarze/slowacja-wobec-agresji-rosji-na-ukraine-kontekst-spoleczny/.

23 Emese Vig, "Felmérés: a magyarok Románia legoroszpártibb közössége, ami az Orbán-kormány Erdélyben is terjesztett propagandájának köszönhető" [Survey: Hungarians are the most pro-Russian community in Romania, which is due to the Orbán government's propaganda spread in Transylvania], *Transtelex,* February 24, 2023, https://transtelex.ro/kozelet/2023/02/24/toro-tibor-eloadas-erdelyi-magyarok-orban-putyin-nemzetegyesites.

24 Sytas, Andrius, "Estonia's Kallas in First Place in Parliamentary Election." *Reuters,* March 5, 2023. https://www.reuters.com/world/europe/estonia-goes-polls-test-pro-kyiv-government-2023-03-05/.

25 Carsten Schmiedl, "Reflecting on One Year of War: The Decisive Element of Black Sea Strategy," Center for Maritime Strategy, February 3, 2023, http://centerformaritimestrategy.org/publications/reflecting-on-one-year-of-war-the-decisive-element-of-black-sea-strategy/.

26 Układ otwarty – Igor Janke, "Strategia dla Polski: silny blok. Szczery wywiad po opuszczeniu Kancelarii Prezydenta – Jakub Kumoch" [Strategy for Poland: a strong bloc. A candid interview after leaving the presidential chancellery – Jakub Kumoch], January 22, 2023, YouTube video, 62:55–63:48, https://www.youtube.com/watch?v=BTQ7H_TZ_0s.

27 Kancelaria Prezydenta (@prezydentpl) "Prezydent @AndrzejDuda wręczył dziś listy uwierzytelniające ambasadorom RP, udającym się na placówki dyplomatyczne. Listy uwierzytelniające z rąk Prezydenta RP otrzymali: [...] @SolochPawel – Ambasador Nadzwyczajny i Pełnomocny RP w Rumunii." [Today President Andrzej Duda handed over the credentials to ambassadors of the Republic of Poland who are on their way to diplomatic missions. Credentials from the president of the Republic of Poland were received by [...] Paweł Soloch—Ambassador Extraordinary and Plenipotentiary to Romania.] Twitter, June 23, 2023, 6:50 pm. https://twitter.com/prezydentpl/status/1672285944500609024.

28 Rupert Wingfield-Hayes, "US Secures Deal on Philippines Bases to Complete Arc around China," *BBC News,* February 2, 2023, https://www.bbc.com/news/world-asia-64479712.

29 See the changes taking place in the December 2022 Japanese National Defense Strategy (https://www.mod.go.jp/j/approach/agenda/guideline/strategy/pdf/strategy_en.pdf).

30 In-person background talks conducted in Poland in September-October 2022.

31 "Remarks by President Biden and President Andrzej Duda of Poland after Bilateral Meeting" The White House, February 21, 2023, https://www.whitehouse.gov/briefing-room/speeches-remarks/2023/02/21/remarks-by-president-biden-and-president-andrzej-duda-of-poland-after-bilateral-meeting/.

32 A "historic turning point" in German foreign policy, announced by Chancellor Olaf Scholz shortly after the Russian invasion, that marks the beginning of a new era in which Berlin spends significantly more on defense and breaks away from its former pro-Russian foreign policy.

33 Bálint Ablonczy, "A vétó a gyengeség jele – a harcos magyar uniós diplomácia mérlege" [The veto is a sign of weakness – the scale of combative Hungarian EU diplomacy], *Válasz Online*, March 1, 2023, https://www.valaszonline.hu/2023/03/01/magyar-unios-diplomacia-kulpolitika-veto-szijjarto/.

34 Jon Henley, "Missile That Hit Poland Likely Came from Ukraine Defences, Say Warsaw and Nato," *The Guardian*, November 16, 2022, https://www.theguardian.com/world/2022/nov/16/poland-president-missile-strike-probably-ukrainian-stray.

35 R.Ch., "Abolicja dla Polaków walczących na Ukrainie" [Amnesty for Poles fighting in Ukraine], *Portal-Mundurowy.pl*, December 25, 2022, https://portal-mundurowy.pl/index.php/component/k2/item/16526-abolicja-dla-polakow-walczacych-na-ukrainie.

36 "Ustawa o wyłączeniu odpowiedzialności karnej za podjęcie służby w Siłach Zbrojnych Ukrainy." [Act on the exclusion of criminal liability for service in the Armed Forces of Ukraine], 2022, https://orka.sejm.gov.pl/Druki9ka.nsf/Projekty/9-020-1106-2022/$file/9-020-1106-2022.pdf.

37 Wojciech Moskwa and Jenny Leonard, "Poland Says It Has Approached US about Sharing Nuclear Weapons," *Bloomberg*, October 5, 2022, https://www.bloomberg.com/news/articles/2022-10-05/poland-is-in-talks-with-us-about-nuclear-weapons-president-says.

38 I am grateful to Krisztián Jójárt for this comment.

39 "Nordic Countries Plan Joint Air Defence to Counter Russian Threat," March 24, 2023, https://www.reuters.com/world/europe/nordic-countries-plan-joint-air-defence-counter-russian-threat-2023-03-24/.

40 Baazil, Diederik, "Dutch Military Merges Its Land Combat Units with Germany," *Bloomberg*, March 30, 2023, https://www.bloomberg.com/news/articles/2023-03-30/dutch-military-merges-its-land-combat-units-with-germany.

41 Ministry of Foreign Affairs of the Republic of Poland, *Information on the Principles and Objectives of Poland's Foreign Policy*. https://www.sejm.gov.pl/media9.nsf/files/MPRA-CQUBZR/%24File/Information%20on%20the%20principles%20and%20objectives%20of%20Poland%E2%80%99s%20foreign%20policy.pdf.

42 Ibid. 14.

43 Ibid. 19.

44 Ministry of National Defence of the Republic of Poland. *"Poland and Romania, Equipping Armed Forces with Similar Equipment, Ensure the Security of the Entire Eastern Flank of NATO."* https://www.gov.pl/web/national-defence/poland-and-romania-equipping-armed-forces-with-similar-equipment-ensures-the-security-of-the-entire-eastern-flank-of-nato.

45 Ministry of Foreign Affairs of the Republic of Poland. *Information on the Principles and Objectives of Poland's Foreign Policy*. 15.

46 Ibid. 16.

47 Ibid. 17.

48 (Panel) discussions organized under Chatham House rules during the 2021 Warsaw Security Forum pointed towards envisioning a lesser role for the Visegrád Group, and an enhanced role for other platforms.

49 See the chapter of Bálint Madlovics and Bálint Magyar in this volume.

50 In terms of military logistics and the transport of equipment to Ukraine, the airport of Rzeszów-Jasionka (a hub near the Via Carpathia communication axis) became the most important logistics center.

51 "In the Riga Summit Leaders of the 3SI Member States Highlight Closer Cooperation with Ukraine and Appreciate the United States Contribution to the 3SI Investment Fund," Three Seas Initiative, 2022, https://3seas.eu/media/news/in-the-riga-summit-leaders-of-the-3si-member-states-highlight-closer-cooperation-with-ukraine-and-appreciate-asv-contribution-to-the-3si-investment-fund.

52 Joanna Hyndle-Hussein, "Tajwan zwiększa zaangażowanie kapitałowe w litewskim sektorze high-tech" [Taiwan increases its capital investment in Lithuanian high-tech sector], Centre for Eastern Studies, January 20, 2023, https://www.osw.waw.pl/pl/publikacje/analizy/2023-01-20/tajwan-zwieksza-zaangazowanie-kapitalowe-w-litewskim-sektorze-high.

53 BNS, "Australia Opens Trade and Investment Office in Vilnius," *Lrt.lt*, February 10, 2023, https://www.lrt.lt/en/news-in-english/19/1886950/australia-opens-trade-and-investment-office-in-vilnius.

54 See "Centrum Badawcze Inicjatywy Trójmorza" [Research center of the Three Seas Initiative], *Instytut Studiów Politycznych PAN*, accessed March 5, 2023, https://isppan.waw.pl/centrum-badawcze-inicjatywy-trojmorza/.

55 In December 2022, one of the Ministry's undersecretaries of state was promoted to the rank of vice minister, entrusted with the task of fostering closer trade cooperation with East Asian countries. See "W planach MSZ na 2023 rok dalsze wsparcie Ukrainy, wizyty w Azji i sejmowe expose ministra Zbigniewa Raua" [The plans of the MFA for 2023 include further support for Ukraine, visits to Asia and a parliamentary report by minister Zbigniew Rau," *Polskieradio.pl*, January 1, 2023, https://www.polskieradio.pl/399/7975/artykul/3095927.

56 "Joint Declaration of President of Ukraine Volodymyr Zelenskyy, President of Lithuania Gitanas Nausėda and President of Poland Andrzej Duda Following the Second Summit of the Lublin Triangle" President of Ukraine, January 11, 2023, https://www.president.gov.ua/en/news/spilna-deklaraciya-prezidenta-ukrayini-volodimira-zelenskogo-80321.

57 "Comprehensive Research: How the War Changed Me and the Country. Summary of the Year," Rating Group, February 21, 2023, https://ratinggroup.ua/en/research/ukraine/kompleksne_dosl_dzhennya_yak_v_yna_zm_nila_mene_ta_kra_nu_p_dsumki_roku.html.

58 "Ukraina przestawia się na europejskie tory. Do końca 2023 r. ma powstać nowa linia" [Ukraine is switching to European tracks. A new line is to be built by the end of 2023], *Money.pl*, March 3, 2023, https://www.money.pl/gospodarka/ukraina-przestawia-sie-europejskie-tory-do-konca-2023-r-ma-powstac-nowa-linia-6872366874643168a.html.

59 Maciej Szopa, "Polska sprzedała Kraby Ukrainie. Rekordowy kontrakt."[Poland sold Krabs to Ukraine. A record contract.], Defence24.pl, June 1, 2022, https://defence24.pl/przemysl/polska-sprzedala-kraby-ukrainie-rekordowy-kontrakt

60 See Ustawa z dnia 12 marca 2022 r. o pomocy obywatelom Ukrainy w związku z konfliktem zbrojnym na terytorium tego państwa, Dz.U. 2022 poz. 583 (2022) ["Act of March 12 2022 on the help of Ukrainian citizens in regards to the armed conflict on the territory of said state"], https://isap.sejm.gov.pl/isap.nsf/download.xsp/WDU20220000583/U/D20220583Lj.pdf

61 The 2022 Russian invasion made large numbers of Ukrainian men working in Poland go back to fight. This group was substituted mainly by Ukrainian women—Polish companies needed to adjust to this situation, e.g., by changing production norms. In selected sectors (such as healthcare), the influx of refugees helped mitigating effects of long-term structural unemployment as well. See Zsombor Zeöld, "Migráció és menekültek: a Lengyelország előtt álló kihívások 2022. február 24-e után" [Migration and refugees: challenges Poland faces after February 24, 2022], Migrációkutató Intézet, May 17, 2022, https://www.migraciokutato.hu/2023/05/17/horizont-2023-5-migracio-es-menekultek-a-lengyelorszag-elott-allo-kihivasok-2022-februar-24-e-utan/.

62 Patryk Kugiel and Piotr Kościński, "Międzynarodowa pomoc dla Ukrainy. Szanse dla polskich firm i organizacji" [International aid for Ukraine. Opportunities for Polish companies and organizations], The Polish Institute for International Affairs, October 5, 2015, 78-79, https://pism.pl/publikacje/Raport_PISM__Mi_dzynarodowa_pomoc_dla_Ukrainy__Szanse_dla_polskich_firm_i_organizacji.

63 Małgorzata Kaliszewska, "PAIH o odbudowie Ukrainy: 1750 Polskich firm zgłosiło się do polskiego projektu" [PAIH on the reconstruction of Ukraine: 1750 Polish companies have applied for the Polish project], *Rzeczpospolita*, February 24, 2022, https://www.rp.pl/finanse/art38017961-paih-1750-polskich-firm-zglosilo-sie-do-polskiego-projektu-odbudowy-ukrainy.

64 Ibid. "[O]znacza konieczność przyswojenia specyfiki ukraińskiego systemu prawnego oraz dostosowanie się do regulacji, które przygotowywane są w Polsce, a będą dedykowane współpracy z Ukrainą [...] [o]rganizuje m.in. szkolenia z zakresu prawa zamówień publicznych dla wciąż rosnącej grupy firm, które wyraziły gotowość do udziału w odbudowanie Ukrainy." "[It m]eans the necessity to adopt the specificities of the Ukrainian legal system, and adjusting to those regulations that are being prepared in Poland and will be dedicated to the cooperation with Ukraine [...] training is organized *inter alia* in the field of public procurement for a continuously growing group of companies who have expressed readiness in taking part in the reconstruction of Ukraine." [trans. Zs.Z.]

65 For a collection of CEE countries' military procurement plans, see "Wschodnia flanka NATO po roku wojny – mobilizacja różnych prędkości" [NATO's eastern flank after a year of war – mobilization at different speeds], Centre for Eastern Studies, February 21, 2023, https://www.osw.waw.pl/pl/publikacje/komentarze-osw/2023-02-21/wschodnia-flanka-nato-po-roku-wojny-mobilizacja-roznych.

66 See e.g. "Układ otwarty – Igor Janke," 44:42 – 44:58 and 46:00 – 46:50.

67 For a recent political messaging about this, see "Wspólna deklaracja Ministrów Spraw Zagranicznych Estonii, Łotwy, Litwy i Polski o pogłębieniu współpracy w regionie Ryga, 31 stycznia" [Joint declaration of the foreign ministers of Estonia, Latvia, Lithuania, and Poland on strengthening diplomatic relations in the region], Ministry of Foreign Affairs, Republic of Poland, January 31, 2023, https://www.gov.pl/web/dyplomacja/wspolna-deklaracja-ministrow-spraw-zagranicznych-estonii-lotwy-litwy-i-polski-o-poglebieniu-wspolpracy-w-regionie-ryga-31-stycznia.

68 See Tamás Maráczi, "'Oroszország agresszivitása a gyengeség jele' – Tálas Péter elemzése a Mandineren" ['Russia's aggression is a sign of weakness – Péter Tálas' analysis for *Mandiner*], *Mandiner*, November 26, 2022, https://mandiner.hu/cikk/20221126_oroszorszag_agresszivitasa_a_gyengeseg_jele_talas_peter_elemzese_a_mandineren.

69 Wiktor Kazanecki, "Białoruś: Zniszczony cmentarz żołnierzy AK. „Barbarzyńcy zrównali go z ziemią" [Belarus. Destroyed cemetery of Home Army soldiers. 'The barbarians leveled it to the ground']" *Interia*, August 25, 2022, https://wydarzenia.interia.pl/zagranica/news-bialorus-zniszczony-cmentarz-zolnierzy-ak-barbarzyncy-zrowna,nId,6243054.

70 "Whitewashed: Church Mural of Soviet Military Defeat Painted over by Belarusian Authorities," *Radio Free Europe/Radio Liberty*, March 1, 2023, https://www.rferl.org/a/belarus-soviet-defeat-mural-painted-over/32294548.html.

71 "Andrzej Poczobut skazany na osiem lat kolonii karnej" [Andrzej Poczobut sentenced to eight years in a penal colony], *Polityka*, February 8, 2023, https://www.polityka.pl/tygodnikpolityka/swiat/2200956,1,andrzej-poczobut-skazany-na-osiem-lat-kolonii-karnej.read.

72 Bogdan Neagu, "Romania Issues 'Memorandum' Blocking Chinese Firms from Public Infrastructure Projects," *Euractiv*, February 2, 2021, https://www.euractiv.com/section/economy-jobs/news/romania-issues-memorandum-blocking-chinese-firms-from-public-infrastructure-projects/.

73 "According to securitisation theory, political issues are constituted as extreme security issues to be dealt with urgently when they have been labelled as 'dangerous,' 'menacing,' 'threatening,' 'alarming' and so on by a 'securitising actor' who has the social and institutional power to move the issue 'beyond politics.'" Claras Eroukhmanoff, "Securitisation Theory: An Introduction," January 14, 2018, 1, https://www.e-ir.info/pdf/72393.

74 In August 2022, the International Republican Institute conducted a poll on various European countries' perceptions on China that covered *inter alia* the Baltic States, the Czech Republic, Poland, Slovakia, and Romania. See "Public Perceptions of China in 13 European Countries," International Republican Institute, August 2022, https://www.iri.org/resources/public-perceptions-of-china-in-13-european-countries-august-2022/.

75 "Anatomy of a Scandal: Why Zelenskyy Launched a Corruption Crackdown in Ukraine," *Financial Times*, January 27, 2023, https://www.ft.com/content/80a0a3e0-e9e4-45bc-b601-615a676e2637.

76 László Gál, "Magyarország és Románia együtt lép fel az ukrán kisebbségvédelmi törvény ellen" [Hungary and Romania are working together against Ukraine's minority protection law], *Transtelex*, January 26, 2023, https://transtelex.ro/kulfold/2023/01/26/magyarorszag-es-romania-egyutt-lep-fel-az-ukran-kisebbsegvedelmi-torveny-ellen.

77 "Comunicat de presă privind poziția MAE referitoare la adoptarea, de către Rada Supremă a Ucrainei, a Legii privind minoritățile naționale (comunitățile) din Ucraina" [Press release regarding the position of the MFA on the adoption by the Supreme Rada of Ukraine of the Law on National Minorities (Communities) of Ukraine], Ministry of Foreign Affairs of Romania, December 22, 2022, https://www.mae.ro/node/60649.

78 See the figure on page 4 in Dmytro Tuzhanskyi, "How Ukraine Must Develop Its Minority Policy to Avoid the "Ethnic Trap" During EU Accession Negotiations, and How International Partners Could Help," Globsec, February 16, 2023, https://www.globsec.org/what-we-do/publications/how-ukraine-must-develop-its-minority-policy-avoid-ethnic-trap-during-eu.

79 „Nasi przedsiębiorcy mają rozbudowane sieci kontaktów wśród Ukraińców, mają know–how, polski sektor budowlany jest w bardzo dobrej kondycji, a bliskość kulturowa sprawia, że możemy być naturalnym partnerem dla Ukrainy w procesie odbudowy. Nasz biznes i rzesza polskich obywateli zatrudniona w przemyśle budowlanym bardzo na to liczą – nasza dyplomacja musi wspierać ten proces! To jest nasze ogromne sąsiedzkie i gospodarcze zadanie." [Our entrepreneurs have extensive networks amongst Ukrainians, have know-how, the Polish construction sector is in a very good condition, the cultural closeness makes us natural partners for Ukraine in the process of reconstruction. Our businesses and masses of Polish citizens employed in the construction sector count on this very much—our diplomacy must support this process! This is our tremendous neighborly and economic task.] President Duda's speech before the Polish diplomatic corps, June 19, 2023, https://www.prezydent.pl/aktualnosci/biuro-polityki-miedzynarodowej/aktualnosci/wystapienie-prezydenta-rp-podczas-spotkania-z-ambasadorami-rp,70199.

80 "Media: Germany Refuses to Create Leopard Tank Repair Center in Poland," *European Pravda*, July 12, 2023, https://www.eurointegration.com.ua/eng/news/2023/07/12/7165598/.

81 "We will strive to make the Three Seas Initiative an institutional flywheel that will drive Ukraine's post-war reconstruction—a process that must take place in parallel with its EU accession, that is to say the expansion of appropriate infrastructure links." Ministry of Foreign Affairs of the Republic of Poland. *Information on the Principles and Objectives of Poland's Foreign Policy*, 18.

82 Nominacje dla specjalnych przedstawicieli Prezydenta RP do zadań z zakresu polityki zagranicznej [Nominations for special representatives of the President of the Republic of Poland's for tasks concerning foreign policy], July 4, 2023, https://www.prezydent.pl/aktualnosci/nominacje/nominacje-dla-specjalnych-przedstawicieli-prezydenta-rp-do-zadan-z-zakresu-polityki-zagranicznej,71124.

Hungary's Dubious Loyalty: Orbán's Regime Strategy in the Russia-Ukraine War

Bálint Madlovics and Bálint Magyar

1. Hungary's patronal autocracy and the full-scale invasion

Hungary today is a post-communist mafia state. In 2010, an autocratic breakthrough replaced the world of competing corrupt networks, i.e., a patronal democracy, and established a single-pyramid patronal network, led by the chief patron, Viktor Orbán (Figure 1). With a two-thirds majority in the parliament, Orbán was able to rewrite the constitution and the electoral law one-sidedly; and in the last years, referring to different types of crisis situations (migration, the pandemic, and the Russian-Ukrainian war) he has ruled by decree without any democratic restraint. He has also been able appoint his own clients to head the institutions that would normally serve to check and balance state power in a democratic regime (constitutional court, media authority, national council overseeing the courts, election monitoring bodies, etc.) without the need for consensus. The creation of unlimited constitutional and appointing powers has emptied the formal institutional system: the people who hold the majority of public power are in practice political front men, at various levels, who do not exercise the authority of their position autonomously, but merely execute in the sphere of legality decisions made outside of legally defined institutions. The decisions made by the informal patronal network, Orbán's adopted political family, can be described and understood by the twin motives of concentration of power and accumulation of wealth, carried out through bloodless means of state coercion applied with wide amplitude of arbitrariness. Hence, the regime is a patronal autocracy, and the state in such a regime can be identified as a mafia state.[1]

Between 2010 and February 2022, Orbán and his party, Fidesz, were re-elected twice with a two-thirds majority in manipulated elections.[2] In foreign policy, the same period saw growing tensions between Hungary and its Western partners, as well as increasing formal and informal dependencies on Russia. Several clashes with the EU over the latter's criticisms of de-democratization in Hungary took place while Russian gas-diplomacy, the ongoing expansion of the Paks Nuclear Power Plant, and other similar deals put Hungary in an obliged, dependent position in exchange for private benefit.

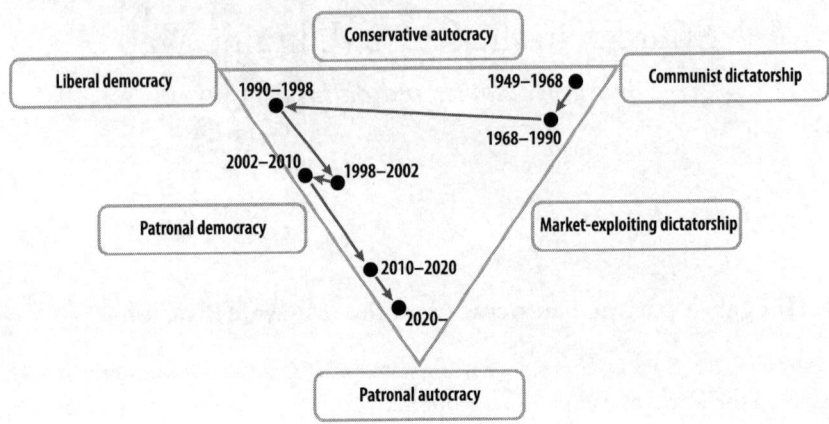

Figure 1. Modeled trajectory of Hungary (1949-2023).

```
                    Conservative autocracy
    Liberal democracy    1990–1998      1949–1968    Communist dictatorship
                                        1968–1990
                    2002–2010  1998–2002
    Patronal democracy                  Market-exploiting dictatorship
                         2010–2020
                         2020–
                    Patronal autocracy
```

Source: Magyar and Madlovics (2022, 218).

When the full-scale Russian military invasion of Ukraine started on February 24, 2022, Hungarian politics was preoccupied with the upcoming elections in April. The frightening news of war in a neighboring country combined with the increasing flow of Ukrainian refugees immediately elevated the topic to the center of the campaign. While the unified opposition had a hard time finding a unified response to the events, the war created an unexpected situation for Orbán's patronal autocracy as well.

In this chapter, we analyze Orbán's response to the Russian invasion in the context of his regime (rather than the country), strategy, as well as the patron-client relationship that has been developing with Putin's Russia since 2010. In the pre-invasion period, Orbán's regime strategy on the geopolitical level was focused on protecting his mafia state's corrupt operations from the EU and expanding them towards Russia. In the next sections, we explain Hungary's position in the EU, the steps in developing the patron-client relationship with Putin, and analyze the two narratives that Orbán, as an ideology-applying populist, has carefully crafted as part of his regime strategy: a negative, de-legitimizing one for the EU ("we won't be a colony") and a positive, de-stigmatizing one for Putin's Russia ("Eastern opening").

Steven Levitsky and Lucan Way argue in their famous book on competitive authoritarianism that Western linkage and leverage leads to a country's democratization.[3] In contrast, when the full-scale Russian invasion started, Orbán's mafia state was in Western linkage and under Russian leverage. The result—which is analyzed in the second half of the chapter—suggests the opposite of democratic change: the crisis in Hungary's "bridge role" between West and East, Orbán's subsequent attempts to maintain it anyway, and his anti-Ukrainian campaign on the domestic scene and pro-Russian steps on the international stage point to the prolonged existence of a mafia state on the EU's periphery.

2. An EU member in Russia's criminal ecosystem: the situation in Orbán's Hungary before the invasion

2.1. The Hungarian mafia state and the European Union

In the years since 2010, Orbán's patronal autocracy has sought to consolidate its position by breaking down the autonomies that potentially threaten its power: autonomous media, autonomous NGOs, the autonomy of entrepreneurs, and the autonomy of citizens, although it has been able to curtail individual freedoms least of all. This is at least partially explained by the fact that Hungary is a member of the European Union (EU).[4]

On the other hand, Hungary is the only mafia state in the EU. While corruption is endemic in other post-communist countries that have joined the EU, such as Romania and Bulgaria, the proportional election systems and divided executive power in these countries have prevented the emergence of a single-pyramid patronal network.[5] The type of autocratic regime that Orbán has established in Hungary is very different from Jarosław Kaczyński's autocratic attempt in Poland as well, despite the similarities in their ideological panels. (By "panels," we mean pre-prepared ideological explanations and arguments that can be drawn out at any time and used to legitimize and defend the regime against critics.) While Orbán's regime seeks wealth, and key decisions are made through informal mechanisms instead of through formal institutions, Kaczyński is conducting a conservative-autocratic experiment which is driven as much by ideology as by the quest for power.[6] Neither informal patronalism nor centrally organized corruption appear in the Polish case, only party nepotism[7] and the extension of formal powers of the state through nationalization.[8]

The EU was founded on the presumption of regime homogeneity, that is, that all its members would be liberal democracies, and even if their respective leaders were to disagree or wish to follow different interests they would have a joint platform of common norms to work out their differences. Therefore, it lacks the appropriate mechanisms to deal with regime heterogeneity. Whereas a majority of the EU members are Western liberal democracies, they are accompanied by a conservative autocratic attempt (Poland), patronal democracies (Bulgaria, Romania, and Slovakia), and a patronal autocracy (Hungary). Of these, patronal autocracy is the most subversive because it is incompatible with Western member states, as well as with both the EU's political foundations (liberal democracy) and its economic foundations (market economy).

While the lack of effective defensive mechanisms that would foster regime homogeneity is a structural-design flaw of the EU, the rationality of common values as declared by the EU have clashed with the rationality of geopolitics with its pressure of circumstances. More specifically, Central Europe (and within it, Orbán's mafia state) is situated on the periphery of empires, between Western Europe, on the one hand, and the patronal autocracy that is Russia, on the other. Before the invasion of Ukraine, the EU saw the dilemma as follows: a move to admit the post-communist countries of the Balkans and Eastern Europe as members of the Union would lead to a catastrophic decline in the system of common values; however, a flat out rejection of these countries, let alone an expulsion of autocratic regimes from within the EU, would give the Russian empire, currently in the process of reincarnation, the opportunity to expand towards the West.

This perception pushed the EU towards the creation of a "buffer zone"—countries situated within the EU, but largely outside the Eurozone. In giving up their romantic beliefs and original mission following the collapse of the Berlin Wall, the Western European political elite began to consider the buffer-zone countries like Hungary not as companions who had fallen behind culturally, but only as areas to be influenced economically. The EU aimed to achieve its geopolitical objectives through support granted to the buffer states; at the same time, however, the EU itself was equipped only for addressing ad hoc violations of common European values by means of mediation, persuasion, and judicial avenues, and lacked the tools for preventing the systematic erosion of liberal democracy. This discrepancy has been exploited by Orbán, using EU funds—which comprise transfers amounting to around 4 percent of the Hungarian GDP every year[9]—to finance his clients and subsequently strengthen his autocratic regime.[10]

2.2. Regime strategy instead of country strategy: mafia state geopolitics and the de-stigmatization of Russia

A criminal organization, whether private or public, has two basic functions. First, it tries to accumulate wealth for its members, which necessitates some source of money and the ability to launder it; second, it needs to be able to ensure impunity for its members, deactivating control mechanisms,[11] such as law enforcement and prosecution, which would prevent them from spending their accumulated wealth.[12] Domestically, Orbán has the political power, both formally (through his supermajority) and informally (through his clients), to achieve these goals.[13] Internationally, he has to achieve these goals within a specific geopolitical environment with different actors, countries, and international organizations with different facilitating and hindering aspects.

After his victory in 2010, Orbán faced a wealth accumulation–impunity conundrum. On the one hand, there was the EU, which provided funds to Hungary (wealth accumulation) but which also included the possibility of oversight (threatened impunity). On the other hand, there were Eastern autocrats, who—being patronal actors themselves—would not complain about corruption risks or rule of law issues regarding international trade deals (impunity) but who had yet to establish relations with Orbán's adopted political family (no wealth accumulation). The logic of the mafia state, however, dictated weakening ties with the EU, reducing the relationship as much as possible to material support, while strengthening ties with Eastern autocrats and with Putin's Russia in particular. The ultimate goal of this strategy was to establish a "bridge role" in the above-mentioned buffer zone situated on the periphery of the West and the East. Orbán intended to secure his regime "while 'taxing two empires': obtaining structural and cohesion funds from the EU, while energy agreements with the Russian empire provided an additional supply of funds."[14] But such a geopolitical equilibrium necessitated opposing movements towards the EU and Russia.

All this reflects a regime strategy instead of a country strategy. While the latter would position Hungary as a country in the geopolitical space, Orbán's actions reflected predominantly regime interests of maintaining, expanding, and preserving patronal autocratic rule. The ideological "country strategy" of the government, making use of ideological panels such as "national sovereignty" and "Eastern opening,"[15] came together as a value-incoherent but functionally coherent combination. On the basis of the so-called "Eastern opening," national sovereignty was surrendered to Putin's Russia, on which both the country and Orbán himself have become significantly and increasingly dependent (see below). On the other hand, the panel of "national sovereignty" appeared only to deflect Western criticisms of de-democratization and corruption in Hungary, while it conspicuously never surfaced in relation to Russia which was embraced on the grounds of the "Eastern opening."

Based on the regime strategy of opposing movements towards the EU and Putin's Russia, functional coherence manifested itself in the symmetrical interpretation of these two foreign entities (Table 1). Ideological panels were carefully selected to fit two narratives, tailored to the mafia state's geopolitical positions: a negative narrative where the elements were tuned to delegitimize the EU's role and oversight; and a positive narrative where the elements were tuned to legitimize the new relations with Putin's Russia. While the former position is necessarily confrontational, generating and aggravating social resentments, the latter position is non-confrontational and aims to pacify society with its new geopolitical allies.

Using the argument of national sovereignty in relation to the EU, Orbán has argued that only "we, Hungarians" have the right to decide on cases of national interest, whereas foreign interference amounts to the violation of this right, the illegitimate narrowing of the room for maneuver for the legitimate, national government. As he declared on March 15, 2012, on the national holiday commemorating the Hungarian revolution of 1848, Hungary "will not be a colony" of the EU.[16]

Table 1. Symmetrical interpretations of the EU and the East in the Orbán regime's narrative.

In relation to the EU (negative narrative)	In relation to Putin's Russia (positive narrative)
de-legitimation:	**legitimation:**
the national interest is legitimately defined by domestic and not foreign actors (emphasizing costs over benefits)	the national interest is to develop new economic relations while respecting foreign regimes and their leaders (emphasizing benefits over costs)
stigmatization:	**de-stigmatization:**
framing the EU as the supporter of "them" against "us," building on existing social resentments (against migrants, LGBT, etc.)	framing Russia as the supporter of "us" against "them," taming existing social resentments (against communists, etc.)

Orbán's "national freedom fight" is a mafia state's fight for impunity within the EU. National sovereignty was used by Fidesz politicians to justify Hungary's refusal to join the European Public Prosecutor's Office,[17] and more regularly to deflect criticisms in rule of law and democracy debates. The responses to detailed criticisms such as the Tavares and the Sargentini reports[18] transformed the mere reference to national sovereignty into a broader narrative of the clash of visions about Europe's future as a "Europe of nations" or an imperial "United States of Europe," as Orbán explained in the European Parliament in 2013.[19] Indeed, Orbán's "Europe of nations" program is simply a demand for a new relationship with the EU: to maintain the obligation for the transfer of European funds for convergence, while ensuring autonomy for the establishment of distinct national democracies, namely, autocracies.

On the other hand, countries like Putin's Russia are embedded in a positive context in the symbolic slogan of an "Eastern opening." Orbán first spoke of an "Eastern wind blowing in the world economy" in 2010, a metaphor he used several times later in his speeches.[20] In this context, the national interest is identified with seeking "the most intensive cooperation possible with China, Russia, the Arab world, and the emerging Central Asian region," as Orbán explained to Hungarian diplomats in 2011.[21] As opposed to the delegitimizing EU narrative, which emphasizes the limitations imposed on the regime by the European community, the legitimizing Eastern narrative emphasizes the (economic) benefits of these incipient relationships while omitting to mention any possible (political) costs.

Between 2010 and 2022, Orbán met Putin 11 times, both in Moscow and in Budapest.[22] These diplomatic meetings were typically followed by press releases on both the Russian and Hungarian sides, praising the other country and looking forward to developing closer economic relations. In 2013, Orbán explained that "it is in Hungary's basic interest to have good relations and maintain close cooperation with Russia," and that "we, Hungarians are aware of [...] Russia's weight and importance, but the respect we have for Russia is not primarily due to Russia's size, but to its culture, and our respect for Russian culture is the basis for our good economic cooperation."[23]

The symmetry of the de-legitimation of the EU and the legitimation of Russia was accompanied by a similar symmetry of stigmatization and de-stigmatization, respectively. Since 2015, there have been several nationwide state-sponsored campaigns against the EU in Hungary, portraying "Brussels" as an ally of George Soros and a supporter of illegal migration and LGBT propaganda.[24] Intensive hate and fear campaigns reached beyond Fidesz's own voter base: in a referendum about the alleged threat of sex reassignment treatments for underage children in 2022, around 3.6 million people voted "no," as the Fidesz campaign suggested, exceeding the number of Fidesz's list votes of around 3 million.[25]

As Putin's autocracy moved from the side of "them" to that of "us" in Orbán's populist narrative, a similar movement of de-stigmatization, or the taming existing social resentments, could be seen as well. Earlier, as an opposition politician, Orbán was highly critical of Putin, publicly condemning Russia's military invasion of Georgia in 2008, and arguing that Hungary must not become "Gazprom's happiest barrack" (a reference to Hungary being called the "happiest barrack" of the Eastern bloc before the regime change). To legitimize Hungary's new geopolitical line, Orbán's task was to reverse this rhetoric, and portray Putin and Russia in a positive light.

Instead of a direct campaign, the combined effect of three elements should be mentioned. The first is the reinterpretation of anti-communism. Orbán started his political career before the regime change, positioning himself against the Soviet Union and Russian oppression. This was clearly stated in a memorably radical speech on June 16, 1989, urging the removal of Soviet troops from Hungary, which later became a point of reference in Fidesz's interpretation of the history of the regime change.[26] Anti-communism has been a strong pillar of the Fidesz identity, but the term has become a general negative group marker over time. Just as Putin who, relying on the Russian historical experience, identifies all his opponents as "Nazis" (such as the Ukrainians, for example), untethering the term from its historical or factual meaning, Fidesz has used the term "communist" for its opponents, de-selecting the Russian component from the term's historical meaning. Before 2010, the epithet was used by Fidesz for the socialist-liberal coalition (MSZP-SZDSZ); later, it became a slur for both Fidesz's opposition and the EU. As Orbán stated in his speech on the national holiday of October 23, 2013:

> We know that Hungarian freedom has not only had heroes but has also had traitors as well. We know that all of our revolutions have been crushed from outside. We also know that there have always been those who have helped the external enemy. Austro-Russian collaborators, communist militiamen, Red Barons—depending on what was in fashion at the time. [...] We know that there were those and there will always be those who are ready to give Hungary to the colonizers again. [...] [They want to take] away the chance for us Hungarians to really decide about our own lives. Not about politics and not about political parties—but about our own lives.[27]

The second element in Russia's de-stigmatization is the spread of Kremlin propaganda by public media and patronalized private media, portraying Russia in a positive light in Hungarian news programs and news services.[28] The replication of Russian fake news and self-legitimizing narratives—such as Russia's fight against "decadent" Western tendencies like LGBT rights—was particularly impactful given the dominated media environment that the Orbán regime has built.[29]

Finally, the widely and positively publicized meetings of high-ranking political actors from Hungary and Russia—primarily Orbán and Putin, but also ministers of foreign affairs Péter Szijjártó and Sergey Lavrov—also contributed to the growing public acceptance of Eastern actors, particularly in contrast to the harsh criticism leveled against the West. The overall effect of de-stigmatization was Putin's relative popularity in Hungary, particularly among Fidesz voters. In 2017, 53% of the population maintained that Hungary should stand somewhere between West and East, with only 39% saying that it should stand on the side of the West; at the same time, 44% of the population had positive attitudes toward Putin (the highest such figure among the Visegrád countries), which was also 6 percentage points higher than Merkel's support, and only 1 percentage point lower than Orbán's. Among Fidesz voters, Putin had a sympathy index of 54% in 2018, well above the average (43%) and significantly above Merkel's index (29%).[30] Further research that same year found that Putin was the most popular foreign leader in Hungary in the 18-59 age group, especially among those without a diploma.[31]

2.3. Growing dependence on Putin: becoming Russia's "sub-sovereign mafia state"

The fundamental change in Orbán's public stance regarding Russia came in 2009, as two journalists explain in a long investigative article on the Orbán-Putin relationship.[32] As they write:

In November 2009, Orbán, already a favorite of the upcoming elections, met Russian leader Vladimir Putin in Saint Petersburg. The purpose of that meeting was for the two politicians, who had never met before, to get to know each other. [Later,] two influential Hungarian businessmen [travelled to] Moscow weeks before Hungary's April 2010 parliamentary election. Both men belonged to the inner circle of [...] Orbán [...]. One of them was Lajos Simicska, a longtime friend of Orbán and his ally in making Fidesz the dominant political force in Hungary. The other person was Zsolt Nyerges, one of Simicska's associates and an old friend of the Orbán family. [...] The goal of Simicska and Nyerges' trip was to establish new business relations between the leaderships of the two countries. [...] One source described it as an "introductory visit." Another said that the FSB official told Simicska and Nyerges that, if they need help in business, they "can rely on Russia."

While there had been unconfirmed rumors of earlier corrupt deals between Orbán and Russia in the 1990s,[33] the above-described meetings marked a turn in Orbán's politics which cannot be explained on ideological grounds. Rather, it followed the needs of the mafia state which looks for sources of money while ensuring the opportunities of money laundering as well as impunity. The two meetings described above appear as a "job interview" for the position of client to the chief patron of Russia. This has resulted in the deepening international dependency of Hungary on Russia and of Orbán, personally, on Putin.

Since 2010, Hungarian foreign policy, going against the grain of EU and transatlantic obligations, has consisted of the search for legitimization and the quest for financial favors from Putin and other Eastern autocrats. This is nothing more but the expansion of the adopted political family's scope of operations, that is, of their power and wealth accumulation through the tools of foreign policy. Simply put, foreign policy and foreign trade policy have been replaced by family business, and the multiple-phase transformation of the institutional system of foreign policy has also been carried out in view of this objective.[34] Before, foreign policy had been led by the ministry for foreign affairs, mainly staffed with career diplomats, while foreign trade policy had been overseen by the ministry for economy. The appointment in 2012 of former Fidesz spokesperson and later head of Orbán's cabinet and press, international, and organizational staff, Péter Szijjártó, as secretary of state for foreign affairs and ministerial coordinator of Hungary's foreign trade with the East was a sign of impending changes in the tasks of foreign policy.

As the chief patron's direct delegate, Szijjártó was tasked with visiting a host of autocratic regimes, from Saudi Arabia to Azerbaijan, from Moscow to Beijing. If we look at the business aspect of the forming relationships, the other members of the Visegrád Group have clearly managed to achieve more dynamic trade growth with Eastern countries. What is growing in Hungary is the proportion of foreign trade deals linked to the adopted political family. Unlike the EU, Eastern autocracies do not grant transfers to the Orbán regime—what they grant are corruption opportunities. They appear as an alternative source of wealth on Orbán's radar because they are willing to make trade deals where there is no requirement or opportunity of control. While EU funds are given for specific purposes, and their misuse may bring consequences for the respective country, contracts concluded with Eastern autocrats are devoid of requirements pertaining to high corruption risk, overpricing, or any other issues related to transparency and the rule of law. Whether the money involved is either loaned to Hungary or is spent directly from the Hungarian budget, the freedom afforded to the subsequent business structures allows for the large-scale, more efficient expropriation of Hungarian taxpayers' money.

Four key deals between Orbán's Hungary and Putin's Russia may be mentioned in this regard:

1. After a confidential meeting with Putin in 2013, Orbán committed himself to the expansion of the Paks nuclear power plant, to be funded for the most part by a EUR 10 billion Russian loan. The deal was announced unexpectedly as the details had been worked out in secret, whereas the documents of the transaction were classified for 30 years. According to estimates, the construction costs, defined in contracts that were granted with no public tendering and with the proceeds thus going straight into the pockets of the adopted political family, account for approximately 40% of the total budget.[35]

2. The public Hungarian electricity company Magyar Villamos Művek (MVM) concluded a host of new contracts with energy trader MET Holding AG, partly owned by offshore companies. The model of a centrally operated cash pump—with the participation of parliament, the government, a mammoth public company, and an offshore private company—resulted in dividends of around HUF 50 billion (ca. EUR 160 million). While this model did not officially involve the Russian state, a Russian private actor was among the owners of the offshore company, and the deal was not opposed by Gazprom even though it clearly violated their interests. Experts and background sources also confirm Russian involvement in the case.[36]

3. The Hungarian government prioritized Russian interests over Hungarian interests when it decided to finance a Russian company instead of the Hungarian winner of an Egyptian tender for the purchase of 1,300 railway carriages worth many hundreds of billions of forints.[37]

4. Putin found an eager partner in the Orbán government in his project to bring one of the former Soviet Bloc's institutions, the International Investment Bank (IIB), back to life. Suspected of espionage, the bank relocated its

headquarters from Moscow to Budapest while receiving many privileges from the Hungarian government. The bank plays the role of an alternative source of money for the mafia state, which can be given loans and support for projects which the EU would not finance.[38]

Hungary, however, has little in the way of solvent goods other than disloyalty towards the EU and NATO, in addition to the petty adopted political family dealings. The Orbán regime routinely channels subversive Russian propaganda and helps erode European trust in the EU, NATO, and liberal democracy in general[39] while also providing a home for Russian secret service activity.[40] Hungary's critique of Western sanctions during the annexation of Crimea, describing them as an ineffective measure not conducive to a solution, was a show of loyalty towards Putin and a gesture aimed to bolster legitimization, as was the lifting of Putin's diplomatic quarantine and his warm welcome in Budapest in February 2015.

The geopolitical relationship between the Hungarian and Russian patronal autocracies can be interpreted in the terms of world-systems theory, although with a spin on its usual categories. In the world-systems theory, the "core" refers to the countries where the benefits of the global division of labor concentrate, and the "periphery," where the costs are to be found.[41] While this theory was developed to analyze formal and legal economic actors (particularly the US and its relations to other countries), we can move the focus to informal and illegal economic actors and their systemic interrelations, insofar as they constitute a so-called criminal ecosystem.[42] Thus, we may say that Russia is the core of a criminal ecosystem, whereas Hungary has become its "semi-periphery" where the core state's illegal deals are made with the main holders of political power, i.e., with the local chief patron who receives benefits but who also enters into a patron-client relationship with the core state's chief patron. The deals described above, while they serve the goals of Orbán's mafia state, also tie it into Putin's criminal ecosystem in a semi-peripheral vassal position.

In short, the program of the Eastern Opening in Hungarian foreign policy aims to secure socially unchecked, freely expendable resources for the adopted political family through its connections to Putin and other autocrats. Three aspects need to be understood here:

1. this is not classical commerce, for the chief merchandise is Hungary's disloyalty to the EU, for which the adopted political family gains financial favors;
2. it is not the countries and nations but the autocrats between whom the Eastern Opening serves to create an intimate, family atmosphere;
3. the Orbán–Putin relationship is not a partnership of "two criminal equals" but one of subordination.

Orbán gains access to corrupt deals with Russia, but the reverse does not occur: Putin does not expect corrupt monies from Hungary but rather growing imperial influence. Although a mutually beneficial exchange, the fact that illegal material benefits are received by Orbán and not Putin creates a dependency relation which Orbán cannot renounce. On the formal side, the Hungarian government becomes a useful tool for Moscow's offensive energy diplomacy designed to gain influence; not only does it do nothing for reducing Hungary's Eastern energy dependency, it even exacerbates it. On the informal side, Orbán's adopted political family becomes entangled in Putin's informal patronal network from which there is no free exit.

3. The mafia state and the war: Western linkage and Russian leverage

3.1. The crisis in the bridge role between West and East

With the full-scale Russian invasion of Ukraine, Orbán had to face the fact that the bridge role which had ensured wealth accumulation with impunity for his regime practically disappeared. On the one hand, the antipathy and sense of danger generated by the invasion on the part of Western countries removed the geopolitical reality of tolerating semi-autocratic regimes in the buffer zone. There is no room for intermediaries in war, especially not for actors within the EU serving Russian interests. On the other hand, Orbán, who had previously found allies in Western populist circles for all his populist campaigns, was confronted with a previously unimaginable Western unity against Russia in the face of the Russian invasion. The moral discrediting of the Putin regime is such that the Western populist parties that were previously (openly or indirectly) pro-Russian could no longer be supporters of Orbán's two-track policy.

Domestic politics were also shaken by the unexpected invasion which started on February 24, only 38 days before the 2022 Hungarian national elections (April 3). The event seemingly caught the Hungarian government by surprise, both in terms of communication and in action. Within a short period of time, huge numbers of refugees began to flow into the country from Ukraine. In a week, around 128 thousand refugees had come through the Hungarian-Ukrainian border; a week later, a flow of refugees arriving at the same pace appeared at the Hungarian-Romanian border as well. The daily average of refugees coming in between February 24 and May 8 was 13,655.[43] Although most of the refugees did not want to stay in Hungary, the Hungarian social services were not prepared to manage such a flow, especially because of the neglect of the asylum system in line with the anti-migrant rhetoric of previous years. The task was taken up by the spontaneous action of civil society, NGOs, and private individuals. Notably, this was in contrast to the previous rhetoric of the Orbán regime which attacked NGOs, in particular ones like Migration Aid that assisted refugees.

The number of Hungarians providing aid and shelter and volunteering in helping the Ukrainian refugees indicated that a mass of sympathy had been generated towards the refugees. Earlier, Orbán's fear campaigns against migration had stigmatized "illegal migrants" from the Middle East with different cultural, ethnic, and religious backgrounds. In that case, already existing resentments were effectively increased from a moderate or average level to an extreme via a government campaign.[44] Now, however, some of the refugees were Transcarpathian Hungarians coming from the close vicinity of the border, but even apart from them most of the Ukrainian refugees were white, Christian women and children. Rather than fear-generating potential, which is the normal criterion for selecting a group for stigmatization in ideology-applying campaigns, Ukrainian refugees had sympathy-generating potential. This potential was evident in the case of Ukraine as a country as well, owing to the obviousness of the Russian aggression and the visualization and media presentation of the attack and subsequent war crimes. The fact that a week after the beginning of the invasion 64 percent of Fidesz voters did not find the offensive justified created a previously unseen division in the Fidesz camp.[45]

Orbán, however, was caught in a dependency relationship with Putin's Russia. With the outbreak of the war, he found himself in a situation where the victim was supported by his previously attacked ally, the EU (and with it, the US), while he himself was tied to the aggressor, Russia, in a patron-client relationship. He did not want to give up on the bridge role he had been building nor did he want to sever his ties to Russia and clearly devote himself to the West, which threatened to cut off his regime's funding or cease its impunity. Thus, Orbán had to completely reverse the people's emerging sympathy towards Ukraine; he had to formally support Western sanctions while maintaining his existing corrupt relations with Russia; and he had to use his veto powers to blackmail the EU to secure funding, minimize control and, in several cases, act in the interests of Russia.

3.2. Orbán's anti-Ukraine campaign: generating fear, reversing solidarity, and encouraging selfishness

While the Ukrainian refugees lacked fear-generating potential, Orbán was still able to build his electoral campaign on the high fear-generating potential of the war itself. On this basis, he redrew the fault lines in domestic politics between those serving and those betraying the national interest. Already in February, he stressed that Hungary "must be left out of this conflict" and therefore he "rejected proposals from the Left urging the government to send troops and weapons to Ukraine."[46] The message was repeated on all government channels: the security of the Hungarian people was the top priority for Fidesz, while the opposition position in favor of Ukraine would put the Hungarian people in danger.

The amorphous fear of war became a group fear projected onto the opposition. The opposition was used in Orbán's messaging in order to anthropomorphize the fear of war, and in doing so the government succeeded in transforming the position of not going to war into a group conflict between the "peace-seeking" and the "warmongering" parties. Setting the context was greatly facilitated by an early statement by Péter Márki-Zay, the opposition's joint candidate for prime minister, who said that if the Euro-Atlantic alliance (referring to Hungary's membership in NATO) decided to do so, Hungary could even send weapons and soldiers to Ukraine. Presenting Márki-Zay's conditional statement as a straight-on assertion, this interview fragment was used during the campaign as a basis for claiming the opposition would take Hungary into war.

The second element of the campaign after re-drawing the fault lines and generating fear according to the abovementioned parameters was to curb the solidarity-generating potential of the Ukrainian side. It was not possible to launch a direct stigmatization campaign against the influx of refugees, and they were regularly referred to as *refugees* rather than *migrants* in the government's communications, as opposed to those arriving from the Middle East in 2015–2016. However, the regime did try to reduce the visibility of the refugees. In opposition to the spontaneous civil unity that emerged, the representatives of the government quickly declared it a state responsibility to care for the refugees, who were transported by bus to the BOK Sports Hall in Budapest. In many cases, their care was not resolved there,[47] and NGOs and journalists who had previously reported on the refugee influx with empathy in the media were excluded from the hall. The sports hall was cordoned off and access to it was at the discretion of the police.[48]

To delegitimize solidarity with the Ukrainian state, Orbán portrayed the Russian invasion as a Slavic internal affair, which Hungary had nothing to do with. As he clearly stated in an interview:

> We've never been involved in the debate about how many states the great Slavic sea to the east of us actually consists of, how many nations it comprises. We've never been involved in the debate about what kind of military-security agreement they conclude with one another: whether Russia gives Ukraine a security guarantee, whether Ukraine gives Russia a security guarantee, whether or not Ukraine can join NATO. That's not a debate for us, it's not a debate that we needed to be involved in or will need to be involved in: it's a debate between two other countries.[49]

Note that Orbán uses Russian narrative elements about the country's security needs and the problem of Ukraine joining NATO. Later, in his programmatic speech in Băile Tușnad, Orbán described this in more detail and repeated the Russian position, practically word for word, about the real cause of the war being the West "rejecting the offer" of stopping NATO's expansion. He also maintained that the way the West interprets the situation is completely wrong because Ukraine will not win the war with Western weapons and trainers because of the superiority of the Russian army; sanctions will not sway Moscow while they hit Europe harder; and "most of the world is demonstrably not on [Ukraine's] side" including China, India, Brazil, South Africa, the Arab world, and Africa.[50]

The media of the Orbán regime also sought to stir up direct resentment by highlighting grievances against Hungarians in Ukraine, particularly in relation to the controversial Ukrainian language law introduced in previous years. The message of "it's none of our business" and "Ukraine deserved its fate" was then further reinforced by the pro-government media which continued to broadcast Kremlin propaganda during the campaign period.[51] Indeed, the percentage of terms used to describe Russian aggression that were in line with Russian propaganda (e.g. "military operation," "liberation") or were obfuscatory (e.g., "conflict," "situation," "crisis") could be found significantly more often in the largest Hungarian news portals than in Western media like the BBC.[52]

In pro-government circles, conspiracy theories such as that Ukrainian President Volodymyr Zelensky was an American agent and that Russia was merely defending itself by launching the attack became commonplace. Orbán himself called Zelensky an adversary in his victory speech after the elections.[53] The regime has sought to relativize events such as the Bucha massacre, which attracted a great deal of media attention and clearly indicated war crimes committed by Russia. Orbán refused to explicitly condemn Russia over the Bucha massacre, saying that an investigation should come first since "we live in a time of mass manipulation"—a statement which was criticized by Kaczyński as well.[54]

The final element of the campaign, which endured even after the electoral period, was an appeal to collective egoism. This concept refers to an element of populism which morally absolves the voters from the burdens of solidarity In presenting populist voters ("us") as the victims, they can become indifferent towards the fate of everyone else ("the others") and indulge themselves in openly asserted egoism in the name of the collective, i.e., the national interest.[55]

In Orbán's campaign, the first message along these lines appeared already in February, when he said that Hungarians "should not pay the price of war."[56] This message was mainly tied to matters of energy in general and possible sanctions on gas imports in particular. In Hungary, Russian gas accounts for 36% of primary energy use, far exceeding the exposure of other EU countries, and this is further exacerbated by the country's own gas storage which is the second lowest after Bulgaria.[57] On the basis of this dependence, which he has not reduced but increased in recent years, Orbán made it a key element of his campaign that a positive relationship with the Russian government was fundamental to maintaining the utility price cuts—a propagandistic policy that had been introduced several years before. Hence, the material self-interest of the Hungarians was declared more important than any sacrifice in the name of solidarity. Fidesz voters were absolved from showing solidarity with the victims, the Ukrainian people. After all, *we* have been the victims since the Treaty of Trianon: everyone owes us, we do not owe anyone—the self-pity of the average Hungarian goes, whose individual selfishness was legitimized by the campaign in a single collective "national" selfishness.[58] Solidarity with the Ukrainian nation, already weakened by the elements mentioned above, has been set against the national interest, taking the burden of solidarity off the shoulders of the electorate and legitimizing and even encouraging the latter to embrace open selfishness instead.

Collective egoism was most palpable after the elections in Orbán's anti-sanctions campaign. The main message here was that sanctions do not work but they do hurt us, causing the country severe economic problems such as record-high inflation. Orbán repeated several times that the war was to be blamed for all economic hardships, and that without the sanctions energy prices would stop rising and inflation would be halved immediately.[59] This message with the wording "sanction inflation" and "war inflation" was spread in social media ads and by the state and patronal media as well. Most notably, the government began a nation-wide mobilization campaign called a "national consultation," which involved billboards visually depicting an actual falling bomb with the inscription "sanctions" on it. Next to the bomb, the message read: "the sanctions of Brussels are ruining us."[60]

The campaign against sanctions linked collective egoism to Orbán's geopolitical regime strategy. It stigmatized and de-legitimized the EU and the West in the eyes of the people, while simultaneously attacking, on the communications front, the sanctions that had been implemented against Putin's Russia.

Propaganda has succeeded in reshaping public opinion. A poll conducted between February 28 and March 3 found that 72 percent of the population considered Russia's attack unjustified, including two-thirds of Fidesz voters.[61] By the end of the month, 43 percent of Fidesz voters opined that Russia's aggression was justified, while only 37 percent of them condemned the invasion.[62] In May, Fidesz voters gave Putin an average score of 47 out of 100 based on their preference (against a score of 22 among the opposition and 37 among non-partisan voters), while 55 percent of them held that if Hungary had to choose, it should choose closer relations with Russia than with other geopolitical players (24 percent responded with the US for this question). The latter figure was 65 percent among young Fidesz voters between the age of 18 and 39.[63] Finally, a representative poll conducted in October found that among Fidesz voters:

- the majority blamed the US for the war, followed by Ukraine in second place, and Russia only in third;
- 90% maintained that the sanctions were hitting EU citizens harder than Russia, with only 3% saying the opposite;
- 71% fully agreed and another 9% agreed with the statement that Hungary should remain neutral and Ukraine should not be supported "in any way";
- 70% fully agreed and another 11% agreed that Ukraine will "inevitably" lose, and peace should be concluded even if it means that Ukraine loses some of its territory to Russia.[64]

Such opinions reach beyond the Fidesz camp. Already in April, a global poll found that 90% of the Hungarian people believed that their country should not get militarily involved in the war (the global average was 72%) and only 53% agreed that Hungary must support sovereign countries when they are attacked (the global average was 70%).[65] By May, the proportion of those who saw Russia as an aggressor had fallen from 64% to 56%, and 25% believed that the invasion was a defensive move on Russia's part. Some 72% of the respondents answered no to the question "Would you support sanctions against Russia that would cost you more for your energy," with a 94% negative reply from Fidesz voters.[66]

3.3. Regime strategy in the war: instead of "Huxit," subversion as a client autocrat in the West

Orbán's regime strategy is always dressed in the most suitable ideological garb. Three key speeches should be mentioned here, which do not reveal the patronalism or the twin motives of the mafia state but legitimize major milestones in its development.

1. In 2009, Orbán spoke in Kötcse about the "realistic possibility that the next 15–20 years of Hungarian politics will not be determined by a dual power structure." Instead, "a large governing party, a central field of political force […] will be able to articulate national issues—not in a constant debate, but by representing them by its own nature."[67] This was the speech of *autocratic breakthrough*, pointing to the strategy of establishing a single-pyramid patronal network by doing away with the competitive world of patronal democracy.
2. In 2014, Orbán explained in Băile Tuşnad that "the new state that we are constructing in Hungary is an illiberal state, a non-liberal state," and that the "stars of the international analysts today" are the "not Western, not liberal" regimes that have made their nations successful like "Singapore, China, India, Russia and Turkey."[68] This was the speech of *autocratic consolidation* which, after reporting the success of creating a new regime, proclaimed it to be the new normal and envisaged its further expansion and stabilization.

3. In 2022, Orbán presented the speech of *the geopolitics of a client autocrat*. In a private event, Orbán (according to the edited version of his speech published by his political director) argued that the Russian invasion and its aftermath had brought back "the bloc-based international order of the Cold War era," from which Hungary "must stay out" or it will become a periphery of the West. Speaking of the war and the sanctions as two equal wrongs that "make the trade routes between East and West impassable," Orbán argued that Hungary must keep and increase its number of interstate connections instead of severing them: "no to decoupling, yes to connectivity."[69]

The last speech mentioned above reflects the ambition to maintain Hungary's bridge role, despite its apparent crisis. Besides representing the ideal geopolitical equilibrium which Orbán has been working for, preservation of the bridge role is also logical for the mafia state as well because it means avoiding a clear and unquestionable integration into the West, which could entail stronger control through the rule of law, an increased need to conform at the regime level, and less leverage to mobilize resources for the regime's mafia interests. On the Eastern side, being "connected" is a necessity: first, there is no free exit from the patronal relationship with Putin, and second, the bridge role helps Orbán keep his options open in case he needs an escape route to preserve his autocratic rule. Unlike the leaders ousted in color revolutions who fled to Putin,[70] or Vladimir Plahotniuc who left Moldova with his patron's court in a private jet,[71] Orbán—who is more threatened by international than domestic political processes—would prefer "fleeing" with his country. Leaving the Western bloc for the East might not seem reasonable as a country strategy, but the situation could become such that, as a regime strategy, i.e., from the perspective of maintaining power concentration and wealth accumulation, it becomes the least bad scenario for the adopted political family.

However, "Huxit," or Hungary leaving the EU, seems unlikely in the middle run for three reasons. First, Orbán will remain in the EU as long as his two goals of wealth accumulation through EU funds and impunity are guaranteed. Since the full-scale invasion, the former has been questioned as the EU has started a rule of law procedure against Hungary and has frozen a substantial part of the funds until a series of (anti-corruption) measures are adopted.[72] The EU sanctions, however, are normative and do not target the perpetrator, i.e., the adopted political family directly,[73] and Orbán has been able to unfreeze some of the funds by blackmailing the EU with vetoes (see below). Second, the European single market and the "four freedoms"—the free movement of goods, capital, services, and people—generate economic benefits for the regime (e.g., through the presence of multinational companies and increased tax revenues) and they remain highly popular among the Hungarian population, although critical attitudes toward the EU have been stronger during anti-EU governmental campaigns.[74] Third, Huxit would not be beneficial from a Russian perspective either as Orbán would lose his most valuable currency, i.e., his influence and subversive capacity within the EU.

Instead of Huxit, the rational regime strategy for the Hungarian mafia state is to maintain Russian ties while trying not to damage Western ones too severely. This is reflected in the actions taken by Orbán since the start of the full-scale war. He condemned the Russian invasion, but has never once mentioned Putin by name or questioned his personal responsibility (he outright refused to call Putin a war criminal;[75] instead, he has named Joe Biden, George Soros, and long-time domestic opponent Ferenc Gyurcsány as the key warmongers);[76] he reluctantly voted in favor of every sanctions package but has constantly sought to soften them, trying to remove Russian oligarchs from sanctions lists (see below) and negotiating an exemption for Hungary from the oil embargo and the price cap on Russian oil. (Due to the strong anti-sanctions propaganda, half of Fidesz voters think that Orbán did not vote for the sanctions at all.)[77]

Instead of decreasing its dependency on Russia in the field of energy as other Western countries have done, Hungary remains committed to the Paks II Nuclear Plant contract, as well as to the 15-year (non-public) contract with Gazprom which was concluded in 2021 and which was extended with an extra 700 million m^3 of natural gas in July 2022.[78] While the ideological cover for this was ensuring cheap and secure gas for the country, Orbán eventually bought gas for the highest price in Eastern Europe. While the average price of Russian import gas in November 2022 was 191 eurocents per m^3, Hungary received it for 237 eurocents.[79] It is legitimate to ask whether the exceptionally high Russian gas prices to Hungary are part of a bad political calculation or a corrupt deal.

At this point we should mention Minister of Foreign Affairs and Trade, Péter Szijjártó, who travelled to Moscow in October 2022 to meet Gazprom CEO Alexey Miller to secure the company's "long-term plans" with Hungary.[80] Szijjártó, who was awarded the Order of Friendship in Moscow in December 2021 by Lavrov, never returned the award and has continued negotiations with the Russian party during the course of the war. Besides travelling to Russia a number of times to meet Lavrov, Szijjártó also met him in New York in September 2022, despite the EU's explicit request not to,[81] and he participated in an international forum on nuclear energy in Moscow (as the only Western participant) in November.[82] In February 2023, he visited Minsk where he was greeted by his Belarusian counterpart, Sergei Aleinik. He repeated the government's panels of "keeping the channels of communication open" and that "Hungarians are in favor of peace," and criticized Western actors who speak "the rhetoric of war" and supply weapons to Ukraine, risking the prolonging or escalation of the war.[83] Aleinik was invited to Budapest in April, where he welcomed the fact that Hungary, like Belarus, was also in favor of peace; Szijjártó, standing next to him, stressed the importance of economic relations between the two countries.[84] In July, Hungary hosted Russian Health Minister Mikhail Murashko, becoming the first Russian cabinet minister to visit an EU country since the start of the war.[85]

While almost every EU member state has expelled Russian spies operating under diplomatic cover, no Russian diplomat has been expelled from Hungary since the start of the invasion. Instead, Budapest remains a spy hub for the Russian secret service.[86] In 2021, 46 accredited diplomats worked at the Russian embassy in Budapest; in 2022, their number was 56 (four times the number in Warsaw and six times the number in Prague). While Bulgaria, the Czech Republic, Romania, and Slovakia terminated their membership in the International Investments Bank (IIB) already in March 2022, Hungary decided to remain in the espionage-suspected bank.[87] It was not until the US sanctioned the Hungarian vice president of the bank that Hungary quit IIB in April 2023.[88]

Besides not cutting ties with Russia, Orbán continues to serve Russian interests as a client autocrat in the EU. On the military front, Hungary—unlike the Western countries and the other Visegrád members—has systematically refused to provide any kind of support to the Ukrainian armed forces, withholding not only weapons (both lethal and non-lethal) but protective helmets or bulletproof vests as well.[89] At the same time, Orbán claimed that Ukraine has become so dependent on Western support that it is no longer a sovereign country, and the US could make ceasefire and peace talks happen "tomorrow morning," which would be the best course of action.[90] On the sanctions front, a strong symbolic gesture to Russia was the EU's removal of Patriarch Kirill from the sanctions blacklist after Hungary's objection. Referring to "the sanctity of religious freedom," the Hungarian mafia state protected the Patriarch—a strong supporter of Putin and the invasion, and a billionaire oligarch himself—from having his assets frozen and his visa banned.[91] In June 2023, Patriarch Kirill awarded the First Degree of the Order of Glory and Honor to Orbán for his "persistent efforts" to foster Hungary's development, maintain independent foreign policy, and protect Christian values.[92]

According to anonymous diplomatic sources, Hungary also tried to have several Russian oligarchs removed from the sanctions list three times, in September 2022, and in January and February 2023.[93] The latter attempt was confirmed by Szijjártó in an interview with the Russian state news agency *Ria Novosti*, where he said that Hungary worked for lifting sanctions against nine people who were "responsible members of the business community" and who had made "very important investments" in Central Asia.[94] Although these attempts have been unsuccessful so far, they suggest either an "irrefusable offer" from the Russian chief patron or corrupt relations between the Hungarian regime and the Russian oligarchs in question.

Matters went beyond symbolic gestures when Orbán vetoed the EU's joint loan for Ukraine in December 2022, arguing that Hungary would prefer bilateral agreements instead.[95] Eventually, this veto was dropped when the rest of the EU members agreed to a joint loan excluding Hungary. Still, the argument for bilateral agreements underlines a characteristic feature of Orbán's regime strategy. Indeed, Hungary opted to stay out of not just the joint loan and the above-mentioned oil embargo but also out of the joint gas procurement scheme with the other EU states as well. While the common leverage of the EU members is considerably greater than Hungary's alone, and therefore a joint procurement should result in lower prices (which were promised to the people in the propaganda), such country-strategic considerations are secondary to regime-strategic ones. What the regime considers is that bilateral agreements are much easier to corrupt since, on the one hand, it is much simpler to have the private interests of the adopted political family taken into consideration in the deal, and, on the other, a bilateral deal is more suitable for setting conditions, i.e., for blackmail. The non-transparency of bilateral contracts makes them a preferred method for a mafia state, as has been evident in Hungary's deals with Russia and other Eastern autocracies (like Azerbaijan) and dictatorships (like China).[96]

The fundamental pattern of the Orbán regime's veto policy reveals both the representation of the Russian patron's interests in the European space and the tactics of using veto powers as a means of blackmail to increase the regime's bargaining position in (otherwise unrelated) issues. In relation to the EU, the blocking of the NATO accession of Finland and Sweden should be mentioned. While the two countries applied for membership as a response to the Russian threat in May 2022, Fidesz MPs repeatedly voted against having the issue on the Parliament's agenda, where it was finally discussed in March 2023—only to have the decision postponed, at least until a Hungarian delegation could have "clarifying discussions" with the representatives of the Finnish and Swedish governments about their previous "blatant lies" about democracy and the rule of law in Hungary.[97] Eventually, the Parliament ratified Finland's NATO membership on March 27,[98] but Orbán made support for Swedish membership conditional on support from Turkey.[99] The stalling and the new excuses we have seen from the government over the past year on the issue are both a gesture towards the Russian and Turkish autocratic regimes and a clear indication of the Orbán regime's intent to use the issue for blackmail and political agitation against the West.[100]

The more the war forces the EU to deal with the Hungary problem, and the stronger the measures it implements to curb the mafia state's interests, the more motivated Orbán will be in securing his position either on the EU's periphery or outside the EU. The EU, however, can only limit and isolate Hungary as it has neither the means nor the power (nor the will, for that matter) to intervene in the regime's internal functioning or to expel the country from its ranks. Meanwhile, both Orbán and his patron, Putin, have a vested interest in keeping Hungary in the EU. It seems that with the latest budget, the Hungarian government is settling in for a longer-term drying up of EU funding, a price it is willing to pay to ensure its unaccountability (to protect its autocratic functioning) and impunity (to protect its patronal functioning). This could result in a legal stalemate whereby the Orbán regime is "in the EU as if it were out." Ironically, we might say that Hungary is on the way to become to the EU what Transnistria is to Moldova: a sub-sovereign mafia state and transmission belt of Russian (and probably Chinese) interests, which cannot be operatively influenced by the "mother country" but remains within the latter's borders for the foreseeable future.

4. Conclusion: Hungary in the trap of regime strategy

On August 20, 2023, the national day of the founding of the Hungarian state, Orbán welcomed the following line of guests in his office: Recep Tayyip Erdoğan, President of Turkey; Ilham Aliyev, President of Azerbaijan; Shavkat Mirziyoyev, President of Uzbekistan; Tamim bin Hamad al-Sani, Emir of Qatar; Sadyr Japarov, President of Kyrgyzstan; Aleksandar Vučić, President of Serbia; Serdar Berdimuhamedow, President of Turkmenistan; Milorad Dodik, President of the Republic of Srpska (the Serbian-majority entity of Bosnia-Herzegovina); Andrej Babiš, former Prime Minister of the Czech Republic; Sebastian Kurz, former Austrian Chancellor; and Rustam Minnikhanov, Head of Tatarstan (a member state of the Russian Federation).[101] These people, whom Orbán referred to as his "friends," provide symbolic illustration to the geopolitical position in which the Hungarian chief patron has placed himself and his country. The majority of patronal autocrats from the East—including the aggressor, Russia—is as telling as the absence of leading politicians from the West (except for Kurz, who has resigned and now is under indictment, and Babiš, who attempted patronal transformation in the Czech Republic but failed). Orbán's turn to the East and his isolation in the Western alliance system were exacerbated during the Russia-Ukraine war, but had already begun earlier, after his autocratic breakthrough in 2010.

The pre- and post-invasion phases of Orbán's geopolitics may be described as initiative and reactive, respectively. In the initiative phase, Orbán set the goals for how he wanted to rearrange geopolitical relations, and defined his populist narrative accordingly. Being the chief patron of a mafia state, Orbán's main goals—wealth accumulation and ensuring impunity—could be achieved by loosening relations with the EU and developing relations with Eastern autocracies, particularly Putin's Russia. By stigmatizing and de-legitimizing the EU while legitimizing and de-stigmatizing Russia, Orbán was able to navigate Hungary through corrupt business deals and increasing energy dependence into a semi-peripheral position in the Russian criminal ecosystem.

In the second, reactive phase it was no longer the intentions but the constraints within which they had to be realized that played the lead role. Following the Russian invasion of Ukraine, the situation was no longer about developing a system of relations between the Orbán regime and Putin's Russia, it concerned the reaction to a sudden geopolitical event within the confines of the pre-existing geopolitical system. After more than a decade of strengthening Russian dependencies, Orbán now found himself in a situation where he was financially tied to an aggressor state. Therefore, he was forced to effect a remarkable turn—change the anti-Russian and pro-Ukraine sentiments of the Hungarian people, and go against the Western world (including his own previous allies) in a carefully developed, anti-Ukrainian and pro-Russian populist narrative. This was accompanied by actions on the international scene in the web of Western linkage and Russian leverage, with Orbán operating in the EU according to his self-declared role of being "the sand in the gears of the machinery, the stick caught in the spokes, the thorn in the flesh."[102]

The pre- and post-invasion phases can also be traced in terms of Orbán's position within the EU. In the initiative phase, Orbán tried to extend his patronal influence in Central Europe. This includes not only the redefinition of V4 and patronalizing Hungarian minorities in Romania and Serbia, but also—with consequences for the EU—the attempt to create a blackmailing alliance with the autocratic leaders of the region. This "autocrat international" included mainly patronal actors (Janez Janša in Slovenia, Aleksandar Vučić in Serbia, Robert Fico in Slovakia, Andrej Babiš in the Czech Republic) as well as the conservative Kaczyński in Poland. This experiment was already looking precarious after the 2019 European elections,[103] but its real downfall came with the full-scale invasion after February 2022. The Polish-Ukrainian reconciliation, the significance of which is comparable to the Franco-German reconciliation that led to the founding of the EU, points towards the creation of a new Eastern European power center involving the Baltic countries and Romania as well. Hungary is left out of this alliance, the existence of which diametrically opposes not simply Orbán's leaning towards Russia but his dependence on the Putin regime. By 2023, the only one left of Orbán's "autocrat international" is Vučić, who is also balancing between Putin and the West, and whom Orbán has since sought to assure of his support.[104]

Rather than competing country strategies, we should see that, while the liberal democratic member states of the EU do follow policy-specific country (or regional) strategies, Hungary is more like Russia: it follows regime and empire-specific strategies. (There is even a similarity in rhetoric: while Putin talks about imperial interests, Orbán in his third programmatic speech envisioned Hungary's "middle power status.") This reflects two opposite kinds of rationality: one is grounded in civic legitimacy, in which the rationality of a policy or strategy is judged by society through structured processes of public deliberation; the other considers an action rational or irrational from the point of view of regime survival, while the consequences for the country become irrelevant. This is why a regime can "successfully" survive in the face of the country's objectively deteriorating political, social, and mental position. While the EU and Ukraine are fighting a battle for freedom, Hungary's regime strategy results in an increasingly vulnerable, dependent position to a larger, imperial patronal autocracy.

Notes

1. See our introductory chapter in the first volume. For details of the case of Hungary, see Bálint Magyar, *Post-Communist Mafia State: The Case of Hungary* (Budapest: CEU Press, 2016).
2. Bálint Magyar and Bálint Madlovics, "Hungary 2022: Election Manipulation and the Regime's Attempts at Electoral Fraud," CEU Democracy Institute, March 31, 2022, https://democracyinstitute.ceu.edu/articles/balint-magyar-and-balint-madlovics-election-manipulation-and-electoral-fraud-hungary.
3. Steven Levitsky and Lucan Way, *Competitive Authoritarianism: Hybrid Regimes after the Cold War* (Cambridge University Press, 2010).
4. András Bozóki and Dániel Hegedűs, "An Externally Constrained Hybrid Regime: Hungary in the European Union," *Democratization* 25, no. 7 (2018): 1173–89.
5. Venelin I. Ganev, "Post-Accession Hooliganism: Democratic Governance in Bulgaria and Romania after 2007," *East European Politics and Societies* 27, no. 1 (2013): 26–44.
6. Wojciech Sadurski, *Poland's Constitutional Breakdown* (Oxford: Oxford University Press, 2019).
7. Edit Zgut, "Informal Exercise of Power: Undermining Democracy under the EU's Radar in Hungary and Poland," *Hague Journal on the Rule of Law* 14 (2022): 287–308.
8. Piotr Kozarzewski and Maciej Bałtowski, "Return of State-Owned Enterprises in Poland," Paper presented at Seventh Annual Conference of the Leibniz Institute for East and Southeast European Studies, Regensburg, Germany, May 30, 2019, https://www.researchgate.net/publication/333480750_Return_of_State-owned_Enterprises_in_Poland.
9. D. Kovács Ildikó and Vitéz F. Ibolya, "Alig látszana gazdasági növekedés az uniós támogatások nélkül" [Economic growth would be almost invisible without EU transfers], *24.hu*, May 2, 2022, https://24.hu/fn/gazdasag/2022/05/02/eu-unios-tamogatas-gazdasagi-novekedes-gdp-petschnig-maria-zita/.
10. István János Tóth and Miklós Hajdu, "Cronyism in the Orbán Regime: An Empirical Analysis of Public Tenders, 2005–2021," in *Dynamics of an Authoritarian System: Hungary, 2010–2021*, by Mária Csanádi et al. (Budapest–Vienna–New York: CEU Press, 2022), 230–74.
11. Dávid Jancsics, "From Local Cliques to Mafia State: The Evolution of Network Corruption," in *Twenty-Five Sides of a Post-Communist Mafia State*, ed. Bálint Magyar and Júlia Vásárhelyi (Budapest–New York: CEU Press, 2017), 129–47.
12. Alexander Cooley, John Heathershaw, and J. C. Sharman, "Laundering Cash, Whitewashing Reputations," *Journal of Democracy* 29, no. 1 (2018): 39–53.
13. Magyar, *Post-Communist Mafia State*.
14. Attila Ara-Kovács, "Nemzeti Diplomácia Helyett Családi Üzlet: Az Orbán Kormány Külpolitikája" [Family business instead of national diplomacy: The Orbán administration's foreign policy], in *Magyar Polip 2 - A Posztkommunista Maffiaállam*, ed. Bálint Magyar and Júlia Vásárhelyi (Budapest: Noran Libro, 2014), 265.
15. Bálint Ablonczy, "General Narrative: The Struggle for Sovereignty," in *The Second Term of Viktor Orbán: Beyond Prejudice and Enthusiasm*, ed. John O'Sullivan and Kálmán Pócza (London: Social Affairs Unit, 2015), 53–66.
16. Viktor Orbán, "Nem Leszünk Gyarmat!" [We will not be a colony!], Website of the Hungarian Government, March 16, 2012, http://2010-2014.kormany.hu/hu/miniszterelnokseg/miniszterelnok/beszedek-publikaciok-interjuk/orban-viktor-miniszterelnok-unnepi-beszede-a-kossuth-lajos-teren.
17. Transparency International, "The European Public Prosecutor's Office and Hungary: Challenge or Missed Opportunity?" (2021), https://transparency.hu/wp-content/uploads/2021/02/europai_ugyeszseg_eng_VEGSO.pdf.
18. See Rui Tavares, "Draft Report on the Situation of Fundamental Rights: Standards and Practices in Hungary" (Committee on Civil Liberties, Justice and Home Affairs, 2013); Judith Sargentini,

"REPORT on a Proposal Calling on the Council to Determine, Pursuant to Article 7(1) of the Treaty on European Union, the Existence of a Clear Risk of a Serious Breach by Hungary of the Values on Which the Union Is Founded" (European Parliament: Committee on Civil Liberties, Justice and Home Affairs, July 4, 2018).

19 Quoted in G. Fodor Gábor, *Az Orbán-szabály: Tíz fejezet az Orbán-korszak első tíz évéről* [The Orbán-rule: Ten chapters on the first ten years of the Orbán era], Új idők (Budapest: Közép- és Kelet-európai Történelem és Társadalom Kutatásáért Közalapítvány, 2021), 154–55.

20 András Rácz, "Kétes politikai sikerek, totális gazdasági kudarcok: A keleti nyitás valós mérlege" [Doubtful political successes, total economic failures: The real balance of opening to the east]," *Válasz Online*, August 11, 2019, https://www.valaszonline.hu/2019/08/11/keleti-nyitas-racz-andras-elemzes/.

21 Zoltán Haszán, "Orbán úgy dicséri a világ sok pénzen ülő diktátorait, mint senki más" [Orbán praises the world's dictators with lots of money like no one else], *444*, April 9, 2015, https://444.hu/2015/04/09/orban-ugy-dicseri-a-vilag-sok-penzen-ulo-diktatorait-mint-senki-mas.

22 Katalin Erdélyi, "Orbán Viktor 11 alkalommal találkozott Putyinnal 2010 óta, legtöbbször Moszkvában [Orbán met Putin 11 times since 2010, most of the times in Moscow]," *atlatszo.hu* (blog), February 28, 2022, https://atlatszo.hu/kozugy/2022/02/28/orban-viktor-11-alkalommal-talalkozott-putyinnal-2010-ota-legtobbszor-moszkvaban/.

23 Viktor Orbán, "Még gyümölcsözőbb kapcsolatot szeretnénk oroszországgal" [We want even more fruitful relations with Russia]," Website of the Hungarian Government, January 31, 2013, https://2010-2014.kormany.hu/hu/miniszterelnokseg/hirek/egyetertes-az-energetikai-egyuttmukodesben.

24 Bálint Madlovics, "It's Not Just Hate: Attitudes toward Migrants in a Dominated Sphere of Communication in Hungary," in *After the Fence: Approaches and Attitudes about Migration in Central Eastern Europe*, ed. Dániel Mikecz, 1st ed. (Budapest: European Liberal Forum - Republikon Intézet, 2017), 6–31.

25 András Hont and Krisztián Szabó, "Nem váltók – Népszavazás és választás [Reassignment of sex and votes: Referendum and the elections]," *Atlatszo.hu*, April 19, 2022, https://atlatszo.hu/adat/2022/04/19/nem-valtok-nepszavazas-es-valasztas/.

26 Anna Szilágyi and András Bozóki, "Playing It Again in Post-Communism: The Revolutionary Rhetoric of Viktor Orbán in Hungary," *Advances in the History of Rhetoric* 18, no. S1 (April 13, 2015): S153–66.

27 Viktor Orbán, "A nagyság dicsőségét hagyták örökül 1956 hősei [The legacy of the heroes of 1956 is the glory of greatness], Website of the Hungarian Government, October 23, 2013, http://2010-2014.kormany.hu/hu/miniszterelnokseg/miniszterelnok/beszedek-publikaciok-interjuk/a-nagysag-dicsoseget-hagytak-orokul-1956-hosei.

28 "The Impact of Russia's State-Run Propaganda Apparatus on Online Media in Hungary – 2010–2017,"Corruption Research Center Budapest, March 19, 2018,

29 Leonárd Máriás et al; "An Illiberal Model of Media Markets – Soft Censorship 2017," Mérték Booklets 15 (July 2018), http://mertek.eu/wp-content/uploads/2018/08/MertekFuzetek15.pdf; Leonárd Máriás et al., "Soft Censorship in Hungary 2016: When Propaganda Rules Public Discourse," Mérték Booklets 12 (May, 2017), https://mertek.eu/wp-content/uploads/2017/10/MertekFuzetek12.pdf.

30 Péter Krekó, "Oroszország a magyar közvéleményben" [Russia in Hungarian public ppinion], in *Társadalmi Riport 2019*, ed. István György Tóth (Budapest: TÁRKI, 2019), 382–96.

31 Ténygyár, "Putyin elnyerte a magyarok szívét [Putin has won the Hungarians' heart]," *24.hu*, July 25, 2018, https://24.hu/kulfold/2018/07/25/vlagyimir-putyin-donald-trump-angela-merkel-nepszeruseg/.

32 András Pethő and András Szabó, "Orbán's Game: The Inside Story of How Hungary Became Close to Putin," *Direkt36* (blog), March 12, 2018, https://www.direkt36.hu/en/orban-jatszmaja/.

33 Anastasia Kirilenko, "Чемодан От Солнцевских: У Путина Есть Видеокомпромат На Лидера Венгрии? [Suitcase from Solntsevo: Does Putin have a compromising video on the Hungarian leader?]," *The Insider*, February 2, 2017, https://theins.ru/korrupciya/43801.

34 Attila Ara-Kovács, "Diplomacy of the Orbán Regime," in *Twenty-Five Sides of a Post-Communist Mafia State*, ed. Bálint Magyar and Júlia Vásárhelyi (Budapest–New York: CEU Press, 2017), 611–35.

35 András Deák, "Captured by Power: The Expansion of the Paks Nuclear Power Plant," in *Twenty-Five Sides of a Post-Communist Mafia State*, ed. Bálint Magyar and Júlia Vásárhelyi (Budapest–New York: CEU Press, 2017), 323–44.

36 Pethő and Szabó, "Orbán's Game."

37 Szabolcs Panyi and András Szabó, "Spies, Business Deals and Criminals. How Orbán Favors Russian Interests Instead of Western Ones," *Direkt36* (blog), March 1, 2022, https://www.direkt36.hu/en/kemek-bizniszek-bunozok-amikor-orbanek-az-oroszoknak-kedveztek-a-nyugati-erdekek-helyett/.

38 András Szabó, "Buzgó szereplője lett az Orbán-kormány az oroszok pénzügyi terjeszkedésének [The Orbán government became an eager agent of Russian financial expansion]," *Direkt36* (blog), September 3, 2018, https://www.direkt36.hu/buzgo-szereploje-lett-az-orban-kormany-az-oroszok-penzugyi-terjeszkedesenek/.

39 Dalibor Rohac, Edit Zgut, and Lóránt Győri, "Populism in Europe and Its Russian Love Affair" (American Enterprise Institute, 2017), http://www.aei.org/wp-content/uploads/2017/01/Populism-in-Europe-and-Its-Russian-Love-Affair.pdf.

40 Ferenc Katrein, "Hungarian Secret Agent Reveals How Serious the Russian Threat Is," interview by Szabolcs Panyi, *Index.hu*, March 21, 2017, http://index.hu/english/2017/03/21/hungarian_secret_agent_reveals_how_serious_the_russian_threat_is/.

41 Immanuel Wallerstein, *World-Systems Analysis: An Introduction* (Durham: Duke University Press, 2004).

42 Bálint Magyar and Bálint Madlovics, "Criminal State and the Criminal Ecosystem: New Aspects for Empirical Corruption Research," *Zhurnal Zarubezhnogo Zakonodatel'stva i Sravnitel'nogo Pravovedeniya = Journal of Foreign Legislation and Comparative Law*, no. 5 (2019): 65–78.

43 Mizsur András and Barkó-Nagy Ferenc, "Alig maradnak itt az ukrajnai menekültek, alig kérnek segítséget az államtól, és azt is nehezen kapják meg [Ukrainian refugees hardly stay here, hardly ask for help from the state, and find it hard to get it]," *Telex*, May 9, 2022, sec. Belföld, https://telex.hu/belfold/2022/05/09/orosz-ukran-haboru-menekultek-menedekes-statusz-magyar-helsinki-bizottsag-budapest-migration-aid.

44 The level of xenophobia in Hungary increased from 41% to 53% in 2015-2016. In 2016, 82% of all Hungarians claimed that accepting refugees would have no positive effects at all. See Endre Sik, "The Socio-Demographic Basis of Xenophobia in Contemporary Hungary," in *The Social Aspects of the 2015 Migration Crisis in Hungary*, ed. Bori Simonovits and Anikó Bernát (Budapest: Tárki, 2016), 41–47, http://www.tarki.hu/hu/news/2016/kitekint/20160330_refugees.pdf.

45 Márton Sándor Németh, "Kiderült, mit gondolnak a magyar emberek az orosz–ukrán háborúról [What Hungarians think about the Russian-Ukrainian war is revealed]," *Index.hu*, March 7, 2022, https://index.hu/belfold/2022/03/07/kiderult-hogy-mit-gondolnak-a-magyarok-az-orosz-ukran-haborurol/.

46 Viktor Orbán, "Hungary Must Be Left out of This Conflict," Cabinet Office of the Prime Minister, February 23, 2022, https://miniszterelnok.hu/hungary-must-be-left-out-of-this-conflict/.

47 Mizsur and Barkó-Nagy, "Alig maradnak itt az ukrajnai menekültek, alig kérnek segítséget az államtól, és azt is nehezen kapják meg" [Ukrainian refugees hardly stay here, hardly ask for help from the state, and find it hard to get it].

48 Csenge Pelva, "Nem látják szívesen a sajtót a kormány újonnan kialakított menekültszállójában [The press is not welcome in the government's newly established refugee shelter]," *168.Hu*, March 22, 2022, https://168.hu/itthon/nem-latjak-szivesen-a-sajtot-a-kormany-ujonnan-kialakitott-menekultszallojaban-230132.

49   Viktor Orbán, "Interview with Prime Minister Viktor Orbán on the Hír Televízió programme Daily Update Extra," Cabinet Office of the Prime Minister, https://miniszterelnok.hu/interview-with-prime-minister-viktor-orban-on-the-hir-televizio-programme-daily-update-extra/.
50   Viktor Orbán, "Speech by Prime Minister Viktor Orbán at the 31st Bálványos Summer Free University and Student Camp," Cabinet Office of the Prime Minister, July 23, 2022, https://miniszterelnok.hu/speech-by-prime-minister-viktor-orban-at-the-31st-balvanyos-summer-free-university-and-student-camp/.
51   "Russian Disinformation in Hungarian Public Broadcast Media: Complaint to the European Commission," Political Capital, March 29, 2022, https://politicalcapital.hu/news.php?article_id=2982.
52   István János Tóth and Júlia Varga, "Tompítás, elkenés, elbizonytalanítás és manipuláció. Az ukrajnai orosz agresszióról hírt adó, a háború első 15 napjában megjelent cikkek tartalomelemzése négy magyar hírportál és a BBC cikkei alapján" [Mitigation, whitewashing, obfuscation and manipulation. Content analysis of articles on the Russian aggression in Ukraine during the first 15 days of the war, based on publications in four Hungarian news portals and the BBC], Corruption Research Center Budapest, December 13, 2022, https://www.crcb.eu/?p=3213.
53   "Hungary Election: PM Viktor Orban Criticises Ukraine's Zelensky as He Wins Vote," *BBC News*, April 4, 2022, sec. Europe, https://www.bbc.com/news/world-europe-60977917.
54   Victor Jack, "Poland's Kaczyński Slams Orbán for Refusing to Condemn Bucha Killings," *Politico*, April 8, 2022, https://www.politico.eu/article/poland-kaczynski-slams-hungary-orban-for-refusing-to-condemn-bucha-killings/.
55   Bálint Madlovics and Bálint Magyar, "Populism as a Challenge to Legal-Rational Legitimacy: The Cases of Orbán and Trump," *Social Research: An International Quarterly* 88, no. 4 (2021): 827–55.
56   Kristóf Ábel Tarnay, "Orbán Viktor: Aki azt mondja, hogy ebben a háborúban nincs kockázat magyarország számára, Az nem mond igazat" [Viktor Orbán: Whoever says that there is no risk for Hungary in this war is not telling the truth], *Hvg.Hu*, February 27, 2022, https://hvg.hu/itthon/20220227_Orban_interju.
57   Manfred Stamer and Katharina Utermöhl, "Who Should Be Afraid of a Stop in Russian Energy Supply?" Allianz Trade, May 11, 2022, https://www.allianz-trade.com/en_global/news-insights/economic-insights/europe-russia-gas-supply.html.
58   On the role of Trianon in Hungarian nationalism, see János Széky, "A Tradition of Nationalism: The Case of Hungary," *New Eastern Europe* 11, no. 2 (2014): 108–15.
59   "PM Orbán Calls for the End of EU Sanctions," About Hungary, September 23, 2022, https://abouthungary.hu//news-in-brief/pm-orban-calls-for-the-end-of-eu-sanctions.
60   Fruzsina Előd and Bálint Nagy, "EU sanctions depicted as actual bomb in Hungarian government's anti-sanctions propaganda," trans. Horváth Kávai Andrea, *Telex*, October 18, 2022, https://telex.hu/english/2022/10/18/eu-sanctions-depicted-as-actual-bomb-in-hungarian-governments-anti-sanctions-propaganda.
61   "Publicus: Tízből nyolc magyar szerint oroszország jogtalanul támadt ukrajnára [Publicus: Eight out of ten Hungarians say Russia has attacked Ukraine illegally]," *Hvg.hu*, March 7, 2022, https://hvg.hu/itthon/20220307_Publicus_kozvelemenykutatas_haboru_kulpolitika.
62   "Medián: A Fidesz győzelme szinte biztosra vehető, csak a mértéke lehet kétséges [Median: Fidesz's victory is almost certain, only its extent can be doubted]," *hvg.hu*, March 30, 2022, https://hvg.hu/360/20220330_Median_valasztas_2022_Fidesz_ellenzek_mandatumbecsles_kozvelemeny_kutatas.
63   Dániel Pál Rényi, "Ugyanolyan rossz véleménnyel vannak a magyarok Ukrajnáról, mint Oroszországról [Hungarians have as bad an opinion of Ukraine as of Russia]," *444*, May 9, 2022, https://444.hu/2022/05/09/ugyanolyan-rossz-velemennyel-vannak-a-magyarok-ukrajnarol-mint-oroszorszagrol.
64   "A Fidesz-szavazók fele szerint a kormány nem szavazta meg a szankciókat – kutatás az orosz-ukrán háborúval kapcsolatos attitűdökről" [Half of Fidesz voters say the government did not vote for

sanctions – research on attitudes towards the Russia-Ukraine war], *Political Capital*, November 16, 2022, https://politicalcapital.hu/hirek.php?article_id=3107.

65   "The World's Response to the War in Ukraine: A 27-Country Global Advisor Survey," Ipsos, April 2022, https://www.ipsos.com/sites/default/files/ct/news/documents/2022-04/Global%20Advisor%20-%20War%20in%20Ukraine%20-%20April%202022%20-%20Graphic%20Report.pdf.

66   Hat a propaganda, egyre kevesebben tartják agressziónak ukrajna lerohanását, a magyarok egynegyede szerint oroszország csak védekezik [Propaganda is effective, the invasion of Ukraine is considered less and less aggressive, a quarter of Hungarians say Russia is only defending itself]," *Népszava*, May 13, 2022, https://nepszava.hu/3156769_oroszorszag-haboru-ukrajna-felmeres-publicus-intezet-nepszava.

67   Viktor Orbán, "Megőrizni a létezés magyar minőségét [Preserving the Hungarian quality of existence]," *Nagyítás*, February 17, 2010, http://tdyweb.wbteam.com/Orban_Megorizni.htm.

68   Viktor Orbán, "A munkaalapú állam korszaka következik [The era of the work-based state is upon us]," Website of the Hungarian Government, https://2015-2019.kormany.hu/hu/a-miniszterelnok/beszedek-publikaciok-interjuk/a-munkaalapu-allam-korszaka-kovetkezik.

69   Balázs Orbán, "Nem a szétbontásra, igen az összekapcsolásra – ez Orbán stratégiája a következő évtizedre! [No to decoupling, yes to connectivity – this is Orbán's strategy for the next decade!]," *Mandiner*, January 4, 2023, https://mandiner.hu/cikk/20230104_nem_a_szetbontasra_igen_az_osszekapcsolasra_a_magyar_strategia.

70   Julia Gerlach, *Color Revolutions in Eurasia* (London: Springer, 2014).

71   Vladimir Solovyov, "Moldovan Regime Change Is Rare Example of Russian-Western Teamwork," *Carnegie Moscow Center* (blog), June 19, 2019, https://carnegie.ru/commentary/79333.

72   Lili Bayer, "Commission Proposes €7.5B Funding Cut for Hungary but Opens Compromise Path," *Politico*, September 18, 2022, https://www.politico.eu/article/commission-suggests-funding-cut-for-hungary-but-opens-compromise-path/.

73   Magyar, *Post-Communist Mafia State*, 283–90.

74   "Medián: Már Kétharmadnyian Mondják, Hogy Rossz Irányba Megy Az Ország" [Medián: Two thirds say the country is going in the wrong direction], *hvg.hu*, December 21, 2022, https://hvg.hu/360/20221221_Unnepromlas.

75   "One Cannot Negotiate Peace While Calling the Other Party a 'War Criminal', Says Viktor Orbán," Hungary Today, June 27, 2023, https://hungarytoday.hu/one-cannot-negotiate-peace-while-calling-the-other-party-a-war-criminal-says-viktor-orban/.

76   János Haász, "Orbán Lists His Opponents: A Harsh Outburst against the West at the Fidesz-KDNP Caucus Meeting," trans. Andrea Horváth Kávai, *Telex*, February 23, 2023, https://telex.hu/english/2023/02/23/orban-lists-his-opponents-a-harsh-outburst-against-the-west-at-the-fidesz-kdnp-caucus-meeting.

77   "A Fidesz-szavazók fele szerint a kormány nem szavazta meg a szankciókat – kutatás az orosz-ukrán háborúval kapcsolatos attitűdökről [Half of Fidesz voters say the government did not vote for sanctions – research on attitudes towards the Russia-Ukraine war]."

78   Katalin Erdélyi, "Titkolja a Gazprommal kötött szerződéseket a kormány, perelünk a nyilvánosságukért [Government hides contracts with Gazprom, we sue for their disclosure]," *atlatszo.hu*, October 7, 2022, https://atlatszo.hu/kozpenz/2022/10/07/titkolja-a-gazprommal-kotott-szerzodeseket-a-kormany-perelunk-a-nyilvanossagukert/.

79   Zoltán Jandó, "Más országoknál is sokkal drágábban kapja az orosz gázt Magyarország [Hungary gets Russian gas at a much higher price than other countries]," *g7.hu*, January 25, 2023, https://g7.hu/penz/20230125/mas-orszagoknal-is-sokkal-dragabban-kapja-az-orosz-gazt-magyarorszag/.

80   Zsolt Hanula, "Szijjártó from Moscow: I am happy to report that Gazprom has long-term plans with Hungary!," trans. Andrea Horváth Kávai, *Telex*, October 13, 2022, https://telex.hu/english/2022/10/13/szijjarto-from-moscow-i-am-happy-to-report-that-gazprom-has-long-term-plans-with-hungary.

81 Hanga Zsófia Aradi, "Szijjártó met with Lavrov despite the EU's explicit request not to," trans. Andrea Horváth Kávai, *Telex*, September 23, 2022, https://telex.hu/english/2022/09/23/szijjarto-met-with-lavrov-despite-the-eus-explicit-request.

82 "Hungary's Foreign Minister Travels to Russia for Energy Expo," *Radio Free Europe*, November 21, 2022, https://www.rferl.org/a/hungary-foreign-minister-szijjarto-russia-visit-nuclear/32141314.html.

83 Ferenc Szalma Baksi, "'Many will attack me for this' – Hungarian FM in Belarus," trans. Andrea Horváth Kávai, *Telex*, February 13, 2023, https://telex.hu/english/2023/02/13/many-will-attack-me-for-this-hungarian-fm-on-visiting-belarus.

84 Sándor Czinkóczi, "Szijjártó Péter fontosnak tartotta, hogy Budapestre hívja a fehérorosz külügyminisztert" [Péter Szijjártó thought it was important to invite the Belarusian Foreign Minister to Budapest], *444*, April 12, 2023, https://444.hu/2023/04/12/szijjarto-peter-fontosnak-tartotta-hogy-budapestre-hivja-a-feherorosz-kulugyminisztert.

85 Boldizsar Gyori, "Hungary Hosts Russian Cabinet Minister, Aims to 'Keep Channels Open,'" *Reuters*, July 5, 2023, https://www.reuters.com/world/europe/hungary-hosts-russian-cabinet-minister-aims-keep-channels-open-2023-07-05/.

86 Szabolcs Panyi, "Getting to the Bottom of Hungary's Russian Spying Problem," *Balkan Insight*, November 30, 2022, https://balkaninsight.com/2022/11/30/getting-to-the-bottom-of-hungarys-russian-spying-problem/.

87 "Hungary Left Isolated as All Other EU States Announce They Are Quitting IIB and IBEC," *bne Intellinews*, March 3, 2022, https://www.intellinews.com/hungary-left-isolated-as-all-other-eu-states-announce-they-are-quitting-iib-and-ibec-236820/.

88 Marton Dunai, "Hungary Quits Russian-Controlled Investment Bank in Orbán U-Turn," *Financial Times*, April 13, 2023, https://www.ft.com/content/21d2da37-ec3d-42dc-a398-84772820e27c.

89 Marianna Bíró, "Jégtörőből a semlegesség gleccsere: A kormány kommunikációja az orosz–ukrán háborúban [From icebreaker to the glacier of neutrality: Government communication in the Russo-Ukrainian war]," *Telex*, March 4, 2022, https://telex.hu/belfold/2022/03/04/orosz-ukran-haboru-magyar-kormanyzati-kommunikacio-orban-putyin.

90 Viktor Orbán, Prime Minister Viktor Orbán on the Kossuth Radio programme "Good Morning Hungary," Cabinet Office of the Prime Minister, July 14, 2023, https://miniszterelnok.hu/en/prime-minister-viktor-orban-on-the-kossuth-radio-programme-good-morning-hungary-2023-07-14/.

91 András Stumpf, "Orbán Viktor megint győzött: A KGB-s Kirill dollármilliárdjait is megvédte [Viktor Orbán wins again: He also defended the billions of dollars of the KGB's Kirill]," *Válasz Online*, June 2, 2022, https://www.valaszonline.hu/2022/06/02/kirill-patriarka-orban-viktor-brusszel-velemeny/.

92 Mercédesz Hetzmann, "PM Viktor Orbán Receives Russian Order of Glory and Honour," *Daily News Hungary*, June 2, 2023, https://dailynewshungary.com/pm-viktor-orban-receives-russian-order-of-glory-and-honour/.

93 Rikard Jozwiak, "Hungary Looks to Remove Nine People from EU Sanctions List Imposed in Wake of Russia Invasion of Ukraine," *Radio Free Europe*, January 17, 2023, https://www.rferl.org/a/hungary-eu-sanctions-list-russia-ukraine/32227730.html.

94 Péter Szíjjártó, "Венгрия добивается снятия санкций ЕС с девяти россиян из бизнес-кругов" [Hungary seeks lifting of EU sanctions on nine business Russians], interview by Alan Bulkaty, *RIA Novosti*, February 24, 2023, https://ria.ru/20230224/sanktsii-1854079016.html.

95 Márton Balázs, "Hungary Vetoes Joint Loan for Ukraine," trans. Andrea Horváth Kávai, *Telex*, December 6, 2022, https://telex.hu/english/2022/12/06/hungary-vetoes-joint-loan-for-ukraine.

96 "Hungary PM Orban's Ally to Co-Build Chinese Railway for $2.1 Billion," *Reuters*, June 12, 2019, sec. Emerging Markets, https://www.reuters.com/article/us-hungary-china-railways-opus-global-idUSKCN1TD1JG.

[97] Viktor Orbán, "Prime Minister Viktor Orbán on the Kossuth Radio programme 'Good Morning Hungary,'" Cabinet Office of the Prime Minister, February 24, 2023, https://miniszterelnok.hu/en/prime-minister-viktor-orban-on-the-kossuth-radio-programme-good-morning-hungary-2023-02-24/.

[98] Lili Bayer, "Finland on Course for NATO Membership after Hungarian Vote," *Politico*, March 27, 2023, https://www.politico.eu/article/hungary-parliament-backs-finland-nato-bid/.

[99] As of early July, Sweden's membership is still yet to be ratified by Hungary (and Turkey). "Hungary Says It'll Back Sweden's NATO Entry Once Turkey Moves," *Bloomberg.com*, July 4, 2023, https://www.bloomberg.com/news/articles/2023-07-04/hungary-says-it-ll-back-sweden-s-nato-entry-once-turkey-moves.

[100] Tibor Lengyel, "Tíz jel, hogy zsarolásra és politikai hangulatkeltésre használja a Fidesz a NATO-bővítés ügyét [Ten signs that Fidesz is using NATO enlargement for blackmail and political agitation]," *hvg.hu*, March 3, 2023, https://hvg.hu/itthon/20230303_nato_bovites_fidesz_zsarolas_keslekedes.

[101] Gergely Tóth, "Orbán's Illiberal Mini-Summit," trans. Andrea Horváth Kávai, *Telex*, August 22, 2023, https://telex.hu/english/2023/08/22/orban-and-the-illiberal-powerhouse.

[102] Viktor Orbán, "Commemoration Speech on the 65th Anniversary of the 1956 Revolution and Freedom Fight," Cabinet Office of the Prime Minister, October 23, 2021, https://miniszterelnok.hu/prime-minister-viktor-orbans-commemoration-speech-on-the-65th-anniversary-of-the-1956-revolution-and-freedom-fight/.

[103] Bálint Magyar and Bálint Madlovics, "Hungary's Mafia State Fights for Impunity," *Project Syndicate*, June 18, 2019, https://www.project-syndicate.org/commentary/hungary-mafia-state-viktor-orban-impunity-by-balint-magyar-and-balint-madlovics-2019-06.

[104] On losing the support of Kaczyński's Poland, see Patrik Galavits and Szabolcs Panyi, "How Viktor Orbán Angered His Closest Friends in Europe," *Telex*, May 16, 2023, https://telex.hu/direkt36/2023/05/16/how-viktor-orban-angered-his-closest-friends-in-europe.

Defensive Submission, Lucrative Neutrality, and Silent Detachment: Post-Soviet Patronal Autocracies in the Shadow of the Russian Invasion

Anatoly Reshetnikov

1. Divergent responses to the war in Russia's neighborhood

If the reaction of liberal democracies to the drastic intensification of the Russia-Ukraine war on February 24, 2022 was relatively consonant—almost all of them supported Ukraine—patronal autocracies did not speak in one voice either for or against Russia's aggression. As the voting in the UN General Assembly on March 2, 2022 has shown, they chose different strategies in response to the conflict.[1] Some patronal autocracies like Hungary condemned the aggression by supporting the General Assembly's resolution, but preserved and nurtured discursive ambiguity at home.[2] Other patronal autocracies, especially the ones located in Russia's immediate neighborhood, chose to be more cautious. Some simply did not participate in the respective UN session, refusing to take any stance (e.g. Azerbaijan, Turkmenistan, and Uzbekistan). Others were present but abstained from voting, manifesting their neutrality and thus indirectly encouraging Russia's actions (e.g. Kazakhstan). Yet others voted against the resolution, showing their wholehearted support for the intervention (e.g. Belarus).

Of particular interest to this analysis are those regimes that have very close geographic, economic, and political connections with (and, in many cases, dependencies on) Russia. Despite these ties, as well as all the similarities in these countries' histories and political regimes,[3] they have to maneuver in the circumstances where their regional hegemon is seemingly making mistakes that could have negative regional and global repercussions. Balancing between maintaining good relations with Russia and trying to find a viable strategy for navigating through the unleashed international crisis, post-Soviet patronal autocracies are forced to reinvent themselves to stay afloat in the new political realities. In doing so, they are somewhat limited by their previous political choices and trajectories, as well as by their own economic and resource potentials. Yet they retain a few degrees of freedom in planning their projected development, and are actively trying to use them to minimize possible damage.

While a detailed analysis of all patronal autocracies from the post-Soviet space and their responses to the Russia-Ukraine war remains beyond the scope of this chapter, I would like to concentrate on the three seemingly polar reactions exhibited by these regimes. I call these reactions: (1) *defensive submission* (most purely practiced by Belarus), (2) *lucrative neutrality* (adopted by Azerbaijan),[4] and (3) *silent detachment* (attempted by Kazakhstan). It would be safe to assume that, as patronal autocracies, these regimes, along with formal and public diplomatic channels, would also rely on informal channels in their domestic and international politics.[5] These informal communications, however, are too recent and, for the time being, will remain hidden from view.

2. Theoretical foundations and research design

As a scholar of discourse, I resort to the official political rhetoric produced during the war by the presidents of Belarus, Azerbaijan, and Kazakhstan, as well as compare it to the rhetoric they produced shortly before the most recent invasion. In doing so, I reject the clear-cut opposition between the real motives of chief patrons and their rhetorical smokescreens. The main point here is not that the patrons cannot lie and manipulate their audiences (they do this all the time), but that we, as scholars, "have no systematic way of talking about—and, hence, analyzing—[their hidden motives] without returning to publicly meaningful notions."[6] A stranger's heart is a deep well—for anyone, including scholars. Therefore, to be able to *attribute* motives, one always needs and has to rely on the interpersonal public manifestations of the other's wants and desires.

Almost all governments (regardless of their regime type) find it necessary to maintain and regularly update the websites that contain nothing else but their official statements. This rhetoric may be manipulative and insincere, and may also differ substantially from what is expressed behind closed doors. Still, it remains vital in public relations and serves an important function in showcasing one's political strategies and ambitions. When properly contextualized and interpreted, it can also shed light on the possible underlying motives, desires, and fears of the given political actors. In this chapter, I intend to provide such contextualization and interpretation of the official discourse produced by the presidents of Belarus, Azerbaijan, and Kazakhstan in the aftermath, as well as shortly before Russia's invasion of Ukraine in February 2022.

I collected my data from the official presidential websites: *www.president.gov.by*, *www.president.az*, and *www.akorda.kz*. All three websites are trilingual and also publish their documents in both English and Russian, in addition to the main local language (Belarusian, Azeri, and Kazakh respectively). The presentation style of the presidents' speeches and statements varies both across the three websites and across the three languages. Sometimes a webpage contains the full transcript of a speech or the relevant Q&A session. At other times, a webpage includes a third-person summary of an event with extensive quotations from the speech delivered by the president. One and the same event may sometimes be presented differently in different language versions. I mainly worked with the English versions of the documents, but also frequently cross-checked them with the Russian versions, which sometimes brought interesting revelations (see especially Kazakhstan's section below).

The cut off point for my data collection was January 31, 2023. The starting point varied across the three case studies (for reasons described below), but fell into the interval between December 1, 2021 and June 12, 2019. I used the search function of the three websites to find and download all the statements made by the presidents that contained the word "Ukraine." When mentions of Ukraine were exceedingly rare, as was the case with the president of Kazakhstan, Kassym-Jomart Tokayev, I added other relevant programmatic speeches that touched upon the evolution of the state's political regime and the president's vision of global affairs (e.g. state of the nation addresses and speeches at the UN).

In the case of Kazakhstan, I also added Tokayev's speech delivered at his first inauguration ceremony on June 12, 2019. The main reason for this was that, unlike Belarus's Alexander Lukashenko and Azerbaijan's Ilham Aliyev, who have been the chief patrons of their regimes for decades (since 1994 and 2003 respectively), Tokayev came to power only recently and in the circumstances where the previous chief patron, Nursultan Nazarbayev, remained, for the time being, an important political figure and served as the Chairman of the Security Council and the Chairman of Nur Otan, Kazakhstan's ruling party. Still, arguably, Nazarbayev's decision to step down as president could be interpreted as an important nodal point in the evolution of Kazakhstan's patronal autocracy, which culminated in his removal from all positions following the protests in Kazakhstan in January 2022 and the adoption of the new constitution in June 2022. Thus, the specifics of Kazakhstan's response to the Russian offensive in Ukraine can be better grasped if one also considers the narratives that Tokayev promoted from the very beginning of his presidency. For the relatively entrenched and unvaried patronal regimes in Azerbaijan and Belarus which have continuously legitimized themselves using sets of narratives which have remained relatively stable through recent years, I decided to use starting points that preceded the 2022 Russian invasion by only a few months, i.e., December or November 2021.

As a result, I compiled three datasets, comparable in size, and worked through all the speeches paying specific attention to the mentions of Ukraine and Russia, as well as the contexts in which they were mentioned. I also focused on statements that expressed the presidents' vision of their country's place and role in global affairs, in regional politics, and in the Russia-Ukraine war. Finally, I took note of the most frequently present identity statements that described the political nature of each of the three regimes, their future aspirations and prospects, as well as their main political Others.[7] In the following sections, I present the results of my analysis along with brief contextualizations of each regime's political trajectories vis-à-vis Russia and Ukraine before and after February 2022.

3. Belarus: defensive submission

3.1. Background

Out of all post-Soviet states, independent Belarus has always preserved the closest ties with Russia. The speedy rapprochement of the two countries started with the project of the Union State of Russia and Belarus, which was launched during Boris Yeltsin's presidency in 1996, went through several stages of integration and attendant disagreements regarding the final design,[8] and has remained on the back burner ever since. In return for its openness to cooperation and exceptional loyalty, Russia offered Belarus not only unencumbered access to its market,[9] but also subsidized prices for oil and gas, as well as generous loans and grants.[10]

Politically, Belarus developed in a very similar direction as did its partner from the Union State, outpacing and anticipating many autocratic tendencies and moves that later also blossomed in Russia (especially Putin's Russia). Lukashenko manipulated and rigged presidential elections,[11] organized populist referenda that were supposed to solve the problem of "only two" consecutive presidential terms,[12] and effectively destroyed Belarus's party system.[13] Already by the end of the 1990s, Belarus became a fully consolidated patronalistic[14] and autocratic[15] regime with a disproportionate share of powers concentrated in the hands of the president,[16] who effectively assumed the role of chief patron.

At the same time, the relations between Belarus and Russia did not develop as an equal partnership. Rather, it could be described as a patron-client relationship projected into the sphere of international politics.[17] In other words, it was always obvious for attentive observers that there exists a fair degree of unconditionality and inequality within the Putin-Lukashenko tandem. This inequality often shines through even in official speeches (see below). However, for a long time, Lukashenko managed to skillfully navigate this dependency preserving some degree of autonomy and even leverage over Russia,[18] which are privileges that clients normally do not enjoy. As late as February 2019, when Lukashenko came to Sochi to yet again discuss energy cooperation with Russia, he played tough and fended off all insinuations that Belarus could ever lose its sovereignty to Russia and threatened in return that Russia could "los[e] the only ally it has to the West of it," if Russia's economic pressure continued.[19]

Arguably, the possibility of such nuanced balancing came to an end during the rigged 2020 presidential elections, when Belarus witnessed the largest street protests in its modern history.[20] Lukashenko's legitimacy was virtually destroyed in the eyes of the wider public, and he could stay in power only thanks to the use of unrestrained intimidation and violence.[21] In dire straits, Lukashenko turned to Putin for Russia's support and received some limited security guarantees,[22] as well as a USD 1.5 billion loan[23]—presumably, to cover the costs of clamping down on the swelling unrest and withstanding the new Western-imposed sanctions.[24]

Lukashenko and his regime have carried this troubling baggage of increasing dependency on Russia and deteriorating domestic legitimacy all the way to the present. Allegedly, this limited Lukashenko's room for maneuver when it came to helping prepare and carry out Russia's major offensive against Ukraine. Belarus opened its borders to Russian soldiers and weaponry under the pretext of joint military exercises. These forces were later used to attack Ukraine.

3.2. *Analysis*

Reflecting the growing, and thus controversial, dependency on Russia, Lukashenko's baseline discursive position was, and remains, ambivalent. On the one hand, he expressed his wholehearted support of Russia's actions both before and after the invasion. For instance, when Lukashenko met with his generals on November 29, 2021, he shifted blame for the potential conflict onto the collective West, and warned that "if they again start a war in the Donbass or somewhere on the border with Russia, Belarus will not stand aside [and it] is clear whose side Belarus will be on" (11.29.2021).[25] Immediately after Russia attacked Ukraine, Lukashenko asserted that "we [i.e., Belarus] will not be traitors, and we will not allow you [i.e., the collective West] to shoot the Russian people in the back" (02.24.2022). Allegedly, this metaphor about Belarus having Russia's back struck a chord with Lukashenko and he used it at least five more times in his subsequent speeches (03.10.2022, 03.11.2022, 07.03.2022, 10.04.2022 and 10.10.2022). Lukashenko also admitted that Belarus and Russia were tightly entangled, both economically and culturally. For him, Russia was "a fraternal state [...], the closest state in the world" (07.03.2022), while its people were "kin people growing from the same root" (03.17.2022) and the same "civilization" (12.02.2021), so, in fact, the two peoples "have always been one" (05.09.2022). In economic terms, Belarus and Russia were presented as "deeply integrated into [each other's] production system[s] [forming] a single market." They "are practically one whole in terms of manufacturing, economy, sales market, [as well as] militarily" (03.17.2022).

On the other hand, Lukashenko adamantly insisted that Belarus was a fully independent and sovereign state that always made up its own mind and maintained complete control over its borders. Sometimes he brought up and harshly criticized the position that Belarus could be incorporated into Russia. He emphasized that both "independent states" were "smart enough not to incorporate each other," and that in the 30 years that passed since the dissolution of the Soviet Union "the looming takeover or incorporation," which everyone waited for, had not happened (06.30.2022). In the context of Russia's military presence in Belarus, the issue of control over the state borders seemed particularly sensitive for Lukashenko. Immediately before, but also after, the start of the full-scale invasion, he spoke about border control remarkably often. In the analyzed dataset, Lukashenko mentions borders and border control more than sixty (!) times, insisting that "the security of [Belarus] begins with the border, because [Belarus's] sovereignty is safe within [its] border" (01.24.2022). It was near the Belarusian border where "Ukrainian nationalists" allegedly set up "training camps [to prepare] 'volunteers' to participate in the Belarusian events" (03.01.2022). Certainly, Lukashenko also promised retaliation "once [Belarus's] border is violated," emphasizing that "the response will be immediate" (03.10.2022). This obsession with borders and their violation was epitomized in a metaphor that compared Belarus to the Brest Fortress, which became the symbol of frontier defense due to its heroic and lengthy (even if strategically pointless) resistance during the first month of Operation Barbarossa in 1941 (12.02.2021). With such semantics, Lukashenko's rhetoric directly echoed the widespread conspiratorial narrative about "Fortress Russia."[26]

Despite all the attempts to present Belarus as inviolable and fully independent, as well as equal to Russia in all respects, Lukashenko could not hide his acceptance of and submission to geopolitical hierarchies. As he put it, describing the intensified global rivalry, "our elections, 'dictatorship,' Lukashenko are not the problem. [...] Geopolitics is" (12.14.2021). According to him, amidst that global rivalry, there are more powerful actors, including the US and Russia, who are running the show and can do whatever they want with the weaker polities. Such a view not only translated into the persistent zombification of Ukraine, often presented as controlled by Western puppet masters (03.01.2022, 03.17.2022, 05.05.2022, 05.09.2022, 10.04.2022 etc.), but also into an indirect recognition of Belarus's complete submission to Russia. Lukashenko made a revealing comment along these lines in an interview with Japanese television, when he attested that "Russia offers Ukraine such things that we have here in Belarus. Ukraine should become a country like Belarus, with certain nuances." This, in his understanding, was "an absolutely acceptable deal," and "if Zelensky fails to [accept] it, [...] he will soon have to sign an act of capitulation" (03.17.2022).

As the Russian offensive dragged on, rebuffed by Ukraine's resilience and resistance, Lukashenko's defensive submission acquired increasingly pessimistic and even fatalistic undertones. Already in May 2022, he admitted in an interview with the Associated Press that, in his opinion, the "operation [was] taking too long" (05.05.2022). In July, he dropped the "denazification" narrative, which had been prominent in his earlier speeches (e.g. 03.01.2022, 03.17.2022, and 03.22.2022), admitting that "denazification and so on is a philosophy [while the] main thing is the security of Russia" (07.21.2022). Finally, in an October interview with NBC, Lukashenko predicted a "looming deadlock" where Putin was not winning, but neither was the West, but at least "Putin has suggested solutions" (10.14.2022).

In sum, the evolution of Lukashenko's discursive position reflected ambiguity, but also the lack of alternatives conditioned by the increasing dependence of his regime on Russia. Having taken Russia's side in the conflict, Lukashenko forwent the flexibility which he could exercise in his relations with Putin before 2020. He accepted both dependence and hierarchy. Notwithstanding his attempts to defend Belarusian autonomy, Lukashenko's regime is getting progressively taken over by Russia on all fronts: from the strengthening of Russian cultural hegemony inside Belarus[27] to the actual formation of joint military forces (10.10.2022) and Russia's censorship of Belarus's cyberspace.[28] As a result, it is currently difficult to imagine a future for Lukashenko's regime that could be significantly different from that of Putin's Russia.

4. Azerbaijan: lucrative neutrality

4.1. Background

Since the dissolution of the Soviet Union, independent Azerbaijan has developed regime features that have made it very similar to contemporary Russia and Belarus. All three countries are highly patronalistic,[29] presidentialist,[30] and autocratic.[31] Just like in Russia, Azerbaijan's patronal network "features a transformed secret service at its core," while its first post-Soviet chief patron, Heydar Aliyev, had previously made a successful career in the Soviet KGB.[32] Like Russia, Azerbaijan largely relies and depends on exports of oil and gas, both as a source of income for the national economy and as a source of corruption rent for its ruling clan.[33] Like Belarus, Azerbaijan more than once organized populist referenda to concentrate virtually unlimited power in the president's hands and to prolong his time in office. For instance, in 2009, the new chief patron of Azerbaijan, Ilham Aliyev (Heydar's son) carried out a controversial referendum that allowed him to abolish presidential term limits and to curtail the freedom of the press. In 2016, he extended the presidential term from five to seven years, and also gave himself the power to dissolve the parliament.[34] As a patronal autocracy as consolidated as Lukashenko's, Ilham Aliyev's regime has also confronted and successfully suppressed attempted color revolutions, resorting to excessive repression and violence.[35] The originally strong and well-organized political opposition to the Aliyev regime was rather quickly incapacitated and further marginalized in both of its two incarnations: formally political and more civil society-oriented.[36]

However, unlike Belarus, post-Soviet Azerbaijan initially had rather chilly relations with Russia, mostly due to the latter's support of Armenia in the Nagorno-Karabakh conflict and from pressure to join the Collective Security Treaty Organization, which Azerbaijan eventually left in 1999.[37] When Putin came to power in 2000 and as the regimes converged in their patronalistic tendencies, embracing high-level corruption, Azerbaijan and Russia found mutually beneficial ways to cooperate and their relations became significantly warmer and more pragmatic. This stage of relations between Azerbaijan and Russia saw many joint projects and economic exchanges based on mutual sympathies between Putin and Aliyev as two chief patrons.[38]

Russia's intervention in Georgia in 2008 sent an alarming signal to Azerbaijan, which had its own unresolved territorial disputes with Armenia. Georgia, which was aiming to reestablish its territorial integrity, as recognized by the international community and international law, was attacked by Russia, which acted in contravention of international law, as interpreted by Azerbaijan. Since one of the foundational narratives of Aliyev's regime was based on proclaiming the unlawfulness of Armenia's actions in Nagorno-Karabakh in the beginning of the 1990s, Azerbaijan both promoted the supremacy of the legal consensus adopted by international organizations and criticized Russia for ignoring it (later on, Aliyev grew disillusioned with the ineffectiveness of international institutions and called for a major reform of the UN Security Council; see below). Consequently, Azerbaijan adopted a more cautious position in its relations with Russia, avoiding direct antagonism while also trying to preserve neutrality in all political and economic issues that did not immediately affect Azerbaijan's national interests. Anar Valiyev compared this policy choice to "Finlandization," equating Azerbaijan's position to the one adopted by Finland after World War II in the face of potential military threats coming from Finland's hostile Eastern neighbor.[39]

In the context of Russia's aggression towards Ukraine, Aliyev tried to preserve neutrality, refusing to take sides. In the winter of 2022, he visited both Zelensky (01.14.2022) and Putin (02.22.2022), paying his respects to both leaders and proposing the further development of bilateral cooperation. The joint declarations that followed both summits emphasized possible economic, cultural, and strategic synergies between Azerbaijan and its regional partners. At the same time, while

Ukraine's protest against the violation of its territorial integrity resonated well with Azerbaijan's struggle for territorial justice, it did not prevent Aliyev from entering into a strategic partnership with Russia, "the format of relations [that he deemed] the highest" (02.23.2022). In the following section, I analyze how Azerbaijan discursively used its neutrality to reap benefits from its non-aligned status.

4.2. Analysis

It so happened that Ilham Aliyev was on an official visit to Moscow one day before Russia attacked Ukraine in February 2022. It was then that Aliyev and Putin signed the Declaration of Allied Cooperation, which made Russia and Azerbaijan strategic partners. When Aliyev gave a press conference to the Russian mass media that same day, he was asked if anything could change in Russia-Azerbaijan relations should the international political climate undergo some qualitative transformations. In his response, the president assured that "there will be no correction in the position of the Azerbaijani and Russian sides in connection with the events that have happened and the events that may still happen in our region" (02.23.2022). Given the centrality of the tensions rising in connection with Ukraine, it would be safe to assume that Russia's intervention was included in the horizon of events that could potentially happen in the region.

At the same time, this does not mean that Azerbaijan has chosen a side in the looming conflict. Aliyev emphasized more than once that his position was that of neutrality, despite its strategic alliance with Russia. In fact, he was markedly proud of his diplomatic accomplishments, presenting the new state of affairs as "a historic achievement," which manifested itself in the fact that Azerbaijan now "[had] allied relations with two great countries, two neighbors," i.e. Russia and Turkey, one of which was a NATO member, while the other—the "de facto leader of the CSTO" (02.23.2022). What is more, in Aliyev's rendering, instead of being ideologically motivated, these allied relations were "based on shared interests, pragmatism and similarity" (02.23.2022).

Indeed, after Russia invaded Ukraine on February 24, Aliyev did not change his rhetoric. He insisted on "the independent character of Azerbaijan's foreign policy, which [was] based on [its] national interests" which prioritized "security and cooperation." According to Aliyev, "without security, there will be no cooperation, and there will be no economic benefits" (04.29.2022). Economic benefits were and remain the main objectives which Aliyev frequently sets in his speeches. Unlike Lukashenko, who presented Belarus's economic entanglement with Russia more as an objective constraint which Belarus had to accommodate for other non-economic reasons (cultural similarity, kindred blood, etc.), Aliyev presented his neutral stance as making the most economic sense, while other non-economic factors were deemed secondary.

According to Aliyev, Azerbaijan's importance in the new international realities is actually growing, both as a "regional transportation hub" with "export[s] through Azerbaijan from Central Asia and China [having grown by] more than 20%," but also as a "corridor [that] has [...] become very important [...] for Russian companies, which now have difficulties exporting their goods to European destinations because of the sanctions" (09.02.2022f). Aliyev also happily revealed that Azerbaijan received "requests from more than ten European countries concerning either increasing or starting the existing [sic] supplies [of energy resources]," and that, for now, the country does "not have enough gas to satisfy all the requests" (11.25.2022). In other words, because of the Russia-Ukraine war, the demand for Azerbaijan's natural resources is booming. Aliyev also reported that during his meeting with Ursula von der Leyen in Baku they discussed energy supplies to the European Union and that he had "big plans to increase the volume of electric energy [supplied] to Europe" (11.25.2022). In sum, Aliyev and his patronal network seem comfortable with how things have developed, since "the role of Azerbaijan is increasing [...] and we [i.e. the country] must take advantage of that" (01.10.2023). Certainly, as befits patronal autocracies, the advantages and gains Aliyev is talking about will not be redistributed evenly among all citizens of Azerbaijan.

Aliyev's choice of lucrative neutrality may also be conditioned by reasons other than sheer economic gain. As becomes evident from his speeches, Azerbaijan takes its participation in the Non-Aligned Movement rather seriously. In the entire dataset, Aliyev mentions the Non-Aligned Movement at least ten times, often reminding his audience that Azerbaijan is chairing it at the moment and emphasizing the need to improve its real political influence, for example, through acquiring better representation at the UN (e.g. 04.22.2022, 01.10.2023, 01.28.2023). The UN itself, however, at least in its current setup, does not receive much credit from Aliyev. Even though he always rhetorically affirms the importance of upholding international law (and hints that Russia has violated it to the detriment of the existing international order [09.02.2022g]), he also expresses dissatisfaction with the UN's performance and design. Since the organization proved unable to resolve the Nagorno-Karabakh conflict at its inception, when international institutions were supposed to be on Azerbaijan's side, it requires reform that would make the organization more diverse, impartial, and inclusive. In particular, Aliyev maintained that "the composition of the Security Council should be revised," since the victors of World War II can no longer decide the destinies of the world, when "World War Three is raging" (01.10.2023). He proposed to reserve one permanent seat for an Islamic country and another one for a country from the Non-Aligned Movement.

In a nutshell, Azerbaijan's patronal autocracy has not suffered much from the Russia-Ukraine war and its global consequences. On the contrary, Aliyev's regime perceived this as an opportunity to boost Azerbaijan's international presence, and to reap additional economic benefits by taking over some share of Russia's energy exports. Moreover, Azerbaijan has become an important connection and transportation hub used by both sides of the conflict: those who want to obey the sanction regime and isolate/bypass Russia, and those Russian companies that want to find new, unsanctioned routes to reach their customers. While the currently existing capacities of Azerbaijan's companies and infrastructure cannot accommodate the growing demand, the country's patronal network is working on devising solutions.

5. Kazakhstan: silent detachment

5.1. Background

Unlike the Baltic states and some other former Soviet republics, Soviet Kazakhstan did not foster any massive anti-authoritarian, pro-independence movements before the fall of the USSR. The republic certainly did have a tradition of local nationalism[40] and even experienced upheavals that could be described as primarily motivated by nationalist sentiment (e.g., the Jeltoqsan, or December uprising of 1986). Still, neither the Kazakh political elites nor the population at large had any radical anti-Soviet disposition. Some scholars of the region went as far as to call post-Soviet Kazakhstan a country "born by default," implying that Moscow simply withdrew its support for the local regime in 1991, and the Kazakhstani elite simply had to proclaim independence, becoming the last Soviet republic to do so (just ten days before the Soviet Union ceased to exist).[41] This story of spontaneous independence may certainly be inaccurate. Yet, one thing is certain: instead of receiving an impulse for democratic transition, as did many other former Soviet republics, Kazakhstan's political system got bogged down in its own political legacies. After becoming independent, Kazakhstan originally reproduced its old political regime under a new label, while its former communist leader, Nursultan Nazarbayev, became the country's first president.

Herbert Kitschelt and his colleagues define the type of communism that had been constructed in Soviet Kazakhstan (and in Soviet Belarus and Azerbaijan as well) as "patrimonial,"[42] i.e. "based on personal networks of loyalty and mutual exchange, combined with patronage, corruption, and nepotism."[43] It was from this baseline condition that independent Kazakhstan started its political development. Patrimonial, or patronal, legacies proved resilient in many post-Soviet states, even in those that are now considered democratic like Kyrgyzstan.[44] Yet, according to Magyar and Madlovics, in its post-Soviet trajectory, Kazakhstan "has been the closest to ideal typical patronal autocracy."[45] Nazarbayev, as Kazakhstan's chief patron and one of the longest-ruling non-royal leaders in the world, successfully transformed bureaucratic patrimonial communism into informal autocratic patronalism as early as 1995, when he modified the constitution, significantly expanding his powers and extending the presidential term.[46] Prior to the two referenda held in April and August 1995, which legalized the highly presidentialist nature of Kazakhstan's regime, Nazarbayev had also intimidated the parliament, inviting it to dissolve in December 1993, and effectively incapacitated all serious systemic challenges to his undivided rule.[47] From then on, he and his adopted political family were able to enjoy the benefits of a fully consolidated patronal autocracy until 2019, when Nazarbayev decided to resign after three decades of presidency.

Initially, Nazarbayev's resignation did not negatively affect his position as chief patron, as he retained a number of important offices under his control. Among these were the "Leader of the Nation" *(Elbasy)*, a position specifically created for Nazarbayev a few years prior to his resignation, and the chairmanships of both Kazakhstan's Security Council and the ruling party Nur Otan. These positions gave Nazarbayev legal immunity, as well as veto rights and *de facto* executive powers over policy decisions.[48] His handpicked successor, a career diplomat Kassym-Jomart Tokayev, was supposed to be a safe bet, as a veteran of Nazarbayev's political system.[49] And a safe bet he was, all the way up to the country-wide protests that broke out in January 2022. Initially, the protests were a reaction to a sudden spike in liquefied gas prices, but later they transformed into openly political protests centered on the citizens' dissatisfaction with the government, as well as the rampant inequality and corruption.[50]

In reaction to the protests, Tokayev chose a response that could be described as *balanced* from the point of view of an autocratic leader, and as *radical* from the point of view of a successor to a chief patron who remained active on the country's political stage. On the one hand, Tokayev invited the CSTO—in effect, Russian troops—to protect his power and quell the unrest.[51] On the other hand, after the situation calmed down, he launched a widespread attack on Nazarbayev and his adopted political family, gradually stripping the Leader of the Nation of all his privileges and titles.[52] He also presented his plan for a fundamental democratic reform of Kazakhstan's political system and has stuck to this rhetoric ever since, Russia's invasion of Ukraine notwithstanding.

When it comes to Kazakhstan's relations with Russia, from very early on, they were friendly, but not exclusive. The "multivector foreign policy,"[53] which independent Kazakhstan adopted as its preferred diplomatic strategy and which anticipated good relations with Russia while also seeking rapprochement with China and the US, never disappeared from the agenda. Tokayev embraced this stance and asserted his independence and autonomy from Russia's influence rather frequently. One clear example was when Tokayev called Luhansk and Donetsk "quasi-state entities" which Kazakhstan would never recognize, while sitting in the same panel as Putin at the Saint Petersburg International Economic Forum (06.18.2022).

In general, Tokayev continues to follow the line about Kazakhstan's autonomy quite consistently, even despite the military assistance he had to request from the CSTO (i.e., Russia) to suppress the protests in January 2022.

5.2. *Analysis*

When one attempts to form an opinion about Tokayev's position on the Russia-Ukraine war reading his speeches published on the president's official website, one receives the impression that he chooses to keep almost pristine silence on the issue. Whenever he mentions Ukraine, he always emphasizes the diplomatic and humanitarian sides of the conflict, avoiding any discussion of the military aspect. For instance, in his conversation with the Federal President of Germany, Frank-Walter Steinmeier, on March 7, 2022, he described the Ukrainian crisis as "quite complex in its origin," and urged the two sides to seek "new diplomatic opportunities [...] for a peaceful solution of the conflict." He also committed "to provide humanitarian assistance to the Ukrainian people with medicines and other necessary products" (03.07.2022). Similarly, in his talk with Volodymyr Zelensky, Tokayev emphasized "the importance of reaching an agreement through negotiations in order to stop and cease further hostilities in Ukraine." Meanwhile, Kazakhstan could offer "cooperation [...] in the humanitarian sphere" (03.02.2022). When speaking with Turkey's Recep Tayyip Erdoğan, he commended the latter's "peacekeeping efforts for the peaceful settlement of the situation in Ukraine" (04.04.2022). In Saint Petersburg, when Tokayev, sitting at the same stage as Putin, was asked about the attitudes in Kazakhstan towards Russia's actions in Ukraine, he answered evasively that "there are different opinions, [since Kazakhstan has] an open society" (06.18.2022).

Meanwhile, Tokayev did not take close cooperation with Russia off the table because of the war. During the second month of invasion, in his conversation with Putin, Tokayev agreed "to intensify cooperation between [Kazakhstan and Russia] on the most important commodities [...] to maintain the dynamics of bilateral trade" (04.02.2022). Similarly, in November 2022, he praised the "mutually beneficial strategic partnership" between Kazakhstan and Russia, as well as the growing amount of Russian investments in Kazakhstan's economy, and promised to do his best "to ensure the security of [those] investments and attract [more]" (11.28.2022). However, such friendliness with Russia was always presented in the framework of Kazakhstan's multivector diplomacy. Good relations with Russia are as desirable for Tokayev as are good relations with "China and brotherly countries of Central Asia." What is more, he also aspires "to develop multifaceted cooperation with the United States, the European Union, the states of Asia, the Middle East and Transcaucasia, as well as with all interested countries" (11.26.2022). In this sense, unlike the case with Belarus, but much like that with Azerbaijan, Russia represents for Kazakhstan one vector of relations among many.

In the context of the discussion about post-Soviet patronal autocracies and their transformations, it is important to note that, out of all three chief patrons, Tokayev is the only one who frequently talks about democratic values and human rights, as well as the democratization of his country. What is more, such pro-democratic sentiment is present across the board, that is, in both domestic and international speeches. For instance, in his speech at the UN in September 2021, he mentioned the need to nurture bottom-up democracy, to help refugees, and to abolish the death penalty, in addition to expressing Kazakhstan's willingness to join the UN Human Rights Council (09.23.2021). Similarly, in his several state of the nation addresses, Tokayev spoke about strengthening human rights institutions and the importance of citizens' participation in political processes (03.16.2022 and 06.06.2022). In his rhetoric and proposed reforms (e.g. the reform of the party system), Tokayev somewhat resembles Dmitry Medvedev in the early years of his presidency in Russia (2008-2011). Yet, unlike Medvedev, who failed to weaken the grip of his chief patron who originally promoted him to his position, Tokayev has successfully managed to hustle *his* chief patron away, forcing him to call it a day.

To what extent Tokayev's ambition to democratize Kazakhstan is genuine remains to be seen. At the moment, his rhetoric still exhibits plenty of patronalistic tendencies and problematic shortcuts: from his favorite formula "Strong President—Authoritative Parliament—Accountable Government" (e.g. 09.20.2022) to some indications of fine-tuning the signals sent to different audiences. While the impression that the latter practice takes place may be explained by simple mistakes and the human factor, existing discrepancies still deserve to be mentioned. Perhaps, the most illustrative example is Tokayev's discussion of media reform, one of the crucial aspects of democratization. In his state of the nation address, delivered on March 16, 2022, Tokayev presented ten points that he perceived as his main tasks to accomplish. The seventh point was related to the reform of the media, which anticipated some liberalization, but also virtually legitimized the propagandistic approach to the national media, demanding patriotic fervor from Kazakh journalists and media resources. Interestingly, this point—which would probably not resonate well with the Western audience—was excluded from the English translation of Tokayev's speech (03.16.2022). In the Russian and Kazakh versions of the transcript, the two languages in which the address was originally delivered, the seventh point is present. Also, since the presentation style of Tokayev's speeches sometimes varies across the three languages (full transcript vs. third-person summary with extensive citations), this technically allows the possibility to highlight or hide those messages that need to be emphasized or omitted. Thus, the "irreversible" nature of Kazakhstan's "ongoing democratization and socio-political transformation," which Tokayev mentions in his original speech in front of the foreign diplomatic missions, and which remains present in its English transcript, changes its context in the Russian-language summary with citations (11.04.2022). Mentioned originally in the context of the media reform, it turns into a decontextualized third-person comment, while the media reform is omitted.

Just like Azerbaijan, Kazakhstan abstained from taking sides in the Russia-Ukraine war, and continued its cooperation with Russia, which was framed as a continuation of its multivector diplomacy and sovereign autonomy. The concrete tactics Tokayev has chosen to adopt is to say nothing about the issue whenever possible. In those instances when avoiding discussion was impossible, Tokayev trod carefully, trying not to antagonize either side. At the same time, he insistently emphasized Kazakhstan's autonomy and its willingness to build partnerships with all its neighbors, as well as all global actors. In addition, he consistently promoted democracy- and human rights-related discourse, which was still interspersed with patronalistic elements, and called for a limited democratic transformation of Kazakhstan. Through this ambition, Tokayev has allegedly tried to move his regime further away from Russia, which is evidently developing in the opposite direction.

6. Conclusion

In the shadow of Russia's most recent invasion of Ukraine, post-Soviet patronal autocracies faced important dilemmas. Siding with Russia, their regional hegemon and a kindred regime, meant undermining their relations with a sizable portion of the rest of the world, including those established partners who condemned the invasion (e.g. Turkey, the US, and the EU). Siding with Ukraine meant spoiling relations with Russia, with whom they had been economically integrated and whom they perceived as a security guarantor in the region. In addition, the move attempted by the Russian regime seemed risky and incautious, as it could potentially damage the regime's stability. Therefore, most post-Soviet patronal autocracies, except one, exercised caution and avoided taking sides, while devising ways to benefit from the invasion (e.g. by taking over some share of the supply of now sanctioned Russian goods and resources to Europe and other destinations). I visualize some emerging rhetorical patters in Table 1.

Table 1. Categories used and not used for the Russia-Ukraine war by post-Soviet chief patrons.

		Lukashenko (Belarus)	Aliyev (Azerbaijan)	Tokayev (Kazakhstan)
Russia's narrative	"special military operation"	++	–	+[54]
	"Security of Russia"	+	–	–
	"Nazi"	++	–	–
Descriptive	"crisis"	–	+	+
	"conflict"	++	++	+
	"war"	++	++	–
Russia critical	"invasion"	–	–	–
	"[Russia's] aggression"	–	–	–
	"war crime"	–	–	–

Legend: "++" means frequently used (more than 3 times), "+" means used (1–3 times), "-" means not used (0 times).

Azerbaijan's reaction seems to be the purest manifestation of such a cautious stance. Having proclaimed his neutrality and skipping the voting in the UN, Aliyev immediately started planning how Azerbaijan could take advantage of the war, and which infrastructural investments were necessary to maximize his country's ability to partially take over, but also facilitate, Russia's sanctioned exports. At the same time, he did not shy away from describing the conflict as "the Russian-Ukrainian war," stopping short of calling it an "invasion" and "aggression." Kazakhstan's chief patron also chose neutrality, but generally preferred to hush up the issue in his official communications. At the same time, Tokayev attempted to implement a democratic reform that was supposed to distance Kazakhstan from its currently almost perfectly implemented ideal type of patronal autocracy. To what extent his motivation is genuine and how far he is prepared to go remains to be seen.

Admittedly, Belarus is an important exception in this group of post-Soviet patronal autocracies. Lukashenko not only supported Russia wholeheartedly on the discursive level but also opened Belarusian borders for Russian soldiers and weaponry, thus helping organize the most recent invasion of Ukraine. However, Lukashenko's support of Russia's actions does not seem to be completely voluntary and enthusiastic. That is, Lukashenko's alliance seems to be conditioned by his previous political choices and agreements with Putin, who was the only kindred autocrat who threw a lifeline when Lukashenko's regime was hanging by a thread in 2020.

Reference list of presidential speeches

Aliyev, Ilham. 2022a. *The Presidents of Azerbaijan and Ukraine made press statements.* January 14. https://president.az/en/articles/view/55259.

Aliyev, Ilham. 2022b. *Ilham Aliyev, President of Russia Vladimir Putin, held a one-on-one meeting.* February 22. https://president.az/en/articles/view/55493.

Aliyev, Ilham. 2022c. *Ilham Aliyev met with the heads of Russia's top mass media outlets at TASS headquarters.* February 23. https://president.az/en/articles/view/55507.

Aliyev, Ilham. 2022d. *Speech by Ilham Aliyev at the 5th Congress of World Azerbaijanis in Shusha.* April 22. https://president.az/en/articles/view/55859.

Aliyev, Ilham. 2022e. *Ilham Aliyev attended the international conference themed "South Caucasus: Development and Cooperation" at ADA University.* April 29. https://president.az/en/articles/view/55909.

Aliyev, Ilham. 2022f. *Ilham Aliyev was interviewed by the Italian "Il Sole 24 Ore" newspaper in Cernobbio.* September 2. https://president.az/en/articles/view/57095.

Aliyev, Ilham. 2022g. *Speech by Ilham Aliyev at the international forum in Cernobbio, Italy.* September 2. https://president.az/en/articles/view/57093.

Aliyev, Ilham. 2022h. *Ilham Aliyev attended the opening of the conference under the motto "Along the Middle Corridor: Geopolitics, Security and Economy."* November 25. https://president.az/en/articles/view/57968.

Aliyev, Ilham. 2023a. *Ilham Aliyev was interviewed by local TV channels.* January 10. https://president.az/en/articles/view/58555.

Aliyev, Ilham. 2023b. *Presidents of Azerbaijan and Egypt made press statements.* January 28. https://president.az/en/articles/view/58741.

Lukashenko, Alexander. 2021a. *Meeting on military security.* November 29. https://president.gov.by/en/events/coveshchanie-po-voprosam-voennoy-bezopasnosti-1638192456.

Lukashenko, Alexander. 2021b. *Meeting with Chairman of Russia's State Duma Vyacheslav Volodin.* December 2. https://president.gov.by/en/events/vstrecha-s-predsedatelem-gosudarstvennoy-dumy-rossii-vyacheslavom-volodinym-1638447372.

Lukashenko, Alexander. 2021c. *Meeting with senior officials of Mogilev Oblast.* December 14. https://president.gov.by/en/events/vstrecha-s-aktivom-mogilevskoy-oblasti-1639577224.

Lukashenko, Alexander. 2022a. *Aleksandr Lukashenko approves decision on guarding Belarus' state border for 2022.* January 24. https://president.gov.by/en/events/utverzhdenie-resheniya-na-ohranu-gosudarstvennoy-granicy-organami-pogranichnoy-sluzhby-v-2022-godu.

Lukashenko, Alexander. 2022b. *Special meeting with the military.* February 24. https://president.gov.by/en/events/operativnoe-soveshchanie-s-voennymi-1645711415.

Lukashenko, Alexander. 2022c. *Meeting with members of Security Council, leadership of Council of Ministers.* March 1. https://president.gov.by/en/events/soveshchanie-s-chlenami-soveta-bezopasnosti-i-rukovodstvom-soveta-ministrov-1646152770.

Lukashenko, Alexander. 2022d. *Meeting with high-ranking officials of Belarus' Defense Ministry.* March 10. https://president.gov.by/en/events/soveshchanie-s-rukovodstvom-ministerstva-oborony-1646912559.

Lukashenko, Alexander. 2022e. *Negotiations with Russian President Vladimir Putin.* March 11. https://president.gov.by/en/events/peregovory-s-prezidentom-rossii-vladimirom-putinym-1647076145.

Lukashenko, Alexander. 2022f. *Interview with TBS Television from Japan.* March 17. https://president.gov.by/en/events/intervyu-yaponskomu-telekanalu-tbs-1647515901.

Lukashenko, Alexander. 2022g. *Address to compatriots on occasion of Khatyn tragedy anniversary.* March 22. https://president.gov.by/en/events/obrashchenie-prezidenta-belarusi-po-sluchayu-godovshchiny-hatynskoy-tragedii-1647946252.

Lukashenko, Alexander. 2022h. *Interview with Associated Press.* May 5. https://president.gov.by/en/events/intervyu-mezhdunarodnomu-informacionnomu-agentstvu-associated-press-1651753515.

Lukashenko, Alexander. 2022i. *Victory Day celebrations.* May 9. https://president.gov.by/en/events/torzhestvennye-meropriyatiya-v-chest-dnya-pobedy-1652100852.

Lukashenko, Alexander. 2022j. *Meeting with Russia's Minister of Foreign Affairs Sergey Lavrov.* June 30. https://president.gov.by/en/events/vstrecha-s-ministrom-inostrannyh-del-rossii-sergeem-lavrovym-1656591143.

Lukashenko, Alexander. 2022k. *Wreath-laying ceremony at Mound of Glory memorial.* July 3. https://president.gov.by/en/events/ceremoniya-vozlozheniya-cvetov-i-venkov-v-memorialnom-komplekse-kurgan-slavy-1656865820.

Lukashenko, Alexander. 2022l. *Interview to Agence France-Presse.* July 21. https://president.gov.by/en/events/interview-to-agence-france-presse.

Lukashenko, Alexander. 2022m. *Meeting to discuss military security.* October 4. https://president.gov.by/en/events/soveshchanie-po-voprosam-voennoy-bezopasnosti-1664894227.

Lukashenko, Alexander. 2022n. *Meeting on security.* October 10. https://president.gov.by/en/events/soveshchanie-po-voprosam-bezopasnosti-1665472043.

Lukashenko, Alexander. 2022o. *Interview with U.S. National Broadcasting Company NBC.* October 14. https://president.gov.by/en/events/intervyu-amerikanskoy-telekompanii-nbc-1665750675.

Tokayev, Kassym-Jomart. 2021. *Kazakhstan President Kassym-Jomart Tokayev's video statement at the General Debate of the 76th session of the UN General Assembly.* September 23. https://www.akorda.kz/en/kazakhstan-president-kassym-jomart-tokayevs-video-statement-at-the-general-debate-of-the-76th-session-of-the-un-general-assembly-228202.

Tokayev, Kassym-Jomart. 2022a. *President Kassym-Jomart Tokayev had a telephone conversation with President Vladimir Putin of Russia*. March 2. https://www.akorda.kz/en/president-kassym-jomart-tokayev-had-a-telephone-conversation-with-president-vladimir-putin-of-russia-225420.

Tokayev, Kassym-Jomart. 2022b. *President Kassym-Jomart Tokayev had a telephone conversation with Federal President Frank-Walter Steinmeier of Germany*. March 7. https://www.akorda.kz/en/president-kassym-jomart-tokayev-had-a-telephone-conversation-with-federal-president-frank-walter-steinmeier-of-germany-725355.

Tokayev, Kassym-Jomart. 2022c. *State of the nation address*. March 16. https://www.akorda.kz/en/state-of-the-nation-address-by-president-of-the-republic-of-kazakhstan-kassym-jomart-tokayev-17293.

Tokayev, Kassym-Jomart. 2022d. *President Kassym-Jomart Tokayev had a telephone conversation with President Vladimir Putin of Russia*. April 2. https://www.akorda.kz/en/president-kassym-jomart-tokayev-had-a-telephone-conversation-with-president-vladimir-putin-of-russia-235634.

Tokayev, Kassym-Jomart. 2022e. *President Kassym-Jomart Tokayev had a telephone conversation with President Recep Tayyip Erdogan of Türkiye*. April 4. https://www.akorda.kz/en/kassym-jomart-tokayev-had-a-telephone-conversation-with-president-recep-tayyip-erdogan-of-trkiye-433153.

Tokayev, Kassym-Jomart. 2022f. *President Kassym-Jomart Tokayev's Address to the people of Kazakhstan*. June 6. https://www.akorda.kz/en/president-kassym-jomart-tokayevs-address-to-the-people-of-kazakhstan-65338.

Tokayev, Kassym-Jomart. 2022g. *Kazakhstan's President Addresses Challenging Issues on International Agenda and Relations with Russia at Saint Petersburg Economic Forum*. June 18. https://www.gov.kz/memleket/entities/mfa/press/news/details/390248?lang=en.

Tokayev, Kassym-Jomart. 2022h. *Speech by the President of Kazakhstan Kassym-Jomart Tokayev at the General Debate of the 77th session of the UN General Assembly*. September 20. https://www.akorda.kz/en/speech-by-the-president-of-kazakhstan-kassym-jomart-tokayev-at-the-general-debate-of-the-77th-session-of-the-un-general-assembly-2082327.

Tokayev, Kassym-Jomart. 2022i. *Speech by the President of the Republic of Kazakhstan Kassym-Jomart Tokayev at a meeting with the heads of foreign diplomatic missions accredited in Kazakhstan*. November 4. https://www.akorda.kz/en/speech-by-the-president-of-the-republic-of-kazakhstan-kassym-jomart-tokayev-at-a-meeting-with-the-heads-of-foreign-diplomatic-missions-accredited-in-kazakhstan-4101217.

Tokayev, Kassym-Jomart. 2022j. *Speech by President of Kazakhstan Kassym-Jomart Tokayev at the Inauguration ceremony.* November 26. https://www.akorda.kz/en/speech-by-the-president-of-kazakhstan-kassym-jomart-tokayev-at-the-inauguration-ceremony-26102635.

Tokayev, Kassym-Jomart. 2022k. *President Kassym-Jomart Tokayev addressed the 18th Interregional Cooperation Forum of Kazakhstan and Russia.* November 28. https://www.akorda.kz/en/president-kassym-jomart-tokayev-attends-the-18th-interregional-cooperation-forum-2810415

Notes

1. European External Action Service (EEAS), "UN General Assembly Demands Russian Federation Withdraw All Military Forces from the Territory of Ukraine," EEAS, March 2, 2022, https://www.eeas.europa.eu/eeas/un-general-assembly-demands-russian-federation-withdraw-all-military-forces-territory-ukraine_en.
2. See the chapter of Bálint Madlovics and Bálint Magyar in this volume.
3. As Oleksandr Fisun has argued, the convergence of these regimes was conditioned by "the expropriation of the resources controlled by powerful economic actors (oligarchs), the elimination of any significant political leverage they may exercise, and, ultimately, the decline in the role played by the parliament and political parties." According to Fisun, these processes transformed "the regime into a type of bureaucratic neopatrimonialism." Oleksandr Fisun, "Rethinking Post-Soviet Politics from a Neopatrimonial Perspective," SSRN Scholarly Paper (Rochester, NY: Social Science Research Network, March 1, 2012), 96, https://papers.ssrn.com/abstract=2645304.
4. Even though I refer to the Azerbaijan's official position as neutral, its media discourse is most pro-Ukrainian out of all South Caucasian states. Azerbaijani television routinely calls Russian soldiers "occupiers" and condemns the war crimes they commit. Admittedly, Azerbaijani state media have more freedom in expressing the pro-Ukrainian position than politicians and diplomats. See, e.g., Taras Kuzio, "Azerbaijan Support for Ukraine," *Daily News*, December 29, 2022, https://www.hurriyetdailynews.com/azerbaijan-support-for-ukraine-op-ed-179693.
5. Bálint Magyar and Bálint Madlovics, *The Anatomy of Post-Communist Regimes: A Conceptual Framework* (Budapest–New York: CEU Press, 2020), 75–84; Alena Ledeneva, *The Global Encyclopaedia of Informality*, vol. 1 (UCL Press, 2018).
6. Patrick Thaddeus Jackson, *Civilizing the Enemy: German Reconstruction and the Invention of the West* (Ann Arbor: University of Michigan Press, 2006), 24.
7. On the importance of Others, with capital O, see Viatcheslav Morozov and Bahar Rumelili, "The External Constitution of European Identity: Russia and Turkey as Europe-Makers," *Cooperation and Conflict* 47, no. 1 (2012): 28–48.
8. Audrius Žulys, "Towards a Union State of Russia and Belarus," *Lithuanian Foreign Policy Review*, no. 15–16 (2005): 148–69.
9. Uladzimir Rouda, "Is Belarus a Classic Post-Communist Mafia State?," in *Stubborn Structures: Reconceptualizing Post-Communist Regimes*, ed. Bálint Magyar (Budapest–New York: CEU Press, 2019), 254.
10. Randall Newnham, "Russia and Belarus: Economic Linkage in a Patron-Client Relationship," *Journal of Belarusian Studies* 9, no. 1 (2020): 3–26.
11. Konstantin Ash, "The Election Trap: The Cycle of Post-Electoral Repression and Opposition Fragmentation in Lukashenko's Belarus," *Democratization* 22, no. 6 (2015): 1030–53.
12. Magyar and Madlovics, *The Anatomy of Post-Communist Regimes*, 333.
13. Magyar and Madlovics, 161; Andrei Kazakevich, "The Belarusian Non-Party Political System: Government, Trust and Institutions 1990-2015," in *Stubborn Structures: Reconceptualizing Post-Communist Regimes*, ed. Bálint Magyar (Budapest–New York: CEU Press, 2019), 353–69.
14. Henry E. Hale, *Patronal Politics: Eurasian Regime Dynamics in Comparative Perspective* (Cambridge: Cambridge University Press, 2015), 60.
15. János Kornai, "The System Paradigm Revisited: Clarification and Additions in the Light of Experiences in the Post-Communist Region," in *Stubborn Structures: Reconceptualizing Post-Communist Regimes*, ed. Bálint Magyar (Budapest–New York: CEU Press, 2019), 45.
16. Hale, *Patronal Politics*, 459.
17. Newnham, "Russia and Belarus."
18. Alexei Pikulik, "Belarus, Russia, and Ukraine as Post-Soviet Rent-Seeking Regimes," in *Stubborn Structures: Reconceptualizing Post-Communist Regimes*, ed. Bálint Magyar (Budapest–New York: CEU Press, 2019), 497.

[19] Cited by Emily Sherwin, "Could Russia and Belarus Trade Oil for National Sovereignty?," *Dw.Com*, February 13, 2019, https://www.dw.com/en/could-russia-and-belarus-trade-oil-for-national-sovereignty/a-47502343.

[20] Shaun Walker, "Tens of Thousands Gather in Minsk for Biggest Protest in Belarus History," *The Guardian*, August 16, 2020, sec. World news, https://www.theguardian.com/world/2020/aug/16/belarus-prepares-for-biggest-protest-yet-after-week-of-anger.

[21] On the class composition of the 2020-2021 Belarusian protests, as well as its gender aspect, see, respectively, Elena Gapova, "Class, Agency, and Citizenship in Belarusian Protest," *Slavic Review* 80, no. 1 (2021): 45–51; Elizaveta Gaufman, "The Gendered Iconography of the Belarus Protest," *New Perspectives* 29, no. 1 (March 1, 2021): 80–89.

[22] Andrew Higgins and Ivan Nechepurenko, "Under Siege in Belarus, Lukashenko Turns to Putin," *The New York Times*, August 15, 2020, sec. World, https://www.nytimes.com/2020/08/15/world/europe/belarus-russia-Lukashenko-Putin.html.

[23] Sarah Rainsford, "Belarus Protests: Putin Pledges $1.5bn Loan at Lukashenko Meeting," *BBC News*, September 14, 2020, sec. Europe, https://www.bbc.com/news/world-europe-54144644.

[24] Victoria Leukavets, "EU Sanctions against Belarus in 2020–2022: Time for a Reappraisal," SCEEUS Report No. 7, December 2, 2022, https://sceeus.se/publikationer/eu-sanctions-against-belarus-in-2020-2022-time-for-a-reappraisal/.

[25] Here and below, when I refer to the official speeches of presidents, I use the dates of speeches to give a better sense of the temporal context in which those speeches were delivered. At the end of the chapter, a reference list of all cited presidential speeches is provided with the respective dates of the speeches together with the web-links to the original documents.

[26] Ilya Yablokov, *Fortress Russia: Conspiracy Theories in the Post-Soviet World* (Cambridge, UK ; Medford, MA: Polity, 2018); Andrei Melville, "'Fortress Russia': Geopolitical Destiny, Unintended Consequences, or Policy Choices," in *The Return of Geopolitics*, ed. Albert J. Bergesen and Christian Suter (Berlin: LIT-Verlag, 2018), 97–112; Sergei Akopov, "Russia's 'Fortresses of Solitude': Social Imaginaries of Loneliness after the Fall of the USSR," *Social Science Information* 59, no. 2 (2020): 288–309.

[27] Aleksandr Burakov, "Русские дома в Беларуси: в чем проблема?" [Russian houses in Belarus: What's the problem?], *DW*, December 13, 2022, https://www.dw.com/ru/russkie-doma-v-belarusi-v-cem-problema/a-64067741.

[28] Mikhail Poloznyakov, "'Мегазадача Белоруссия.' Как Роскомнадзор цензурирует беларуский интернет" ["Mega-task Belarus': How Roskomnadzor is censoring Belarusian internet], Mediazona Belarus, February 8, 2023, https://mediazona.by/article/2023/02/08/rknby; Anna Myroniuk, "Leaked document reveals alleged Kremlin plan to take over Belarus by 2030," *The Kyiv Independent*, February 22, 2023, https://kyivindependent.com/investigations/leaked-document-reveals-alleged-kremlin-plan-to-take-over-belarus-by-2030.

[29] Hale, *Patronal Politics*, 60.

[30] Hale, *Patronal Politics*, 459.

[31] Kornai, "The System Paradigm Revisited," 45.

[32] Magyar and Madlovics, *The Anatomy of Post-Communist Regimes*, 677–78.

[33] Magyar and Madlovics, *The Anatomy of Post-Communist Regimes*, 700, 706.

[34] Ronald J. Hill and Stephen White, "Russia, the Former Soviet Union and Eastern Europe," in *Referendums Around the World*, ed. Matt Qvortrup, eBook (Palgrave Macmillan UK, 2018), 130–31.

[35] Julia Gerlach, *Color Revolutions in Eurasia* (London: Springer, 2014); Valerie J. Bunce and Sharon L. Wolchik, *Defeating Authoritarian Leaders in Postcommunist Countries* (Cambridge: Cambridge University Press, 2011), 177–90.

[36] Shahla Sultanova, "Challenging the Aliyev Regime: Political Opposition in Azerbaijan," *Demokratizatsiya* 22, no. 1 (2014): 15–37; Jody LaPorte, "Hidden in Plain Sight: Political Opposition and Hegemonic Authoritarianism in Azerbaijan," *Post-Soviet Affairs* 31, no. 4 (2015): 339–66.

[37] Anar Valiyev, "Azerbaijan-Russian Relations after Five Day War: Friendship, Enmity or Pragmatism," *Turkish Policy Quarterly*, 2011, 134.

38. Valiyev, "Azerbaijan-Russian Relations after Five Day War."
39. Valiyev, "Azerbaijan-Russian Relations after Five Day War," 134–35.
40. On late Soviet and post-Soviet nation-building projects in Kazakhstan, see Diana T. Kudaibergenova, *Rewriting the Nation in Modern Kazakh Literature: Elites and Narratives* (Lanham, Boulder, New York, and London: Lexington Books, 2017) and Diana T. Kudaibergenova, "'Imagining community' in Soviet Kazakhstan. An historical analysis of narrative on nationalism in Kazakh-Soviet literature," *Nationalities Papers* 41.5 (2013): 839-854.
41. Sally Cummings, *Kazakhstan: Power and the Elite* (London; New York: I.B. Tauris, 2005), 1.
42. Herbert Kitschelt et al., *Post-Communist Party Systems: Competition, Representation, and Inter-Party Cooperation*, First edition (Cambridge: Cambridge University Press, 1999), 39.
43. Kitschelt et al., 21.
44. Barbara Junisbai and Azamat Junisbai, "Regime Type versus Patronal Politics: A Comparison of 'Ardent Democrats' in Kazakhstan and Kyrgyzstan," *Post-Soviet Affairs* 35, no. 3 (2019): 240–57.
45. Magyar and Madlovics, *The Anatomy of Post-Communist Regimes*, 643–45.
46. Hale, *Patronal Politics*, 140.
47. Cummings, *Kazakhstan*, 24–26.
48. Magyar and Madlovics, *The Anatomy of Post-Communist Regimes*, 351.
49. On the controversies that surrounded Kazakhstan's 2019 presidential elections, see Paul Stronski, "Nine Things to Know about Kazakhstan's Election," Carnegie Endowment for International Peace, June 5, 2019, https://carnegieendowment.org/2019/06/05/nine-things-to-know-about-kazakhstan-s-election-pub-79264.
50. Georgi Kantchev, "Kazakhstan's Elite Got Richer on Natural Resources. Then Came the Unrest.," *The Wall Street Journal*, January 7, 2023, sec. World, https://www.wsj.com/articles/kazakhstans-elite-got-richer-on-natural-resources-then-came-the-unrest-11641572839.
51. Lamiat Sabin and Rory Sullivan, "Russian Troops Arrive in Kazakhstan to Quell Unrest as Police Say Officer Beheaded," *The Independent*, January 6, 2022, https://www.independent.co.uk/asia/central-asia/kazakhstan-protests-oil-russia-troops-ctso-b1987634.html.
52. Catherine Putz, "Kazakhstan Annuls Law 'On the First President,'" *The Diplomat*, January 11, 2023, https://thediplomat.com/2023/01/kazakhstan-annuls-law-on-the-first-president/; "Law on Privileges for Nazarbayev, His Family Members Declared Void in Kazakhstan - Presidential Order," *Interfax*, February 15, 2023, https://interfax.com/newsroom/top-stories/87990/.
53. Sally Cummings, "Eurasian Bridge or Murky Waters between East and West? Ideas, Identity and Output in Kazakhstan's Foreign Policy," *Journal of Communist Studies and Transition Politics* 19, no. 3 (2003): 147.
54. The collocation "special military operation" was used on the website of Kazakhstan's president only once. It was used in the third-person summary of Tokayev's visit to Saint Petersburg and was put in quotation marks to emphasize that this was the wording of the question addressed to Tokayev.

The Russia-Ukraine War and China: Neutrality with Imperial Characteristics

Gyula Krajczár

1. Introduction

If we look at China's aspirations and concerns in the global space, it is safe to say that the war in Ukraine has been a distinctly disturbing factor for China. As Qin Gang, the then ambassador to Washington who has since become foreign minister, put it, it is an "unwanted conflict."[1] We do not know whether Xi Jinping encouraged Vladimir Putin when they met in Beijing on February 4, just before the war broke out, or whether there was no talk of war, which is hard to imagine, given that hundreds of thousands of Russian troops were already on the Ukrainian border. The lengthy Sino-Russian agreement signed at the time, which covers a lot of ground, does not mention Ukraine, but it does state—and the Chinese use this in countless arguments—that the parties oppose the further enlargement of NATO, and call on the North Atlantic Alliance to abandon ideological Cold War approaches, to respect the sovereignty, security, and interests of other countries and their civilizational, cultural and historical diversity, and to contribute fairly and objectively to the peaceful development of other states.[2] The treaty also states that the friendship of the two countries shall "have no limits" and that there are no forbidden areas of cooperation. Twenty days later, these phrases took on a special significance, certainly in the sense of whether they would stand up in the new situation as applied to war.

The elements of China's strategy that can be applied to international relations—a multipolar world, economic globalization, peaceful development, civilizational diversity, respect for sovereignty, and so on—are essentially based on a combination of its own interests and identity. What is relatively constant in this is that its interests revolve around two axes: one is its internal focus, China-centricity, and the other is stability. All ideas and risks are measured against this position.

Since 1992–93, China's actions in the international arena have been determined by the need to demand and promote economic globalization and the desire to participate in world governance, in accordance with the internal needs of the economy, the policy of opening-up, and the external guarantees of stability. In the changed external and internal environment since 2008–2010, major internal structural transformations and new industrial policies on China's part have led to a perceptibly more aggressive pursuit of the same international objectives, made more pronounced by the county's significantly increased economic, developmental, military, diplomatic, and cultural weight. In this process of transformation, China has increasingly become a global competitor to the United States. The interests of the two countries have come into conflict in many areas, and this has begun to significantly reshape China's external relations. Its strategic vision has not changed significantly, but the adaptation has brought with it a whole new set of circumstances.

The Ukraine war is not the first time that China has been confronted with a conflict between its declared principles and its interests in the Ukraine war. Nor is it the first time that it has had to resolve a problem in which two countries, with each of which it has good and important relations, are at odds. These are tactical challenges for Chinese foreign policy making. But relations with the peoples and state formations to its north have been a strategic issue throughout its history. This has included Russia from the 17th century, then the Soviet Union for much of the 20th century, and finally the post-Soviet states. For China, the relationship has always been inescapable in terms of security, economy, infrastructure, and intercultural relations. Throughout history, it has shaped a range of solutions, behaviors, and attitudes, and these traditions continue to influence Chinese strategic thinking today.

In this study, we will first examine the theoretical basis and difficulties of China's perception of sovereignty as a foreign policy in general, as well as its policy of defining its relationship to the war in Ukraine and, more broadly, to the post-Soviet world. We will then examine the relationship between China and the relevant post-Soviet states, with a particular focus on military-industrial cooperation, and how the war has shaped these relations. We will then address the motives for Chinese behavior in relation to the war and, finally, make a brief attempt at assessing the hopes and risks that the changes hold for China.

2. Chinese foreign policy before the war: imperial sovereignty and economic imperialism

2.1. For China, the other side is the West

For a long time, it has been almost a truism among experts that China, like many post-colonial or newly developing countries, has a very rigid concept of sovereignty. This is suggested by the five principles of peaceful coexistence on which it is based and which originally formed the introduction to the 1954 India-China Agreement.[3] The principles are based on mutual respect for sovereignty and territorial integrity, mutual non-aggression, non-interference in internal affairs, and peaceful coexistence.

These principles are generally adhered to very strictly, although their practical application with respect to international law often involves ambiguities, which are reflected in the Chinese attitude towards such law and institutions. The fact that Chinese foreign relations have traditionally been characterized by a middle-consciousness, Confucian hierarchy, and moral approaches based on this, plays a significant role here. And although the Chinese state has been trying to integrate into the international community since the beginning of the 20th century (at the latest), and to adopt norms based on Western legal developments, its way of thinking remains strongly influenced by cultural, political-moral and imperial attitudes and traditions. The applicability of imperial traditions—or "Chinese characteristics," as they are often called – is underlined by the fact that they must still govern a vast complex country with a specific culture.

All of this leads to facts such as the Chinese for a long time not involving themselves in peacekeeping because they do not interfere in the internal affairs of other countries, although they have recently become involved because that is what is expected of a great country with responsibilities. Another example is that they have no problem in cooperating with unacceptable regimes, saying that it is none of their business what happens in the country concerned. This often looks like cynicism from the outside, but there is a system to it, based on their own imperial considerations. This mixture of adaptation, desire to modernize, domestic interests, and traditionalism always has surprises in store, as the Chinese saying "China sleeps in the same bed but dreams differently" can be applied to this situation.

When the referendum on secession from Ukraine was held in Crimea on March 16, 2014, China abstained from the UN vote both before and afterwards. The preceding vote in the Security Council was on a resolution declaring the referendum invalid, while the subsequent one in the General Assembly was on a resolution calling on members not to recognize any change in Crimea's international status. The term "neutrality" was not used, but several Chinese spokespersons mentioned China's lack of support for either side in the UN discussions. It is typical that in the Chinese discourse, the West was already portrayed as one side and Russia as the other, on the basis that in the UN, Western countries supported one position and Russia the other. Prime Minister Li Keqiang, at a press conference at the time, said of Ukraine itself and its territory, "We respect Ukraine's independence, sovereignty, and territorial integrity." He added that "the Ukraine issue has added to the complexity of the geopolitical situation and has affected the process of the global economic recovery."[4] Typically, Zhang Lihua, a Chinese author working in the Western analytical ecosystem, notes that the pursuit of balance is very characteristic of the Chinese mentality, with the traditional philosophical view, indoctrinated by the imperial empire, that all beings have both yin and yang to some degree, or, as he puts it, "one yin and one yang is the way."[5]

2.2. Try to love Russia

After the annexation of Crimea, China sought to maintain good relations with both Russia and Ukraine. However, it was the nexus with Russia that was obviously more pronounced and visible, both in terms of size and importance. This relationship has become exceptionally close since Xi Jinping came to power in 2012.

On the other hand, there is no great tradition of good Russian-Chinese relations. Over time, Russia has proven to be an unpleasant neighbor in the Far East. Once the Russian empire caught China in its sights, it constantly behaved as an aggressor and colonizer, and even in the form of the Soviet Union this was more of a modulation than anything else, the essence having remained the same. In other words, the Chinese conception of sovereignty and security, burdened with imperial traditions, encountered and struggled with another country's conception of sovereignty and security, also burdened with imperial traditions. Even after the Chinese Communists took power, relations between the two countries were only good for a brief moment in historical terms. From the second half of the 1980s, relations began to normalize, but Deng Xiaoping considered the Soviet Union to be the greatest security threat throughout his life.

As China's growth took off and the policies based on it became more pragmatic, the public discourse in relation to Russia became more and more about energy, raw materials, and the economic potential of the Far East. The most important thing was that the borders were fixed. This required considerable self-restraint on the part of the Chinese, since it is known that large areas of the Qing empire had come under Russian-Soviet control, and even Mao Zedong and later Deng Xiaoping did not consider this matter closed. China initially appeared to be more active in the normalization of relations, with the focus mainly on economic issues, such as the purchase of energy resources and the construction of the necessary pipeline systems and networks, the construction and interconnection of transport and trade infrastructure, and the facilitation of Chinese employment in Russia. The latter was a particularly sensitive issue that has been very much in the public discourse in China ever since, although it is only sporadically allowed into the media. From the late 1980s, citizens in the Soviet Union and then later in the Russian Federation became free to move, and the already sparsely populated Far East subsequently suffered a major population loss due to relocations to the European part of the country. At the same time, the nearby Chinese provinces, known as Dongbei, has long been a region with acute unemployment problems and where the crisis in heavy industry has created one of the most extensive rust belts. The "Sinophobia" that still exists in Russian political thinking (the fear that the Chinese could flood into Siberia) has prevented a more flexible stance on work permits. Moreover, Moscow's thinking in the 1990s still viewed Russia as a European state, and relations with the Far East were kept at a moderate level.

The deterioration of Russia's relations with the West cannot be linked to a single point in time. Rather, it has been a long process, one accompanied by a parallel process of increasing openness towards its Asian neighbors, including China. This has assumed its most obvious form in energy and other economic-infrastructural cooperation. However, the process has also been uneven on the Chinese side. From 1994 onwards, they have signed inter-state agreements from time to time, using various linguistic formulas to describe their increasingly intimate relations: a "cooperative partnership" in 1994, a "strategic cooperative partnership" in 1996, and a "good neighborliness, friendship, and cooperation" treaty in 2001.[6] They agreed on a series of international events, such as the war in the former Yugoslavia, Kosovo, the war in Iraq, and sanctions against Iran. There is also the view that the Arab Spring was the series of events that really brought the two countries closer together.[7]

However, it should be noted that, according to Medeiros, for example, the "Chinese threat" is not exclusively an American or Western European invention, but is also alive in Russia, mostly in the form of and based on the aforementioned Sinophobia. Strong negative stereotypes are at work: despite administratively difficult employment, small and large Chinatowns have sprung up in Russian cities in Siberia and the Far East, and news of fights and Chinese-bashings are frequent.

The image of Russians in Chinese public opinion is not good either. The memory of old history is full of negative symbols, such as the "unequal treaties" and the pogroms in Blagoveshchensk. During the conflict with the Soviet Union, Chinese propaganda for decades pitted public opinion against the Soviets (Russians), while since the break-up of the Soviet Union, the ideological-political discourse has been heavily influenced by the bad policies that led to the abandonment of the socialist course in the Soviet Union. This picture has changed a lot over the past decade or so of friendliness, but it is still a curious situation that Chinese public opinion has become divided over the Ukraine war,[8] as both anti-Russian and pro-Russian readings of Chinese nationalism are available in this respect.

2.3. Building a trade belt is the road

With the break-up of the Soviet Union, China became bordered by Kazakhstan, Kyrgyzstan, and Tajikistan in addition to Russia, and its immediate surroundings included the other two Central Asian countries of Uzbekistan and Turkmenistan. Qin Gang interpreted the responses to the break-up differently at the two ends of the Eurasian continent. On the European side, the decision to expand NATO eastwards had caused the current problems between Russia and the West. On the Asian side, however, the creation of the so-called "Shanghai Five" mechanism and the signing in 1996 of the Treaty on Deepening Military Trust in Border Regions between China and all four of its post-Soviet neighbors essentially resolved border problems.[9] Although Tajikistan was ravaged by a long civil war and Kyrgyzstan by regime changes, repeatedly backed by mass demonstrations, the region's overall political and security situation was balanced. The region's relations with its larger neighbors and the influence posed by them differed, however. Although the region's countries were particularly concerned about their independence, they nevertheless oriented themselves towards Moscow from a cultural, security, and infrastructural point of view. At the same time, Russia was no longer able to provide the same level of assistance in material terms, and this enabled China to step into the vacuum through its companies and became the region's most important partner in terms of trade and investment. Moreover, it was with the intention of building infrastructure links to these countries that the very first phase of the Chinese Belt and Road Initiative was begun. The culmination of this process is currently the Trans-Asian Gas Pipeline from Turkmenistan to China, which connects to the Trans-Caspian Pipeline under the Caspian Sea and to the Russian network. It can also be said that the Chinese have emerged as a culturally alien element in these essentially secular but largely Muslim countries, and their level of acceptance is nowhere near that afforded to the Russians. Moreover, this has been reinforced in recent years by a sense of public solidarity with the problems facing the Uighurs in China.

A very different relationship has developed with Ukraine, which the Chinese view as distant yet having great business potential. In 2013, the two countries entered into a strategic partnership. After Kyiv's association agreement with the European Union entered into force in 2017, Beijing saw a growing potential of including the country in the Belt and Road Initiative through various projects. By the early 2020s, China had become Ukraine's largest trading partner. In 2021, an intergovernmental infrastructure development agreement was signed. President Volodymyr Zelensky said at the time that Ukraine would become China's bridge to Europe.[10] According to the Ukrainian Embassy in Beijing, trade between the two countries in 2021 was $18.97 billion, with a slight surplus on the Chinese side. Ukrainian exports ranged from ores and grains to machinery and wood products.[11] Ukraine has become a very important supplier of agricultural products, accounting for 80 percent of China's corn imports. For example, the Chinese company COFCO, which trades agricultural products internationally, has built up a complete value chain for a range of agricultural products, from production to extensive trade, and not just to China.[12] This has involved significant investment in building new dedicated terminals in four Ukrainian ports: Mykolayiv, Chornomorsk, Yuzhne and Mariupol. In Mariupol, for example, grain transshipment capacity has been tripled. But China has also been involved commercially in projects to reduce Ukraine's dependence on Russia. For example, Chinese technology has been supplied for the conversion of gas-fired power plants dependent on Russian gas to coal-fired ones.

2.4. Chinese intrusion into the military-industrial symbiosis

China has paid close attention to the Ukrainian and Russian defense industries, which are in a special situation. After the break-up of the Soviet Union, a significant part of the former Soviet defense industry was transferred to Ukraine, with the Russian military becoming its main market, while the Ukrainian military became an important market for the Russian defense industry. A contractual system was set up between the two countries, and a division of labor in arms development was effectively established. China, which has been under an arms embargo by the United States and the European Union since 1989, entered this situation as a potential buyer and investor.[13] China itself has pursued and continues to pursue a very intensive and diversified program of military development, trying to overcome its technological disadvantage vis-à-vis the West, and especially the United States (which is still significant in many areas). China's development landscape is very uneven, with some areas where it is absolutely world class, such as anti-ship ballistic missiles (ASBMs), and missile technology in general. At the same time, in many areas, the practice is to buy or try to invest in companies with advanced technologies in parallel with their own development. The West cannot be made a target of this practice, mainly because of the arms embargo.

Sino-Soviet arms development and trade relations date back to 1949. Although for most of the time the two countries were positioned as adversaries, very important aspects of Chinese military development were linked to the Soviet relationship. In the 1950s, complete production structures were adopted, along with Soviet management culture, but even then, the Soviets did not share their state-of-the-art technologies. Moreover, the break between the two countries happened relatively quickly, leaving the Chinese on their own, trying to understand and develop the technologies and production processes in their hands. Typically, this was the case with their nuclear program, which was launched by a Soviet-Chinese treaty in 1951. Under this agreement, China exported uranium ore to the Soviet Union in return for intensive assistance with the program, which began in earnest after the Korean War in 1954. After a little less than a decade, Soviet experts, plans, documentation, and data were withdrawn and the Chinese completed the program on their own.[14]

In the 1980s, the United States and other Western countries slowly relaxed the rules on arms sales to communist China, at which time Western weapons were transferred to the Chinese military. However, this was completely halted in 1989, and the arms embargo has remained in place with minor modifications ever since. From then on, the Soviet Union, and soon Russia and Ukraine, became the target of Chinese military procurement.

From the 1990s onwards, the situation was markedly affected by the fact that cash-strapped Russia (and Ukraine), with a fluctuating economic performance, needed new military industrial plans and new structural approaches, including production for export beyond the former Soviet Union. China became a buyer in a wide variety of areas, buying cruisers, submarines, fighters, and other equipment it was also developing domestically. At the same time, both the Russians and the Chinese sought to position this relationship strategically. The Russians were counting on their sales to influence the direction of Chinese military development in the long term, which was an important business consideration given the soviet legacy. However, traditional fears remained, and they were far from opening up their full technological arsenal to the Chinese. Beijing, on the other hand, was only seeking temporary solutions and essential technologies, aiming for self-development and self-sufficiency in the long term. Thus, the process was not without disagreements.

On several occasions, the Ukrainians stepped in as suppliers when the Russians were reluctant. This was to the Chinese advantage from a risk management point of view, but the Ukrainian defense industry was itself a desirable target for Chinese buyers and investors. Ukraine manufactures missile components, transport aircraft, aircraft engines, gas turbines for ships, armored vehicles, and so on. From Ukraine, for example, China obtained hovercrafts, essential for operations in the South China Sea archipelago, and the Kuznetsov-class "heavy aircraft carrier cruiser" *Varyag* (formerly *Riga*), which was 68% completed at the Mykolayiv shipyards at the moment the Soviet Union broke up, and which served as the basis for the first Chinese aircraft carrier in service, the *Liaoning*. Another indication of the changing Chinese focus on Ukraine was the purchase of a 41 percent stake in the Ukrainian aircraft-engine manufacturer Motor Sich by Skyrizon, a company linked to the well-known Chinese investor Wang Jing. Motor Sich was later effectively re-nationalized by the Ukrainian government under pressure from the US government after Skyrizon was placed on the US so-called Military End User List of sanctioned companies.

The annexation of Crimea radically changed this military-industrial triangle. Russian-Ukrainian military-industrial relations were effectively dismantled, with very serious consequences for both sides, mainly because of the disruption of value chains. At the same time, Ukraine began to orient itself more intensively towards the West. Not surprisingly, China was also quick to find points of contact in the new situation. In Russia, on the one hand, it found increased willingness to cooperate, while in Ukraine, on the other, it sought to take advantage of the fact that it had already made itself compatible with the Ukrainian military industry in many respects. However, as the fate of Motor Sich revealed, slow changes to China's disadvantage were also underway.

The war has had a particular impact on the arms market. Russia, the world's second-largest arms exporter, sold 26% fewer weapons abroad in 2022 for the simple reason that it needed them itself.[15] Arms supplied to Russia are subject to US and

EU sanctions, which, along with other sanctions, are respected by Chinese companies. US President Joe Biden has repeatedly stated that there is "no evidence" that Beijing is supplying arms to Russia, although intelligence sources have repeatedly raised the possibility. The arms trade is now trending in the reverse direction as well (also under sanctions), as China is now a seller, and is being openly touted as a major arms exporter in the future.[16]

3. China and the war: Russia, the US, and the red line of nuclear threat

3.1. Within imperial neutrality, Russia is certainly more important

China has clearly tried to adopt a neutral position since the outbreak of the war in Ukraine. Just as in the case of the formal secession of Abkhazia and South Ossetia and the annexation of Crimea, China has not chosen a declared side and has sought to maintain its existing relations with the relevant parties in each case. However, since relations with Russia have been much more extensive and intense than with Georgia or even Ukraine, the much greater importance of fraternization with Russia has been very clearly visible within their characteristic neutrality. This is, of course, further underplayed by the fact that, in Chinese eyes, Russia is a potential pole of the multipolar world—a pole which, at least for the moment, seems to be one of the counterweights to the pole that is most hostile to Beijing, the United States. From this perspective, the weight of Georgia and Ukraine is less significant for Beijing.

The conflicts themselves, however, take on additional significance in their Chinese interpretation when compared to Xi Jinping's so-called Global Security Initiative,[17] which initially received relatively moderate international attention but was widely reported in the Chinese media, and finally summarized in a voluminous document.[18] In it, Xi has, without mentioning it, essentially interpreted the five principles of peaceful coexistence for a globalized world, complementing it with the concept of "indivisible security." The phrase comes from the 1975 Helsinki Final Act, which reflected a very different world situation, and was intended as a tool for managing the risks of the Cold War.[19] In introducing the initiative at the Boao Forum in 2022, Xi said, among other things, that all parties should "stay committed to abiding by the purposes and principles of the UN Charter, reject the Cold War mentality, oppose unilateralism, and say no to group politics and bloc confrontation." The pro-Russian elements of the Chinese statements on the war in Ukraine derive from this position, namely, that NATO has pushed Russia into a corner by wanting Ukraine (and Georgia) to be one of its members; that NATO has militarized Eastern Europe through its actions, and; that NATO and the United States are benefiting financially from the war.

Chinese politicians and media most often describe the sanctions against Russia as "immoral" and "illegal." This is also what is usually said about sanctions in general, such as those against Iran, arguing that they impede the free flow of goods and services, and hinder the establishment and operation of value and supply chains. The Chinese also object to the idea that laws made in some countries, most notably the United States, can be enforced in other countries (long-arm jurisdiction), namely, that sanctions can be imposed on and enforced in countries other than those where the sanctions were devised. In the case of Russia, however, the Chinese interest in the country's survival is particularly evident. On the one hand, it is true that China and Chinese companies are enforcing the sanctions against Russia; they have essentially pulled out of the Russian tech sector and their large active banks such as ICBC and Bank of China have suspended their financing activities, and are proceeding very cautiously, are avoiding signing new contracts even in areas not seriously affected by sanctions. On the other hand, they openly admit that they do this not for their own pleasure, but because of cost-benefit analyses. At the same time, there is also a sense that China does not want to appear to be supporting Moscow's war at all.[20]

In terms of the Chinese position on sanctions, it is worth noting that it is not just about protecting Russians or value chains more broadly. China is trying to avoid becoming a direct target of sanctions itself. At the same time, it has prepared its own legal system to be able to use sanctions if necessary, and in some cases has already made use of this possibility.[21]

Yan Xuetong, dean of the Institute of International Relations at Tsinghua University, certainly has good reason to argue that China has no ambition to act or play a role in global security affairs. A practical explanation is that there is a huge gap between it and the United States in the military field.[22] Xi Jinping's report to the 20th Party Congress in the autumn of 2022 also only speaks of military capabilities, saying that, among many other things, the country should be able to "win local wars."[23]

In the context of the war in Ukraine, several politicians, analysts, and media have raised the question of Taiwan, whether China will attempt a military occupation of the island, either now or at some point in the near future. The almost unanimous response from China—from spokespersons and academics—has always been the same as the one Yan advocates in his cited article: as long as the United States does not offer military support for Taiwan's de jure independence, it is unlikely that China will abandon the path of peaceful development.[24]

3.2. The Chinese gaze looks everywhere for the United States

The war in Ukraine has proved to be much larger in scale, much longer in duration, and much more drastic in shaping world politics than Russia's former aggressions and annexations. The events have forced all countries in the world to take a stand, at least in the UN. Thus, Chinese policy, which had been tried and tested according to well-known guidelines, has also required considerable retooling. The starting point for this has been the assertion that from China's point of view the war in Ukraine is an "unwanted conflict," and that "China likes peace, opposes war."[25] The most quoted formulation of the position was taken from a telephone conversation between then Foreign Minister Wang Yi and his Spanish counterpart José Manuel Albares: "China is not a party to the crisis, still less wants to be subjected to sanctions, and it has the right to safeguard its legitimate and lawful rights and interests."[26] Additional motives in developing a *de facto* neutral policy have been the important fact that world seems divided on the war in Ukraine, as is evident from the very first votes in the UN, and that China does not want to jeopardize its relations with Europe.

All this suggests that the Chinese interpretation of the conflict is two-layered. On the one hand, there is an explicitly anti-war layer according to which China is not a party to the conflict and wants to see it end as quickly as possible. Moreover, China sees itself as a partner to both sides and maintains its views on full respect for national sovereignty and territorial integrity. On the other hand, there is the broader conflict between NATO and, in particular, the United States, on one side, and Russia, on the other, in which—according to Chinese view—NATO wishes to expand and militarize the Eastern European region. In this view, NATO is seen as an unwanted Cold War construct in its very nature and the bombing of the Chinese embassy in Belgrade by NATO forces on May 7, 1999 is a regular feature of Chinese discourse on this subject. The first layer reflects the approach of a regular state; the second accords with the approach of a great state, or an empire. What does not appear in this interpretation, and what gives the Chinese approach a pro-Russian character (while remaining neutral) is that, while emphasizing Ukraine's sovereignty and territorial integrity, it does not include the legitimate security needs of the Ukrainian people which are entrusted to the Ukrainian state.

China's comprehensive approach was essentially formalized in a 12-point "peace plan," summarizing China's position on the war.[27] This document stresses the recognition of the sovereignty, independence, and territorial integrity of all countries, condemns the Cold War mentality, and calls for a cessation of hostilities and a resumption of peace negotiations. The humanitarian crisis must be resolved, and the civilian population and prisoners of war must be protected. The document also addresses the nuclear issue on two points. On the one hand, it stresses the need to keep nuclear power plants safe and, on the other, states that nuclear weapons should not be used, nuclear war should not be waged, nuclear threats should not be made, and nuclear proliferation should be prevented. The document also refers to chemical and biological weapons, and expresses China's opposition to their research, development, and use under all circumstances. The resolution specifically addresses the issue of "unilateral sanctions," saying that it can only envisage sanctions that have been approved by the UN Security Council.

During his visit to Moscow in March 2023, Xi Jinping repeatedly stressed that there are "no limits" to the friendship between China and Russia. Vladimir Putin welcomed the Chinese "peace plan" in return. Xi later also discussed the proposal with Ukrainian President Volodymyr Zelensky online. Zelensky should, of course, keep all options open, but neither the Russians nor the Ukrainians are inclined to peace talks for the time being. The Chinese special envoy, Li Hui, has held talks in Moscow, Kyiv, and several European capitals, but he has had to admit that the situation is not at all ripe for peace talks. However, these actions have also demonstrated that China is an advocate of peace and peaceful negotiations and that an actor with whom everyone is willing to negotiate.

For China, the real stakes in this conflict concern major developments in the international system and China's position in it, and thus its relationship with the United States. This is the most important factor in the Chinese framing of this issue, which is also conceived as a kind of equilibrium approach. In the Chinese view, the dominance of the United States, the way in which Washington conducts international affairs—a Cold War approach based on a zero-sum game, according to the Chinese—poses an obstacle to Chinese development, whose containment has already been declared an objective by the last two American administrations. At the same time, the United States is in fact the most important partner of the People's Republic of China in all respects, and it is also an important and recognized base for Chinese development. In other words, they want to navigate the Russian nexus and the war by striking the right balance between limiting the influence and reach of the United States and at least maintaining a diverse partnership.

4. Conclusion

The concepts of security, sovereignty, and neutrality are almost taken for granted in international relations as reciprocal categories with mutually necessary guarantees between countries that are legal equals. However, when a country is conferred with the adjective "imperial," it results in profoundly unequal relations, as the Chinese understand them, between that country, say China, and the rest of the world. In all three categories—imperial security, imperial sovereignty, and imperial neutrality—what the imperial actor is entitled to as a right and can demand for protection is almost self-evidently denied to the non-imperial partner.

Imperial security for both the Russians and the Chinese means that while they may pose a threat to other countries, the latter cannot be in the position to threaten them. *Imperial sovereignty* means that, while the imperial party considers its own sovereignty inviolable, it does not consider the sovereignty of the non-imperial party the same way, either economically or militarily. China's Janus-faced "peace plan" recognizes Ukraine's sovereignty but does not demand the withdrawal of Russian troops. An acceptable peace, in China's understanding of such, could comprise a ceasefire with an acknowledgement of the borders presently occupied (at least temporarily) territories, which would be an indirect recognition of Russian-occupied military zone.

Finally, *imperial neutrality* is neutrality interpreted according to China's own interests. Beijing must be experiencing less and less confidence in its original hope that the conflict would end quickly and that only slight modifications would have to made in its old policy towards all the parties concerned. Relatively quickly, they were forced to draw a line in the sand for Russia in its prosecution of the war: nuclear threats, the use of nuclear weapons, and the development and use of chemical and biological weapons were all considered unacceptable. China declares even Russia's threat of using these weapons of mass destruction as a red line because if they were to be used, it would eliminate the possibility of maintaining a neutral intermediate position, and would force China to side with the West in support of Ukraine. China, however, does not want to take either the Russians' or the West's side across the board. It is this imperial neutrality that gives it the most room to maneuver and the opportunity to gain the most benefit from the situation, preferably without risk.

China also wants to maintain its position in Europe, and wants the EU and individual European countries to "not pick sides." At the same time, it is clearly facing the fact that the many European countries perceive the war in Ukraine as a watershed moment, and that significant European political forces are working to limit Chinese activity. This situation foreshadows a tactically reactive, but also very intense, European policy in which pro-Russian Chinese politicking is obviously a major drawback.

The Russians seem to accept Beijing's Russia-policy as expressed in the peace plan (China sets certain limits, but otherwise it will not force or encourage Moscow to do anything on Ukraine), while seeking the broadest possible economic cooperation. For China, this is essential, first and foremost in terms of energy, and secondly in terms of transport logistics. Both require major infrastructure developments, many of which are already underway while others are on the drawing board, and in which the Central Asian countries and Mongolia are increasingly involved as third parties.[28] In this process, sanctions are explicitly a linchpin, but this battle is already being fought with the United States, which China needs enormously as a market, as a source of technology, as a broad partner, and as a key factor in its 21st century development. And here we have come full circle.

Notes

1. Gang Qin, "The Ukraine Crisis and Its Aftermath," *The National Interest*, April 18, 2022, https://nationalinterest.org/feature/chinese-ambassador-ukraine-crisis-and-its-aftermath-201867.
2. "Joint Statement of the Russian Federation and the People's Republic of China on the International Relations Entering a New Era and the Global Sustainable Development," President of Russia, February 4, 2023, http://en.kremlin.ru/supplement/5770.
3. "Agreement between the Republic of India and the People's Republic of China on Trade and Intercourse between Tibet Region of China and India" (INTSer5. Indian Treaty Series, 1954), http://www.commonlii.org/in/other/treaties/INTSer/1954/5.html.
4. "China Premier Says Respects Ukraine Integrity, Won't Be Drawn on Crimea," *Reuters*, March 15, 2015, https://www.reuters.com/article/us-china-parliament-ukraine-idUSKBN0MB05220150315.
5. Lihua Zhang, "Explaining China's Position on the Crimea Referendum," Carnegie Endowment for International Peace, April 1, 2015, https://carnegietsinghua.org/2015/04/01/explaining-china-s-position-on-crimea-referendum-pub-59600.
6. Evan S. Medeiros, *China's International Behavior: Activism, Opportunism, and Diversification* (Santa Monica, CA: RAND Corporation, 2009).
7. Lukács Krajcsír, *A kínai-orosz kooperáció a XXI. század elején: Kína, Oroszország és a Sanghaji Együttműködési Szervezet* [Sino-Russian cooperation at the turn of the 21st century: China, Russia, and the Shanghai Cooperation Organization] (Veszprém: Veszprémi Humán Tudományokért Alapítvány, 2014).
8. Xuetong Yan, "China's Ukraine Conundrum," *Foreign Affairs*, May 2, 2022, https://www.foreignaffairs.com/articles/china/2022-05-02/chinas-ukraine-conundrum.
9. Qin, "Chinese Ambassador."
10. Yunis Sharifli, "Ukraine: China's New Bridge to Europe?," *euractiv*, October 20, 2021, https://www.euractiv.com/section/central-asia/opinion/ukraine-chinas-new-bridge-to-europe/.
11. "Trade and Economic Cooperation," Embassy of Ukraine in the People's Republic of China, May 16, 2022, https://china.mfa.gov.ua/en/partnership/economic-cooperation-en/trade-and-investments.
12. "COFCO around the World: Ukraine - a Solid Partnership with Potential to Grow," COFCO International, August 5, 2021, https://www.cofcointernational.com/stories/cofco-around-the-world-ukraine-a-solid-partnership-with-potential-to-grow/.
13. Sarah Kirchberger, "The End of a Military-Industrial Triangle: Arms-Industrial Co-operation between China, Russia and Ukraine after the Crimea Crisis," *SIRIUS - Zeitschrift für Strategische Analysen* 1, no. 2 (June 12, 2017): 1–19.
14. John W. Lewis and Litai Xue, *China Builds the Bomb*, 1st ed. (Stanford: Stanford University Press, 1991).
15. "Russia Forecasts Drop in Arms Export Revenue," *Defense News*, August 29, 2022, https://www.defensenews.com/global/europe/2022/08/29/russia-forecasts-drop-in-arms-export-revenue/.
16. Vasabjit Banerjee and Benjamin Tkach, "The Coming Chinese Weapons Boom," *Foreign Affairs*, October 11, 2022, https://www.foreignaffairs.com/china/coming-chinese-weapons-boom.
17. "Xi Jinping Delivers a Keynote Speech at the Opening Ceremony of the Boao Forum for Asia Annual Conference 2022," Ministry of Foreign Affairs of the People's Republic of China, April 21, 2022, https://www.fmprc.gov.cn/eng/zxxx_662805/202204/t20220421_10671083.html.
18. "The Global Security Initiative," Ministry of Foreign Affairs of the People's Republic of China, February 21, 2023, https://www.fmprc.gov.cn/mfa_eng/wjbxw/202302/t20230221_11028348.html.
19. Chris Cash, "What Is China's Global Security Initiative?," Council on Geostrategy, September 29, 2022, https://www.geostrategy.org.uk/research/what-is-chinas-global-security-initiative/.

[20] Licci C. Lee, "China's Long Game in Russia: Violating Sanctions? No. Ensuring Russia's Survival? Yes," *Russia Matters*, June 30, 2022, https://www.russiamatters.org/analysis/chinas-long-game-russia-violating-sanctions-no-ensuring-russias-survival-yes.

[21] Evan A. Feigenbaum and Adam Szubin, "What China Has Learned From the Ukraine War," *Foreign Affairs*, February 14, 2023, https://www.foreignaffairs.com/china/what-china-has-learned-ukraine-war.

[22] Yan, "China's Ukraine Conundrum."

[23] "Full Text of the Report to the 20th National Congress of the Communist Party of China." Ministry of Foreign Affairs of People's Republic of China, October 25, 2022, https://www.fmprc.gov.cn/eng/zxxx_662805/202210/t20221025_10791908.html.

[24] Yan, "China's Ukraine Conundrum."

[25] Qin, "Chinese Ambassador."

[26] "FM Holds Phone Talks with Spanish Counterpart," The State Council, March 15, 2022, http://english.www.gov.cn/statecouncil/wangyi/202203/15/content_WS622fe5b4c6d09c94e48a6a56.html.

[27] "China's Position on the Political Settlement of the Ukraine Crisis," *Xinhua*, February 24, 2022, https://english.news.cn/20230224/f6bf935389394eb0988023481ab26af4/c.html.

[28] Gaye Christoffersen, "Central Asia over a Decade: The Shifting Balance in Central Asia between Russia and China," The Asan Forum, November 30, 2022, https://theasanforum.org/central-asia-over-a-decade-the-shifting-balance-in-central-asia-between-russia-and-china/.

Contributors

Kostiantyn Fedorenko is a social scientist with a background in political science. He is a research fellow at the Center for East European and International Studies (ZOiS), Berlin, concentrated on an intersection of contentious politics and migration. He received his M.A. degree in European and European Legal Studies from Europa-Kolleg Hamburg, and a Master degree in Political Science from Kyiv-Mohyla Academy. He is also a doctoral student at the Humboldt University of Berlin. In 2014-2019, he worked as a political analyst for the Institute for Euro-Atlantic Cooperation (Kyiv).

Dóra Győrffy is a political economist. She is a Professor at the Corvinus University of Budapest, Institute of Economics. She holds a BA in Government from Harvard University (class of 2001), an MA (2003) and PhD (2006) in International Relations and European Studies from the Central European University and a Doctor of Science degree in Economics (2015) from the Hungarian Academy of Sciences. Her research deals with issues of international political economy with a particular focus on its post-communist member states. She has published 4 monographs and over 70 journal articles in English and Hungarian on topics important to the CEE region including the problems of distrust and weak institutions, European integration, macroeconomic imbalances, economic convergence, and the rise of populism.

Gyula Krajczár is a journalist, researcher, and China expert. He spent most of his career at the now defunct Hungarian daily *Népszabadság*, as a journalist and senior editor of the economic and later the foreign affairs sections. He spent years in Beijing as a correspondent. For a long time, he was deputy editor-in-chief of the daily. He holds a PhD from the Doctoral School of International Relations at Corvinus University of Budapest. He is currently deputy editor-in-chief and foreign affairs editor of the Hungarian political weekly *Jelen*.

Péter Krekó is a political scientist, social psychologist, and disinformation expert. He is a senior fellow at the Washington-based CEPA think tank and a PopBack Fellow at the University of Cambridge. Earlier, he was a guest researcher at the Europe's Futures – Ideas for Action program of the Vienna-based Institute for Human Sciences (IWM), and a non-resident Associate Fellow at the Johns Hopkins University SAIS Bologna Institute of Policy Research. He is an associate professor with habilitation at the Department of Social Psychology at ELTE PPK. During 2016-2017, Krekó worked as a Fulbright Visiting Professor in the United States at the Central Eurasian Studies Department of Indiana University. He wrote his PhD dissertation on the social psychology of conspiracy theories in 2014, and he habilitated in 2020. His main areas of expertise are the psychology of disinformation and conspiracy theories, Russian political influence in the West.

Lidia Kuzemska is a sociologist with an interdisciplinary interest in forced migration, internal displacement, borders, and citizenship. She is a 2022/2023 Prisma Ukraïna Fellow at the Forum Transregionale Studien (Berlin), a Research Affiliate at the Internal Displacement Research Program (SOAS University of London), and a peer-reviewer of the Knowledge Platform and Connection Hub (UN Network on Migration).

Tamás Lattmann is an international lawyer, currently working as Associate Professor and Head of Department of Social Studies of the Tomori Pál University (Budapest), Associate Professor at the University of New York in Prague (Prague), and the general manager of the Centre for European Progression (Brussels). In 2016-2019, he was a senior researcher at the Institute of International Relations Prague (IIR) and earlier worked at the Eötvös Loránd University (ELTE) and the University of National Defense (ZMNE) and the National University of Public Service (NKE) in Budapest. His research and publication activities cover international and European law.

Bálint Madlovics is a political scientist and economist. He is a Junior Research Fellow at the CEU Democracy Institute, visiting professor at Eötvös Loránd University (ELTE), and a doctoral student of Corvinus University of Budapest (BCE). He holds an MA in Political Science (2018) from Central European University and BAs in sociology and applied economics. He has published peer-reviewed articles, book chapters, and books on post-communist regimes since 2015. He was a research fellow at the Financial Research Institute in Budapest (2018–2019) and visiting professor at BCE (2022).

Bálint Magyar is a sociologist. He is a Senior Research Fellow at the CEU Democracy Institute. He was an activist of the anti-communist dissident movement before the regime change, Member of the Hungarian Parliament (1990–2010), and Minister of Education (1996–1998, 2002–2006). He has been publishing and editing writings on post-communist regimes since 2013. He was an Open Society fellow (2015–2016), Hans Speier Visiting Professor at the New School for Social Research (2017), and Senior Research Fellow at CEU Institute for Advanced Study (2018–2019).

Oksana Mikheieva is a historian and sociologist. She is a DAAD Professor at the European University Viadrina Frankfurt (Oder), Germany, and Professor of Sociology at the Ukrainian Catholic University (Lviv). In 2016, she was a visiting professor in Ukraine European Dialogue at the Institute for Human Science (Vienna), and in 2015 she was Eugene and Daymel Shklar Research Fellow Harvard University, Ukrainian Research Institute. She is a member of Taras Shevchenko Scientific Society and the Ukrainian Sociological Association. Additionally, she serves on the editorial board of the academic peer-reviewed journal *Ukraina Moderna* and the Analytical Information Journal *East (Skhid)*. Her research interests include historical aspects of deviant and delinquent behavior, urban studies, paramilitary motivations, forced displacement, and migration.

Kálmán Mizsei was the founding Head of the European Union's Advisory Mission for Civilian Security Sector Reform in Ukraine in 2014-15. He served as the EU Special Representative for Moldova in 2007-11 and as a High-Level EU Adviser to the Government of Moldova in 2019-22 on issues related to the Transnistrian conflict settlement. Mizsei served as the Regional Director of UNDP for Europe and the CIS in 2001-6 in the rank of UN Assistant Secretary General. Trained as an economist with Ph.D. from the Corvinus University of Budapest, he has experience primarily in economic and political reform of the former socialist countries and in conflict related diplomacy.

Nikolai Petrov is a visiting researcher at Stiftung Wissenschaft und Politik (SWP) in Berlin. In 2019-2022, he was a senior researcher at Russian and Eurasian program, Chatham House. In 2013-2021, he was a professor and head at Laboratory for Regional Development Assessment Methods at Higher School of Economics in Moscow. For many years, he was a scholar in residence at the Carnegie Moscow Center. Petrov is a member of the Program on New Approaches to Research and Security in Eurasia (PONARS Eurasia) and the scientific boards of the *Journal of Power Institutions in Post-Soviet Societies, Russian Politics* and *Russian Politics & Law*. During 1990-1995, he served as an advisor to the Russian parliament, government, and presidential administration. He is the author or editor of numerous publications dealing with the analysis of Russia's political regime, elites, post-Soviet transformation, socioeconomic and political development of Russia's regions, political repressions, and other topics.

András Rácz is a military historian and political scientist. He is Senior Fellow at the German Council on Foreign Relations (DGAP) in Berlin and Senior Lecturer at Corvinus University of Budapest. He defended his Ph.D. at the Eötvös Loránd University in Budapest in 2008. His main field of research is the security and defense policy of countries of the post-Soviet region, primarily Russia, Ukraine, and Belarus. Previously, he worked at the Finnish Institute of International Affairs (2014-2016) and held various research positions in Hungary. He was visiting fellow at the Transatlantic Academy of the German Marshall Fund (2011-2012) in Washington D.C. and a guest researcher at the Yad Vashem Institute in Jerusalem (2004).

Boglárka Rédl is an analyst of Political Capital Institute. She holds a Bachelor's Degree in International Relations from Károli Gáspár University of the Reformed Church and in International Business Economics from Eötvös Loránd University in Budapest. She has a background in journalism, having worked previously as a freelance author at Hungarian investigative portal *atlatszo.hu,* where she specialized on Russian influence and disinformation. She also worked for *azonnali.hu,* publishing mainly on the Western Balkans. Her research interests include geopolitics, authoritarian influence, and migration. In recent years, she has published on the potential "land swap" deal between Serbia and Kosovo and on the challenges of the Central Mediterranean migration route.

Anatoly Reshetnikov is Assistant Professor of International Relations at Webster University in Vienna. He holds a PhD in Political Science from Central European University where he also worked as a Visiting Lecturer (2014-2020). He was a Visiting Researcher at University College London (2015), Lund University (2017), and a Visiting Lecturer at Eötvös Loránd University (2016). His research on Russia and Central and Eastern Europe was published in *European Journal of International Relations*, *Security Dialogue*, and *Nationalities Papers*, among other places. He is an Associate Editor of *New Perspectives*, an interdisciplinary journal of politics and international relations in Central and Eastern Europe.

Kirill Rogov is a political scientist, journalist, and writer. He is a fellow at the Institute for Human Sciences (IWM) in Vienna and the founder of Re: Russia, a policy network. Since 2007, Rogov has held positions at the Gaidar Institute for Economic Policy, the leading Russian think-tank in economics, and at the Academy for the National Economy and Public Policy. In 2010-2011, he was an academic secretary and a member of the editorial committee of the working group on economic growth that formulated the Government Strategy Until 2020 (Strategy-2020). A well-known political analyst in Russia, Rogov is frequently quoted in the West by *The Economist*, *The New York Times*, and *The Washington Post*. His columns and analyses have been published in *Forbes Russia, Vedomosti, Novaya Gazeta, RBC* and also in *Süddeutsche Zeitung* and *Financial Times*.

Viktoriya Sereda is a sociologist. She is a senior fellow of the Forum Transregionale Studien (Berlin) and the director of the project "Prisma Ukraïna: War, Migration and Memory." Prior to this, she was a fellow at the Imre Kertesz Kolleg at the

University of Jena. Since 2020, she has also been a Senior Research Fellow at the Institute of Ethnology of the National Academy of Sciences of Ukraine and a Professor in the Department of Sociology at the Ukrainian Catholic University. In 2021 she was a visiting lecturer at the University of Basel. From 2011 to 2017, she was the head of the sociological team for the project "Region, Nation and Beyond: An Interdisciplinary and Transcultural Reconceptualization of Ukraine," organized by the University of St. Gallen in Switzerland. In 2016/17 and 2019/20, she was the Research Fellow at the Ukrainian Research Institute at Harvard University, where she developed a digital atlas of social changes in Ukraine after the Euromaidan.

Zoltán Sz. Bíró is a historian, researcher of Russia, and a research fellow at the Department of International Relations of Corvinus University of Budapest. His main research interests are the history of Russia in the 19th century, late Soviet history, and history of the political and economic transformation of Russia from 1991 to the present. His most recent books in Hungarian language are *The Failed Constitution-Making: Russia in the Second Half of the Nineteenth Century* (Budapest: Osiris, 2017), *Putin's Russia* (Budapest: Noran Libro, 2019) and *Putin's War* (Budapest: Gondolat, 2023).

Zsombor Zeöld holds Masters degrees from the Jagiellonian University, Poland (MA in Central and Eastern European Affairs) and from the Eötvös Loránd University, Budapest (MA in International Relations). His professional career ties him to Poland; as a former CEPA-HIF Andrássy National Security Fellow, his main research areas include Polish foreign and security policy and security policies in the Central European region—with a particular focus on the Visegrád Cooperation and on the Three Seas Initiative.

Index

Abramovich, Roman, 4–5, 8, 24
Agalarov, Araz, 9, 24
Agranovich, Alexei, 18
Albares, José Manuel, 321
Aleinik, Sergei, 273
Alekperov, Vagit, 5, 8–9, 24
Aliyev, Ilham, 276, 289, 293–97, 302, 303, 308
Aliyev, Heydar, 293
Andropov, Yuri, vii
Åslund, Anders, 162, 166–67, 179, 181
Avakov, Arsen, 81, 99
Aven, Petr, 4–5
Awad, Amin, 184, 195

Babiš, Andrej, 114, 118, 276–77
Babushkin, Igor, 13
Bandera, Stepan, 82, 245
Bastrykin, Alexander, 12
Belozerov, Oleg, 5
Bennett, Naftali, 85
Bensouda, Fatou, 191, 196
Berdimuhamedow, Serdar, 276
Biden, Joe, 234–35, 238–39, 248–49, 273, 319
Bildt, Carl, 141
Bortnikov, Alexander, 12, 23
Brezhnev, Leonid, vii, 51, 57
Brzezinski, Mark, 235
Bukharin, Nikolai, vii
Bukhman, Dmitry, 6
Bukhman, Igor, 6
Busargin, Roman, 19
Bush, George W., 144

Castles, Stephen, 207, 223
Chamberlain, Neville, 53
Chemezov, Sergey, 5, 10

Chubais, Anatoly, 14–15, 21

Dahl, Robert, xv, xx
Daladier, Édouard, 53
Daszyńska-Muzyczka, Beata, 247
Deng, Xiaoping, 314
Denisenko, Alia, 86, 101
Deripaska, Oleg, 5, 8
Dmitriev, Sergey, 6
Dobrodeev, Oleg, 16, 23
Dodik, Milorad, 276
Dodon, Igor, 148
Duda, Andrzej, 247, 248–49, 251, 253
Dugin, Aleksandr, 94, 104, 107
Durov, Pavel, 6
Dvorkovich, Arkady, 15, 25
Dyukov, Aleksandr, 5
Dyumin, Alexey, 13
Dzerzhinsky, Feliks Edmundovich, 67, 75–76
Dzurinda, Mikuláš, 146

Eichengreen, Barry, 176
Erdoğan, Recep Tayyip, xix, 276, 299, 305
Ernst, Konstantin, 16
Erpyleva, Svetlana, 73, 76
Evans, William Andrews, 87, 101

Fedun, Leonid, 9, 24
Filat, Vlad, 146–48, 154
Firtash, Dmytro, 107
Fridman, Mikhail, 4–5
Friedlander, Julia, 167, 179

Gabuev, Alexander, 172, 180
Gaidar, Yegor, ix
Gannushkina, Svetlana, 217, 227
Gavrilita, Natalia, 158

Gavrilov, Roman, 13
Gerasimov, Valery, 12, 36, 108, 122
Gessen, Masha, 77, 92, 97
Golikova, Tatyana, 14
Gorbachev, Mikhail, vii–viii, 13, 56–57, 62
Grabbe, Heather, 152, 163
Gref, German, 5, 11, 21
Gromov, Aleksey, 17, 23
Grozev, Christo, 89, 102
Guryev, Andrey, 9
Gusev, Vladimir, 18
Gyurcsány, Ferenc, 273

Hale, Henry, xv, xx, 307–9
Herpen, Marcel Van, 108, 122
Hitler, Adolf, 52, 54–55, 58
Hufbauer, Gary C., 166, 179

Ilyin, Ivan, 77, 94, 97, 107
Ivanov, Sergei, 57, 74

Janša, Janez, 277
Japarov, Sadyr, 276

Kabaeva, Alina, 17
Kaczyński, Jarosław, 257, 269, 277, 282, 285
Kadyrov, Ramzan, 12–13
Kallas, Kaja, 236, 249
Kharichev, Alexander, 15
Khodorkovsky, Mikhail, x, xvi, 173
Khusnullin, Marat, 14, 23
Kirill (Patriarch Kirill of Moscow), 115, 274, 284
Kiriyenko, Sergey, ix, 9–10, 14–15, 18–19
Kiselyov, Dimitry, 112, 123
Kitschelt, Herbert, 297, 309
Kiva, Ilia, 88
Kochnev, Dmitry, 12
Kogogin, Sergei, 9
Kolokoltsev, Vladimir, 12
Kolomoisky, Igor, 79, 89–91, 98, 102
Konov, Dmitry, 9
Korn, David A., 200, 221
Kornai, János, 180, 307–8

Kostin, Andrey, 5, 10
Kovalchuk, Yuri, 5, 10, 14–17, 19, 25
Kozak, Dmitry, 17–18, 25, 133, 160
Krasnov, Igor, 12
Kropivnitskii, Anatolii, 86, 101
Krugman, Paul, 171, 180
Kudrin, Alexei, 14, 18, 21
Kurenkov, Alexander, 12–13
Kurz, Sebastian, 276
Kuzmichev, Alexey, 4, 5
Kuznetsova, Irina, 217, 221–22, 227
Kynev, Alexander, 18, 25

Lauder, Matthew A., 89, 102
Lavrov, Sergey, 57, 184, 191, 193, 262, 273, 284, 304
Le Pen, Marine, 114, 118
Lebedev, Platon, x
Lenin, Vladimir, 64
Levitin, Igor, 15
Levitsky, Steven, 256, 279
Li, Hui, 322
Li, Keqiang, 313
Likhachev, Alexey, 5, 10
Lisin, Vladimir, 5, 8, 24
Loshak, Marina, 18
Lukashenko, Alexander, 289–93, 294–95, 302, 303–4, 307–8
Lupusor, Adrian, 148
Lvova-Belova, Maria, 216

Mackinder, Sir Halford John, 233, 248
Macron, Emmanuel, 118, 156
Maganov, Ravil, 8, 24
Magnitsky, Sergei, 166, 179
Malofeev, Konstantin, 107
Mandelstam, Osip, 64
Manturov, Denis, 11
Mao, Zedong, 314
Márki-Zay, Péter, 268
Matveeva, Anna, 106, 122
Matvienko, Valentina, 15–16
Mau, Vladimir, 18
Mazepin, Dmitry, 9

McCloskey, Deirdre, 171, 180
Medinsky, Vladimir, 57–58, 66
Medvedchuk, Viktor, 80, 92, 98–99, 103
Medvedev, Dmitry, x–xii, 10–12, 15, 66, 167–68, 300
Melnichenko, Andrey, 5, 8–9
Mikhelson, Leonid, 5, 8
Mikoyan, Anastas, 55
Miller, Alexey, 5, 10, 17, 273
Milner, Yuri, 6
Minnikhanov, Rustam, 276
Mironov, Dmitry, 12–13, 16
Mirziyoyev, Shavkat, 276
Mishustin, Mikhail, 14
Mitchell, A. Wess, 234, 238–39, 248
Molotov, Vyacheslav, viii, 52–57, 62, 74, 109
Moniava, Lida, 218, 227
Mordashov, Alexey, 5, 8
Morozov, Sergey, 13
Moshkovich, Vadim, 9
Murashko, Mikhail, 274
Muratov, Dmitriy, 87
Musk, Elon, 111, 123, 181

Nabiullina, Elvira, 14, 21
Naryshkin, Sergey, 57
Navalny, Alexei, xii, 131
Nazarbayev, Nursultan, 289, 297–98, 309
Nechaev, Sergey, 16
Nikonov, Vyacheslav, 108–9, 122
Nyerges, Zsolt, 263

Orbán, Viktor, xix, 112, 114, 122, 209, 249, 255–78, 279–85

Pankov, Nikolai, 36
Patrushev, Nikolai, 12
Pavlovsky, Gleb, 111
Pelevin, Viktor, 77
Peter I, 51, 64
Plahotniuc, Vlad, 146–48, 272
Poklonskaya, Natalya, 15, 80, 98
Pomerantsev, Peter, 77, 90, 92, 97, 100, 122–23

Pompeo, Mike, 234, 248
Poroshenko, Petro, 30, 78–79, 82–83, 88, 94, 97–99, 103, 145, 161
Potanin, Vladimir, 5, 8
Prigozhin, Yevgeny, 12–13, 25, 35–36, 47, 109, 122
Primakov, Yevgeny, ix
Prokhorov, Mikhail, 8
Ptitsyna, Veronika, 73, 76
Pumpyansky, Dmitry, 8
Putin, Vladimir, ix–xii, xvi–xix, 3–23, 24–25, 28–30, 36, 39–40, 46–47, 51–57, 59–72, 74–75, 77–81, 83, 84–87, 91–92, 94, 97, 99–101, 103, 105, 107–12, 118, 121, 122–24, 127–35, 140, 142–46, 161, 165–67, 169, 173–74, 179–80, 183, 189, 193–94, 197, 217, 256, 259–67, 270, 272–74, 276–77, 280–81, 290–91, 293–95, 298–99, 302, 303–5, 308, 311, 322

Qin, Gang, 311, 315, 324

Rashevsky, Vladimir, 9
Rau, Zbigniew, 241, 247, 251
Recean, Dorin, 158
Reichelgauz, Iosif, 18
Ribbentrop, Joachim von, viii, 52–57, 62, 74
Robinson, James, 171, 180
Rogoff, Kenneth, 176
Roland, Gérard, 176
Romanova, Olga, 36
Rotenberg, Arkady, 5, 8, 14
Rubezhnoy, Alexey, 12
Rybolovlev, Dmitry, 4–5
Ryzhakov, Viktor, 18

Saakashvili, Mikheil, 146, 148
Sakharov, Andrei, vii
Salvini, Matteo, 114
Sandu, Maia, 148, 158
Sargentini, Judith, 260, 279
Sarkozy, Nicolas, 144

Schneider, Gerald, 166, 179
Sechin, Igor, 5, 10–11, 14–15, 19, 25
Shoigu, Sergei, 12, 36
Shuvalov, Igor, 5, 11
Sikorski, Radek, 141
Simicska, Lajos, 263
Simola, Heli, 169–70, 180
Simonyan, Margarita, 17
Skabeeva, Marina, 94
Slutsky, Leonid, 16
Sobyanin, Sergey, 14, 19, 23
Soloch, Paweł, 238, 249
Sonin, Konstantin, 174, 181
Sonnenveld, Jeffrey, 169
Soros, George, 83, 99, 261, 273
Stalin, Joseph, 52–55, 57–58, 61, 64–67, 74–75, 109
Steinmeier, Frank-Walter, 81, 99, 299, 305
Storonsky, Nikolay, 6
Surkov, Vladislav, 81, 94, 99
Szijjártó, Péter, 250, 262–63, 273–74, 283–84
Szydło, Beata, 208, 223

Tamim, bin Hamad al-Sani, 276
Tavares, Rui, 260, 279
Timchenko, Gennady, 5, 8
Timofti, Nicolae, 147
Tinkov, Oleg, 7, 24
Tokarev, Nikolai, 5
Tokayev, Kassym-Jomart, 289, 298–302, 304–6, 309
Travnikov, Maxim, 13
Tregulova, Zelfira, 18
Treisman, Daniel, 4, 24
Trump, Donald, 179, 184, 233–35, 280, 282
Turlov, Timur, 6

Usmanov, Alisher, 5, 8–9, 24

Vaino, Anton, 14
Valiyev, Anar, 294, 308–9
Vekselberg, Viktor, 5, 8

Volodin, Vyacheslav, 15, 19, 25, 65, 75, 88, 101, 191, 303
Volozh, Arkady, 6
Vorobyov, Vadim, 9
Voronin, Vladimir, 146, 154
Voroshilov, Kliment, 54–55, 74
Vučić, Aleksandar, 276–77
Vysotskii, Sergei, 88, 101

Waltzman, Rand, 112, 121, 123–24
Wang, Jing, 318
Wang, Yi, 321
Way, Lucan, 256, 279
Weber, Patrick M., 166, 179
Weiss, Thomas G., 200, 221

Xi, Jinping, 311, 314, 319–20, 322, 324

Yablokov, Ilya, 121, 122, 124, 308
Yakovlev, Andrey, 7, 24
Yan, Xuetong, 320, 324–25
Yanukovych, Viktor, x, xvi, 78, 135, 144–46
Yatseniuk, Arseniy, 161
Yavlinsky, Grigory, 16
Yeltsin, Boris, viii–x, 4–5, 7, 16, 21–22, 24, 56, 64, 72, 290
Yevtushenkov, Vladimir, 8–9
Yumashev, Valentin, 21
Yushchenko, Viktor, xvi, 133

Zelensky, Volodymyr, xvii, 29–32, 34, 38, 40, 45–46, 49, 77–85, 87, 88–94, 97–103, 150, 162, 224, 251–52, 269, 282, 292, 294, 299, 316, 322
Zemsky, Alexei, 17
Zhang, Lihua, 313, 324
Zharov, Alexander, 17
Zhironovsky, Vladimir, 16
Zhupanin, Andrey, 34
Zinichev, Evgeny, 13
Zolotov, Viktor, 12–13
Zuev, Sergey, 18
Zyuganov, Gennady, ix, 16